SITUATIONIST INTERNATIONAL
ANTHOLOGY

Edited and translated from the French by Ken Knabb
Translation collaboration: Nadine Bloch and Joël Cornuault

Published 1981 by the Bureau of Public Secrets (P.O. Box 1044,
Berkeley, CA 94701). Second printing, 1989. Third printing, 1995
(same as first two except for updated bibliography on pages 378–380).
Printed in USA.

ISBN 0-939682-00-1
Library of Congress No. 81-69735

Cover: from a 1957 psychogeographical map of Paris by Guy Debord
Cover design: Jeanne Jambu

TABLE OF CONTENTS

---

†Excerpts.

MAY 1968 DOCUMENTS

INTERNAL S.I. TEXTS

PREFACE

In 1957 a few European avant-garde groups came together to form the Situationist International. Over the next decade the SI developed an increasingly incisive and coherent critique of modern society and of its bureaucratic pseudo-opposition, and its new methods of agitation were influential in leading up to the May 1968 revolt in France. Since then—although the SI itself was dissolved in 1972—situationist theses and tactics have been taken up by radical currents in dozens of countries all over the world.

In this anthology I have tried to present a useful selection of situationist writings while at the same time illustrating the SI's origins and development. Thus some early texts are included even though they express positions that were later repudiated by the situationists. But even the later texts reveal mistakes, contradictions, projects that never materialized, problems that remain to be solved. In other publications I have presented my own views on a few of these issues; but here I have as far as possible let the SI speak for itself.

The major portion of the anthology is drawn from the French journal *Internationale Situationniste* (it includes about a third of the *IS* articles). The rest consists of various shorter publications and documents. I have not included any excerpts from the situationist books, Debord's *The Society of the Spectacle*, Vaneigem's *Treatise on Living for the Young Generations*, Viénet's *Enragés and Situationists in the Occupations Movement* and Debord and Sanguinetti's *The Real Split in the International*. Anyone who is serious will want to read these books in their entirety. The English translations of them that have appeared are all unsatisfactory, but sooner or later someone will publish accurate versions.

The only previous English-language SI anthology, Christopher Gray's *Leaving the Twentieth Century*, is particularly bad. In *Bureau of Public Secrets* #1 I have already criticized the superficiality of Gray's commentaries on the SI. His translations are on the same level. Not only do his chummy paraphrases obscure the precise sense of the original, but there is scarcely a page in which he has not left out sentences or paragraphs without any indication of the omission, or even made completely gratuitous additions of his own.

About half the texts in the present anthology have been translated into English for the first time. All the others have been freshly translated, but I have gone through all the previous translations and incorporated many of their best renderings. I received an immense help from Nadine Bloch and Joël Cornuault, who answered hundreds of questions regarding the French texts, then checked the entire manuscript, correcting many errors and suggesting many further improvements. Dan Hammer also made a number of good suggestions.

Asterisks refer to my notes at the end of the book. The only notes original to the SI are the numbered footnotes in *On the Poverty of Student Life*. Within the text, all annotations in square brackets are mine and my omissions are indicated by [...]. I have not generally annotated references to historical events, etc., that enterprising readers can easily find out about for themselves. Nor have I tried to explain supposed difficulties in the SI's language. After the usual diet of ideological pabulum it may be a momentary shock to be forced to think; but those who are really confronting their lives and therefore this society will soon understand how to use these texts. Those who aren't, won't, regardless of explanations. Situationist language is difficult only to the extent that our situation is. "The path to simplicity is the most complex of all."

K.K.

Pre-SI Texts
(1953–1957)

FORMULARY FOR A NEW URBANISM

SIRE, I AM FROM THE OTHER COUNTRY

We are bored in the city, there is no longer any Temple of the Sun. Between the legs of the women walking by, the dadaists imagined a monkey wrench and the surrealists a crystal cup. That's lost. We know how to read every promise in faces—the latest stage of morphology. The poetry of the billboards lasted twenty years. We are bored in the city, we really have to strain to still discover mysteries on the sidewalk billboards, the latest state of humor and poetry:

> *Shower-Bath of the Patriarchs*
> *Meat Cutting Machines*
> *Notre-Dame Zoo*
> *Sports Pharmacy*
> *Martyrs Provisions*
> *Translucent Concrete*
> *Golden Touch Sawmill*
> *Center for Functional Recuperation*
> *Sainte-Anne Ambulance*
> *Café Fifth Avenue*
> *Prolonged Volunteers Street*
> *Family Boarding House in the Garden*
> *Hotel of Strangers*
> *Wild Street*

And the swimming pool on the Street of Little Girls. And the police station on Rendezvous Street. The medical-surgical clinic and the free placement center on the Quai des Orfèvres. The artificial flowers on Sun Street. The Castle Cellars Hotel, the Ocean Bar and the Coming and Going Café. The Hotel of the Epoch.

And the strange statue of Dr. Philippe Pinel, benefactor of the insane, in the last evenings of summer. To explore Paris.

And you, forgotten, your memories ravaged by all the consternations of two hemispheres, stranded in the Red Cellars of Pali-Kao, without music and without geography, no longer setting out for the hacienda *where the roots think of the child and where the wine is finished off with fables from an old almanac.* Now that's finished. You'll never see the hacienda. It doesn't exist.

The hacienda must be built.

All cities are geological; you cannot take three steps without encountering ghosts bearing all the prestige of their legends. We move within a *closed* landscape whose landmarks constantly draw us toward the past. Certain *shifting* angles, certain *receding* perspectives, allow us to glimpse original conceptions of space, but this vision remains fragmentary. It must be sought in the magical locales of fairy tales and

1

surrealist writings: castles, endless walls, little forgotten bars, mammoth caverns, casino mirrors.

These dated images retain a small catalyzing power, but it is almost impossible to use them in a *symbolic urbanism* without rejuvenating them by giving them a new meaning. Our imaginations, haunted by the old archetypes, have remained far behind the sophistication of the machines. The various attempts to integrate modern science into new myths remain inadequate. Meanwhile abstraction has invaded all the arts, contemporary architecture in particular. Pure plasticity, inanimate, storyless, soothes the eye. Elsewhere other fragmentary beauties can be found—while the promised land of syntheses continually recedes into the distance. Everyone wavers between the emotionally still-alive past and the already dead future.

We will not work to prolong the mechanical civilizations and frigid architecture that ultimately lead to boring leisure.

We propose to invent new, changeable decors. . . .

Darkness and obscurity are banished by artificial lighting, and the seasons by air conditioning; night and summer are losing their charm and dawn is disappearing. The man of the cities thinks he has escaped from cosmic reality, but there is no corresponding expansion of his dream life. The reason is clear: dreams spring from reality and are realized in it.

The latest technological developments would make possible the individual's unbroken contact with cosmic reality while eliminating its disagreeable aspects. Stars and rain can be seen through glass ceilings. The mobile house turns with the sun. Its sliding walls enable vegetation to invade life. Mounted on tracks, it can go down to the sea in the morning and return to the forest in the evening.

Architecture is the simplest means of *articulating* time and space, of *modulating* reality, of engendering dreams. It is a matter not only of plastic articulation and modulation expressing an ephemeral beauty, but of a modulation producing influences in accordance with the eternal spectrum of human desires and the progress in realizing them.

The architecture of tomorrow will be a means of modifying present conceptions of time and space. It will be a means of *knowledge* and a *means of action.*

The architectural complex will be modifiable. Its aspect will change totally or partially in accordance with the will of its inhabitants. . . .

Past collectivities offered the masses an absolute truth and incontrovertable mythical exemplars. The appearance of the notion of *relativity* in the modern mind allows one to surmise the EXPERIMENTAL aspect of the next civilization (although I'm not satisfied with that word; say, more supple, more "fun"). On the bases of this mobile civilization, architecture will, at least initially, be a means of experimenting with a thousand ways of modifying life, with a view to a mythic synthesis.

A mental disease has swept the planet: banalization. Everyone is hypnotized by production and conveniences—sewage system, elevator, bathroom, washing machine.

This state of affairs, arising out of a struggle against poverty, has overshot its ultimate goal—the liberation of man from material cares—and become an obsessive image hanging over the present. Presented with the alternative of love or a garbage disposal unit, young people of all countries have chosen the garbage disposal unit. It has become essential to bring about a complete spiritual transformation by bringing to light forgotten desires and by creating entirely new ones. And by carrying out an *intensive propaganda* in favor of these desires.

We have already pointed out the need of constructing situations as being one of the fundamental desires on which the next civilization will be founded. This need for *absolute* creation has always been intimately associated with the need to *play* with architecture, time and space. . . .

Chirico remains one of the most remarkable architectural precursors. He was grappling with the problems of absences and presences in time and space.

We know that an object that is not consciously noticed at the time of a first *visit* can, by its absence during subsequent visits, provoke an indefinable impression: as a result of this sighting backward in time, *the absence of the object becomes a presence one can feel.* More precisely: although the quality of the impression generally remains indefinite, it nevertheless varies with the nature of the removed object and the importance accorded it by the visitor, ranging from serene joy to terror. (It is of no particular significance that in this specific case memory is the vehicle of these feelings; I only selected this example for its convenience.)

In Chirico's paintings (during his Arcade period) an *empty space* creates a *full-filled time.* It is easy to imagine the fantastic future possibilities of such architecture and its influence on the masses. Today we can have nothing but contempt for a century that relegates such *blueprints* to its so-called museums.

This new vision of time and space, which will be the theoretical basis of future constructions, is still imprecise and will remain so until experimentation with patterns of behavior has taken place in cities specifically established for this purpose, cities assembling—in addition to the facilities necessary for a minimum of comfort and security— buildings charged with evocative power, symbolic edifices representing desires, forces, events past, present and to come. A rational extension of the old religious systems, of old tales, and above all of psychoanalysis, into architectural expression becomes more and more urgent as all the reasons for becoming impassioned disappear.

Everyone will live in his own personal "cathedral," so to speak. There will be rooms more conducive to dreams than any drug, and houses where one cannot help but love. Others will be irresistibly alluring to travelers. . . .

This project could be compared with the Chinese and Japanese gardens of illusory perspectives [*en trompe-l'œil*]—with the difference that those gardens are not designed to be lived in all the time—or with the ridiculous labyrinth in the Jardin des Plantes, at the entry to which is written (height of absurdity, Ariadne unemployed): *Games are forbidden in the labyrinth.*

This city could be envisaged in the form of an arbitrary assemblage of castles, grottos, lakes, etc. It would be the baroque stage of urbanism considered as a means of knowledge. But this theoretical phase is already outdated. We know that a modern building could be constructed which would have no resemblance to a medieval castle but which could preserve and enhance the *Castle* poetic power (by the conservation of a strict minimum of lines, the transposition of certain others, the positioning of openings, the topographical location, etc.).

The districts of this city could correspond to the whole spectrum of diverse feelings that one encounters *by chance* in everyday life.

Bizarre Quarter — Happy Quarter (specially reserved for habitation) — Noble and Tragic Quarter (for good children) — Historical Quarter (museums, schools) — Useful Quarter (hospital, tool shops) — Sinister Quarter, etc. And an *Astrolaire* which would group plant species in accordance with the relations they manifest with the stellar rhythm, a planetary garden comparable to that which the astronomer Thomas wants to establish at Laaer Berg in Vienna. Indispensable for giving the inhabitants a consciousness of the cosmic. Perhaps also a Death Quarter, not for dying in but so as to have somewhere to *live in peace*, and I think here of Mexico and of a principle of cruelty in innocence that appeals more to me every day.

The Sinister Quarter, for example, would be a good replacement for those hellholes that many peoples once possessed in their capitals: they symbolized all the evil forces of life. The Sinister Quarter would have no need to harbor real dangers, such as traps, dungeons or mines. It would be difficult to get into, with a hideous decor (piercing whistles, alarm bells, sirens wailing intermittently, grotesque sculptures, power-driven mobiles, called *Auto-Mobiles*), and as poorly lit at night as it is blindingly lit during the day by an intensive use of reflection. At the center, the "Square of the Appalling Mobile." Saturation of the market with a product causes the product's market value to fall: thus, as they explored the Sinister Quarter, the child and the adult would learn not to fear the anguishing occasions of life, but to be amused by them.

The principal activity of the inhabitants will be the CONTINUOUS DÉRIVE. The changing of landscapes from one hour to the next will result in complete disorientation. . . .

Later, as the gestures inevitably grow stale, this dérive will partially leave the realm of direct experience for that of representation. . . .

The economic obstacles are only apparent. We know that the more a place is *set apart for free play*, the more it influences people's behavior and the greater is its force of attraction. This is demonstrated by the immense prestige of Monaco and Las Vegas—and Reno, that caricature of free love—although they are mere gambling places. Our first experimental city would live largely off tolerated and controlled tourism. Future avant-garde activities and productions would naturally tend to gravitate there. In a few years it would become the intellectual capital of the world and would be universally recognized as such.

IVAN CHTCHEGLOV*
October 1953

4

INTRODUCTION TO A
CRITIQUE OF URBAN GEOGRAPHY

Of all the affairs we participate in, with or without interest, the groping search for a new way of life is the only aspect still impassioning. Aesthetic and other disciplines have proved blatantly inadequate in this regard and merit the greatest detachment. We should therefore delineate some provisional terrains of observation, including the observation of certain processes of chance and predictability in the streets.

The word *psychogeography*, suggested by an illiterate Kabyle as a general term for the phenomena a few of us were investigating around the summer of 1953, is not too inappropriate. It does not contradict the materialist perspective of the conditioning of life and thought by objective nature. Geography, for example, deals with the determinant action of general natural forces, such as soil composition or climatic conditions, on the economic structures of a society, and thus on the corresponding conception that such a society can have of the world. *Psychogeography* could set for itself the study of the precise laws and specific effects of the geographical environment, consciously organized or not, on the emotions and behavior of individuals. The adjective *psychogeographical*, retaining a rather pleasing vagueness, can thus be applied to the findings arrived at by this type of investigation, to their influence on human feelings, and even more generally to any situation or conduct that seems to reflect the same spirit of discovery.

It has long been said that the desert is monotheistic. Is it illogical or devoid of interest to observe that the district in Paris between Place de la Contrescarpe and Rue de l'Arbalète conduces rather to atheism, to oblivion and to the disorientation of habitual reflexes?

The notion of utilitariness should be situated historically. The concern to have open spaces allowing for the rapid circulation of troops and the use of artillery against insurrections was at the origin of the urban renewal plan adopted by the Second Empire. But from any standpoint other than that of police control, Haussmann's Paris is a city built by an idiot, full of sound and fury, signifying nothing. Today urbanism's main problem is ensuring the smooth circulation of a rapidly increasing quantity of motor vehicles. We might be justified in thinking that a future urbanism will also apply itself to no less utilitarian projects that will give the greatest consideration to psychogeographical possibilities.

This present abundance of private cars is nothing but the result of the constant propaganda by which capitalist production persuades the masses—and this case is one of its most astonishing successes—that the possession of a car is one of the privileges our society reserves for its privileged members. (At the same time, anarchical progress negates itself: one can thus savor the spectacle of a prefect of police urging Parisian car owners to use public transportation.)

We know with what blind fury so many unprivileged people are ready to defend their mediocre advantages. Such pathetic illusions of privilege are linked to a general idea of happiness prevalent among the bourgeoisie and maintained by a system of publicity that includes Malraux's aesthetics as well as the imperatives of Coca-Cola—an idea of happiness whose crisis must be provoked on every occasion by every means.

The first of these means are undoubtedly the systematic provocative dissemination of a host of proposals tending to turn the whole of life into an exciting game, and the continual depreciation of all current diversions—to the extent, of course, that they cannot be detourned to serve in constructions of more interesting ambiances. The greatest difficulty in such an undertaking is to convey through these apparently delirious proposals a sufficient degree of *serious seduction*. To accomplish this we can imagine an adroit use of currently popular means of communication. But a disruptive sort of abstention, or manifestations designed to radically frustrate the fans of these means of communication, could also promote at little expense an atmosphere of uneasiness extremely favorable for the introduction of a few new notions of pleasure.

This idea, that the realization of a chosen emotional situation depends only on the thorough understanding and calculated application of a certain number of concrete techniques, inspired this "Psychogeographical Game of the Week" published, not without a certain humor, in *Potlatch* #1:

"In accordance with what you are seeking, choose a country, a more or less populated city, a more or less busy street. Build a house. Furnish it. Use decorations and surroundings to the best advantage. Choose the season and the time of day. Bring together the most suitable people, with appropriate records and drinks. The lighting and the conversation should obviously be suited to the occasion, as should be the weather or your memories.

"If there has been no error in your calculations, the result should satisfy you."

We need to work toward flooding the market—even if for the moment merely the intellectual market—with a mass of desires whose realization is not beyond the capacity of man's present means of action on the material world, but only beyond the capacity of the old social organization. It is thus not without political interest to publicly counterpose such desires to the elementary desires that are endlessly rehashed by the film industry and in psychological novels like those of that old hack Mauriac. ("In a society based on *poverty*, the *poorest* products are inevitably used by the greatest number," Marx explained to poor Proudhon.)

The revolutionary transformation of the world, of all aspects of the world, will confirm all the dreams of abundance.

The sudden change of ambiance in a street within the space of a few meters; the evident division of a city into zones of distinct psychic atmospheres; the path of least resistance which is automatically followed in aimless strolls (and which has no relation to the physical contour of the ground); the appealing or repelling character of certain places—all this seems to be neglected. In any case it is never envisaged as depending on causes that can be uncovered by careful analysis and turned to account. People are quite aware that some neighborhoods are sad and others pleasant. But they generally simply assume that elegant streets cause a feeling of satisfaction and that poor streets are depressing, and let it go at that. In fact, the variety of possible combinations of ambiances, analogous to the blending of pure chemicals in an infinite number of mixtures, gives rise to feelings as differentiated and complex as any other form of spectacle can evoke. The slightest demystified investigation reveals that the qualitatively or quantitatively different influences of diverse urban decors cannot be determined solely on the basis of the era or architectural style, much less on the basis of housing conditions.

The research that we are thus led to undertake on the arrangement of the elements of the urban setting, in close relation with the sensations they provoke, entails bold hypotheses that must constantly be corrected in the light of experience, by critique and self-critique.

Certain of Chirico's paintings, which are clearly provoked by architecturally originated sensations, exert in turn an effect on their objective base to the point of transforming it: they tend themselves to become blueprints or models. Disquieting neighborhoods of arcades could one day carry on and fulfill the allure of these works.

I scarcely know of anything but those two harbors at dusk painted by Claude Lorrain—which are at the Louvre and which juxtapose two extremely dissimilar urban ambiances—that can rival in beauty the Paris metro maps. It will be understood that in speaking here of beauty I don't have in mind plastic beauty—the new beauty can only be a beauty of situation—but simply the particularly moving presentation, in both cases, of a *sum of possibilities.*

Among various more difficult means of intervention, a renovated cartography seems appropriate for immediate utilization.

The production of psychogeographic maps, or even the introduction of alterations such as more or less arbitrarily transposing maps of two different regions, can contribute to clarifying certain wanderings that express not subordination to randomness but complete *insubordination* to habitual influences (influences generally categorized as tourism, that popular drug as repugnant as sports or buying on credit). A friend recently told me that he had just wandered through the Harz region of Germany while blindly following the directions of a map of London. This sort of game is obviously only a mediocre beginning in comparison to the complete construction of architecture and urbanism that will someday be within the power of everyone. Meanwhile we can distinguish several stages of partial, less difficult realizations, beginning with the mere displacement of elements of decoration from the locations where we are used to seeing them.

For example, in the preceding issue of this journal Mariën proposed that when global resources have ceased to be squandered on the irrational enterprises that are imposed on us today, all the equestrian statues of all the cities of the world be assembled in a single desert. This would offer to the passersby—the future belongs to them—the spectacle of an artificial cavalry charge, which could even be dedicated to the memory of the greatest massacrers of history, from Tamerlane to Ridgway. Here we see reappear one of the main demands of this generation: educative value.

In fact, there is nothing to be expected until the masses in action awaken to the conditions that are imposed on them in all domains of life, and to the practical means of changing them.

"The imaginary is that which tends to become real," wrote an author whose name, on account of his notorious intellectual degradation, I have since forgotten. The involuntary restrictiveness of such a statement could serve as a touchstone exposing various farcical literary revolutions: That which tends to remain unreal is empty babble.

Life, for which we are responsible, encounters, at the same time as great motives for discouragement, innumerable more or less vulgar diversions and compensations. A year doesn't go by when people we loved haven't succumbed, for lack of having clearly grasped the present possibilities, to some glaring capitulation. But the enemy camp objectively condemns people to imbecility and already numbers millions of imbeciles; the addition of a few more makes no difference.

The first moral deficiency remains indulgence, in all its forms.

GUY DEBORD

From *Les Lèvres Nues* #6, September 1955

METHODS OF DETOURNEMENT*

All aware people of our time agree that art can no longer be justified as a superior activity, or even as an activity of compensation to which one could honorably devote oneself. The cause of this deterioration is clearly the emergence of productive forces that necessitate other production relations and a new practice of life. In the civil war phase we are engaged in, and in close connection with the orientation we are discovering for certain superior activities to come, we can consider that all known means of expression are going to converge in a general movement of propaganda which must encompass all the perpetually interacting aspects of social reality.

Regarding the forms and even the very nature of educative propaganda, there are several conflicting opinions, generally inspired by one or another currently fashionable variety of reformist politics. Suffice it to say that in our view the premises for revolution, on the cultural as well as the strictly political level, are not only ripe, they have begun to rot. It is not just returning to the past which is reactionary; even "modern" cultural objectives are ultimately reactionary since they depend in reality on ideological formulations of a past society that has prolonged its death agony to the present. Only extremist innovation is historically justified.

The literary and artistic heritage of humanity should be used for partisan propaganda purposes. It is, of course, necessary to go beyond any idea of scandal. Since the negation of the bourgeois conception of art and artistic genius has become pretty much old hat, [Duchamp's] drawing of a mustache on the *Mona Lisa* is no more interesting than the original version of that painting. We must now push this process to the point of negating the negation. Bertolt Brecht, revealing in a recent interview in the magazine *France-Observateur* that he made some cuts in the classics of the theater in order to make the performances more educative, is much closer than Duchamp to the revolutionary orientation we are calling for. We must note, however, that in Brecht's case these salutary alterations are held within narrow limits by his unfortunate respect for culture as defined by the ruling class— that same respect, taught in the primary schools of the bourgeoisie and in the newspapers of the workers parties, which leads the reddest worker districts of Paris always to prefer *The Cid* over *Mother Courage*.

In fact, it is necessary to finish with any notion of personal property in this area. The appearance of new necessities outmodes previous "inspired" works. They become obstacles, dangerous habits. The point is not whether we like them or not. We have to go beyond them.

Any elements, no matter where they are taken from, can serve in making new combinations. The discoveries of modern poetry regarding the analogical structure of images demonstrate that when two objects are brought together, no matter how far apart their original contexts may be, a relationship is always formed. Restricting oneself to a personal arrangement of words is mere convention. The mutual interference of two worlds of feeling, or the bringing together of two independent expressions, supersedes the original elements and produces a synthetic organization of greater efficacy. Anything can be used.

It goes without saying that one is not limited to correcting a work or to integrating diverse fragments of out-of-date works into a new one; one can also alter the meaning of those fragments in any appropriate way, leaving the imbeciles to their slavish preservation of "citations."

Such parodical methods have often been used to obtain comical effects. But such humor is the result of contradictions within a condition whose existence is taken for granted. Since the world of literature seems to us almost as distant as the Stone Age, such contradictions don't make us laugh. It is therefore necessary to conceive of a parodic-serious stage where the accumulation of detourned elements, far from aiming at arousing indignation or laughter by alluding to some original work, will express our indifference toward a meaningless and forgotten original, and concern itself with rendering a certain sublimity.

Lautréamont advanced so far in this direction that he is still partly misunderstood even by his most ostentatious admirers. In spite of his obvious application of this method to theoretical language in *Poésies* (drawing particularly on the ethical maxims of Pascal and Vauvenargues)—where Lautréamont strives to reduce the argument, through successive concentrations, to maxims alone—a certain Viroux caused considerable astonishment three or four years ago by demonstrating conclusively that *Maldoror* is one vast detournement of Buffon and other works of natural history, among other things. That the prosaists of *Figaro*, such as this Viroux himself, were able to see this as a justification for disparaging Lautréamont, and that others believed they had to defend him by praising his insolence, only testifies to the intellectual debility of these two camps of dotards in courtly combat with each other. A slogan like "Plagiarism is necessary, progress implies it" is still as poorly understood, and for the same reasons, as the famous phrase about the poetry that "must be made by all."

Apart from Lautréamont's work—whose appearance so far ahead of its time has to a great extent preserved it from a precise critique—the tendencies toward detournement that can be observed in contemporary expression are for the most part unconscious or incidental; and it is in the advertising industry, more than in a decaying aesthetic production, that one can find the best examples.

We can first of all define two main categories of detourned elements, without considering whether or not their being brought together is accompanied by corrections introduced in the originals. These are *minor detournements* and *deceptive detournements*.

Minor detournement is the detournement of an element which has no importance in itself and which thus draws all its meaning from the new context in which it has been placed. For example, a press clipping, a neutral phrase, a commonplace photograph.

Deceptive detournement, also termed premonitory proposition detournement, is in contrast the detournement of an intrinsically significant element, which derives a different scope from the new context. A slogan of Saint-Just, for example, or a sequence from Eisenstein.

Extended detourned works will thus usually be composed of one or more sequences of deceptive and minor detournements.

Several laws on the use of detournement can now be formulated:

It is the most distant detourned element which contributes most sharply to the overall impression, and not the elements that directly determine the nature of this impression. For example, in a metagraph [poem-collage] relating to the Spanish Civil War the phrase with the most distinctly revolutionary sense is a fragment from a lipstick ad: "Pretty lips are red." In another metagraph ("The Death of J.H.") 125 classified ads of bars for sale express a suicide more strikingly than the newspaper articles that recount it.

The distortions introduced in the detourned elements must be as simplified as possible, since the main force of a detournement is directly related to the conscious or vague recollection of the original contexts of the elements. This is well known. Let us simply note that if this dependence on memory implies that one must determine one's public before devising a detournement, this is only a particular case of a general law that governs not only detournement but also any other form of action on the world. The idea of pure, absolute expression is dead; it only temporarily survives in parodic form as long as our other enemies survive.

Detournement is less effective the more it approaches a rational reply. This is the case with a rather large number of Lautréamont's altered maxims. The more the rational character of the reply is apparent, the more indistinguishable it becomes from the ordinary spirit of repartee, which similarly uses the opponent's words against him. This is naturally not limited to spoken language. It was in this connection that we objected to the project of some of our comrades who proposed to detourn an anti-Soviet poster of the fascist organization "Peace and Liberty"—which proclaimed, amid images of overlapping flags of the Western powers, "Union makes strength"—by adding onto it a smaller sheet with the phrase "and coalitions make war."

Detournement by simple reversal is always the most direct and the least effective. Thus, the Black Mass reacts against the construction of an ambiance based on a given metaphysics by constructing an ambiance in the same framework that merely reverses—and thus simultaneously conserves—the values of that metaphysics. Such reversals may nevertheless have a certain progressive aspect. For example, Clemenceau [called "The Tiger"] could be referred to as "The Tiger called Clemenceau."

Of the four laws that have just been set forth, the first is essential and applies universally. The other three are practically applicable only to deceptive detourned elements.

The first visible consequences of a widespread use of detournement, apart from its intrinsic propaganda powers, will be the revival of a multitude of bad books, and thus the extensive (unintended) participation of their unknown authors; an increasingly extensive transformation of sentences or plastic works that happen to be in fashion; and above all an ease of production far surpassing in quantity, variety and quality the automatic writing that has bored us so much.

Detournement not only leads to the discovery of new aspects of talent; it addition, clashing head-on with all social and legal conventions, it cannot fail to be a powerful cultural weapon in the service of a real class struggle. The cheapness of its products is the heavy artillery that breaks through all the Chinese walls of understanding. It is a real means of proletarian artistic education, the first step toward a *literary communism.*

Ideas and realizations in the realm of detournement can be multiplied at will. For the moment we will limit ourselves to showing a few concrete possibilities starting from various current sectors of communication—it being understood that these separate sectors are significant only in relation to present-day techniques, and are all tending to merge into superior syntheses with the advance of these techniques.

Apart from the various direct uses of detourned phrases in posters, records or radio broadcasts, the two principal applications of detourned prose are metagraphic writings and, to a lesser degree, the adroit perversion of the classical novel form.

There is not much future in the detournement of complete novels, but during the transitional phase there might be a certain number of undertakings of this sort. Such a detournement gains by being accompanied by illustrations whose relationships to the text are not immediately obvious. In spite of the undeniable difficulties, we believe it would be possible to produce an instructive psychogeographical detournement of George Sand's *Consuelo*, which thus decked out could be relaunched on the literary market disguised under some innocuous title like "Life in the Suburbs," or even under a title itself detourned, such as "The Lost Patrol." (It would be a good idea to reuse in this way many titles of old deteriorated films of which nothing else remains, or of films which continue to stupefy young people in the film clubs.)

Metagraphic writing, no matter how backward may be the plastic framework in which it is materially situated, presents far richer opportunities for detourning prose, as well as other appropriate objects or images. One can get some idea of this from the project, devised in 1951 but then abandoned for lack of sufficient financial means, which envisaged a pinball machine arranged in such a way that the play of the lights and the more or less predictable trajectories of the balls would form a metagraphic-spatial composition entitled *Thermal sensations and desires of people passing by the gates of the Cluny Museum around an hour after sunset in November.* We have since, of course, come to realize that a situationist-analytic work cannot scientifically advance by way of such projects. The means nevertheless remain suitable for less ambitious goals.

It is obviously in the realm of the cinema that detournement can attain its greatest efficacity, and undoubtedly, for those concerned with this aspect, its greatest beauty.

The powers of film are so extensive, and the absence of coordination of those powers is so glaring, that almost any film that is above the miserable average can provide matter for innumerable polemics among spectators or professional critics. Only the conformism of those people prevents them from discovering features just as appealing and faults just as glaring in the worst films. To cut through this absurd confusion of values, we can observe that Griffith's *Birth of a Nation* is one of the most important films in the history of the cinema because of its wealth of new contributions. On the other hand, it is a racist film and therefore absolutely does not merit being shown in its present form. But its total prohibition could be seen as regrettable from the point of view of the secondary, but potentially worthier, domain of the cinema. It would be better to detourn it as a whole, without necessarily even altering the montage, by adding a soundtrack that made a powerful denunciation of the horrors of imperialist war and of the activities of the Ku Klux Klan, which are continuing in the United States even now.

Such a detournement—a very moderate one—is in the final analysis nothing more than the moral equivalent of the restoration of old paintings in museums. But most films only merit being cut up to compose other works. This reconversion of preexisting sequences will obviously be accompanied by other elements, musical or pictorial as well as historical. While the filmic rewriting of history has until now been largely along the lines of Guitry's burlesque re-creations, one could have Robespierre say, before his execution: "In spite of so many trials, my experience and the grandeur of my task convinces me that all is well." If in this case a judicious revival of Greek tragedy serves us in exalting Robespierre, we can conversely imagine a neorealist sort of sequence, at the counter of a truckstop bar, for example, with one of the truckdrivers saying seriously to another: "Ethics was in the books of the philosophers; we have introduced it into the governing of nations." One can see that this juxtaposition illuminates Maximilien's idea,* the idea of a dictatorship of the proletariat.

The light of detournement is propagated in a straight line. To the extent that new architecture seems to have to begin with an experimental baroque stage, the *architectural complex*—which we conceive as the construction of a dynamic environment related to styles of behavior—will probably detourn existing architectural forms, and in any case will make plastic and emotional use of all sorts of detourned objects: calculatedly arranged cranes or metal scaffolding replacing a defunct sculptural tradition. This is shocking only to the most fanatic admirers of French-style gardens. It is said that in his old age D'Annunzio, that pro-fascist swine, had the prow of a torpedo boat in his park. Leaving aside his patriotic motives, the idea of such a monument is not without a certain charm.

If detournement were extended to urbanistic realizations, not many people would remain unaffected by an exact reconstruction in one city of an entire neighborhood of another. Life can never be too disorienting: detournements on this level would really make it beautiful.

Titles themselves, as we have already seen, are a basic element of detournement. This follows from two general observations: that all titles are interchangeable and that they have a determinant importance in several genres. All the detective stories in the "Série Noir" are extremely similar, yet merely continually changing the titles suffices to hold a considerable audience. In music a title always exerts a great influence, yet the choice of one is quite arbitrary. Thus it wouldn't be a bad idea to make a final correction to the title of the "Eroica Symphony" by changing it, for example, to "Lenin Symphony."

The title contributes strongly to a work, but there is an inevitable counteraction of the work on the title. Thus one can make extensive use of specific titles taken from scientific publications ("Coastal Biology of Temperate Seas") or military ones ("Night Combat of Small Infantry Units"), or even of many phrases found in illustrated children's books ("Marvelous Landscapes Greet the Voyagers").

In closing, we should briefly mention some aspects of what we call ultradetournement, that is, the tendencies for detournement to operate in everyday social life. Gestures and words can be given other meanings, and have been throughout history for various practical reasons. The secret societies of ancient China made use of quite subtle recognition signals encompassing the greater part of social behavior (the manner of arranging cups; of drinking; quotations of poems interrupted at agreed-on points). The need for a secret language, for passwords, is inseparable from a tendency toward play. Ultimately, any sign or word is susceptible to being converted into something else, even into its opposite. The royalist insurgents of the Vendée, because they bore the disgusting image of the Sacred Heart of Jesus, were called the Red Army. In the limited domain of political war vocabulary this expression was completely detourned within a century.

Outside of language, it is possible to use the same methods to detourn clothing, with all its strong emotional connotations. Here again we find the notion of disguise closely linked to play. Finally, when we have got to the stage of constructing situations, the ultimate goal of all our activity, it will be open to everyone to detourn entire situations by deliberately changing this or that determinant condition of them.

The methods that we have briefly dealt with here are presented not as our own invention, but as a generally widespread practice which we propose to systematize.

In itself, the theory of detournement scarcely interests us. But we find it linked to almost all the constructive aspects of the presituationist period of transition. Thus its enrichment, through practice, seems necessary.

We will postpone the development of these theses until later.

GUY DEBORD, GIL J. WOLMAN

From *Les Lèvres Nues* #8, May 1956

THE ALBA PLATFORM

From 2 to 8 September a Congress was held in Alba, Italy, convoked by Asger Jorn and Giuseppe Gallizio in the name of the International Movement for an Imaginist Bauhaus, a grouping whose views are in agreement with the Lettrist International's program regarding urbanism and its possible uses (see *Potlatch* #26). Representatives of avantgarde groups from eight countries (Algeria, Belgium, Czechoslovakia, Denmark, France, Great Britain, Holland, Italy) met there to lay the foundations for a united organization. The tasks toward this end were dealt with in all their implications.

Christian Dotremont, who had been announced as a member of the Belgian delegation in spite of the fact that he has for some time been a collaborator in the *Nouvelle Nouvelle Revue Française*, refrained from appearing at the Congress, where his presence would have been unacceptable for the majority of the participants.

Enrico Baj, representative of the "Nuclear Art Movement," was excluded the very first day; and the Congress affirmed its break with the Nuclearists by issuing the following statement: "Confronted with his conduct in certain previous affairs, Baj withdrew from the Congress. He did not make off with the cash-box."

Meanwhile our Czechoslovakian comrades Pravoslav Rada and Kotik were prevented from entering Italy. In spite of our protests, the Italian government did not grant them visas to pass through its national iron curtain until the end of the Alba Congress.

The statement of Wolman, the Lettrist International delegate, particularly stressed the necessity for a common platform defining the totality of current experimentation:

"Comrades, the parallel crises presently affecting all modes of artistic creation are determined by an overall interrelated movement that cannot be resolved outside a general perspective. The process of negation and destruction that has manifested itself at an accelerating rate against all the former conditions of artistic activity is irreversible: it is the consequence of the appearance of superior possibilities of action on the world. . . . Whatever prestige the bourgeoisie may today be willing to accord fragmentary or deliberately retrograde artistic tentatives, creation can now be nothing less than a synthesis aiming at an integral construction of an atmosphere, of a style of life. . . . A unitary urbanism—the synthesis that we call for, incorporating arts and technology—must be created in accordance with new values of life, values which it is henceforth necessary to distinguish and disseminate. . . ."

The final resolution of the Congress expressed a substantial accord in the form of a declaration in six points declaring the "necessity of an integral construction of the environment by a unitary urbanism that must utilize all arts and modern techniques"; the "inevitable outmodedness of any renovation of an art within its traditional limits"; the "recognition of an essential interdependence between unitary urbanism and a future style of life" which must be situated "in the perspective of a greater real freedom and a greater domination of nature"; and finally, "unity of action among the signers on the basis of this program" (the sixth point going on to enumerate the various specifics of mutual support).

Apart from this final resolution—signed by J. Calonne, Constant, G. Gallizio, A. Jorn, Kotik, Rada, Piero Simondo, E. Sottsass Jr., Elena Verrone, Wolman—the Congress unanimously declared itself against any relations with participants in the Festival de la Cité Radieuse, thus following through with the boycott initiated the preceding month.

At the conclusion of the Congress Gil J. Wolman was added to the editorial board of *Eristica*, the information bulletin of the International Movement for an Imaginist Bauhaus, and Asger Jorn was placed on the board of directors of the Lettrist International.

The Alba Congress probably marks one of the difficult stages in the struggle for a new sensibility and a new culture, a struggle which is itself part of the general revolutionary resurgence characterizing the year 1956, visible in the upsurge of the masses in the USSR, Poland and Hungary (although in the latter case we see the dangerously confusing revival of rotten old watchwords of clerical nationalism resulting from the fatal error of the prohibition of any Marxist opposition), in the successes of the Algerian insurrection and in the major strikes in Spain. These developments allow us the greatest hopes for the near future.

From *Potlatch: Information Bulletin of the Lettrist International* #27

2 November 1956

NOTES ON THE FORMATION OF
AN IMAGINIST BAUHAUS

What was the Bauhaus?

The Bauhaus was an answer to the question: What "education" do artists need in order to take their place in the machine age?

How was the Bauhaus idea realized?

It was realized with a "school" in Germany; first at Weimar, then at Dessau; founded by the architect Walter Gropius in 1919—destroyed by the Nazis in 1933.

What is the International Movement for an Imaginist Bauhaus?

It is the answer to the question WHERE AND HOW to find a justified place for artists in the machine age. This answer demonstrates that the education carried out by the old Bauhaus is false.

How has the idea of an International Movement for an Imaginist Bauhaus been realized?

The Movement was founded in Switzerland in 1953 as a tendency for the forming of a united organization capable of promoting an integral revolutionary cultural attitude. In 1954 the experience of the Albissola gathering demonstrated that experimental artists must get hold of industrial means and subject them to their own nonutilitarian ends. In 1955 an imaginist laboratory was founded at Alba. Conclusion of the Albissola experience: complete inflationary devaluation of modern values of decoration (cf. ceramics produced by children). In 1956 the Alba Congress dialectically defines unitary urbanism. In 1957 the Movement promulgates the watchword of psychogeographical action.

What we want

We want the same economic and practical means and possibilities that are already at the disposal of scientific research, of whose great results everyone is aware.

Artistic research is identical to "human science," which for us means "concerned" science, not purely historical science. This research should be carried out by artists with the assistance of scientists.

The first institute ever formed for this purpose is the experimental laboratory for free artistic research founded 29 September 1955 at Alba. Such a laboratory is not an instructional institution; it simply offers new possibilities for artistic experimentation.

The leaders of the old Bauhaus were great masters with exceptional talents, but they were bad teachers. The pupils' works were only pious imitations of their masters. The real influence of the latter was indirect, by force of example: Ruskin on Van de Velde, Van de Velde on Gropius.

This is not at all a critique, it is simply a statement of fact from which the following conclusions may be drawn: The direct transfer of artistic gifts is impossible; artistic adaptation takes place through a series of contradictory phases: Stupefaction—Wonder—Imitation—Rejection—Experience—Possession.

None of these phases can be avoided, although they need not all be gone through by any one individual.

Our practical conclusion is the following: we are abandoning all efforts at pedagogical action and moving toward experimental activity.

ASGER JORN

1957

REPORT ON THE CONSTRUCTION OF SITUATIONS AND ON THE INTERNATIONAL SITUATIONIST TENDENCY'S CONDITIONS OF ORGANIZATION AND ACTION

(excerpts)

Revolution and Counterrevolution in Modern Culture

First of all we think the world must be changed. We want the most liberating change of the society and life in which we find ourselves confined. We know that this change is possible through appropriate actions.

Our specific concern is the use of certain means of action and the discovery of new ones, means more easily recognizable in the domain of culture and mores, but applied in the perspective of an interaction of all revolutionary changes.

What is termed culture reflects, but also prefigures, the possibilities of organization of life in a given society. Our era is fundamentally characterized by the lagging of revolutionary political action behind the development of modern possibilities of production which call for a superior organization of the world. [. . .]

One of the contradictions of the bourgeoisie in its phase of liquidation is that while it respects the abstract principle of intellectual and artistic creation, it at first resists actual creations, then eventually exploits them. This is because it must maintain a sense of criticality and experimental research among a minority, but must channel this activity toward strictly compartmentalized utilitarian disciplines and avert any concerted overall critique and research. In the domain of culture the bourgeoisie strives to divert the taste for innovation, which is dangerous for it in our era, toward certain degraded, innocuous and confused forms of novelty. Through the commercial mechanisms that control cultural activity, avant-garde tendencies are cut off from the segments of society that could support them, segments already limited because of the general social conditions. The people in these tendencies who become well known are generally accepted as exceptional individuals, on the condition that they accept various renunciations: the essential point is always the renunciation of a comprehensive contestation and the acceptance of fragmentary work susceptible to diverse interpretations. This is what gives the very term "avant-garde," which in the final analysis is always controlled and manipulated by the bourgeoisie, a ridiculous and dubious aspect.

The very notion of a collective avant-garde, with the militant aspect it implies, is a recent product of historical conditions that are simultaneously giving rise to the necessity for a coherent revolutionary program in culture and to the necessity to struggle against the forces that impede the development of such a program. Such groups are led to transpose into their sphere of activity organizational methods created by revolutionary politics, and their action is henceforth inconceivable without some connection with a political critique. In this regard there is a notable progression from futurism through dadaism and surrealism to the movements formed after 1945. At each of these stages, however, one discovers the same totalistic will for change; and the same rapid crumbling away when the inability to change the real world profoundly enough leads to a defensive withdrawal to the very doctrinal positions whose inadequacy had just been revealed.

Futurism, whose influence spread from Italy in the period preceding World War I, adopted an attitude of revolutionizing literature and the arts which introduced a great number of formal innovations, but which was only based on an extremely oversimplified application of the notion of mechanical progress. Futurism's puerile technological optimism vanished with the period of bourgeois euphoria that had sustained it. Italian futurism collapsed, going from nationalism to fascism without ever attaining a more complete theoretical vision of its time.

Dadaism, constituted in Zurich and New York by refugees and deserters from World War I, aimed at embodying the refusal of all the values of a bourgeois society whose bankruptcy had just become so grossly evident. Its violent manifestations in postwar Germany and France aimed mainly at the destruction of art and literature and to a lesser degree at certain forms of behavior (deliberately imbecilic spectacles, speeches, excursions). Its historic role is to have delivered a mortal blow to the traditional conception of culture. The almost immediate dissolution of dadaism was a result of its purely negative definition. But it is certain that the dadaist spirit has influenced all the movements that have come after it; and that a dadaist-type negation must be present in any later constructive position as long as the social conditions that impose the repetition of rotten superstructures—conditions that have intellectually already been definitively condemned—have not been wiped out by force.

The creators of surrealism, who had participated in the dadaist movement in France, endeavored to define the terrain of a constructive action on the basis of the spirit of revolt and the extreme depreciation of traditional means of communication expressed by dadaism. Setting out from a poetic application of Freudian psychology, surrealism extended the methods it had discovered to painting, to film and to some aspects of everyday life; and its influence, in more diffuse forms, spread much further. Now, what is important in an enterprise of this nature is not whether it is absolutely or relatively right, but whether it succeeds in catalyzing for a certain time the desires of an era. Surrealism's period of progress, marked by the liquidation of idealism and a moment of rallying to dialectical materialism, came to a halt soon after 1930, but its decay only became evident after World War II. Surrealism had by then spread to numerous countries. It had also initiated a discipline whose rigor must not be overestimated, a discipline which was often tempered by commercial considerations, but which was nevertheless an effective means of struggle against the confusionist mechanisms of the bourgeoisie.

The surrealist program, asserting the sovereignty of desire and surprise, proposing a new use of life, is much richer in constructive possibilities than is generally thought. Certainly the lack of material means of realization seriously limited the scope of surrealism. But the devolution of its original proponents into spiritualism, and above all the mediocrity of its epigones, obliges us to search for the negation of the development of surrealist theory in the very origin of this theory.

The error that is at the root of surrealism is the idea of the infinite richness of the unconscious imagination. The cause of the ideological failure of surrealism was its belief that the unconscious was the finally discovered ultimate force of life, and its having revised the history of ideas accordingly and stopped it there. We now know that the unconscious imagination is poor, that automatic writing is monotonous, and that the whole genre of ostentatious surrealist "weirdness" has ceased to be very surprising. The formal fidelity to this style of imagination ultimately leads back to the antipodes of the modern conditions of imagination: back to traditional occultism. The extent to which surrealism has remained in dependence on its hypothesis regarding the unconscious can be seen in the work of theoretical investigation attempted by the second-generation surrealists: Calas and Mabille relate everything to the two successive aspects of the surrealist practice of the unconscious—the one to psychoanalysis, the other to cosmic influences. In fact, the discovery of the role of the unconscious was a surprise, an innovation, not a law of future surprises and innovations. Freud had also ended up discovering this when he wrote, "Everything conscious wears out. What is unconscious remains unaltered. But once it is set loose, does it not fall into ruins in its turn?"

Opposing an apparently irrational society in which the clash between reality and the old but still vigorously proclaimed values was pushed to the point of absurdity, surrealism made use of the irrational

to destroy its superficially logical values. The very success of surrealism has a lot to do with the fact that the most modern side of this
society's ideology has renounced a strict hierarchy of factitious values
and openly uses the irrational, including vestiges of surrealism. The
bourgeoisie must above all prevent a new setting out of revolutionary
thought. It was aware of the danger of surrealism. Now that it has
been able to dissolve it into ordinary aesthetic commerce, it would like
people to believe that surrealism was the most radical and disturbing
movement possible. It thus cultivates a sort of nostalgia for surrealism
at the same time that it discredits any new venture by automatically
reducing it to a surrealist déjà-vu, that is, to a defeat which according
to it is definitive and can no longer be brought back into question by
anyone. The refusal of the alienation in the society of Christian morality has led some people to a respect for the completely irrational
alienation of primitive societies, that's all. It is necessary to go further
and rationalize the world more—the first condition for impassioning
it. [. . .]

The Role of Minority Tendencies in the Ebbing Period

[. . .] Between 1930 and World War II surrealism continually declined
as a revolutionary force at the same time that its influence was being
extended beyond its control. The postwar period led to the rapid liquidation of surrealism by the two elements that had already blocked
its development around 1930: the lack of possibilities for theoretical
renewal and the ebbing of revolution, elements which were reflected
in the political and cultural reaction in the workers movement. This
second element is directly determinant, for example, in the disappearance of the surrealist group of Rumania. On the other hand, it is above
all the first of these elements which condemned the Revolutionary
Surrealism movement in France and Belgium to a rapid breaking up.
Except in Belgium, where a fraction issuing from surrealism has held
to a valid experimental position [the *Lèvres Nues* group], all the surrealist tendencies scattered around the world have joined the camp of
mystical idealism.

Rallying a part of the Revolutionary Surrealism movement, an
"Experimental Artists' International"—which published the journal
Cobra (Copenhagen-Brussels-Amsterdam)—was formed between 1949
and 1951 in Denmark, Holland and Belgium, and subsequently extended to Germany. The merit of these groups was to have understood
that such an organization is necessitated by the complexity and extent
of present-day problems. But their lack of ideological rigor, the limitation of their pursuits to largely plastic experimentation, and above
all the absence of a comprehensive theory of the conditions and perspectives of their experience led to their breaking up.

Lettrism, in France, had started off with a complete opposition to
the entire known aesthetic movement, whose continual decaying it
correctly analyzed. Having in view the uninterrupted creation of new
forms in all domains, the lettrist group carried on a salutary agitation

between 1946 and 1952. But the group generally took it for granted that aesthetic disciplines should take a new departure within a general framework similar to the former one, and this idealist error limited its productions to a few paltry experiments. In 1952 the lettrist left wing organized itself into a "Lettrist International" and expelled the backward fraction.* In the Lettrist International the quest for new methods of intervention in everyday life was pursued amidst sharp struggles among different tendencies.

In Italy, with the exception of the antifunctionalist experimental group that in 1955 formed the most solid section of the International Movement for an Imaginist Bauhaus, the efforts toward avant-garde formations attached to the old artistic perspectives have not even attained a theoretical expression.

During the same period the most innocuous and massified aspects of Western culture have been massively imitated from the United States to Japan. (The US avant-garde, which tends to congregate in the American colony in Paris, lives there in the most tame, insipidly conformist manner, isolated ideologically, socially and even ecologically from everything else going on.) As for the productions of peoples who are still subject to cultural colonialism (often caused by political oppression), even though they may be progressive in their own countries, they play a reactionary role in the advanced cultural centers. Critics who have based their entire career on outdated systems of creation pretend to discover engaging new advances in Greek films or Guatemalan novels—an exoticism of the antiexotic, of the revival of old forms long since exploited and exhausted in other countries; an exoticism which does, however, serve the primary purpose of exoticism: escape from the real conditions of life and creation.

In the workers states only the experimentation conducted by Brecht in Berlin, in its putting into question the classic spectacle notion, is close to the constructions that matter for us today. Only Brecht has succeeded in resisting the stupidity of Socialist Realism in power.

Now that Socialist Realism is falling apart, we can expect much from a revolutionary irruption of the intellectuals in the workers states into the real problems of modern culture. If Zhdanovism has been the purest expression not only of the cultural degeneration of the workers movement but also of the conservative cultural position in the bourgeois world, those in the East who are presently rising against Zhdanovism cannot do so—whatever their subjective intentions— merely in the name of a greater creative freedom à la Cocteau, for example. A negation of Zhdanovism objectively means the negation of the Zhdanovist negation of "liquidation."* The sole possible supersession of Zhdanovism will be the real exercise of freedom, which is consciousness of present necessity.

Here, too, the recent years have at most been a period of confused resistance to the confused reign of retrograde imbecility. There weren't many of us really working against it. But we should not linger over the tastes or trivial findings of this period. The problems of cultural creation can be resolved only in relation with a new advance of world revolution.

Platform for a Provisional Opposition

[. . .] The union of several experimental tendencies for a revolutionary front in culture, begun at the congress held at Alba, Italy, at the end of 1956, presupposes that we not neglect three important factors.

First of all, we must insist on a complete accord among the persons and groups that participate in this united action; and this accord must not be facilitated by allowing certain of its consequences to be dissimulated. Jokers or careerists who have the unconsciousness to think they can make a career in this way must be rebuffed.

Next, we must recall that while any genuinely experimental attitude is usable, that word has very often been misused in the attempt to justify some artistic action within a present structure, that is, a structure previously discovered by others. The sole valid experimental proceeding is based on the accurate critique of existing conditions and the deliberate supersession of them. It must be understood once and for all that something that is only a personal expression within a framework created by others cannot be termed a creation. Creation is not the arrangement of objects and forms, it is the invention of new laws on that arrangement.

Finally, we have to eliminate the sectarianism among us that opposes unity of action with possible allies for specific goals and prevents our infiltration of parallel organizations.* From 1952 to 1955 the Lettrist International, after some necessary purges, continually moved toward a sort of absolutist rigor leading to an equally absolute isolation and ineffectuality, and ultimately to a certain immobility, a degeneration of the spirit of critique and discovery. We must definitively supersede this sectarian conduct in favor of real actions. This should be the sole criterion on which we join with or separate from comrades. Naturally this does not mean that we should renounce breaks, as everyone urges us to do. We think, on the contrary, that it is necessary to go still further in breaking with habits and persons.

We should collectively define our program and realize it in a disciplined manner, by all means, even artistic ones.

Toward a Situationist International

Our central idea is that of the construction of situations, that is to say, the concrete construction of momentary ambiances of life and their transformation into a superior passional quality. We must develop a methodical intervention based on the complex factors of two components in perpetual interaction: the material environment of life and the comportments which it gives rise to and which radically transform it.

Our perspectives of action on the environment ultimately lead us to the notion of unitary urbanism. Unitary urbanism is defined first of all by the use of the ensemble of arts and technics as means contributing to an integral composition of the milieu. This ensemble must be envisaged as infinitely more far-reaching than the old domination of architecture over the traditional arts, or than the present sporadic application to anarchic urbanism of specialized technology or of scientific investigations such as ecology. Unitary urbanism must, for example, dominate the acoustic environment as well as the distribution of different varieties of food and drink. It must include the creation of new forms and the detournement of previous forms of architecture, urbanism, poetry and cinema. Integral art, which has been talked about so much, can only be realized at the level of urbanism. But it can no longer correspond to any of the traditional aesthetic categories. In each of its experimental cities unitary urbanism will act by way of a certain number of force fields, which we can temporarily designate by the classic term "quarter." Each quarter will tend toward a specific harmony, divided off from neighboring harmonies; or else will play on a maximum breaking up of internal harmony.

Secondly, unitary urbanism is dynamic, that is, in close relation to styles of behavior. The most elementary unit of unitary urbanism is not the house, but the architectural complex, which combines all the factors conditioning an ambiance, or a series of clashing ambiances, on the scale of the constructed situation. The spatial development must take into account the emotional effects that the experimental city will determine. One of our comrades has advanced a theory of states-of-mind quarters according to which each quarter of a city would be designed to provoke a specific basic sentiment to which the subject would knowingly expose himself. It seems that such a project draws opportune conclusions from the current tendency of depreciation of the randomly encountered primary sentiments, and that its realization could contribute to accelerating that depreciation. The comrades who call for a new, free architecture must understand that this new architecture will primarily be based not on free, poetic lines and forms—in the sense that today's "lyrical abstract" painting uses those words— but rather on the atmospheric effects of rooms, hallways, streets, atmospheres linked to the gestures they contain. Architecture must advance by taking emotionally moving situations, rather than emotionally moving forms, as the material it works with. And the experiments conducted with this material will lead to unknown forms. Psychogeographical research, "the study of the exact laws and specific effects of the action of the geographical environment, consciously organized or not, on the emotions and behavior of individuals," thus takes on a double meaning: active observation of present-day urban agglomerations and development of hypotheses on the structure of a situationist city. The progress of psychogeography depends to a great extent on the statistical extension of its methods of observation, but above all on experimentation by means of concrete interventions in urbanism. Before this stage is attained we cannot be certain of the objective truth of the first psychogeographical findings. But even if these findings should turn out to be false, they would still be false solutions to what is certainly a real problem.

Our action on behavior, linked with other desirable aspects of a revolution in mores, can be briefly defined as the invention of games of an essentially new type. The most general goal must be to extend the nonmediocre part of life, to reduce the empty moments of life as much as possible. One could thus speak of our action as an enterprise of quantitatively increasing human life, an enterprise more serious than the biological methods currently being investigated. This automatically implies a qualitative increase whose developments are unpredictable. The situationist game is distinguished from the classic conception of the game by its radical negation of the element of competition and of separation from everyday life. The situationist game is not distinct from a moral choice, the taking of one's stand in favor of what will ensure the future reign of freedom and play. This perspective is obviously linked to the inevitable continual and rapid increase of leisure time resulting from the level of productive forces our era has attained. It is also linked to the recognition of the fact that a battle of leisure is taking place before our eyes whose importance in the class struggle has not been sufficiently analyzed. So far, the ruling class has succeeded in using the leisure the revolutionary proletariat wrested from it by developing a vast industrial sector of leisure activities that is an incomparable instrument for stupefying the proletariat with by-products of mystifying ideology and bourgeois tastes. The abundance of televised imbecilities is probably one of the reasons for the American working class's inability to develop any political consciousness. By obtaining by collective pressure a slight rise in the price of its labor above the minimum necessary for the production of that labor, the proletariat not only extends its power of struggle, it also extends the terrain of the struggle. New forms of this struggle then arise alongside directly economic and political conflicts. It can be said that revolutionary propaganda has so far been constantly overcome in these new forms of struggle in all the countries where advanced industrial development has introduced them. That the necessary changing of the infrastructure can be delayed by errors and weaknesses at the level of superstructures has unfortunately been demonstrated by several experiences of the twentieth century. It is necessary to throw new forces into the battle of leisure, and we will take up our position there.

A rough experimentation toward a new mode of behavior has already been made with what we have termed the *dérive*, which is the practice of a passional journey out of the ordinary through rapid changing of ambiances, as well as a means of study of psychogeography and of situationist psychology. But the application of this will to playful creation must be extended to all known forms of human relationships, so as to influence, for example, the historical evolution of sentiments like friendship and love. Everything leads us to believe that the essential elements of our research lie in our hypothesis of constructions of situations.

The life of a person is a succession of fortuitous situations, and even if none of them is exactly the same as another the immense majority of them are so undifferentiated and so dull that they give a perfect impression of similitude. The corollary of this state of things is that the rare intensely engaging situations found in life strictly confine and limit this life. We must try to construct situations, that is to say, collective ambiances, ensembles of impressions determining the quality of a moment. If we take the simple example of a gathering of a group of individuals for a given time, it would be desirable, while taking into account the knowledge and material means we have at our disposal, to study what organization of the place, what selection of participants and what provocation of events produce the desired ambiance. The powers of a situation will certainly expand considerably in both time and space with the realizations of unitary urbanism or the education of a situationist generation. The construction of situations begins on the ruins of the modern spectacle. It is easy to see to what extent the very principle of the spectacle—nonintervention—is linked to the alienation of the old world. Conversely, the most pertinent revolutionary experiments in culture have sought to break the spectator's psychological identification with the hero so as to draw him into activity by provoking his capacities to revolutionize his own life. The situation is thus made to be lived by its constructors. The role played by a passive or merely bit-part playing "public" must constantly diminish, while that played by those who cannot be called actors but rather, in a new sense of the term, "livers," must steadily increase.

So to speak, we have to multiply poetic subjects and objects—which are now unfortunately so rare that the slightest ones take on an exaggerated emotional importance—and we have to organize games of these poetic objects among these poetic subjects. This is our entire program, which is essentially transitory. Our situations will be ephemeral, without a future; passageways. The permanence of art or anything else does not enter into our considerations, which are serious. Eternity is the grossest idea a person can conceive of in connection with his acts. [. . .]

The situationist minority first constituted itself as a tendency in the lettrist left wing, then in the Lettrist International which it ended up controlling. The same objective movement has led several avant-garde groups of the recent period to similar conclusions. Together we must eliminate all the relics of the recent past. We consider today that an accord for a united action of the revolutionary avant-garde in culture must be carried out on the basis of such a program. We have neither guaranteed recipes nor definitive results. We only propose an experimental research to be collectively led in a few directions that we are presently defining and toward others that have yet to be defined. The very difficulty of succeeding in the first situationist projects is a proof of the newness of the domain we are penetrating. That which changes our way of seeing the streets is more important than what changes our way of seeing painting. Our working hypotheses will be reexamined at each future upheaval, wherever it comes from. [. . .]

GUY DEBORD
June 1957*

Soundtracks of Two Films by Guy Debord (1959–1961)

ON THE PASSAGE OF A FEW PERSONS
THROUGH A RATHER BRIEF PERIOD OF TIME

Voice 1 (male "announcer"): This neighborhood* was made for the wretched dignity of the petty bourgeoisie, for respectable occupations and intellectual tourism. The sedentary population of the upper floors was sheltered from the influences of the street. This neighborhood has remained the same. It was the strange setting of our story. Here a systematic questioning of all the diversions and works of a society, a total critique of its idea of happiness, was expressed in acts.

These people also scorned "subjective profundity." They were interested in nothing but an adequate and concrete expression of themselves.

Voice 2 (Debord, monotone): Human beings are not fully conscious of their real life ... usually groping in the dark; overwhelmed by the consequences of their acts; at every moment groups and individuals find themselves confronted with results they have not wished.

Voice 1: They said that oblivion was their ruling passion. They wanted to reinvent everything each day; to become the masters and possessors of their own lives.

Just as one does not judge a man according to the conception he has of himself, one cannot judge such periods of transition according to their own consciousness; on the contrary, one must explain the consciousness through the contradictions of material life, through the conflict between social conditions and the forces of social production.

The progress achieved in the domination of nature was not yet matched by a corresponding liberation of everyday life. Youth passed away among the various controls of resignation.

Our camera has captured for you a few aspects of a provisional microsociety.

The knowledge of empirical facts remains abstract and superficial as long as it is not concretized by its integration into the whole—which

29

alone permits the supersession of partial and abstract problems so as to arrive at their *concrete essence*, and implicitly at their meaning.

This group was on the margins of the economy. It tended toward a role of pure consumption, and first of all the free consumption of its time. It thus found itself directly engaged in qualitative variations of daily life but deprived of any means to intervene in them.

The group ranged over a very small area. The same times brought them back to the same places. No one went to bed early. Discussion on the meaning of all this continued. . . .

Voice 2: "Our life is a journey — In the winter and the night. — We seek our passage . . ."

Voice 1: The abandoned literature nevertheless exerted a delaying action on new affective formulations.

Voice 2: There was the fatigue and the cold of the morning in this much-traversed labyrinth, like an enigma that we had to resolve. It was a looking-glass reality through which we had to discover the possible richness of reality. On the bank of the river evening began once again; and caresses; and the importance of a world without importance. Just as the eyes have a blurred vision of many things and can see only one clearly, so the will can strive only incompletely toward diverse objects and can completely love only one at a time.

Voice 3 (young girl): No one counted on the future. It would never be possible to be together later, or anywhere else. There would never be a greater freedom.

Voice 1: The refusal of time and of growing old automatically limited encounters in this narrow, contingent zone, where what was lacking was felt as irreparable. The extreme precariousness of the means of getting by without working was at the root of this impatience which made excesses necessary and breaks definitive.

Voice 2: One never really contests an organization of existence without contesting all of that organization's forms of language.

Voice 1: When freedom is practiced in a closed circle, it fades into a dream, becomes a mere representation of itself. The ambiance of play is by nature unstable. At any moment "ordinary life" can prevail once again. The geographical limitation of play is even more striking than its temporal limitation. Any game takes place within the contours of its spatial domain. Around the neighborhood, around its fleeting and threatened immobility, stretched a half-known city where people met only by chance, losing their way forever. The girls there, because they were legally under the control of their families until the age of eighteen, were often recaptured by the defenders of that detestable institution. They were generally confined under the guard of those creatures who among all the bad products of a bad society are the most ugly and repugnant: nuns.

What usually makes documentaries so easy to understand is the arbitrary limitation of their subject matter. They describe the atomization of social functions and the isolation of their products. One can, in contrast, envisage the entire complexity of a moment which is not resolved into a work, a moment whose movement indissolubly contains facts and values and whose meaning does not yet appear. The subject matter of the documentary would then be this confused totality.

Voice 2: The epoch had arrived at a level of knowledge and technical means that made possible, and increasingly necessary, a *direct* construction of all aspects of a liberated affective and practical existence. The appearance of these superior means of action, still unused because of the delays in the project of liquidating the commodity economy, had already condemned aesthetic activity, whose ambitions and powers were both outdated. The decay of art and of all the values of former mores had formed our sociological background. The ruling class's monopoly over the instruments we had to control in order to realize the collective art of our time had excluded us from a cultural production officially devoted to illustrating and repeating the past. An art film on this generation can only be a film on its absence of real works.

Everyone unthinkingly followed the paths learned once and for all, to their work and their homes, to their predictable future. For them duty had already become a habit, and habit a duty. They did not see the deficiency of their city. They thought the deficiency of their life was natural. We wanted to break out of this conditioning, in quest of another use of the urban landscape, in quest of new passions. The atmosphere of a few places gave us intimations of the future powers of an architecture it would be necessary to create to be the support and framework for less mediocre games. We could expect nothing of anything we had not ourselves altered. The urban environment proclaimed the orders and tastes of the ruling society just as violently as the newspapers. It is man who makes the unity of the world, but man has extended himself everywhere. Men can see nothing around them that is not their own image; everything speaks to them of themselves. Their very landscape is alive. There were obstacles everywhere. There was a coherence in the obstacles of all types. They maintained the coherent reign of poverty. Everything being connected, it was necessary to *change everything* by a unitary struggle, or nothing. It was necessary to link up with the masses, but we were surrounded by sleep.

Voice 3: The dictatorship of the proletariat is a desperate struggle, bloody and bloodless, violent and peaceful, military and economic, educational and administrative, against the forces and traditions of the old world.

Voice 1: In this country it is once again the men of order who have rebelled. They have reinforced their power. They have been able to aggravate the grotesqueness of the ruling conditions according to their will. They have embellished their system with the funereal ceremonies of the past.

Voice 2· Years, like a single instant prolonged to this point, come to an end.

Voice 1: That which was directly lived reappears frozen in the distance, fit into the tastes and illusions of an era carried away with it.

Voice 2: The appearance of events that we have not made, that others have made against us, obliges us from now on to be aware of the passage of time, its results, the transformation of our own desires into events. What differentiates the past from the present is precisely its out-of-reach objectivity; there is no more should-be; being is so consumed that it has ceased to exist. The details are already lost in the dust of time. Who was afraid of life, afraid of the night, afraid of being taken, afraid of being kept?

Voice 3: That which should be abolished continues, and we continue to wear away with it. We are engulfed. We are separated. The years pass and we have not changed anything.

Voice 2: Once again morning in the same streets. Once again the fatigue of so many similarly passed nights. It is a walk that has lasted a long time.

Voice 1: Really hard to drink more.

Voice 2: Of course one might make a film of it. But even if such a film succeeds in being as fundamentally incoherent and unsatisfying as the reality it deals with, it will never be more than a re-creation—poor and false like this botched traveling shot.

Voice 3: There are now people who flatter themselves that they are authors of films, as others were authors of novels. They are even more backward than the novelists because they are ignorant of the decomposition and exhaustion of individual expression in our time, ignorant of the end of the arts of passivity. They are praised for their sincerity since they dramatize, with more personal depth, the conventions of which their life consists. There is talk of the liberation of the cinema. But what does it matter to us if one more art is liberated through which Pierre or Jacques or François can joyously express their slave sentiments? The only interesting venture is the liberation of everyday life, not only in the perspectives of history but for us and right away. This entails the withering away of alienated forms of communication. The cinema, too, has to be destroyed.

Voice 2: In the final analysis, stars are created by the need we have for them, and not by talent or absence of talent or even by the film industry or advertising. Miserable need, dismal, anonymous life that would like to expand itself to the dimensions of cinema life. The imaginary life on the screen is the product of this real need. The star is the projection of this need.

The images of the advertisements during the intermissions are more suited than any others for evoking an intermission of life.

To really describe this era it would no doubt be necessary to show many other things. But what would be the point? Better to grasp the totality of what has been done and what remains to be done than to add more ruins to the old world of the spectacle and of memories.

1959

CRITIQUE OF SEPARATION

We don't know what to say. Words form themselves into sequences and gestures recognize each other. Outside us. Of course some methods are mastered, some results verified. It's often pleasant. But so many things we wanted have not been attained; or only partially and not like we thought. What communication have we desired, or experienced, or only simulated? What true project has been lost?

The cinematic spectacle has its rules, which enable one to produce satisfactory products. But dissatisfaction is the reality that must be taken as a point of departure. The function of the cinema is to present a false, isolated coherence, dramatic or documentary, as a substitute for a communication and an activity that are absent. To demystify documentary cinema it is necessary to dissolve what is called its subject matter.

A well-established rule is that anything in a film that is said other than by way of images must be repeated or else the spectators will miss it. That may be true. But this sort of incomprehension is present everywhere in everyday encounters. Something must be specified, made clear, but there's not enough time and you are not sure of having been understood. Before you have done or said what was necessary, you've already gone. Across the street. Overseas. There will never be another chance.

After all the dead time and lost moments, there remain these endlessly traversed postcard landscapes; this distance organized between each and everyone. Childhood? It's right here; we have never gotten out of it.

Our epoch accumulates powers and dreams of itself as being rational. But no one recognizes these powers as his own. There is no entering into adulthood: only the possible transformation, someday, of this long restlessness into a routine somnolence. Because no one ceases to be held under guardianship. The problem is not that people live more or less poorly; but that they live in a way that is always out of their control.

At the same time, it is a world in which we have been taught change.

Nothing stops. It changes more every day; and I know that those who day after day produce it against themselves can appropriate it for themselves.

The only adventure, we said, is to contest the totality, whose center is this way of living, where we can test our strength but not use it. In reality no adventure is directly formed for us. The adventures form part of the whole range of legends transmitted by cinema or in other ways; part of the whole spectacular sham of history.

Until the environment is collectively dominated, there will be no individuals—only specters haunting the things anarchically presented to them by others. In chance situations we meet separated people moving randomly. Their divergent emotions neutralize each other and maintain their solid environment of boredom. As long as we are unable to make our own history, to freely create situations, the effort toward unity will introduce other separations. The quest for a central activity leads to the formation of new specializations.

And only a few encounters were like signals emanating from a more intense life, a life that has not really been found.

What cannot be forgotten reappears in dreams. At the end of this type of dream, half asleep, the events are still for a brief moment taken as real. And the reactions they give rise to become clearer, more distinct, more reasonable; like, so many mornings, the memory of what one drank the night before. Then comes the awareness that it's all false; that "it was only a dream"; that there are no new realities and no going back into it. Nothing you can hold on to. These dreams are flashes from the unresolved past. They unilaterally illuminate moments previously lived in confusion and doubt. They strikingly publicize those of our needs that have not been answered. Here is daylight, and here are perspectives that now no longer mean anything. The sectors of a city are, at a certain level, decipherable. But the personal meaning they have had for us is incommunicable, like all that clandestinity of private life regarding which we possess nothing but pitiful documents.

Official news is elsewhere. The society sends back to itself its own historical image as a merely superficial and static history of its rulers. Those who incarnate the external fatality of what is done. The sector of rulers is the very sector of the spectacle. The cinema suits them well. Moreover, the cinema everywhere and with everything it deals with presents exemplary conduct and heroes modeled on the same old pattern as the rulers.

All existing equilibrium, however, is brought back into question each time unknown people try to live differently. But it's always far away. We learn of it through the papers and newscasts. We remain outside of it, confronted with just another spectacle. We are separated from it by our own nonintervention. It makes us disappointed in ourselves. At what moment was choice postponed? We have let things go.

I have let time slip away. I have lost what I should have defended.

This general critique of separation obviously contains and covers some particulars of memory. A less recognized pain, the awareness of a less explainable indignity. Exactly what separation was it? How quickly we have lived! It is to this point in our unreflecting history that I bring us back.

Everything that concerns the sphere of loss—that is to say, the past time I have lost, as well as disappearance, escape, and more generally the flowing past of things, and even what in the prevalent and therefore most vulgar social sense of the use of time is called wasted time—all this finds in that strangely apt old military expression, *"en enfants perdus,"** its meeting ground with the sphere of discovery, adventure, avant-garde. It is the crossroads where we have found and lost ourselves.

All this, it must be admitted, is not clear. It is a completely typical drunken monologue, with its incomprehensible allusions and tiresome delivery. With its vain phrases which do not await response, and its overbearing explanations. And its silences.

The poverty of means has to plainly express the scandalous poverty of the subject.

The events that happen in individual existence as it is organized, the events that really concern us and require our participation, are generally precisely those that merit nothing more than our being distant, bored, indifferent spectators. In contrast, the situation that is seen in some artistic transposition is rather often attractive, something that would merit our participating in it. This is a paradox to reverse, to put back on its feet. This is what must be realized in acts. And this idiotic spectacle of the fragmented and filtered past, full of sound and fury: it is not a question now of transmitting it—of "rendering" it, as is said—in another neatly ordered spectacle that would play the game of neatly ordered comprehension and participation. No. Any coherent artistic expression already expresses the coherence of the past, already expresses passivity. It is necessary to destroy memory in art. To destroy the conventions of its communication. To demoralize its fans. What a task! As in blurry drunken vision, the memory and language of the film fade out simultaneously. At the extreme, the miserable subjectivity is reversed into a certain sort of objectivity: a documentary on the conditions of noncommunication.

For example, I don't talk about her. False face. False relationship. A real person is separated from the interpreter of that person, if only by the time passed between the event and its evocation, by a distance that continually increases, that is increasing at this very moment. Just as the conserved expression itself remains separated from those who hear it abstractly and without any power over it.

The spectacle in its entirety is the era, an era in which a certain youth has recognized itself; it is the gap between this image and its results; the gap between the vision, the tastes, the refusals and the projects that previously defined it and the way it has advanced into ordinary life.

We have invented nothing. We adapt ourselves, with a few variations, into the network of possible courses. We get used to it, it seems.

No one has the enthusiasm on returning from a venture that they had on setting out on it. My dears, adventure is dead.

Who will resist? It is necessary to go beyond this partial defeat. Of course. And how to do it?

This is a film that interrupts itself and does not come to an end.

All conclusions remain to be drawn, everything has to be recalculated.

The problem continues to be posed, its expression is becoming more complicated. We have to resort to other measures.

Just as there was no profound reason to begin this abstract message, so there is none for concluding it.

I have scarcely begun to make you understand that I don't intend to play the game.

1961

French SI Journals
(1958–1969)

THE SOUND AND THE FURY

There is a lot of talk these days about angry, raging youth. People are fond of talking about them because, from the Swedish adolescents' aimless riots to the proclamations of England's "Angry Young Men" trying to form a literary movement, there is the same utter innocuousness, the same reassuring flimsiness. Products of a period in which the dominant ideas and ways of living are decomposing, a period of major breakthroughs in the domination of nature without any corresponding increase in the real possibilities of everyday life, reacting often crudely against the world they find themselves stuck in, these youth outbursts are roughly reminiscent of the surrealist state of mind. But they lack surrealism's points of leverage in culture, and its revolutionary hope. Hence the tone underlying this spontaneous negativity of American, Scandinavian and Japanese youth is one of resignation. Saint-Germain-des-Prés had already, during the first years after World War II, served as a laboratory for this kind of behavior (misleadingly termed "existentialist" by the press); which is why the present intellectual representatives of that generation in France (Françoise Sagan, Robbe-Grillet, Vadim, the atrocious Buffet) are all such extreme caricatural images of resignation.

Although this intellectual generation exhibits more aggressivity outside France, its consciousness still ranges from simple imbecility to premature self-satisfaction with a very inadequate revolt. The rotten egg smell exuded by the idea of God envelops the mystical cretins of the American "Beat Generation" and is not even entirely absent from the declarations of the Angry Young Men (e.g. Colin Wilson). These latter have discovered, thirty years behind the times, a certain moral subversiveness that *England* had managed to completely hide from them all this time; and they think they're being daringly scandalous by declaring themselves republicans. "Plays continue to be produced," writes Kenneth Tynan, "that are based on the ridiculous idea that people still fear and respect the Crown, the Empire, the Church, the University and Polite Society." This statement is indicative of how tepidly *literary* the Angry Young Men's perspective is. They have simply come to change their opinions about a few social conventions without even noticing the whole *change of terrain* of all cultural activity so evident in every avant-garde tendency of this century. The Angry Young Men are in fact particularly reactionary in their attribution of a privileged, redemptive value to the practice of literature: they are defending a mystification that was denounced in Europe around 1920 and whose survival today is of greater counterrevolutionary significance than that of the British Crown.

In all this revolutionary babble there is a common lack of understanding of the meaning and scope of surrealism (itself naturally distorted by its bourgeois artistic success). A continuation of surrealism would in fact be the most consistent attitude to take if nothing new arose to replace it. But because the young people who now adopt it are aware of surrealism's profound exigency while being incapable of overcoming the contradiction between this exigency and the immobility accompanying its pseudosuccess, they take refuge in the reactionary aspects present within surrealism from its inception (magic, belief in a golden age elsewhere than in history to come). Some of them even congratulate themselves on still being there, so long after the period of real struggle, under surrealism's *arc de triomphe*. There they will remain faithful to their tradition, says Gérard Legrand proudly (*Surréalisme même* #2), "a small band of youthful souls resolved to keep alive the true flame of surrealism."

A movement more liberating than the surrealism of *1924*—a movement Breton promised to rally to if it were to appear—cannot easily be formed because its liberativeness now depends on its seizing the more advanced material means of the modern world. But the surrealists of 1958 have not only become incapable of rallying to such a movement, they are even determined to combat it. But this does not eliminate the necessity for a revolutionary movement in culture to appropriate, with greater effectiveness, the freedom of spirit and the concrete freedom of mores claimed by surrealism.

For us, surrealism has been only a beginning of a revolutionary experiment in culture, an experiment that almost immediately ground to a halt practically and theoretically. We have to go further. Why can we no longer be surrealists? Certainly not in obedience to the ruling class's constant encouragement of "avant-garde" movements to dissociate themselves from the scandalous aspects of surrealism. (This encouragement is not made in the name of promoting originality at all costs—how could it be, when the ruling order has nothing really new to propose to us, nothing going beyond surrealism? On the contrary, the bourgeoisie stands ready to applaud any regressions we might lapse into.) If we are not surrealists it is *because we don't want to be bored.*

Decrepit surrealism, raging and ill-informed youth, well-off adolescent rebels lacking perspectives but far from lacking a cause—boredom is what they all have in common. The situationists will execute the judgment that contemporary leisure is pronouncing against itself.

PRELIMINARY PROBLEMS IN
CONSTRUCTING A SITUATION

"The construction of situations begins on the ruins of the modern spectacle. It is easy to see the extent to which the very principle of the spectacle—nonintervention—is linked to the alienation of the old world. Conversely, the most pertinent revolutionary experiments in culture have sought to break the spectator's psychological identification with the hero so as to draw him into activity . . . . The situation is thus made to be lived by its constructors. The role played by a passive or merely bit-part playing 'public' must constantly diminish, while that played by those who cannot be called actors, but rather, in a new sense of the term, 'livers,' must constantly increase."

—Report on the Construction of Situations

Our conception of a "constructed situation" is not limited to a unitary use of artistic means to create an ambiance, however great the force or spatiotemporal extension of this ambiance may be. The situation is also a unitary ensemble of behavior in time. It is composed of gestures contained in a transitory decor. These gestures are the product of the decor and of themselves. And they in their turn produce other forms of decor and other gestures. How can these forces be oriented? We are not going to limit ourselves to merely empirical experimentation with environments in quest of mechanistically provoked surprises. The really experimental direction of situationist activity consists in setting up, on the basis of more or less clearly recognized desires, a temporary field of activity favorable to these desires. This alone can lead to the further clarification of these primitive desires, and to the confused emergence of new desires whose material roots will be precisely the *new reality* engendered by the situationist constructions.

We must thus envisage a sort of situationist-oriented psychoanalysis in which, in contrast to the goals pursued by the various Freudian currents, each of the participants in this adventure would have to discover precise desires for ambiances *in order to realize them.* Each person must seek what he loves, what attracts him. (And here again, in contrast to certain tentatives of modern writing—Leiris, for example—what is important to us is neither our individual psychological structures nor the explanation of their formation, but their possible application in the construction of situations.) Through this method, elements out of which situations can be constructed can be determined, along with *projects to dynamize these elements.*

Such research is meaningful only for individuals working practically in the direction of a construction of situations. Such people are all, either spontaneously or in a conscious and organized manner, *pre-situationists*—individuals who have felt the objective need for this sort of construction through having recognized the present cultural emptiness and having participated in recent expressions of experimental awareness. They are close to each other because of their common specialization and because of their having taken part in the same historical avant-garde of that specialization. It is thus likely that they will share a number of common situationist themes and desires, which will increasingly diversify once they are brought into a phase of real activity.

The constructed situation is necessarily collective in its preparation and development. It would seem, however, that at least for the period of the first rough experimentations a given situation requires one individual to play a preeminent role as "director." If we imagine a particular situation project in which, for example, a research team has arranged an *emotionally moving gathering* of a few people for an evening, we would no doubt have to distinguish: a *director* or producer responsible for coordinating the basic elements necessary for the construction of the decor and for working out certain *interventions* in the events (alternatively, several people could work out their own interventions while being more or less unaware of each other's plans); the *direct agents* living the situation, who have taken part in creating the collective project and worked on the practical composition of the ambiance; and finally, a few passive *spectators* who have not participated in the constructive work, who should be *reduced to action*.

This relation between the director and the "livers" of the situation must naturally never become a permanent specialization. It is a purely temporary subordination of a whole team of situationists to the person responsible for a particular project. These perspectives, or the provisional terminology describing them, should not be taken to mean that we are talking about some continuation of theater. Pirandello and Brecht have already expressed the destruction of the theatrical spectacle and pointed out a few of the requirements for going beyond it. It could be said that the construction of situations will replace the theater in the same sense that the real construction of life has tended more and more to replace religion. Clearly the principal domain we are going to replace and *fulfill* is poetry, which burned itself out by taking its position at the vanguard of our time and has now completely disappeared.

Real individual fulfillment, which is also involved in the artistic experience that the situationists are discovering, entails the collective takeover of the world. Until this happens there will be no real individuals—only specters haunting the things anarchically presented to them by others. In chance situations we meet separated beings moving at random. Their divergent emotions neutralize each other and maintain their solid environment of boredom. We are going to undermine these conditions by raising at a few points the incendiary beacon heralding a *greater game*.

In our time functionalism, an inevitable expression of technological advance, is attempting to entirely eliminate play, and the partisans of "industrial design" complain that their projects are spoiled by people's tendency toward play. At the same time, industrial commerce crudely exploits this tendency by diverting it to a demand for constant superficial renovation of utilitarian products. We obviously have no interest in encouraging the continuous artistic renovation of refrigerator designs. But a moralizing functionalism is powerless to confront the problem profoundly. The only progressive way out is to liberate the tendency toward play elsewhere and on a larger scale. Short of this, all the naive indignation of the theorists of industrial design will not change the basic fact that the private automobile, for example, is primarily an idiotic toy and only secondarily a means of transportation. As opposed to all the regressive forms of play—which are regressions to its infantile stage, and always associated with reactionary politics— it is necessary to promote the experimental forms of a game of revolution.

DEFINITIONS

constructed situation: A moment of life concretely and deliberately constructed by the collective organization of a unitary ambiance and a game of events.

situationist: Having to do with the theory or practical activity of constructing situations. One who engages in the construction of situations. A member of the Situationist International.

situationism: A meaningless term improperly derived from the above. There is no such thing as situationism, which would mean a doctrine of interpretation of existing facts. The notion of situationism is obviously devised by antisituationists.

psychogeography: The study of the specific effects of the geographical environment, consciously organized or not, on the emotions and behavior of individuals.

psychogeographical: Relating to psychogeography. That which manifests the geographical environment's direct emotional effects.

psychogeographer: One who explores and reports on psychogeographical phenomena.

dérive: A mode of experimental behavior linked to the conditions of urban society: a technique of transient passage through varied ambiances. Also used to designate a specific period of continuous dériving.

unitary urbanism: The theory of the combined use of arts and techniques for the integral construction of a milieu in dynamic relation with experiments in behavior.

detournement: Short for: detournement of preexisting aesthetic elements. The integration of present or past artistic production into a superior construction of a milieu. In this sense there can be no situationist painting or music, but only a situationist use of these means. In a more primitive sense, detournement within the old cultural spheres is a method of propaganda, a method which testifies to the wearing out and loss of importance of those spheres.

culture: The reflection and prefiguration of the possibilities of organization of everyday life in a given historical moment; a complex of aesthetics, feelings and mores through which a collectivity reacts on the life that is objectively determined by its economy. (We are defining this term only in the perspective of the creation of values, not in that of the teaching of them.)

decomposition: The process in which the traditional cultural forms have destroyed themselves as a result of the emergence of superior means of dominating nature which enable and require superior cultural constructions. We can distinguish between an active phase of the decomposition and effective demolition of the old superstructures—which came to an end around 1930—and a phase of repetition which has prevailed since then. The delay in the transition from decomposition to new constructions is linked to the delay in the revolutionary liquidation of capitalism.

THE SITUATIONISTS AND AUTOMATION

(excerpts)

It is rather astonishing that almost no one until now has dared to examine the ultimate implications of automation. As a result, there are no real perspectives concerning it. One has rather the impression that engineers, scientists and sociologists are trying to surreptitiously smuggle automation into the society.

Yet automation is now at the heart of the problem of the socialist domination of production and of the preeminence of leisure over labor time. The question of automation is the one most pregnant with positive and negative possibilities.

[. . .] Automation thus contains two opposing perspectives: it deprives the individual of any possibility of adding anything personal to automated production, which is a *fixation* of progress; and at the same time it saves human energy by massively liberating it from reproductive and uncreative activities. The value of automation thus depends on projects that supersede it and open the way for expression of human energies on a higher plane. [. . .]

The new leisure time appears as an empty space that present-day society can fill only by multiplying the pseudoplay of ridiculous hobbies. But this leisure is at the same time the basis on which can be built the most magnificent cultural construction that has ever been imagined. [. . .] *Automation can develop rapidly only once it has established as a goal a perspective contrary to its own establishment, and only if it is known how to realize such a general perspective in the process of the development of automation.* [. . .]

Pierre Drouin (*Le Monde*, 5 January 1957), discussing the extension of hobbies as a realization of the potentialities that workers cannot express in their professional activity, concludes that "a creator lies dormant" in each person. This old banality is today of vital importance if one relates it to the real material possibilities of our time. The sleeping creator must be awakened, and his waking state can be termed "situationist."

The idea of standardization is an effort to reduce and simplify the greatest number of human needs to the greatest equality. It is up to us whether this standardization opens up domains of experience more interesting than those it closes. Depending on the outcome, we may arrive at a total degradation of human life or at the possibility of continually discovering new desires. But these new desires will not appear by themselves in the oppressive context of our world. There must be a collective action to detect, express and realize them.

ASGER JORN

NO USELESS LENIENCY

(excerpts)

An intellectual or artistic sort of collaboration in a group devoting itself to the type of experimentation we engage in involves our everyday life. It is always accompanied with a certain friendship.

Consequently, when we think of those who have participated in this common activity and then been excluded from it, we are obliged to admit that they were once our friends. Sometimes the memory is pleasant. In other cases it's ridiculous and embarrassing.

On the whole, later developments have confirmed the correctness of our reproaches and the irredeemability of the people who have not been able to remain with us. Few of them (though there have been some) have ended up joining the Church or the colonial troops. The others have generally found a place in the intelligentsia. There they grow old. [. . .]

The recent formation of the Situationist International has given a new relevance to the questions of accord and breaking. A period of discussions and negotiations on a footing of equality between several groups, beginning with the Alba Congress, has been concluded at Cosio d'Arroscia in favor of a disciplined organization. The result of these new objective conditions has been to force certain opportunist elements into open opposition, leading to their immediate elimination (the purging of the Italian section). Certain wait-and-see attitudes have also ceased to be tolerable, and those of our allies who have not seen fit to join us immediately have thereby unmasked themselves as adversaries. It is on the basis of the program since developed by the majority of the SI that all the new elements have joined us, and we would risk cutting ourselves off from these elements, and especially from those we will meet in the future, if we consented to pursue the slightest dialogue with those who, since Alba, have demonstrated that their creative days are over.

We have become stronger and therefore more seductive. We don't want innocuous relationships and we don't want relationships that could serve our adversaries. [...]

We will say flatly that all the situationists will maintain the enmities inherited from the former groupings that have constituted the SI, and that there is no possible return for those whom we have ever been forced to despise. But we don't have an idealist, abstract, absolute conception of breaking. It is necessary to see when an encounter in a concrete collective task becomes impossible, but also to see if such an encounter, in changed circumstances, does not once again become possible and desirable between persons who have been able to retain a certain respect for each other.

[...] It's true that a collective project like we have undertaken and are pursuing cannot avoid being accompanied by friendship, as I said at the beginning. But it is also true that it cannot be identified with friendship and that it should not be subject to the same weaknesses. Nor to the same modes of continuity or looseness.

MICHÈLE BERNSTEIN

ACTION IN BELGIUM AGAINST THE INTERNATIONAL ASSEMBLY OF ART CRITICS

On 12 April, two days before the gathering in Brussels of an international general assembly of art critics, the situationists widely distributed an address to that assembly signed—in the name of the Algerian, Belgian, French, German, Italian and Scandinavian sections of the SI—by Khatib, Korun, Debord, Platschek, Pinot-Gallizio and Jorn:

> To you this gathering is just one more boring event. The Situationist International, however, considers that while this assemblage of so many art critics as an attraction of the Brussels Fair is laughable, it is also significant.
>
> Inasmuch as modern cultural thought has proved itself completely stagnant for the last twenty-five years, and inasmuch as a whole period that has understood nothing and changed nothing is now becoming aware of its failure, its spokesmen are striving to transform their activities into institutions. They thus solicit official recognition from the completely outmoded but still materially dominant society, for which most of them have been loyal watchdogs. The main deficiency of modern art criticism is to have never conceived of the culture as a whole and the

conditions of an experimental movement that is perpetually superseding it. At this point in time the increased domination of nature permits and necessitates the use of superior powers in the construction of life. These are today's problems; and those intellectuals who hold back, through fear of a general subversion of a certain form of existence and of the ideas which that form has produced, can no longer do anything but struggle irrationally against each other as defenders of one or another detail of the old world—of a world whose day is done and whose meaning they have not even known. And so we see art critics assembling to exchange the crumbs of their ignorance and their doubts. We know of a few people here who are presently making some effort to understand and support new ventures; but by coming here they have accepted being mixed up with an immense majority of mediocrities, and we warn them that they cannot hope to retain the slightest interest on our part unless they break with this milieu.

Vanish, art critics, partial, incoherent and divided imbeciles! In vain do you stage the spectacle of a false encounter. You have nothing in common but a role to cling to; you are only in this market to parade one of the aspects of Western commerce: your confused and empty babble on a decomposed culture. History has depreciated you. Even your audacities belong to a past now forever closed.

Disperse, fragments of art critics, critics of fragments of art. The Situationist International is now organizing the unitary artistic activity of the future. You have nothing more to say.

The Situationist International will leave no place for you. We will starve you out.

Our Belgian section carried out the necessary direct attack. Beginning 13 April, on the eve of the opening of the proceedings, when the art critics from two hemispheres, led by the American Sweeney, were being welcomed to Brussels, the text of the situationist proclamation was brought to their attention in several ways. Copies were mailed to a large number of critics or given to them personally. Others were personally telephoned and read all or part of the text. A group forced its way into the Press Club where the critics were being received and threw the leaflets among the audience. Others were tossed onto the sidewalks from upstairs windows or from a car. (After the Press Club incident art critics were seen coming out in the street to pick up the leaflets so as to remove them from the curiosity of passersby.) In short, all steps were taken to leave the critics no chance of being unaware of the text. These art critics did not shrink from calling the police, and used their World Exposition influence in order to block the reprinting in the press of a text harmful to the prestige of their convention and their specialization. Our comrade Korun is now being threatened with prosecution for his role in the intervention.

THEORY OF THE DÉRIVE

Among the various situationist methods is the *dérive* [literally: 'drift-ing'], a technique of transient passage through varied ambiances. The dérive entails playful-constructive behavior and awareness of psycho-geographical effects; which completely distinguishes it from the clas-sical notions of the journey and the stroll.

In a dérive one or more persons during a certain period drop their usual motives for movement and action, their relations, their work and leisure activities, and let themselves be drawn by the attractions of the terrain and the encounters they find there. The element of chance is less determinant than one might think: from the dérive point of view cities have a psychogeographical relief, with constant currents, fixed points and vortexes which strongly discourage entry into or exit from certain zones.

But the dérive includes both this letting go and its necessary con-tradiction: the domination of psychogeographical variations by the knowledge and calculation of their possibilities. In this latter regard, ecological science—despite the apparently narrow social space to which it limits itself—provides psychogeography with abundant data.

The ecological analysis of the absolute or relative character of fis-sures in the urban network, of the role of microclimates, of the distinct, self-contained character of administrative districts, and above all of the dominating action of centers of attraction, must be utilized and completed by psychogeographical methods. The objective passional ter-rain of the dérive must be defined in accordance both with its own logic and with its relations with social morphology.

In his study *Paris et l'agglomération parisienne* (Bibliothèque de Sociologie Contemporaine, P.U.F., 1952) Chombart de Lauwe notes that "an urban neighborhood is determined not only by geographical and economic factors, but also by the image that its inhabitants and those of other neighborhoods have of it." In the same work, in order to illustrate "the narrowness of the real Paris in which each individual lives . . . within a geographical area whose radius is extremely small," he diagrams all the movements made in the space of one year by a student living in the 16th arrondissement. Her itinerary delineates a small triangle with no deviations, the three apexes of which are the School of Political Sciences, her residence and that of her piano teacher.

Such data—examples of a modern poetry capable of provoking sharp emotional reactions (in this case, indignation at the fact that there are people who live like that)—or even Burgess's theory of Chicago's social activities as being distributed in distinct concentric zones, doubtedly prove useful in developing dérives.

Chance plays an important role in dérives precisely be methodology of psychogeographical observation is still in its infancy. But the action of chance is naturally conservative and in a new setting tends to reduce everything to an alternation between a limited number of variants, and to habit. Progress is nothing other than breaking through a field where chance holds sway by creating new conditions more favorable to our purposes. We can say, then, that the randomness of the dérive is fundamentally different from that of the stroll, but also that the first psychogeographical attractions discovered run the risk of fixating the dériving individual or group around new habitual axes, to which they will constantly be drawn back.

An insufficient awareness of the limitations of chance, and of its inevitably reactionary use, condemned to a dismal failure the celebrated aimless ambulation attempted in 1923 by four surrealists, beginning from a town chosen by lot: wandering in the open country is naturally depressing, and the interventions of chance are poorer there than anywhere else. But this mindlessness is pushed much further by a certain Pierre Vendryes (in *Médium*, May 1954), who believes he can put this anecdote in the same category with various probability experiments on the grounds that they all are supposedly involved in the same sort of antideterminist liberation. He gives as an example the random distribution of tadpoles in a circular aquarium, adding, significantly, "It is necessary, of course, that such a population be subject to no external guiding influence." In these conditions, the palm really should go to the tadpoles, who have the advantage of being "as stripped as possible of intelligence, sociability and sexuality," and consequently "truly independent from one another."

At the opposite pole from these imbecilities, the primarily urban character of the dérive, in its element in the great industrially transformed cities—those centers of possibilities and meanings—could be expressed in Marx's phrase: "Men can see nothing around them that is not their own image; everything speaks to them of themselves. Their very landscape is alive."

One can dérive alone, but all indications are that the most fruitful numerical arrangement consists of several small groups of two or three people who have reached the same awakening of consciousness, since the cross-checking of these different groups' impressions makes it possible to arrive at objective conclusions. It is preferable for the composition of these groups to change from one dérive to another. With more than four or five participants, the specifically dérive character rapidly diminishes, and in any case it is impossible for there to be more than ten or twelve people without the dérive fragmenting into several simultaneous dérives. The practice of such subdivision is in fact of great interest, but the difficulties it entails have so far prevented it from being organized on a sufficient scale.

The average duration of a dérive is one day, considered as the time between two periods of sleep. The times of beginning and ending have no necessary relation to the solar day, but it should be noted that the ast hours of the night are generally unsuitable for dérives.

But this duration is merely a statistical average. For one thing, the dérive rarely occurs in its pure form: it is difficult for the participants to avoid setting aside an hour or two at the beginning or end of the day for taking care of banal tasks; and toward the end of the day fatigue tends to encourage such an abandonment. But even more importantly, the dérive often takes place within a deliberately limited period of a few hours, or even fortuitously during fairly brief moments; or over a period of several days without interruption. In spite of the cessations imposed by the need for sleep, certain dérives of a sufficient intensity have been sustained for three or four days, or even longer. It is true that in the case of a series of dérives over a rather long period of time it is almost impossible to determine precisely when the state of mind peculiar to one dérive gives way to that of another. One sequence of dérives was pursued without notable interruption for around two months. Such an experience gives rise to new objective conditions of behavior, which bring about the disappearance of a good number of the old ones.*

The influence of weather on dérives, although real, is a determining factor only in the case of prolonged rains, which make them virtually impossible. But storms or other types of precipitation are rather favorable for dérives.

The spatial field of the dérive may be precisely delimited or vague, depending on whether the activity is aimed at studying a terrain or at emotional disorientation. It must not be forgotten that these two aspects of the dérive overlap in many ways so that it is impossible to isolate one of them in a pure state. But the use of taxis, for example, can provide a clear enough line of demarcation between them: if in the course of a dérive one takes a taxi, either to get to a specific destination or simply to move twenty minutes to the west, one is concerned primarily with a personal trip outside one's usual surroundings. If, on the other hand, one sticks to the direct exploration of a particular terrain, one is concentrating primarily on research for a psychogeographical urbanism.

In every case the spatial field depends first of all on the point of departure—the residence of the solo dériver or the meeting place selected by a group. The maximum area of this spatial field does not extend beyond the entirety of a large city and its suburbs. At its minimum it can be limited to a small self-contained ambiance: a single neighborhood or even a single block of houses if it's worth it (the extreme case being the static-dérive of an entire day within the Saint-Lazare train station).

The exploration of a fixed spatial field thus presupposes the determining of bases and the calculation of directions of penetration. It is here that the study of maps comes in—ordinary ones as well as ecological and psychogeographical ones—along with their rectification and improvement. It should go without saying that we are not at all interested in any mere exoticism that may arise from the fact that one is exploring a neighborhood for the first time. Besides its unimportance, this aspect of the problem is completely subjective and rapidly disappears in the process of the dérive.

In the "possible rendezvous," on the other hand, the element of exploration is minimal in comparison with that of behavioral disorientation. The subject is invited to come alone to a specified place at a specified time. He is freed from the bothersome obligations of the ordinary rendezvous since there is no one to wait for. But since this "possible rendezvous" has brought him without warning to a place he may or may not know, he observes the surroundings. It may be that the same spot has been specified for a "possible rendezvous" for someone else whose identity he has no way of knowing. Since he may never have even seen the other person before, he will be incited to start up conversations with various passersby. He may meet no one, or he may by chance meet the person who has arranged the "possible rendezvous." In any case, particularly if the time and place have been well chosen, the subject's use of time will take an unexpected turn. He may even telephone someone else who doesn't know where the first "possible rendezvous" has taken him, in order to ask for another one to be specified. One can see the virtually unlimited resources of this pastime.

Thus a loose lifestyle and even certain amusements considered dubious that have always been enjoyed among our entourage—slipping by night into houses undergoing demolition, hitchhiking nonstop and without destination through Paris during a transportation strike in the name of adding to the confusion, wandering in subterranean catacombs forbidden to the public, etc.—are expressions of a more general sensibility which is nothing other than that of the dérive. Written descriptions can be no more than passwords to this great game.

The lessons drawn from the dérive permit the drawing up of the first surveys of the psychogeographical articulations of a modern city. Beyond the discovery of unities of ambiance, of their main components and their spatial localization, one comes to perceive their principal axes of passage, their exits and their defenses. One arrives at the central hypothesis of the existence of psychogeographical pivotal points. One measures the distances that effectively separate two regions of a city, distances that may have little relation with the physical distance between them. With the aid of old maps, aerial photographs and experimental dérives, one can draw up hitherto lacking maps of influences, maps whose inevitable imprecision at this early stage is no worse than that of the first navigational charts; the only difference is that it is a matter no longer of precisely delineating stable continents, but of changing architecture and urbanism.

Today the different unities of atmosphere and of dwellings are not precisely marked off, but are surrounded by more or less extended and indistinct bordering regions. The most general change that the dérive leads to proposing is the constant diminution of these border regions, up to the point of their complete suppression.

Within architecture itself, the taste for dériving tends to promote all sorts of new forms of labyrinths made possible by modern techniques of construction. Thus in March 1955 the press reported the construction in New York of a building in which one can see the first signs of an opportunity to dérive inside an apartment:

53

"The apartments of the helicoidal house will have the form of slices of cake. One will be able to augment or diminish them by shifting movable partitions. The half-floor gradations avoid limiting the number of rooms, since the tenant can request the use of the adjacent section on either upper or lower levels. This system permits the transformation of three four-room apartments into one twelve-room apartment in less than six hours."

(*To be continued.*)

GUY DEBORD
1956*

DETOURNEMENT AS NEGATION
AND PRELUDE

Detournement, the reuse of preexisting artistic elements in a new ensemble, has been a constantly present tendency of the contemporary avant-garde both before and since the establishment of the SI. The two fundamental laws of detournement are the loss of importance of each detourned autonomous element—which may go so far as to lose its original sense completely—and at the same time the organization of another meaningful ensemble that confers on each element its new scope and effect.

Detournement has a peculiar power which obviously stems from the double meaning, from the enrichment of most of the terms by the coexistence within them of their old senses and their new, immediate senses. Detournement is practical because it is so easy to use and because of its inexhaustible potential for reuse. Concerning the negligible effort required for detournement, we have already said, "The cheapness of its products is the heavy artillery that breaks through all the Chinese walls of understanding" (*Methods of Detournement*, May 1956). But these points would not by themselves justify recourse to this method, which the same text describes as "clashing head-on against all social and legal conventions." Detournement has a historical significance. What is it?

"Detournement is a game made possible by the capacity of *devaluation*," writes Jorn in his study *Detourned Painting* (May 1959), and he goes on to say that all the elements of the cultural past must be "reinvested" or disappear. Detournement is thus first of all a negation of the value of the previous organization of expression. It arises and grows increasingly stronger in the historical period of the decomposition of artistic expression. But at the same time, the attempts to reuse the "detournable bloc" as material for other ensembles express the search for a vaster construction, a new genre of creation at a higher level.

The SI is a very special kind of movement, of a nature different from preceding artistic avant-gardes. Within culture the SI can be likened to a research laboratory, for example, or to a party in which we are situationists but nothing that we do is situationist. This is not a disavowal for anyone. We are partisans of a certain future of culture, of life. Situationist activity is a definite craft which we are not yet practicing.

Thus the signature of the situationist movement, the sign of its presence and contestation in contemporary cultural reality (since we cannot represent any common style whatsoever), is first of all the use of detournement. We may mention, on the level of detourned expression, Jorn's altered paintings; Debord and Jorn's book *Mémoires*, "composed entirely of prefabricated elements," in which the writing on each page runs in all directions and the reciprocal relations of the phrases are invariably uncompleted; Constant's projects for detourned sculptures; and Debord's detourned documentary film, *On the Passage of a Few Persons Through a Rather Brief Period of Time*. On the level of what *Methods of Detournement* calls "ultradetournement, that is, the tendencies for detournement to operate in everyday social life" (e.g. passwords or the wearing of disguises, belonging to the sphere of play), we might mention, at different levels, Gallizio's industrial painting; Wyckaert's "orchestral" project for assembly-line painting with a division of labor based on color; and numerous detournements of buildings that were at the origin of unitary urbanism. But we should also mention in this context the SI's very forms of "organization" and propaganda.

At this point in the world's development all forms of expression are losing all grip on reality and being reduced to self-parody. As the readers of this journal can frequently verify, present-day writing always has an element of parody. "It is necessary," states *Methods of Detournement*, "to conceive of a parodic-serious stage where the accumulation of detourned elements, far from aiming at arousing indignation or laughter by alluding to some original work, will express our indifference toward a meaningless and forgotten original, and concern itself with rendering a certain sublimity."

The parodic-serious expresses the contradictions of an era in which we find ourselves confronted with both the urgent necessity and the near impossibility of bringing together and carrying out a totally innovative collective action. An era in which the greatest seriousness advances masked in the ambiguous interplay between art and its negation; in which the essential voyages of discovery have been undertaken by such astonishingly incapable people.

SITUATIONIST THESES ON TRAFFIC

1

The mistake made by all urbanists is to consider the private automobile (and its by-products like the motorcycle) essentially as a means of transportation. Such a misconception is a major expression of a notion of happiness that developed capitalism tends to spread throughout the society. The automobile is at the center of this general propaganda, both as sovereign good of an alienated life and as essential product of the capitalist market: It is being generally said this year that American economic prosperity is soon going to depend on the success of the slogan "Two cars per family."

2

Commuting time, as Le Corbusier rightly pointed out, is a surplus labor which correspondingly reduces the amount of "free" time.

3

We must replace travel as an adjunct to work with travel as a pleasure.

4

To want to redesign architecture to accord with the needs of the present massive, parasitical existence of private automobiles reflects the most unrealistic misapprehension of where the real problems lie. It is necessary to transform architecture to accord with the whole development of the society, criticizing all the transitory values linked to condemned forms of social relationships (in the first rank of which is the family).

5

Even if during a transitional period we temporarily accept a rigid division between work zones and residence zones, we must at least envisage a third sphere: that of life itself (the sphere of freedom, of leisure—the truth of life). Unitary urbanism acknowledges no boundaries; it aims to form a unitary human milieu in which separations such as work/leisure or public/private will finally be dissolved. But before this, the minimum action of unitary urbanism is to extend the terrain of play to all desirable constructions. This terrain will be at the level of complexity of an old city.

6

It is not a question of combating the automobile as an evil in itself. It is its extreme concentration in the cities that has led to the negation of its role. Urbanism should certainly not ignore the automobile, but even less should it accept it as its central theme. It should reckon on its gradual phasing out. In any case, we can foresee that the central areas of certain new complexes, as well as of a few old cities, will become closed to automobile traffic.

7

Those who believe that the automobile is eternal are not thinking, even from a strictly technological standpoint, of other future forms of transportation. For example, certain models of one-man helicopters presently being tested by the US Army will probably have spread to the general public within twenty years.

8

The breaking up of the dialectic of the human milieu in favor of automobiles (the projected freeways in Paris will entail the demolition of thousands of houses and apartments although the housing crisis is continually growing worse) masks its irrationality under pseudopractical justifications. But it is practically necessary only in terms of a specific social set-up. Those who believe that the particulars of the problem are permanent want in fact to believe in the permanence of the present society.

9

Revolutionary urbanists will not limit their concern to the circulation of things and of human beings trapped in a world of things. They will try to break these topological chains, paving the way with their experiments for a human journey through authentic life.

GUY DEBORD

GANGLAND AND PHILOSOPHY

(excerpts)

[. . .] " 'Protection' is the key word in the Garment Center racket. The process is as follows: one day you receive a visit from a gentleman who kindly offers to 'protect' you. If you are really naive you ask, 'Protection against what?' " (S. Groueff and D. Lapierre, *The Gangsters of New York.*) [. . .]

How can we comprehend the formation of our culture and our philosophical and scientific information? Modern psychology has eliminated many of the doctrines that used to obscure the question. It seeks motives: why do we accept or refuse an "idea" or an imperative? [. . .] For example, someone becomes aware of situationist activity. He "understands" it and "rationally" follows its arguments. Then, in spite of his momentary intellectual agreement, he relapses. The next day he no longer understands us. We propose a slight modification of the psychological description quoted above, in order to grasp the play of forces that have prevented him from considering various things as "practicable" or even "thinkable" when we know they are *possible*. Let us examine this striking experimental reaction: "The trial of Dio and his accomplices begins. Then something extraordinarily scandalous takes place. The first witness, Gondolfo Miranti, refuses to talk. He denies all the depositions he has made before the FBI. The judge loses all patience. Furious, he resorts to the ultimate argument: 'I order you to answer. If you do not, you will be sentenced to five years imprisonment!' Without hesitation Miranti accepts the five long years of prison. In the defendants' box Johnny Dio, well dressed and smooth shaven, smiles ironically." (*Op. cit.*) It is difficult not to recognize an analogous comportment in someone who doesn't dare speak of problems as he knows they are. We have to ask: Is he a victim of intimidation? He certainly is. What is the mechanism common to these two sorts of fear?

Miranti lived in *Gangland* since his youth; this explains many things. "Gangland," in Chicago gangster slang, means the domain of crime, of rackets. I propose to study the basic functioning of "the Organization," in spite of the risks of getting involved: "And as for the man who would try to set them free and lead them up to the light, do you not think that they would seize him and kill him if they could?" (Plato, *The Republic*, Book VII.) Philosophy must not forget that it has always spoken its part in the most burlesque, melodramatic setting.

We should develop a *glossary of detourned words*. I propose that "neighborhood" should often be read *Gangland*. Social organization: *protection*. Society: *racket*. Culture: *conditioning*. Leisure activity: *protected crime*. Education: *premeditation*. [. . .]

ATTILA KOTÁNYI

THE ADVENTURE

(excerpts)

The conditions of the SI's activity explain both its discipline and the forms of hostility it encounters. The SI is interested not in finding a niche in the present artistic edifice, but in undermining it. The situationists are in the catacombs of visible culture.

Anyone who is at all familiar with the social milieu of those with special status in cultural affairs is well aware of how everyone there despises and is bored by almost everyone else. This situation is not even hidden, they are all quite aware of it; it is even the first thing they talk about. What is their resignation due to? Clearly to the fact that they are incapable of being bearers of a common project. Each one thus recognizes in the others his own insignificance and conditioning: the resignation he had to subscribe to in order to participate in this separate milieu and its established aims.

Within such a community people have neither the need nor the objective possibility for any sort of collective discipline. Everyone always politely agrees about the same things and nothing ever changes. Personal or ideological disagreements remain secondary in comparison with what they have in common. But for the SI and the struggle it sets for itself, exclusion is a possible and necessary weapon.

It is the only weapon of any group based on complete freedom of individuals. None of us likes to control or judge; if we do so it is for a practical purpose, not as a moral punishment. The "terrorism" of the SI's exclusions can in no way be compared to the same practices in political movements by bureaucracies holding some power. It is, on the contrary, the extreme ambiguity of the situation of artists, who are constantly tempted to integrate themselves into the modest sphere of social power reserved for them, that makes some discipline necessary in order to clearly define an incorruptible platform. Otherwise there would be a rapid and irremediable osmosis between this platform and the dominant cultural milieu because of the number of people going back and forth. It seems to us that the present-day cultural avant-garde question can only be posed at an integral level, a level not only of collective works but of collectively interacting problems. This is why certain people have been excluded from the SI. Some of them have rejoined the world they previously fought; others merely console themselves in a pitiful community with each other, although they have nothing in common but the fact that we broke with them—often for opposite reasons. Others retain a certain dignity in isolation, and we have been in a good position to recognize their talents. Do we think that in leaving the SI they have broken with the avant-garde? Yes, we do. There is, for the moment, no other organization constituted for a task of this scope.

The sentimental objections to these breaks seem to us to reflect the greatest mystification. The entire socioeconomic structure tends to make the past dominate, to freeze living man, to reify him as a commodity. A sentimental world in which the same sorts of tastes and relations are constantly *repeated* is the direct product of the economic and social world in which *gestures must be repeated* every day in the slavery of capitalist production. The taste for false novelty expresses its unhappy nostalgia.

The violent reactions against the SI, especially those coming from people who were previously excluded from its collective activity, are first of all a measure of the personal passion that this enterprise has been able to bring into play. Reversed into a boundless hostility, this passion has spread it about that we are loafers, Stalinists, imposters and a hundred other clever characterizations. One had it that the SI was a cunningly organized economic association for dealing in modern art; others have suggested that it was rather for the purpose of dealing in drugs. Still others have declared that we have never sold any drugs since we have too great a propensity for taking them ourselves. Others go into detail about our sexual vices. Others have gotten so carried away as to denounce us as social climbers.

These attacks have long been whispered around us by the same people who publicly pretend to be unaware of our existence. [. . .]

To the question, Why have we promoted such an impassioned regrouping in this cultural sphere whose present reality we reject? the answer is: Because culture is the center of meaning of a society without meaning. This empty culture is at the heart of an empty existence, and the reinvention of a project of generally transforming the world must also and first of all be posed on this terrain. To give up demanding power in culture would be to leave that power to those who now have it.

We know quite well that the culture to be overthrown will really fall only with the totality of the socioeconomic structure that supports it. But without waiting any longer, the Situationist International intends to confront it in its entirety, on every front, to the point of imposing an autonomous situationist control and instrumentation against those held by existing cultural authorities, that is, to the point of *a state of dual power in culture.*

THE FOURTH S.I. CONFERENCE IN LONDON

(excerpts)

The 4th Conference of the Situationist International was held in London, at a secret address in the East End, 24–28 September 1960, seventeen months after the Munich Conference (April 1959). The situationists assembled in London were: Debord, Jacqueline de Jong, Jorn, Kotányi, Katja Lindell, Jørgen Nash, Prem, Sturm, Maurice Wyckaert and H.P. Zimmer. [. . .]

The discussion of these perspectives leads to posing the question: To what extent is the SI a political movement? Various responses state that the SI is political, but not in the ordinary sense. The discussion becomes somewhat confused. Debord proposes, in order to bring out clearly the opinion of the Conference, that each person respond in writing to a questionnaire asking if he considers that there are "forces in the society that the SI can count on? What forces? In what conditions?" This questionnaire is agreed upon and filled out. The first responses express the view that the SI aims to establish a program of overall liberation and to act in accord with other forces on a social scale. (Kotányi: "To rely on what we call free." Jorn: "We are against specialization and rationalization, but not against them as means. . . . The movements of social groups are determined by the character of their desires. We can accept other social movements only to the extent that they are moving in our direction. We are the new revolution . . . we should act with other organizations that seek the same path.") The session is then adjourned.

At the beginning of the second session, 26 September, Heimrad Prem reads a declaration of the German section in response to the questionnaire. This very long declaration attacks the tendency in the responses read the day before to count on the existence of a revolutionary proletariat, for the signers strongly doubt the revolutionary capacities of the workers against the bureaucratic institutions that have dominated their movement. The German section considers that the SI should prepare to realize its program on its own by mobilizing the avant-garde artists, who are placed by the present society in intolerable conditions and can count only on themselves to take over the weapons of conditioning. Debord responds with a sharp critique of these positions. [. . .] Kotányi reminds the German delegates that even if since 1945 they have seen apparently passive and satisfied workers in Germany and legal strikes organized with music to divert union members, in other advanced capitalist countries "wildcat" strikes have multiplied. He adds that in his opinion they vastly underestimate the German workers themselves. [. . .] Debord proposes that the majority openly declare that it rejects the German theses. It is agreed that the two tendencies separately decide on their positions. The German minority withdraws to an adjoining room to deliberate. When it returns Zimmer announces, in the name of his group, that they retract the preceding declaration, not because they think it unimportant, but in order not to impede present situationist activity. He concludes: "We declare that we are in complete agreement with all the acts already done by the SI, with or without us, and with those that will be done in the foreseeable future. We are also in agreement with all the ideas published by the SI. We consider the question debated today as secondary in relation to the SI's overall development, and propose to reserve further discussion of it for the future." Everyone agrees to this. Kotányi and Debord, however, ask that it be noted in the minutes that they do not consider that the question discussed today is secondary. The German situationists agree to delete their reference to it as such. The session is adjourned, very late at night. [. . .]

INSTRUCTIONS FOR TAKING UP ARMS

If it seems somewhat ridiculous to talk of revolution, this is obviously because the organized revolutionary movement has long since disappeared from the modern countries where the possibilities of a decisive transformation of society are concentrated. But *everything else* is even more ridiculous, since it implies accepting the existing order in one way or another. If the word "revolutionary" has been neutralized to the point of being used in advertising to describe the slightest change in an ever-changing commodity production, this is because the possibilities of a central *desirable* change are no longer expressed anywhere. Today the revolutionary project stands accused before the tribunal of history—accused of having failed, of having engendered a new alienation. This amounts to recognizing that the ruling society has proved capable of defending itself, on all levels of reality, much better than revolutionaries expected. Not that it has become more tolerable. Revolution has to be reinvented, that's all.

This poses a number of problems that will have to be theoretically and practically overcome in the next few years. We can briefly mention a few points that it is urgent to resolve.

Of the tendencies toward regroupment that have appeared over the last few years among various minorities of the workers movement in Europe, only the most radical current is worth preserving: that centered on the program of workers councils. Nor should we overlook the fact that a number of simply confusionist elements are seeking to insinuate themselves into this debate (see the recent common accord among "leftist" philosophico-sociological journals of different countries).

The greatest difficulty confronting groups that seek to create a new type of revolutionary organization is that of establishing new types of human relationships within the organization itself. The forces of the society exert an omnipresent pressure against such an effort. But unless this is accomplished, by methods yet to be experimented with, we will never be able to escape from specialized politics. The demand for participation on the part of everyone often degenerates into a mere abstract ideal, when in fact it is an absolute practical necessity for a really new organization and for the organization of a really new society. Even if militants are no longer mere executants of decisions made by masters of the organization, they still risk being reduced to the role of spectators of those among them who are the most qualified in politics conceived as a specialization; and in this way the passivity relation of the old world is reproduced.

People's creativity and participation can only be awakened by a collective project explicitly concerned with all aspects of lived experience. The only way to "arouse the masses" is to expose the appalling contrast between the possible constructions of life and its present poverty. Without a critique of everyday life, a revolutionary organization is a separated milieu, as conventional and ultimately as passive as those holiday camps that are the specialized terrain of modern leisure. Sociologists, such as Henri Raymond in his study of Palinuro, have shown how in such places the spectacular mechanism recreates, on the level of play, the dominant relations of the society as a whole. But then they go on naively to commend the "multiplicity of human contacts," for example, without seeing that the mere quantitative increase of these contacts leaves them just as insipid and inauthentic as they are everywhere else. Even in the most libertarian and antihierarchical revolutionary group, communication between people is in no way guaranteed by a shared political program. The sociologists naturally support efforts to reform everyday life, to organize compensation for it in vacation time. But the revolutionary project cannot accept the classical idea of play, of a game limited in space, in time and in qualitative depth. The revolutionary game, the creation of life, is opposed to all memories of past games. To provide a three-week break from the kind of life led during forty-nine weeks of work, the holiday villages of the Club Méditerranée draw on a shoddy Polynesian ideology—a bit like the French Revolution presenting itself in the guise of republican Rome, or like the revolutionaries of today who define themselves principally in accordance with how well they fill the Bolshevik or some other style of *militant role*. The revolution of everyday life cannot draw its poetry from the past, but only from the future.

The experience of the empty leisure produced by modern capitalism has naturally provided a critical correction to the Marxist idea of the *extension of leisure time*. It is true that full freedom of time requires first of all a transformation of work and the appropriation of this work in view of goals, and under conditions, that are utterly different from those of the forced labor that has prevailed until now (see the activity of the groups that publish *Socialisme ou Barbarie* in France, *Solidarity** in England and *Alternative* in Belgium). But those who put all the stress on the necessity of changing work itself, of rationalizing it, of interesting people in it, and who neglect the idea of the free content of life (i.e. the development of a materially equipped creative power beyond the traditional categories of work time and rest and recreation time), run the risk of providing an ideological cover for a harmonization of the present production system in the direction of *greater efficiency and profitability* without at all having called in question the experience of this production or the necessity of this kind of life. The free construction of the entire space-time of individual life is a demand that will have to be defended against all sorts of dreams of harmony in the minds of aspiring managers of social reorganization.

The different moments of situationist activity until now can only be understood in the perspective of a reappearance of revolution, a revolution that will be social as well as cultural and whose field of action will right from the start have to be broader than during any of its previous tentatives. Thus the SI does not want to recruit disciples or partisans, but to bring together people capable of applying themselves to this task in the years to come, by every means and without worrying about labels. This means that we must reject the vestiges not only of specialized artistic activity, but also those of specialized politics; and particularly the post-Christian masochism characteristic of so many intellectuals in this area. We don't claim to be developing a new revolutionary program all by ourselves. We say that this program in the process of formation will one day practically contest the ruling reality, and that we will participate in that contestation. Whatever may become of us individually, the new revolutionary movement will not be formed without taking into account what we have sought together; which could be summed up as the passage from the old theory of limited permanent revolution to a theory of generalized permanent revolution.

ELEMENTARY PROGRAM OF THE BUREAU OF UNITARY URBANISM

1. NOTHINGNESS OF URBANISM AND NOTHINGNESS OF THE SPECTACLE

Urbanism* doesn't exist; it is only an "ideology" in Marx's sense of the word. Architecture does really exist, like Coca-Cola: though coated with ideology, it is a real production, falsely satisfying a falsified need. Urbanism is comparable to the advertising propagated around Coca-Cola—pure spectacular ideology. Modern capitalism, which organizes the reduction of all social life to a spectacle, is incapable of presenting any spectacle other than that of our own alienation. Its urbanistic dream is its masterpiece.

2. URBAN PLANNING AS CONDITIONING AND FALSE PARTICIPATION

The development of the urban milieu is the capitalist domestication of space. It represents the choice of one specific materialization, to the exclusion of other possible ones. Like aesthetics, whose course of decomposition it is going to follow, it can be considered as a rather neglected branch of criminology. However, what characterizes it at the "city planning" level—as opposed to its merely architectural level—is its insistence on popular consent, on individual integration into the inauguration of this bureaucratic production of conditioning.

All this is imposed by means of a blackmail of utility, which hides the fact that the architecture and conditioning are really useful only in reinforcing reification. Modern capitalism dissuades people from making any criticism of architecture with the simple argument that they need a roof over their heads, just as television is accepted on the grounds that they need information and entertainment. People are

made to overlook the obvious fact that this information, this entertainment and this kind of dwelling place are not made for them, but
without them and against them.

The whole of urban planning can be understood only as a society's
field of publicity-propaganda, i.e. as the organization of participation
in something in which it is impossible to participate.

3. TRAFFIC CIRCULATION, SUPREME STAGE OF URBAN PLANNING

Traffic circulation is the organization of universal isolation. In this
regard it constitutes the major problem of modern cities. It is the opposite of encounter, it absorbs the energies that could otherwise be
devoted to encounters or to any sort of participation. In it one's status
is determined by one's residence and mobility (personal vehicles). For
in fact one doesn't live somewhere in the city; one lives somewhere in
the hierarchy. At the summit of this hierarchy the ranks can be as-
certained by the extent of mobility. Power is objectively expressed in
the necessity of being present each day at more and more places (business dinners, etc.) further and further removed from each other. One
could characterize the modern VIP as a man who has appeared in
three different capitals in the course of a single day.

4. DISTANCIATION FROM THE URBAN SPECTACLE

The totality of the spectacle which tends to integrate the population
manifests itself as both organization of cities and as permanent information network. It is a solid framework to secure the existing conditions of life. Our first task is to enable people to stop identifying with
their surroundings and with model patterns of behavior. This is inseparable from a possibility of free mutual recognition in a few initial
zones set apart for human activity. People will still be obliged for a
long time to accept the era of reified cities. But the attitude with which
they accept it can be changed immediately. We must spread skepticism
toward those bleak, brightly colored kindergartens, the new dormitory
cities of both East and West. Only a mass awakening will pose the
question of a conscious construction of the urban milieu.

5. AN INDIVISIBLE FREEDOM

The main achievement of contemporary city planning is to have
made people blind to the possibility of what we call unitary urbanism,
namely a living critique, fueled by all the tensions of daily life, of this
manipulation of cities and their inhabitants. Living critique means
the setting up of bases for an experimental life, the coming together
of those creating their own lives on terrains equipped to their ends.
Such bases cannot be reservations for "leisure" activities separated
from the society. No spatiotemporal zone is completely separable. In
fact there is continual pressure from the whole society on its present
vacation "reservations." Situationist bases will exert pressure in the
opposite direction, acting as bridgeheads for an invasion of the whole
of daily life. Unitary urbanism is the contrary of a specialized activity;

to accept a separate urbanistic domain
urbanistic lie and the falsehood perme

Urbanism promises happiness. It sha
coordination of artistic and scientific me
to a complete denunciation of existing c

6. THE LANDING

All space is already occupied by the ene
its elementary laws, its geometry, to its
banism will appear when the absence of
certain zones. What we call construction st
by the *positive void* concept developed by _____ .... material-
izing freedom means beginning by appropriating a few patches of the
surface of a domesticated planet.

7. THE ILLUMINATION OF DETOURNEMENT

The basic practice of the theory of unitary urbanism will be the
transcription of the whole theoretical lie of urbanism, detourned for
the purpose of de-alienation: we constantly have to defend ourselves
from the poetry of the bards of conditioning—to jam their messages,
to turn their songs inside out.

8. CONDITIONS OF DIALOGUE

The functional is what is practical. The only thing that is practical
is the resolution of our fundamental problem: our self-realization (our
escape from the system of isolation). This and nothing else is useful
and utilitarian. Everything else is nothing but minor by-products of
the practical, the mystification of the practical.

9. RAW MATERIAL AND TRANSFORMATION

The situationist destruction of present conditioning is already at the
same time the construction of situations. It is the liberation of the
inexhaustible energies trapped in a petrified daily life. With the advent of unitary urbanism, present city planning (that geology of lies)
will be replaced by a technique for defending the permanently threatened conditions of freedom, and individuals—who do not yet exist as
such—will begin freely constructing their own history.

10. END OF THE PREHISTORY OF CONDITIONING

We are contending not that people must return to some stage previous to the era of conditioning, but rather that they must move beyond it. We have invented the architecture and the urbanism that
cannot be realized without the revolution of everyday life—without
the appropriation of conditioning by everyone, its endless enrichment,
its fulfillment.

ATTILA KOTÁNYI, RAOUL VANEIGEM

PERSPECTIVES FOR CONSCIOUS
ALTERATIONS IN EVERYDAY LIFE

To study everyday life would be a completely absurd undertaking, unable even to grasp anything of its object, if this study was not explicitly for the purpose of transforming everyday life.

The lecture, the exposition of certain intellectual considerations to an audience, being an extremely commonplace form of human relations in a rather large sector of society, itself forms a part of the everyday life that must be criticized.

Sociologists, for example, are only too inclined to remove from everyday life things that happen to them every day, and to transfer them to separate and supposedly superior spheres. In this way habit in all its forms—beginning with the habit of handling a few *professional* concepts (concepts produced by the division of labor)—masks reality behind privileged conventions.

It is thus desirable to demonstrate, by a slight alteration of the usual procedures, that everyday life is right here. These words are being communicated by way of a tape recorder, not, of course, in order to illustrate the integration of technology into this everyday life on the margin of the technological world, but in order to seize the simplest opportunity to break with the appearance of pseudocollaboration, of artificial dialogue, established between the lecturer "in person" and his spectators. This slight discomforting break with accustomed routine could serve to bring directly into the field of questioning of everyday life (a questioning otherwise completely abstract) the conference itself, as well as any number of other forms of using time or objects, forms that are considered "normal" and not even noticed, and which ultimately condition us. With such a detail, as with everyday life as a whole, alteration is always the necessary and sufficient condition for experimentally bringing into clear view the object of our study, which would otherwise remain uncertain—an object which is itself less to be studied than to be altered.

I have just said that the reality of an observable entity designated by the term "everyday life" stands a good chance of remaining hypothetical for many people. Indeed, the most striking feature of the present "Group for Research on Everyday Life" is obviously not the fact that it has not yet discovered anything, but the fact that the very existence of everyday life has been disputed from its very inception, and increasingly so with each new session of this conference. Most of the talks we have heard so far have been by people who are not at all convinced that everyday life exists, since they haven't encountered it anywhere. A group for research on everyday life with this attitude is comparable in every way to an expedition in search of the Yeti, which might similarly come to the conclusion that its quarry was merely a popular hoax.

68

To be sure, everyone agrees that certain gestures rep[...]
such as opening doors or filling glasses, are quite real; [...]
tures are at such a trivial level of reality that it is righ[...]
that they are not of sufficient interest to justify a new s[...]
branch of sociological research. A number of sociologists seem[...]
clined to recognize any aspects of everyday life beyond these tri[...]
ties. They thus accept the definition of it proposed by Henri Lefebvre[...]
"whatever remains after one has eliminated all specialized activities"—but draw a different conclusion: that everyday life is nothing.
The majority of sociologists—and we know how much they are in their
element in specialized activities, in which they generally have the
blindest faith!—recognize specialized activities everywhere and everyday life nowhere. Everyday life is always elsewhere. Among others. In
any case, in the nonsociologistic classes of the population. Someone
said here that it would be interesting to study the workers as guinea
pigs who have probably been infected with this virus of everyday life
because they, having no access to specialized activities, have *only*
everyday life to live. This condescending manner of investigating the
common people in search of an exotic primitivism of everyday life—
and above all this ingenuously avowed self-satisfaction, this naive
pride in participating in a culture whose glaring bankruptcy no one
can dream of denying, this radical inability to understand the world
that produces this culture—all this never ceases to astonish.

There is in this an evident will to hide behind a development of
thought based on the separation of artificial, fragmentary domains so
as to reject the useless, vulgar and disturbing concept of "everyday
life." Such a concept covers an uncatalogued and unclassified residue
of reality, a residue some people are averse to confronting because it
at the same time represents the standpoint of the totality; it would
imply the necessity of an integral political judgment. Certain intellectuals seem to flatter themselves with an illusory personal participation in the dominant sector of society through their possession of
one or more cultural specializations; these specializations, however,
have placed them in the best position to realize that the whole of this
dominant culture is manifestly moth-eaten. But whatever one's opinion of the coherence of this culture or of the interest of one or another
of its fragments, the particular alienation it has imposed on these
intellectuals is to make them think, from their position in the heaven
of the sociologists, that they are quite outside the everyday life of the
common people, or to give them an exaggerated idea of their rank on
the scale of human powers, as if their lives, too, were not *impoverished*.

Specialized activities certainly exist; they are even, in a given period, put to a certain general use which should be recognized in a
demystified manner. Everyday life is not everything—although its osmosis with specialized activities is such that in a sense we are never
outside of everyday life. But to use a facile spatial image, we still have
to place everyday life at the center of everything. Every project begins
from it and every realization returns to it to acquire its real significance. Everyday life is the measure of all things: of the fulfillment or
rather the nonfulfillment of human relations; of the use of lived time;
of artistic experimentation; of revolutionary politics.

ll that the old stereotypical image of the
er is fallacious in any case. It must be
observation is even less possible here than
es for the difficulty of even recognizing a
ot only the fact that it has already become
ind of an empirical sociology and a concep-
he fact that it presently happens to be the
renewal of culture and politics.

ay life today means accepting the prolon-
ughly rotten forms of culture and politics,
......s is expressed in increasingly widespread
political apathy and neoilliteracy, especially in the most modern countries. On the other hand, a radical critique in acts of prevailing everyday life could lead to a supersession of culture and politics in the
traditional sense, that is, to a higher level of intervention in life.

"But," you may ask, "how does it happen that the importance of this
everyday life, which according to you is the only real life, is so completely and directly underrated by people who, after all, have no direct
interest in doing so—many of whom are even far from being opposed
to some kind of renewal of the revolutionary movement?"

I think this happens because everyday life is organized within the
limits of a scandalous poverty, and above all because there is nothing
accidental about this poverty of everyday life: it is a poverty that is
constantly imposed by the coercion and violence of a society divided
into classes, a poverty historically organized in line with the evolving
requirements of exploitation.

The use of everyday life, in the sense of a consumption of lived time,
is governed by the reign of scarcity: scarcity of free time and scarcity
of possible uses of this free time.

Just as the accelerated history of our time is the history of accumulation and industrialization, so the backwardness and conservative
tendency of everyday life are products of the laws and interests that
have presided over this industrialization. Everyday life has until now
resisted the historical. This represents first of all a *verdict against the
historical* insofar as it has been the heritage and project of an exploitative society.

The extreme poverty of conscious organization and creativity in
everyday life expresses the fundamental necessity for unconsciousness
and mystification in an exploiting society, in a society of alienation.

Henri Lefebvre has extended the idea of uneven development so as
to characterize everyday life as a lagging sector, out of joint with the
historical but not completely cut off from it. I think that one could go
so far as to term this level of everyday life a colonized sector. We know
that underdevelopment and colonization are interrelated on the level
of global economy. Everything suggests that the same thing applies at
the level of socioeconomic structure, at the level of praxis.

Everyday life, policed and mystified by every means, is a sort of
reservation for good natives who keep modern society running without
understanding it—this society with its rapid growth of technological
powers and the forced expansion of its market. History—the transformation of reality—cannot presently be used in everyday life because

the people of everyday life are the product of a history over which they have no control. It is of course they themselves who make this history, but not freely.

Modern society is viewed through specialized fragments that are virtually incommunicable; and so everyday life, where all questions are liable to be posed in a unitary manner, is naturally the domain of ignorance.

Through its industrial production this society has emptied the gestures of work of all meaning. And no model of human behavior has retained any real relevance in everyday life.

This society tends to atomize people into isolated consumers, to prohibit communication. Everyday life is thus private life, the realm of separation and spectacle.

It is thus also the sphere of the specialists' resignation and failure. It is there, for example, that one of the rare individuals capable of understanding the latest scientific conception of the universe will make a fool of himself by earnestly pondering Alain Robbe-Grillet's aesthetic theories or by sending petitions to the President of the Republic in the hope of convincing him to change his policies. It is the sphere of disarmament, of the avowal of the incapability of living.

Thus the underdevelopment of everyday life cannot be characterized solely by its relative inability to put technology to use. This trait is an important, but only partial, consequence of the everyday alienation as a whole, which could be defined as the inability to invent a technique for the liberation of everyday experience.

In fact many techniques do more or less markedly alter certain aspects of everyday life: the domestic arts, as has already been mentioned here, but also the telephone, television, the recording of music on long-playing records, mass air travel, etc. These elements arise anarchically, by chance, without anyone having foreseen their interrelations or consequences. But on the whole this introduction of technology into everyday life—ultimately taking place within the framework of modern bureaucratized capitalism—certainly tends rather to reduce people's independence and creativity. The new prefabricated cities clearly exemplify the totalitarian tendency of modern capitalism's organization of life: the isolated inhabitants (generally isolated within the framework of the family cell) see their lives reduced to the pure triviality of the repetitive combined with the obligatory absorption of an equally repetitive spectacle.

One can thus conclude that if people censor the question of their own everyday life, it is both because they are aware of its unbearable misery and because sooner or later they sense—whether they admit it or not—that all the real possibilities, all the desires that have been frustrated by the functioning of social life, were focused there, and not at all in the specialized activities or distractions. That is, awareness of the profound richness and energy abandoned in everyday life is inseparable from awareness of the poverty of the dominant organization of this life. Only the perceptible existence of this untapped richness leads to the contrasting definition of everyday life as poverty and as prison; and then, in the same movement, to the negation of the problem.

71

In these conditions, repressing the political question posed by the poverty of everyday life means repressing the depth of the demands bearing on the possible richness of this life—demands that can lead to nothing less than a reinvention of revolution. Of course an evasion of politics at this level is in no way incompatible with being active in the Parti Socialiste Unifié, for example, or with reading *Humanité* with confidence.

Everything effectively depends on the level at which this problem is posed: How is our life? How are we satisfied with it? Dissatisfied? Without for a moment letting ourselves be intimidated by the various advertisements designed to persuade us that we can be happy because of the existence of God or Colgate toothpaste or the CNRS.

It seems to me that this phrase "critique of everyday life" could and should also be understood in this reverse sense: as everyday life's sovereign critique of everything that is external or irrelevant to itself.

The question of the use of technological means, in everyday life and elsewhere, is a political question (and out of all the possible technical means, those that are implemented are in reality selected in accordance with the goal of maintaining one class's domination). When one envisions a future such as that presented in science fiction, in which interstellar adventures coexist with a terrestrial everyday life kept in the same old material indigence and archaic morality, this implies precisely that there is still a class of specialized rulers maintaining the proletarian masses of the factories and offices in their service; and that the interstellar adventures are nothing but the particular enterprise chosen by those rulers, the way they have found to develop their irrational economy, the pinnacle of specialized activity.

Someone posed the question, "What is private life deprived of?" Quite simply of life itself, which is cruelly absent. People are as deprived as possible of communication and of self-realization. Deprived of the opportunity to personally make their own history. Hypotheses responding positively to this question on the nature of the privation can thus only be expressed in the form of projects of enrichment; the project of a different style of life; or in fact simply the project of a style of life . . . Or, if we regard everyday life as the frontier between the dominated and the undominated sectors of life, and thus as the terrain of risk and uncertainty, it would be necessary to replace the present ghetto with a constantly moving frontier; to work ceaselessly toward the organization of new chances.

The question of intensity of experience is posed today—with the use of drugs, for example—in the only terms in which the society of alienation is capable of posing any question: namely, in terms of false recognition of a falsified project, in terms of fixation and attachment. It should also be noted how much the image of love elaborated and propagated in this society has in common with drugs. A passion is first of all presented as a denial of all other passions; then it is frustrated and finally reappears only in the compensations of the reigning spectacle. La Rochefoucauld observed, "What often prevents us from abandoning ourselves to a single vice is that we have several." This is a very constructive observation if we ignore its moralist presuppositions and put it back on its feet as the basis of a program for the realization of

72

human capacities.

All these questions are of present significa, visibly dominated by the emergence of the pro} ing class—the abolition of every class society an human history—and thus also dominated by the this project and by the distortions and failures it ha now.

The present crisis of everyday life takes its place forms of the crisis of capitalism, forms that remain un. who cling to the classical calculation of the date of th crisis of the economy.

The disappearance in developed capitalism of all the old values, of all the frames of reference of past communication; and the impossibility of replacing them by any others before having rationally dominated, within everyday life and everywhere else, the new industrial forces that escape us more and more—these facts produce not only the virtually official dissatisfaction of our time, a dissatisfaction particularly acute among young people, but also the self-negating tendency of art. Artistic activity had always been alone in conveying the clandestine problems of everyday life, albeit in a veiled, deformed, partially illusory manner. Evidence of a destruction of all artistic expression now exists before our eyes: modern art.

If we consider the whole extent of the crisis of contemporary society, I don't think it is possible still to regard leisure activities as a negation of the everyday. It has been recognized here that it is necessary to "study wasted time." But let us look at the recent evolution of this idea of wasted time. For classical capitalism, wasted time was time that was not devoted to production, accumulation, saving. The secular morality taught in bourgeois schools has instilled this rule of life. But it so happens that by an unexpected turn of events modern capitalism needs to increase consumption, to "raise the standard of living" (if we bear in mind that this expression is completely meaningless). Since at the same time production conditions, compartmentalized and clocked to the extreme, have become indefensible, the new morality already being conveyed in advertising, propaganda and all the forms of the dominant spectacle now frankly admits that wasted time is the time spent at work, which latter is only justified by the hierarchized scale of earnings that enable one to buy rest, consumption, entertainments—a daily passivity manufactured and controlled by capitalism.

If we now consider the artificiality of the consumer needs prefabricated and ceaselessly stimulated by modern industry—if we recognize the emptiness of leisure activities and the impossibility of rest—we can pose the question more realistically: What would *not* be wasted time? The development of a society of abundance should lead to an abundance of *what*?

This can obviously serve as a touchstone in many regards. When, for example, in one of those papers where the flabby thinking of "leftist intellectuals" is displayed—I am referring to *France-Observateur*— one reads a title like "The Little Car Out To Conquer Socialism" heading an article that explains that nowadays the Russians are beginning to pursue an American-style private consumption of goods, beginning

cars, one cannot help thinking that one need not have
[...]d all of Hegel and Marx to realize that a socialism that gives
[...] the face of an invasion of the market by small cars is in no way
[...]e socialism for which the workers movement fought. The bureaucratic rulers of Russia must be opposed not on the level of their tactics
or their dogmatism, but fundamentally, on the fact that the meaning
of people's lives has not really changed. And this is not some obscure
fatality of an everyday life doomed to remain reactionary. It is a fatality imposed on everyday life from the outside by the reactionary
sphere of specialized rulers, regardless of the label under which they
plan and regulate poverty in all its aspects.

The present depoliticization of many former leftist militants, their
withdrawal from one type of alienation to plunge into another, that of
private life, represents not so much a return to privacy, a flight from
"historical responsibility," but rather a withdrawal from the specialized political sector that is always manipulated by others—a sector
where the only responsibility they ever took was that of leaving all
responsibility to uncontrolled leaders; and where the communist project was betrayed and frustrated. Just as one cannot simplistically oppose private life to public life without asking: what private life? what
public life? (for private life contains the factors of its negation and
supersession, just as collective revolutionary action harbored the factors of its degeneration), so it would be a mistake to assess the alienation of individuals in revolutionary politics when it is really a matter
of the alienation of revolutionary politics itself. It is right to dialectize
the problem of alienation, to draw attention to the constantly recurring
possibilities of alienation arising within the very struggle against alienation; but we should stress that this applies to the highest level of
research (to the philosophy of alienation as a whole, for example) and
not to the level of Stalinism, the explanation of which is unfortunately
more gross.

Capitalist civilization has not yet been superseded anywhere, but it
continues to produce its own enemies everywhere. The next rise of the
revolutionary movement, radicalized by the lessons of past defeats and
with a program enriched in proportion to the practical powers of modern society (powers already constituting the potential material basis
that was lacking in the so-called utopian currents of socialism)—this
next attempt at a total contestation of capitalism will know how to
invent and propose a different use of everyday life, and will immediately base itself on new everyday practices, on new types of human
relationships (being no longer unaware that any conserving, within
the revolutionary movement, of the relations prevailing in the existing
society imperceptibly leads to a reconstitution of one or another variant of this society).

Just as the bourgeoisie, in its ascending phase, had to ruthlessly
liquidate everything that transcended earthly life (heaven, eternity),
so the revolutionary proletariat—which can never, without ceasing to
be revolutionary, recognize itself in any past or any models—will have
to renounce everything that transcends everyday life. Or rather, everything that claims to transcend it: the spectacle, the "historical" act or
pronouncement, the "greatness" of leaders, the mystery of specializa-

tions, the "immortality" of art and its ...... other words, it must renounce all the by-p..... survived as weapons of the world of the rul.....

The revolution in everyday life, breaking i..... the historical (and to every kind of change), will ...... in which *the present dominates the past* and the ...... life always predominate over the repetitive. We must ...... that the side of everyday life expressed by the concepts o..... misunderstanding, compromise or misuse—will decline c..... in importance in favor of their opposites: conscious choice and ...... .le.

The present artistic calling in question of language—appear...ng at the same time as that metalanguage of machines which is nothing other than the bureaucratized language of the bureaucracy in power— will then be superseded by higher forms of communication. The present notion of a decipherable social text will lead to new methods of writing this social text, in the direction my situationist comrades are presently seeking with unitary urbanism and some preliminary ventures in experimental behavior. The central production of an en- tirely reconverted industrial work will be the organization of new con- figurations of everyday life, the free creation of events.

The critique and perpetual re-creation of the totality of everyday life, before being carried out naturally by all people, must be under- taken in the present conditions of oppression, in order to destroy these conditions.

An avant-garde cultural movement, even one with revolutionary sympathies, cannot accomplish this. Neither can a revolutionary party on the traditional model, even if it accords a large place to criticism of culture (understanding by that term the entirety of artistic and conceptual means through which a society explains itself to itself and shows itself goals of life). This culture and this politics are worn out and it is not without reason that most people take no interest in them. The revolutionary transformation of everyday life, which is not re- served for some vague future but is placed immediately before us by the development of capitalism and its unbearable demands—the al- ternative being the reinforcement of the modern slavery—this trans- formation will mark the end of all unilateral artistic expression stocked in the form of commodities, at the same time as the end of all specialized politics.

This is going to be the task of a new type of revolutionary organiza- tion from its inception.

GUY DEBORD

A tape recording of this talk was presented 17 May 1961 at a confer- ence of the Group for Research on Everyday Life convened by Henri Lefebvre in the Center of Sociological Studies of the CNRS.

GEOPOLITICS OF HIBERNATION

The "balance of terror" between two rival groups of states—which is the most visible of the essential aspects of global politics at this moment—also means a balance of resignation: the resignation of each antagonist to the permanence of the other; and within their frontiers, the resignation of people to a fate that escapes them so completely that the very existence of the planet is far from certain, hinging on the prudence and skill of inscrutable strategists. This involves a generalized resignation to the existing order, to the coexisting powers of the specialists who organize this fate. These powers find an additional advantage in this balance since it permits the rapid liquidation of any original emancipatory experience arising on the margin of their systems, particularly in the present movement of the underdeveloped countries. It was through the same method of neutralizing one menace with another—regardless of who the particular winning protector may be—that the revolutionary impetus of the Congo was crushed by sending in the United Nations Expeditionary Corps (two days after landing, at the beginning of July 1960, the Ghanian troops, the first on the scene, were used to break the transportation strike in Léopoldville) and that of Cuba by the formation of a one-party system (in March 1962 General Lister, whose role in the repression of the Spanish revolution is known, was named Assistant Chief of Staff to the Cuban Army).

The two camps are actually preparing not for war, but for the indefinite preservation of this balance, which is in the image of the internal stabilization of their power. It goes without saying that this will entail an enormous mobilization of resources, since it is imperative to continually escalate the spectacle of possible war. Thus Barry Commoner, who presides over the scientific committee commissioned by the United States government to estimate the destruction that would result from a thermonuclear war, announces that after one hour of such a war 80 million Americans would be killed and that the survivors would have no hope of living normally afterwards. The Chiefs of Staff, who in their projections now count only in *megabodies* (this unit represents one million corpses), have admitted the futility of calculating beyond the first half day since experimental evidence is lacking to make any meaningful estimates at this level of destruction. According to Nicolas Vichney (*Le Monde*, 5 January 1962), one extreme current of American defense doctrine already considers that "the best deterrent would consist of the possession of an enormous thermonuclear bomb buried underground. If the enemy attacked, the bomb would be detonated and the Earth would be blown apart."

The theorists of this "Doomsday System" have certainly found the ultimate weapon for enforcing submission; they have for the first time translated the refusal of history into precise technical powers. But the rigid logic of these doctrinaires only responds to one aspect of the contradictory needs of the society of alienation, whose indissoluble project is to prevent people from living while it organizes their survival (see the opposition of the concepts of life and survival described by Vaneigem in "Basic Banalities"). Thus the Doomsday System, through its contempt for survival—which is still the indispensable condition for the present and future exploitation of human labor—can only play the role of last resort for the ruling bureaucracies: the insane proof of their seriousness. But in order to be fully effectual in reinforcing people's submission, the spectacle of a war to come must henceforth extend its sway over the organization of our present peacetime existence.

In this regard the extraordinary development of fallout shelters during 1961 is certainly a decisive turning point in the Cold War, a qualitative leap that will one day be distinguished as of immense importance in the process of the formation of a cybernetized totalitarian society on a global scale. This movement began in the United States, where Kennedy in his State of the Union Message last January could already assure Congress: "The nation's first serious civil defense shelter program is under way, identifying, marking and stocking fifty million spaces; and I urge your approval of federal incentives for the construction of public fallout shelters in schools and hospitals and similar centers." This state-controlled organization of survival has rapidly spread, more or less secretly, to other major countries of the two camps. West Germany, for example, was first of all concerned with the survival of Chancellor Adenauer and his team, and the disclosure of the plans to this end led to the seizure of the Munich magazine *Quick*. Sweden and Switzerland are at the point of installing collective shelters where workers buried with their factories will be able to continue to produce without interruption until the grand finale of the Doomsday System. But the launching pad of the civil defense policy is the United States, where a number of flourishing companies, such as the Peace o' Mind Shelter Company in Texas, the American Survival Products Corporation in Maryland, Fox Hole Shelter, Inc., in California and the Bee Safe Manufacturing Company in Ohio, advertise and install a multitude of individual shelters built as private property to take care of the survival of each family. This fad is giving rise to a new interpretation of religious morality, certain clergymen expressing the opinion that one's duty will clearly consist of refusing entry to friends or strangers, even by means of arms, in order to guarantee the salvation of one's own family. Morality had to adapt itself in order to cooperate in bringing to perfection that terrorism of conformity that underlies all the publicity of modern capitalism. It was already hard, faced with one's family and neighbors, not to have a given model of automobile which a given salary level enables one to buy on credit (a salary level always recognizable in the American-type urban housing developments because the location of the dwelling is precisely determined by the level of salary). It will be even more difficult not to guarantee one's family's *survival status* once that commodity is on the market.

It is generally estimated that in the United States since 1955 the relative saturation of the demand for "durable goods" has led to an insufficiency of the consumer stimulus necessary for economic expansion. One can thus understand the enormous vogue for gadgets of all sorts, which represent an easily manipulable development in the semidurable goods sector. It is easy to see the important role of the shelters in this necessary boost of expansion. With the installation of shelters and their foreseeable offshoots and by-products, all the appurtenances of life on the surface are to be duplicated for the new duplicate life underground. These subterranean investments in layers as yet unexploited by the affluent society are boosting the sale both of semidurable goods already in use on the surface—as with the boom in canned foods, of which each shelter needs a maximum stock—and of particular new gadgets, such as plastic bags for the bodies of people who will die in the shelter and, naturally, continue to lay there with the survivors.

It is undoubtedly easy to see that these already widespread individual shelters are never effective, if only for such gross technical oversights as the absence of an independent oxygen supply; and that even the most perfected collective shelters would offer only the slightest possibility for survival if thermonuclear war was actually accidentally unleashed. But here, as in every racket, protection is only a pretext. The real use of the shelters is to test—and thereby reinforce—people's submissiveness, and to manipulate this submissiveness in a way favorable to the ruling society. The shelters, as a creation of a new consumable commodity in the affluent society, prove more than any preceding commodity that people can be made to work to satisfy highly artificial needs, needs that most certainly "remain needs without ever having been desires" (*Preliminaries . . .*, 20 July 1960) and without having the slightest chance of becoming desires. The power of this society, its formidable automatic genius, can be measured by this extreme case. If this system were to go to the point of bluntly proclaiming that it imposes such an empty and despairing existence that the best solution for everyone would be to go hang themselves, it would still succeed in managing a healthy and profitable business by producing standardized ropes. But regardless of all its capitalist wealth, the concept of survival means *suicide on the installment plan* through exhaustion, a renunciation of life *every day*. The network of shelters—which are not intended to be used for a war, but right now—presents a still far-fetched and caricatural image of existence under a perfected bureaucratic capitalism. A neo-Christianity has revived its ideal of renunciation with a new humility compatible with a new boost of industry. The world of shelters acknowledges itself as an *air-conditioned vale of tears*. The coalition of all the managers and their various sorts of priests will be able to agree on one unitary program: mass hypnosis plus superconsumption.

Survival as the opposite of life, if rarely voted for so clearly as by the buyers of shelters in 1961, is to be found at all levels of the struggle against alienation. It is found in the old conception of art, which stressed survival through one's works, an admission of a renunciation of life, art as excuse and consolation (principally since the bourgeois epoch of aesthetics, that secular substitute for the religious other-world). And it is found just as much at the level of the most basic needs, those of food and shelter, with the "blackmail of utility" denounced in the "Elementary Program of Unitary Urbanism" (*IS #6*), the blackmail that eliminates any human critique of the environment "by the simple argument that one needs a roof over one's head."

The new habitation that is now taking shape with the large housing developments is not really distinct from the architecture of the shelters; it merely represents a lower level of that architecture. (The two are closely related and the direct passage from one to the other is envisaged: the first example in France is a development presently being built in Nice, the basement of which is already adapted as an atomic shelter for its inhabitants.) The concentration-camp organization of the surface of the earth is the normal state of the present society in formation; its condensed subterranean version merely represents that society's pathological excess. This subterranean sickness reveals the real nature of the normal surface "health." The urbanism of despair is rapidly becoming dominant on the surface, not only in the population centers of the United States, but also in those of much more backward countries of Europe and even, for example, in the Algeria of the neocolonialist period proclaimed since the "Constantine Plan." At the end of 1961 the first version of the national plan for French territorial development (whose formulation was later toned down) complained in its chapter on Paris of "the persistency of an inactive population in living within the capital" despite the fact that the authors of the report, licensed specialists of happiness and practicality, pointed out that "they could live more agreeably outside Paris." The authors therefore urged the elimination of this distressing irrationality by the enactment of legal measures to "systematically discourage this inactive population from living" in Paris.

Since the principal worthwhile activity in this society obviously consists in systematically discouraging the plans made by its managers, to the point of eventually concretely eliminating them, and since those managers are much more constantly aware of this latter danger than are the drugged masses of executants, they erect their defenses in all the modern projects of territorial organization. The planning of shelters for the population, whether in the normal form of dwellings or in the "affluent" form of family tombs to inhabit preventively, is in fact used to shelter the planners' own power. The rulers who control the canning and maximum isolation of their subjects also know how to entrench themselves for strategic purposes. The Haussmanns of the twentieth century no longer stop at facilitating the deployment of their repressive forces by partitioning the old urban clusters into manageable city blocks divided by wide avenues. At the same time that they disperse the population over a vast area in the new prefabricated cities which represent this partitioning in its *purest state* (where the inferiority of the masses, disarmed and deprived of means of communication, is sharply increased compared with the continually more technically equipped police), they erect *capital cities out of reach* where the ruling bureaucracy, for more security, can constitute the whole of the population.

Different stages of development of these government-cities can be noted. The "Military Zone" of Tirana is a section cut off from the city and defended by the army wherein are concentrated the homes of the rulers of Albania, the Central Committee building and the schools, hospitals, stores and diversions for this autarkic elite. The administrative city of Rocher Noir was built in one year to serve as the capital of Algeria when it became evident that the French authorities had become incapable of maintaining themselves normally in a large city; it has exactly the same function as the "Military Zone" of Tirana, though it was erected in open country. Finally, there is the supreme example, Brasília, parachuted into the center of a vast desert. Its inauguration came just at the moment when President Quadros was dismissed by his military and there were premonitions of civil war in Brazil. This bureaucratic capital is also the supreme expression of functionalist architecture.

Things having gone this far, many specialists are beginning to denounce a number of disturbing absurdities. This is due to their having failed to comprehend the central rationality (the rationality of a coherent delirium) that governs these partial, apparently accidental absurdities, to which their own activities inevitably contribute. Their denunciation of the absurd is thus itself inevitably absurd in its forms and its means. What is one to think of the nine hundred professors of all the universities and research institutes of the New York–Boston region who in the *New York Herald Tribune* of 30 December 1961 solemnly addressed themselves to President Kennedy and Governor Rockefeller—a few days before Kennedy proudly issued an initial order for fifty million shelter spaces—in order to convince them of the perniciousness of "Civil Defense" development? Or of the horde of sociologists, judges, architects, policemen, psychologists, teachers, hygienists, psychiatrists and journalists who never cease gathering in congresses, committee meetings and conferences of all sorts, all in search of an urgent solution for *humanizing* housing developments? Humanizing housing developments is as ridiculous a notion as humanizing atomic war, and for the same reasons. The shelters reduce not war but the threat of war to "human proportions"—"human" in modern capitalist terms: marketable human consumption. This sort of investigation into humanization simply aims at the joint working out of the most effective lies for the repression of people's resistance. While boredom and total absence of social life characterize the suburban housing developments in a way as immediate and tangible as a Siberian cold wave, some women's magazines now go to those new suburbs to photograph their fashion models and interview satisfied people. Since the stupefying power of such environments is discernable in the intellectual development of the children, their maladjustment is blamed on their previous slum upbringing. The latest reformist theory places its hopes in a sort of culture center—without using that particular word so as not to frighten anyone away. In the plans of the Seine Architects Union (*Le Monde*, 22 December 1961) the prefabricated "bistro-club" that will everywhere humanize their work is presented as a cubic "plastic cell" ($28 \times 18 \times 4$ meters) comprising "a stable element: the *bistro*, which will sell tobacco and magazines, but not alcohol; the remainder will be reserved for various craft activities. . . .

It should become a seductive showcase. Hence the aesthetic conception and the quality of the materials will be carefully designed to give their full effect night and day. The play of lights should in fact *communicate* the life of the *bistro-club*."

Thus is presented to us, in profoundly revealing terms, the discovery that "could facilitate social integration on a level that would forge the spirit of a small city." The absence of alcohol will be little noticed: in France youth gangs do not even need the aid of alcohol to go on the rampage. The French delinquents seem to have broken with the French tradition of mass alcoholism, which is still so important in the "hooliganism" of the Eastern bloc, while not having yet come around, like American youth, to the use of marijuana or stronger drugs. Although stuck in such an empty transitional period, between the stimulants of two distinct historical stages, they nevertheless express a sharp violence in response to this world we are describing and to the horrible perspective of occupying their niche in it. Leaving aside the factor of revolt, the unionized architects' project is coherent: their glass bistros are intended as an instrument of supplementary control on the way to that *total surveillance* of production and consumption that actually constitutes the famous integration they aim at. The candidly avowed recourse to the aesthetics of the show-window is perfectly illuminated by the theory of the spectacle: in these de-alcoholized bars the consumers themselves become spectacular, as do any objects of consumption, for lack of any other attraction. Perfectly reified man has his place in the show-window as a desirable image of reification.

The internal defect of the system is that it cannot perfectly reify people; it needs to make them act and to obtain their participation, without which the production and consumption of reification would come to a stop. The reigning system is thus in conflict with history—with its own history, which is at once the history of its reinforcement and the history of its contestation.

Today (after a century of struggles and after the traditional or newly formed rulers' liquidation, between the two world wars, of the entire classical workers movement which represented the force of general contestation), in spite of certain appearances, the dominant world *more than ever presents itself as permanent* on the basis of an enrichment and an infinite extension of an irreplaceable model. The comprehension of this world can be based only on contestation. And this contestation is neither true nor realistic except insofar as it is a contestation of the totality.

This explains the astonishing absence of ideas evident in all the acts of culture, politics, organization of life, and everything else—the debility of the modernist builders of functionalist cities is only a particularly blatant example. The intelligent specialists are intelligent only in playing the game of specialists; hence the timid conformity and fundamental lack of imagination that make them grant that this or that product is useful, good, necessary. In fact, the root of the prevailing *absence of imagination* cannot be understood unless one attains the *imagination of the absence*—that is, unless one conceives what is missing, forbidden and hidden, and yet possible, in modern life.

This is not a theory without links to the way people see their own lives; it is, on the contrary, a reality in the minds of people as yet without links with theory. Those who, going far enough in the "cohabitation with the negative" in the Hegelian sense, come to explicitly recognize this absence as their principal force and their program, will bring to light the only *positive project* that can overthrow the wall of sleep; and the measures of survival; and the doomsday bombs; and the megatons of architecture.

THE BAD DAYS WILL END

As the world of the spectacle extends its reign it approaches the climax of its offensive, provoking new resistances everywhere. These resistances are very little known precisely because the goal of the reigning spectacle is the universal hypnotic reflection of submission. But they do exist and are spreading.

Everyone talks about the youth rebellion in the advanced industrial countries, though without understanding much about it (see "Unconditional Defense" in issue #6 of this journal). Militant publications like *Socialisme ou Barbarie* in Paris and *Correspondence* in Detroit have published very well documented articles on workers' continual resistance at work (against the whole organization of work) and on their depoliticization and disaffection from the unions, which have become a mechanism for integrating workers into the society and a supplementary weapon in the economic arsenal of bureaucratized capitalism. As the old forms of opposition reveal their ineffectiveness, or more often their complete inversion into participation in the existing order, the irreducible dissatisfaction spreads subterraneanly, undermining the edifice of the affluent society. The "old mole" that Marx evoked in his "Toast to the Proletarians of Europe" is still digging away, the specter is reappearing in all the nooks and crannies of our televised Elsinore Castle, whose political mists are dissipated as soon as and as long as the workers councils exist and wield power.

Just as the first organization of the classical proletariat was preceded, during the end of the eighteenth century and the beginning of the nineteenth, by a period of isolated "criminal" acts aimed at destroying the machines of production that were depriving people of their work, so we are presently witnessing the first appearance of a wave of vandalism against the *machines of consumption* that are just as certainly depriving us of our life. It is evident that now, as then, the value does not lie in the destruction itself, but in the insubordination which can eventually transform itself into a positive project, to the point of reconverting the machines in a way that increases people's real power. Leaving aside the havoc perpetrated by groups of adolescents, we can point out a few examples of actions by workers that are in large part incomprehensible from the classical "demands" perspective.

On 9 February 1961 in Naples factory workers coming off the day shift found that the streetcars that ordinarily took them home were not running, the drivers having launched a lightning strike because several of them had just been laid off. The workers demonstrated their solidarity with the strikers by throwing various projectiles at the company offices, and then bottles of gasoline which set fire to part of the streetcar station. Then they burned several buses while successfully holding off police and firemen. Numbering several thousand, they spread through the city, smashing store windows and electric signs. During the night troops had to be called in to restore law and order, and armored cars moved on Naples. This totally spontaneous and aimless demonstration was obviously a direct revolt against *commuting time*, which is such a burdensome addition to wage slavery time in modern cities. Sparked by a chance minor incident, this revolt immediately began to extend to the whole decor (recently plastered over the traditional poverty of southern Italy) of consumer society: the store window and the neon sign, being at once its most symbolic and most fragile points, draw the first attacks just as during the rampages of rebellious youth.

On 4 August in France striking miners at Merlebach attacked twenty-one cars parked in front of the management buildings. All the commentators pointed out dumbfoundedly that nearly all these automobiles belonged to the workers' *fellow employees* at the mine. Who can fail to see in this—over and beyond the innumerable reasons that always justify aggression on the part of the exploited—a gesture of self-defense against the central object of consumer alienation?

The strikers of Liège, in setting out to destroy the machinery of the newspaper *La Meuse* on 6 January 1961, attained one of the peaks of consciousness of their movement in thus attacking the *information* apparatus held by their enemies. (Since monopoly of all the means of transmitting information is shared by the government and the leaders of the socialist and union bureaucracies, this was precisely the crucial point of the struggle, the unbreached barrier blocking off workers' "wildcat" struggles from the perspective of power and thus condemning them to disappear.) Another symptom, though less interesting because more contingent on Gaullism's clumsy propagandistic excesses, is nevertheless worth noting in the following joint communiqué of the unions of French journalists and radio and television technicians last 9 February: "Our fellow reporters and technicians who were covering the demonstration Thursday evening *were attacked by the crowd merely because they were bearing the RTF* [French radio-television] *insignia*. This fact is significant. This is why the SJRT and SUT unions consider themselves justified in saying once again in all seriousness that *the lives of our fellow reporters and technicians depend on the respect in which their reports are held.*" Of course, along with the first concrete reactions against the forces of conditioning we cannot close our eyes to the extent to which this conditioning continues to prove successful, even within very combative workers' actions. Thus, when at the beginning of the year the Decazeville miners delegated twenty of their number to go on a hunger strike, they were fighting on the spectacular terrain of the enemy by relying on the tear-jerking potential of twenty stars. They thus necessarily lost, since their only chance of success would have been to extend their collective intervention at all costs beyond their limited sector (the only industry they were blocking had already been losing money anyway). Capitalist social organization and its oppositional by-products have so effectively propagated *parliamentary* and *spectacular* ideas that revolutionary workers often tend to forget that *representation* must always be kept to the essential minimum, used as little as possible. But it isn't only industrial workers who are fighting against brutalization. The Berlin actor Wolfgang Neuss perpetrated a most suggestive act of sabotage in January by placing a notice in the paper *Der Abend* giving away the identity of the killer in a television detective serial that had been keeping the masses in suspense for weeks.

The assault of the first workers movement against the whole organization of the old world came to an end long ago and nothing can bring it back to life. It failed. Certainly it achieved immense results, but not the ones it had originally intended. No doubt such deviation toward partially unexpected results is the general rule in human actions, but the exception to this rule is precisely the moment of revolutionary action, the moment of the qualitative leap, of all or nothing. The classical workers movement must be reexamined without any illusions, particularly without any illusions regarding its various political and pseudotheoretical heirs, for all they have inherited is its failure. The apparent successes of this movement are its fundamental failures (reformism or the installation of a state bureaucracy), while its failures (the Paris Commune or the Asturias revolt) are its most promising successes so far, for us and for the future. This subject must be precisely delineated in time. One could say that the classical workers movement began a couple decades before the official formation of the International, with the first linking up of communist groups of several countries that Marx and his friends organized from Brussels in 1845. And that it was completely finished after the failure of the Spanish revolution, that is, after the Barcelona May days of 1937.

It is necessary to rediscover the whole truth of this period and to reexamine all the oppositions between revolutionaries, all the neglected possibilities, without any longer being impressed by the fact that some won out over others and dominated the movement; for we know that the movement within which they were successful was an overall failure. Marx's thought is obviously the first which must be rediscovered; nor does this present much difficulty in view of the extensive existing documentation and the grossness of the lies about it. But it is also necessary to reassess the anarchist positions in the First International, Blanquism, Luxemburgism, the council movement in Germany and Spain, Kronstadt, the Makhnovists, etc. Without overlooking the practical influence of the utopian socialists. All this, of course, not with the aim of scholarship or academic eclecticism, but solely with the aim of contributing toward the formation of a new revolutionary movement, a movement of which we have seen so many premonitory signs over the last few years, one of which is our own existence. This new movement will be profoundly different. We must understand these signs through the study of the classical revolutionary project and vice versa. It is necessary to rediscover the history of the very movement of history, which has been so thoroughly hidden and distorted. It is, moreover, only in this enterprise—and in a few experimental artistic groups generally linked to it—that seductive modes of behavior have appeared; modes which enable one to take an objective interest in modern society and the possibilities it contains.

There is no other way to be faithful to, or even to understand, the actions of our comrades of the past than to profoundly reconceive the problem of revolution, which has been all the more deprived of thought as it has become posed more intensely in concrete reality. But why does this reconception seem so difficult? Starting from an experience of free everyday life (that is, from a quest for freedom in everyday life) it is not difficult. It seems to us that this question is quite concretely felt today among young people. And to feel it with enough urgency enables one to rediscover *lost history*, to salvage and rejudge it. It is not difficult for thought concerned with questioning everything that exists. It is only necessary not to have *abandoned* philosophy—as have virtually all the philosophers—and not to have abandoned art—as have virtually all the artists—and not to have abandoned contestation of *present reality*—as have virtually all the militants. When they are not abandoned, these questions all converge toward the same supersession. It is only the specialists, whose power is geared to a society of specialization, who have abandoned the *critical* truth of their disciplines in order to preserve the personal advantages of their *function*. But all real researches are converging toward a totality, just as real people are going to come together in order to try once again to escape from their prehistory.

Many people are skeptical about the possibility of a new revolutionary movement, continually repeating that the proletariat has been integrated or that the workers are now satisfied, etc. This means one of two things: either they are declaring themselves satisfied—in which case we will fight them without any equivocation—or they are identifying themselves with a category separate from the workers (artists, for example)—in which case we will fight this illusion by showing them that the new proletariat is tending to encompass almost everybody.

In the same way, apocalyptic fears or hopes regarding the movements of revolt in the colonized or semicolonized countries overlook this central fact: the revolutionary project must be realized in the industrially advanced countries. Until it is, all the movements in the underdeveloped zone seem doomed to follow the model of the Chinese revolution, whose birth accompanied the liquidation of the classical workers movement and whose entire subsequent evolution has been dominated by the mutation it suffered due to that liquidation. It remains true that the existence of these anticolonialist movements, even if they are polarized around the bureaucratic Chinese model, creates a disequilibrium in the external confrontation of the two great counterbalanced blocs, destabilizing any division of the world by their rulers and owners. But the security of the stakes in the planetary poker game is threatened just as much by the internal disequilibrium that still prevails in the factories of Manchester and East Berlin.

The radical minorities that in obscurity managed to survive the crushing of the classical workers movement (whose power the ruse of history transformed into state police) have handed down the truth of that movement, but only as an abstract truth of the past. Their honorable resistance to force has thus far succeeded in preserving a calumniated tradition, but not in reinvesting it into a new force. The formation of new organizations depends on a deeper critique, translated into acts. There must be a complete break with *ideology*, in which revolutionary groups think they possess official titles guaranteeing their function; it is necessary to resume the Marxian critique of the role of ideologies. It is thus necessary to leave the terrain of specialized revolutionary activity—of the self-mystification of political seriousness—because it has long been seen that the possession of this specialization encourages even the best people to demonstrate stupidity regarding all other questions; with the result that they lose any chance of succeeding even in political struggle itself, since the latter is inseparable from all other aspects of the total problem of our society. Specialization and pseudoseriousness are among the first defensive outposts that the organization of the old world occupies in everyone's mind. A revolutionary association of a new type will also break with the old world by permitting and demanding of its members an authentic and creative participation, instead of expecting a participation of militants measurable in *attendance time*, which amounts to recreating the sole control possible in the dominant society: the quantitative criterion of hours of labor. Such impassioned participation on the part of everyone is necessitated by the fact that the classical political militant, who "devotes himself" to his duties, is everywhere disappearing along with classical politics itself; and even more by the fact that devotion and sacrifice always engender *authority* (even if only purely moral authority). *Boredom is counterrevolutionary.* In every way.

The groups that acknowledge the fundamental (not merely circumstantial) failure of the old politics must also acknowledge that they can claim to be a *permanent avant-garde* only if they themselves exemplify a new style of life—a new passion. There is nothing utopian about this lifestyle criterion: it can be observed everywhere in the moments of the emergence and rise of the classical workers movement. We think that in the coming period this will not only hold true to the extent it did in the nineteenth century, but will go much further. Otherwise the militants of these groups would only constitute dull propaganda societies, pushing quite correct and basic ideas but with virtually no one listening. The spectacular unilateral transmission of a revolutionary teaching—whether within an organization or in its action directed toward the outside—has lost all chance of proving effective in the society of the spectacle, which simultaneously organizes a completely different spectacle and infects every spectacle with an element of nausea. Such specialized propaganda thus has little chance of issuing into timely and fruitful intervention whenever the masses are compelled to wage real struggles.

It is necessary to recall and revive the nineteenth century social war of the *poor*. The word can be found everywhere, in songs and in all the declarations of the people who worked for the objectives of the classical workers movement. One of the most urgent tasks confronting the SI and other comrades now advancing along convergent paths is to define the *new poverty*. Certain American sociologists over the last few years have played a role in the exposure of this new poverty analogous to that played by the first utopian philanthropists vis-à-vis workers' action in the previous century: The malady is revealed, but in an idealist and artificial way; because since understanding resides in praxis alone, one can really comprehend the nature of the enemy only in the process of fighting it (this is the terrain on which are situated, for example, G. Keller's and R. Vaneigem's projects of *introducing the aggressivity of the delinquents onto the plane of ideas*).

Defining the new poverty also entails defining the new wealth. To the image propagated by the dominant society—according to which it has evolved (both on its own and in response to acceptable reformist pressure) from an economy of profit to an economy of needs—must be counterposed *an economy of desires*, which could be formulated as: technological society plus the imagination of what could be done with it. The economy of needs is falsified in terms of habit. Habit is the natural process by which desire (accomplished, realized desire) is degraded into need and is confirmed, objectified and universally recognized as need. But the present economy is directly geared to the fabrication of habits, and manipulates people by forcing them to repress their desires.

Complicity with the world's false opposition goes hand in glove with complicity with its false wealth (and thus with a retreat from defining the new poverty). Sartre's disciple Gorz is a good case in point. In *Les Temps Modernes* #188 he confesses how embarrassed he is that, thanks to his career as a journalist (which indeed is nothing to write home about), he can afford the good things of this society: among which he respectfully mentions taxis and trips abroad, at a time when taxis inch forward behind the mass of cars that everyone has been forced to buy; and when trips present us with the same boring spectacle of eternal alienation endlessly duplicated around the Earth. At the same time, he waxes enthusiastic—like Sartre did once upon a time about the "total freedom of criticism in the USSR"—about "the youth" of the only "revolutionary generations," those of Yugoslavia, Algeria, Cuba, China and Israel. The other countries are old, says Gorz, to justify his own debility. He thus relieves himself of the necessity of making any more precise analyses of or distinctions among "the youth" of those or other countries, where not everyone is so old or so visible, and where not every revolt is so Gorz.

Fougeyrollas, the latest thinker to have superseded Marxism, is somewhat disconcerted over the fact that while all previous major stages of historical development were characterized by a change in the mode of production, the communist society heralded by Marx, if it were to come about, would seem to be no more than an extension of the society of industrial production. Go to the back of the class, Fougeyrollas. The next form of society will not be based on industrial production. It will be a society of *realized art*. The "absolutely new type of production supposedly in gestation in our society," whose absence Fougeyrollas asserts in *Marxisme en question*, is the construction of situations, the free construction of the events of life.

THE FIFTH S.I. CONFERENCE IN GÖTEBORG

(excerpts)

The 5th Conference of the Situationist International was held at Göteborg, Sweden, 28–30 August 1961, eleven months after the London Conference. The situationists of nine countries were represented by Ansgar-Elde, Debord, J. de Jong, Kotányi, D. Kunzelmann, S. Larsson, J.V. Martin, Nash, Prem, G. Stadler, Hardy Strid, H. Sturm, R. Vaneigem, Zimmer. [. . .]

Next the Conference hears an orientation report by Vaneigem, who says notably:

· "[. . .] It is a question not of elaborating the spectacle of refusal, but rather of refusing the spectacle. In order for their elaboration to be *artistic* in the new and authentic sense defined by the SI, the elements of the destruction of the spectacle must precisely cease to be works of art. There is no such thing as *situationism* or a situationist work of art or a spectacular situationist. Once and for all. [. . .] Our position is that of combatants between two worlds—one that we don't acknowledge, the other that does not yet exist. [. . .]"

[. . .] Kunzelmann expresses a strong skepticism as to the powers the SI can bring together in order to act on the level envisaged by Vaneigem.

Kotányi responds to Nash and Kunzelmann: "Since the beginning of the movement there has been a problem as to what to call artistic works by members of the SI. It was understood that none of them was a situationist production, but what to call them? I propose a very simple rule: *to call them 'antisituationist.'* We are against the dominant conditions of artistic inauthenticity. I don't mean that anyone should stop painting, writing, etc. I don't mean that that has no value. I don't mean that we could continue to exist without doing that. But at the same time we know that all that will be recuperated* by the society and used against us. Our force is in the elaboration of certain truths which have an explosive power whenever people are ready to struggle for them. At the present stage the movement is only in its infancy regarding the elaboration of these essential points. [. . .]"

The responses to Kotányi's proposal are all favorable. It is noted that would-be avant-garde artists are beginning to appear in different countries who have no connection with the SI but who refer to "situationism" or describe their works as being more or less situationist. This tendency is obviously going to increase and it would be pointless for the SI to try and resist it. While various confused artists nostalgic for a positive art call themselves situationist, *antisituationist* art will be the mark of the best artists, those of the SI, since genuinely situationist conditions have as yet not at all been created. Admitting this is the mark of a situationist.

With one exception, the Conference unanimously decides to adopt this rule of antisituationist art, binding on all members of the SI. Only

Nash objects, his spite and indignation having become sharper and sharper throughout the whole debate, to the point of uncontrolled rage.

[. . .] Prem resumes in more detail the objections of his friends to Kotányi's perspectives. He agrees with calling our art antisituationist; and also with organizing a situationist base. But he does not think the SI's tactics are good. There is talk of people's dissatisfaction and revolt, but in his view, as his tendency already expressed it at London, "Most people are still primarily concerned with comfort and conveniences." Prem considers that the SI systematically neglects its real chances in culture. It rejects favorable occasions to impose itself in existing cultural politics, whereas according to him the SI has no power but its power in culture—a power which could be very great and which is visibly within our reach. The SI majority sabotages the chances of an effective action on the terrain where it is possible. It castigates artists who would be able to succeed in doing something; it throws them out the moment they get the means to do things. [. . .]

Other German situationists strongly oppose Prem, some of them accusing him of having expressed positions in their name that they do not share (but it seems, rather, that Prem simply had the frankness to clearly express the line that dominates in the German section). Finally the Germans come around to agreeing that none of them conceives of theory as separate from its practical results. With this the third session is adjourned in the middle of the night, not without violent agitation and uproar (from one side there are shouts of "Your theory is going to fly right back in your faces!" and from the other, "Cultural pimps!").

[. . .] The German situationists who publish the journal *Spur* [. . .] emphasize the urgency, already made evident by the Conference, for them to unify their positions and projects with the rest of the SI. [. . .] On their request, the Conference adds Attila Kotányi and J. de Jong to the editorial committee of *Spur* in order to verify this process of unification. (But in January this decision is flouted by their putting out, without Kotányi and de Jong's knowledge, an issue #7 marking a distinct regression from the preceding ones—which leads to the exclusion of those responsible.)

[. . .] It is voted to hold the 6th Conference at Anvers, after the rejection of the Scandinavian proposal to hold it clandestinely in Warsaw. The Conference does decide, however, to send a delegation of three situationists to Poland to develop our contacts there. [. . .]

BASIC BANALITIES

1

Bureaucratic capitalism has found its legitimation in Marx. I am not referring here to orthodox Marxism's dubious merit of having reinforced the neocapitalist structures whose present reorganization is an implicit homage to Soviet totalitarianism; I am emphasizing the extent to which Marx's most profound analyses of alienation have been vulgarized in the most commonplace facts, which, stripped of their magical veil and materialized in each gesture, have become the sole substance, day after day, of the lives of an increasing number of people. In a word, bureaucratic capitalism contains the palpable reality of alienation; it has brought it home to everybody far more successfully than Marx could ever have hoped to do, it has banalized it as the diminishing of material poverty has been accompanied by a spreading mediocrity of existence. As poverty has been reduced in terms of mere material survival, it has become more profound in terms of our way of life—this is at least one widespread feeling that exonerates Marx from all the interpretations a degenerate Bolshevism has derived from him. The "theory" of peaceful coexistence has accelerated such an awareness and revealed, to those who were still confused, that exploiters can get along quite well with each other despite their spectacular divergences.

2

"Any act," writes Mircea Eliade, "can become a religious act. Human existence is realized simultaneously on two parallel planes, that of temporality, becoming, illusion, and that of eternity, substance, reality." In the nineteenth century the brutal divorce of these two planes demonstrated that power would have done better to have maintained reality in a mist of divine transcendence. But we must give reformism credit for succeeding where Bonaparte had failed, in dissolving becoming in eternity and reality in illusion; this union may not be as solid as the sacraments of religious marriage, but it is *lasting*, which is the most the managers of coexistence and social peace can ask of it. This is also what leads us to define ourselves—in the illusory but inescapable perspective of duration—as the end of abstract temporality, as the end of the reified time of our acts; to define ourselves—does it have to be spelled out?—at the positive pole of alienation as the end of social alienation, as the end of humanity's term of social alienation.

3

The socialization of primitive human groups reveals a will to struggle more effectively against the mysterious and terrifying forces of nature. But struggling in the natural environment, at once with it and against it, submitting to its most inhuman laws in order to wrest from it an increased chance of survival—doing this could only engender a more evolved form of aggressive defense, a more complex and less primitive attitude, manifesting on a higher level the contradictions that the uncontrolled and yet influenceable forces of nature never ceased to impose. In becoming socialized, the struggle against the blind domination of nature triumphed inasmuch as it gradually assimilated primitive, natural alienation, but in another form. Alienation became social in the fight against natural alienation. Is it by chance that a technological civilization has developed to such a point that social alienation has been revealed by its conflict with the last areas of natural resistance that technological power hadn't managed (and for good reasons) to subjugate? Today the technocrats propose to put an end to primitive alienation: with a stirring humanitarianism they exhort us to perfect the technical means that "in themselves" would enable us to conquer death, suffering, discomfort and boredom. But to get rid of death would be less of a miracle than to get rid of suicide and the desire to die. There are ways of abolishing the death penalty than can make one miss it. Until now the specific use of technology—or more generally the socioeconomic context in which human activity is confined—while quantitatively reducing the number of occasions of pain and death, has allowed death itself to eat like a cancer into the heart of each person's life.

4

The prehistoric food-gathering age was succeeded by the hunting age during which clans formed and strove to increase their chances of survival. Hunting grounds and reserves were staked out from which outsiders were absolutely excluded since the welfare of the whole clan depended on its maintaining its territory. As a result, the freedom gained by settling down more comfortably in the natural environment, and by more effective protection against its rigors, engendered its own negation outside the boundaries laid down by the clan and forced the group to moderate its customary rules in organizing its relations with excluded and threatening groups. From the moment it appeared, socially constituted economic survival implied the existence of boundaries, restrictions, conflicting rights. It should never be forgotten that until now both history and our own nature have developed in accordance with the movement of privative appropriation: the seizing of control by a class, group, caste or individual of a general power over socioeconomic survival whose form remains complex—from ownership of land, territory, factories or capital, all the way to the "pure" exercise of power over people (hierarchy). Beyond the struggle against regimes whose vision of paradise is a cybernetic welfare state lies the necessity of a still vaster struggle against a fundamental and initially natural state of things, in the development of which capitalism plays only an incidental, transitory role; a state of things which will only disappear when the last traces of hierarchical power disappear—along with the "swine of humanity," of course.

5

To be an owner is to arrogate a good from whose enjoyment one excludes other people—while at the same time recognizing everyone's abstract right to possession. By excluding people from the real right of ownership, the owner extends his dominion over those he has excluded (absolutely over nonowners, relatively over other owners), without whom he is nothing. The nonowners have no choice in the matter. The owner appropriates and alienates them as producers of his own power, while the necessity of ensuring their own physical existence forces them in spite of themselves to collaborate in producing their own exclusion and to survive without ever being able to live. Excluded, they participate in possession through the mediation of the owner, a mystical participation characterizing from the outset all the clan and social relationships that gradually replaced the principle of obligatory cohesion in which each member was an integral part of the group ("organic interdependence"). Their guarantee of survival depends on their activity within the framework of privative appropriation. They reinforce a right to property from which they are excluded. Due to this ambiguity each of them sees himself as participating in ownership, as a living fragment of the right to possess, and this belief in turn reinforces his condition as excluded and possessed. (Extreme cases of this alienation: the faithful slave, the cop, the bodyguard, the centurion—creatures who, through a sort of union with their own death, confer on death a power equal to the forces of life and identify in a destructive energy the negative and positive poles of alienation, the absolutely submissive slave and the absolute master.) It is of vital importance to the exploiter that this appearance is maintained and made more sophisticated; not because he is especially machiavellian, but simply because he wants to stay alive. The organization of appearance is bound to the survival of his privileges and to the physical survival of the nonowner, who can thus remain alive while being exploited and excluded from being a person. Privative appropriation and domination are thus originally imposed and felt as a positive right, but in the form of a negative universality. Valid for everyone, justified in everyone's eyes by divine or natural law, the right of privative appropriation is objectified in a general illusion, in a universal transcendence, in an essential law under which everyone individually manages to tolerate the more or less narrow limits assigned to his right to live and to the conditions of life in general.

6

In this social context the function of alienation must be understood as a *condition of survival.* The labor of the nonowners is subject to the same contradictions as the right of privative appropriation. It transforms them into possessed beings, into producers of their own expropriation and exclusion, but it represents the only chance of survival for slaves, for serfs, for workers—so much so that the activity that allows their existence to continue by emptying it of all content ends up, through a natural and sinister reversal of perspective, by taking on a positive sense. Not only has value been attributed to work (in its form of sacrifice in the *ancien régime,* in its brutalizing aspects in bourgeois ideology and in the so-called People's Democracies), but very early on to work for a master, to alienate oneself willingly, became the honorable and scarcely questioned price of survival. The satisfaction of basic needs remains the best safeguard of alienation; it is best dissimulated by being justified on the grounds of undeniable necessities. Alienation multiplies needs because it can satisfy none of them; nowadays lack of satisfaction is measured in the number of cars, refrigerators, TVs: the alienating objects have lost the ruse and mystery of transcendence, they are there in their concrete poverty. To be rich today is to possess the greatest *number* of poor objects.

Up to now surviving has prevented us from living. This is why much is to be expected of the increasingly evident impossibility of survival, an impossibility which will become all the more evident as the glut of conveniences and elements of survival reduces life to a single choice: suicide or revolution.

7

The sacred presides even over the struggle against alienation. As soon as the relations of exploitation and the violence that underlies them are no longer concealed by the mystical veil, there is a breakthrough, a moment of clarity, the struggle against alienation is suddenly revealed as a ruthless hand-to-hand fight with naked power, power exposed in its brute force and its weakness, a vulnerable giant whose slightest wound confers on the attacker the infamous notoriety of an Erostratus. Since power survives, the event remains ambiguous. Praxis of destruction, sublime moment when the complexity of the world becomes tangible, transparent, within everyone's grasp; inexpiable revolts—those of the slaves, the Jacques, the iconoclasts, the Enragés, the Communards, Kronstadt, the Asturias, and—promises of things to come—the hooligans of Stockholm and the wildcat strikes . . . only the destruction of all hierarchical power will allow us to forget these. We aim to make sure it does.

The deterioration of mythical structures and their slowness in regenerating themselves, which make possible the awakening of consciousness and the critical penetration of insurrection, are also responsible for the fact that once the "excesses" of revolution are past, the struggle against alienation is grasped on a theoretical plane, subjected to an "analysis" that is a carryover from the demystification preparatory to revolt. It is at this point that the truest and most authentic aspects of a revolt are reexamined and repudiated by the "we didn't really mean to do that" of the theoreticians charged with explaining the meaning of an insurrection to those who made it—to those who aim to demystify by acts, not just by words.

All acts contesting power call for analysis and tactical development. Much can be expected of:

a) the new proletariat, which is discovering its destitution amidst consumer abundance (see the development of the workers' struggles presently beginning in England, and the attitudes of rebellious youth in all the modern countries);

b) countries that have had enough of their partial, sham revolutions and are consigning their past and present theorists to the museums (see the role of the intelligentsia in the Eastern bloc);

c) the Third World, whose mistrust of technological myths has been kept alive by the colonial cops and mercenaries, the last, over-zealous militants of a transcendence against which they are the best possible vaccination;

d) the force of the SI ("our ideas are in everyone's mind"), capable of forestalling remote-controlled revolts, "crystal nights" and sheepish resistance.

Privative appropriation is bound to the dialectic of particular and general. In the mystical realm where the contradictions of the slave and feudal systems are resolved, the nonowner, excluded as a particular individual from the right of possession, strives to ensure his survival through his labor: the more he identifies with the interests of the master, the more successful he is. He knows the other nonowners only through their common plight: the compulsory surrender of their labor power (Christianity recommended voluntary surrender: once the slave "willingly" offered his labor power, he ceased to be a slave), the search for the optimum conditions of survival, and mystical identification. Struggle, though born of a universal will to survive, takes place on the level of appearance where it brings into play identification with the desires of the master and thus introduces a certain individual rivalry that reflects the rivalry between the masters. Competition develops on this plane as long as the relations of exploitation remain dissimulated behind a mystical opacity and as long as the conditions producing this opacity continue to exist; as long as the degree of slavery determines the slave's consciousness of the degree of lived reality. (We are still at the stage of calling "objective consciousness" what is in reality the consciousness of being an object.) The owner, for his part, depends on the general acknowledgment of a right from which he alone is not excluded, but which is seen on the plane of appearance as a right accessible to each of the excluded taken individually. His privileged position depends on such a belief, and this belief is also the basis for the strength that is essential if he is to hold his own among the other owners; it is his strength. If, in his turn, he seems to renounce exclusive appropriation of everything and everybody, if he poses less as a master than as a servant of public good and defender of collective security, then his power is crowned with glory and to his other privileges he adds that of denying, on the level of appearance (which is the only level of reference in unilateral communication), the very notion of personal appropriation; he denies that anyone has this right, he repudiates the other owners. In the feudal perspective the owner is not integrated into appearance in the same way as the nonowners, slaves, soldiers, functionaries, servants of all kinds. The lives of the latter are so squalid that the majority can live only as a caricature of the Master (the feudal lord, the prince, the major-domo, the taskmaster, the high priest, God, Satan . . .). But the master himself is also forced to play one of these caricatural roles. He can do so without much effort since his pretension to total life is already so caricatural, isolated as he is among those who can only survive. He is already one of our own kind (with the added grandeur of a past epoch, which adds an exquisite savor to his sadness); he, like each of us, was anxiously seeking the adventure where he could find himself on the road to his total perdition. Could the master, at the very moment he alienates the others, see that he reduces them to dispossessed and excluded beings, and thus realize that he is only an exploiter, a purely negative being? Such an awareness is unlikely and would be dangerous. By extending his dominion over the greatest possible number of subjects, isn't he enabling them to survive, giving them their only chance of salvation? ("Whatever would happen to the workers if the capitalists weren't kind enough to employ them?" the high-minded souls of the nineteenth century liked to ask.) In fact, the owner officially excludes himself from all claim to privative appropriation. To the sacrifice of the non-owner, who through his labor exchanges his real life for an apparent one (thus avoiding immediate death by allowing the master to determine his variety of living death), the owner replies by appearing to sacrifice his nature as owner and exploiter; he excludes himself mythically, he puts himself at the service of everyone and of myth (at the service of God and his people, for example). With an additional gesture, with an act whose gratuitousness bathes him in an otherworldly radiance, he gives renunciation its pure form of mythical reality; renouncing common life, he is the poor man amidst illusory wealth, he who sacrifices himself for everyone while all the other people only sacrifice themselves for their own sake, for the sake of their survival. He turns his predicament into prestige. The more powerful he is, the greater his sacrifice. He becomes the living reference point of the whole illusory life, the highest attainable point in the scale of mythical values. "Voluntarily" withdrawn from common mortals, he is drawn toward the world of the gods, and his more or less established participation in divinity, on the level of appearance (the only generally acknowledged frame of reference), consecrates his rank in the hierarchy of the other owners. In the organization of transcendence the feudal lord—and, through osmosis, the owners of some power or production materials, in varying degrees—is led to play the principal role, the role that he really does play in the economic organization of the group's survival. As a result, the existence of the group is bound on every level to the existence of the owners as such, to those who, owning everything because they own everybody, also force everyone to renounce their lives on the pretext of the owners' unique, absolute and divine renunciation. (From the god Prometheus punished by the gods to the god Christ punished by men, the sacrifice of the Owner becomes vulgarized, it loses its sacred aura, is humanized.) Myth thus unites owner and nonowner, it envelops them in a common form in which the necessity of survival, whether merely physical or as a privileged being, forces them to live on the level of appearance and of the inversion of real life, the inversion of the life of everyday praxis. We are still there, waiting to live a life less than or beyond a mystique against which our every gesture protests while submitting to it.

9

Myth, the unitary absolute in which the contradictions of the world find an illusory resolution, the harmonious and constantly harmonized vision that reflects and reinforces order—this is the sphere of the sacred, the extrahuman zone where an abundance of revelations are manifested but where the revelation of the process of privative appropriation is carefully suppressed. Nietzsche saw this when he wrote, "All becoming is a criminal revolt from eternal being, and its price is death." When the bourgeoisie claimed to replace the pure Being of feudalism with Becoming, all it really did was to desacralize Being and resacralize Becoming to its own profit; it elevated its own Becoming to the status of Being, no longer that of absolute ownership but rather that of relative appropriation: a petty democratic and mechanical Becoming, with its notions of progress, merit and causal succession. The owner's life hides him from himself; bound to myth by a life and death pact, he cannot see himself in the positive and exclusive enjoyment of any good except through the lived experience of his own exclusion. (And isn't it through this mythical exclusion that the non-owners will come to grasp the reality of their own exclusion?) He bears the responsibility for a group, he takes on the burden of a god. Submitting himself to its benediction and its retribution, he swathes himself in austerity and wastes away. Model of gods and heroes, the master, the owner, is the true reality of Prometheus, of Christ, of all those whose spectacular sacrifice has made it possible for "the vast majority of people" to continue to sacrifice themselves to the extreme minority, to the masters. (Analysis of the owner's sacrifice should be worked out more subtly: isn't the case of Christ really the sacrifice of the owner's son? If the owner can never sacrifice himself except on the level of appearance, then Christ stands for the real immolation of the owner's son when circumstances leave no other alternative. As a son he is only an owner at a very early stage of development, an embryo, little more than a dream of future ownership. In this mythic dimension belongs Barrès's well-known remark in 1914 when war had arrived and made his dreams come true at last: "Our youth, as is proper, has gone to shed torrents of *our blood*.") This rather distasteful little game, before it became transformed into a symbolic rite, knew a heroic period when kings and tribal chiefs were ritually put to death according to their "will." Historians assure us that these august martyrs were soon replaced by prisoners, slaves or criminals. They may not get hurt any more, but they've kept the halo.

10

The concept of a common fate is based on the sacrifice of the owner and the nonowner. Put another way, the notion of a human condition is based on an ideal and tormented image whose function is to resolve the irresolvable opposition between the mythical sacrifice of the minority and the really sacrificed life of everyone else. The function of myth is to unify and eternalize, in a succession of static moments, the dialectic of "will-to-live" and its opposite. This universally dominant factitious unity attains its most tangible and concrete representation in communication, particularly in language. Ambiguity is most manifest at this level, it leads to an absence of real communication, it puts the analyst at the mercy of ridiculous phantoms, at the mercy of words—eternal and changing instants—whose content varies according to who pronounces them, as does the notion of sacrifice. When language is put to the test, it can no longer dissimulate the misrepresentation and thus it provokes the crisis of participation. In the language of an era one can follow the traces of total revolution, unfulfilled but always imminent. They are the exalting and terrifying signs of the upheavals they foreshadow, but who takes them seriously? The discredit striking language is as deeply rooted and instinctive as the suspicion with which myths are viewed by people who at the same time remain firmly attached to them. How can key words be defined by other words? How can phrases be used to point out the signs that refute the phraseological organization of appearance? The best texts still await their justification. When a poem by Mallarmé becomes the sole explanation for an act of revolt, then poetry and revolution will have overcome their ambiguity. To await and prepare for this moment is to manipulate information not as the last shock wave whose significance escapes everyone, but as the first repercussion of an act still to come.

11

Born of man's will to survive the uncontrollable forces of nature, myth is a public welfare policy that has outlived its necessity. It has consolidated its tyrannical force by reducing life to the sole dimension of survival, by negating it as movement and totality.

When contested, myth homogenizes the diverse attacks on it; sooner or later it engulfs and assimilates them. Nothing can withstand it, no image or concept that attempts to destroy the dominant spiritual structures. It reigns over the expression of facts and lived experience, on which it imposes its own interpretive structure (dramatization). Private consciousness is the consciousness of lived experience that finds its expression on the level of organized appearance.

Myth is sustained by rewarded sacrifice. Since every individual life is based on its own renunciation, lived experience must be defined as sacrifice and recompense. As a reward for his asceticism, the initiate (the promoted worker, the specialist, the manager—new martyrs canonized democratically) is granted a niche in the organization of appearance; he is made to feel at home in alienation. But collective shelters disappeared with unitary societies, all that's left is their later concrete embodiments for the benefit of the public: temples, churches, palaces ... memories of a universal protection. Shelters are private nowadays, and even if their protection is far from certain there can be no mistaking their price.

12

"Private" life is defined primarily in a formal context. It is, to be sure, born out of the social relations created by privative appropriation, but its essential form is determined by the expression of those relations. Universal, incontestable but constantly contested, this form makes appropriation a right belonging to everyone and from which everyone is excluded, *a right one can obtain only by renouncing it.* As long as it fails to break free of the context imprisoning it (a break that is called revolution), the most authentic experience can be grasped, expressed and communicated only by way of an inversion through which its fundamental contradiction is dissimulated. In other words, if a positive project fails to sustain a praxis of radically overthrowing the conditions of life—which are nothing other than the conditions of privative appropriation—it does not have the slightest chance of escaping being taken over by the negativity that reigns over the expression of social relationships: it is recuperated like the image in a mirror, in inverse perspective. In the totalizing perspective in which it conditions the whole of everyone's life, and in which its real and its mythic power can no longer be distinguished (both being both real and mythical), the process of privative appropriation has made it impossible to express life any way except negatively. Life in its entirety is suspended in a negativity that corrodes it and formally defines it. To talk of life today is like talking of rope in the house of a hanged man. Since the key of will-to-live has been lost we have been wandering in the corridors of an endless mausoleum. The dialogue of chance and the throw of the dice no longer suffices to justify our lassitude; those who still accept living in well-furnished weariness picture themselves as leading an indolent existence while failing to notice in each of their daily gestures a living denial of their despair, a denial that should rather make them despair only of the poverty of their imagination. Forgetting life, one can identify with a range of images, from the brutish conqueror and brutish slave at one pole to the saint and the pure hero at the other. The air in this shithouse has been unbreathable for a long time. The world and man as representation stink like carrion and there's no longer any god around to turn the charnel houses into beds of lilies. After all the ages men have died while accepting without notable change the explanations of gods, of nature and of biological laws, it wouldn't seem unreasonable to ask if we don't die because so much death enters—and for very specific reasons—into every moment of our lives.

13

Privative appropriation can be defined notably as the appropriation of things by means of the appropriation of people. It is the spring and the troubled water where all reflections mingle and blur. Its field of action and influence, spanning the whole of history, seems to have been characterized until now by a fundamental double behavioral determination: an ontology based on sacrifice and negation of self (its subjective and objective aspects respectively) and a fundamental duality, a division between particular and general, individual and collective, private and public, theoretical and practical, spiritual and material, intellectual and manual, etc. The contradiction between universal appropriation and universal expropriation implies that the master has been seen for what he is and isolated. This mythical image of terror, want and renunciation presents itself to slaves, to servants, to all those who can't stand living as they do; it is the illusory reflection of their participation in property, a natural illusion since they really do participate in it through the daily sacrifice of their energy (what the ancients called pain or torture and we call labor or work) since they themselves produce this property in a way that excludes them. The master can only cling to the notion of work-as-sacrifice, like Christ to his cross and his nails; it is up to him to authenticate sacrifice, to apparently renounce his right to exclusive enjoyment and to cease to expropriate with purely *human* violence (that is, violence without mediation). The sublimity of the gesture obscures the initial violence, the nobility of the sacrifice absolves the commando, the brutality of the conqueror is bathed in the light of a transcendence whose reign is internalized, the gods are the intransigent guardians of rights, the irascible shepherds of a peaceful and law-abiding flock of "Being and Wanting-To-Be Owner." The gamble on transcendence and the sacrifice it implies are the masters' greatest conquest, their most accomplished submission to the necessity of conquest. Anyone who intrigues for power while refusing the purification of renunciation (the brigand or the tyrant) will sooner or later be tracked down and killed like a mad dog, or worse: as someone who only pursues his own ends and whose blunt conception of "work" lacks any tact toward others' feelings: Troppmann, Landru, Petiot, murdering people without justifying it in the name of defending the Free World, the Christian West, the State or Human Dignity, were doomed to eventual defeat. By refusing to play the rules of the game, pirates, gangsters and outlaws disturb those with good consciences (whose consciences are a reflection of myth), but the masters, by killing the encroacher or enrolling him as a cop, reestablish the omnipotence of "eternal truth": those who don't sell themselves lose their right to survive and those who do sell themselves lose their right to live. The sacrifice of the master is the matrix of humanism, which is what makes humanism—and let this be understood once and for all—the miserable negation of everything human. Humanism is the master taken seriously at his own game, acclaimed by those who see in his apparent sacrifice—that caricatural reflection of their real sacrifice—a reason to hope for salvation. Justice, dignity, nobility, freedom . . . these words that yap and howl, are they anything other than household pets whose masters have calmly awaited their homecoming since the time when heroic lackeys won the right to walk them on the streets? To use them is to forget that they are the ballast that enables power to rise out of reach. And if we imagine a regime deciding that the mythical sacrifice of the masters should not be promoted in such universal forms, and setting about tracking down these word-concepts and wiping them out, we could well expect the Left to be incapable of combating it with anything more than a plaintive battle of words whose every phrase, invoking the "sacrifice" of a previous master, calls for an equally mythical sacrifice of a new one (a leftist master, a power mowing down workers in the name of the proletariat). Bound to the notion of sacrifice, humanism is born of the common fear of masters and slaves: it is nothing but the solidarity of a shit-scared humanity. But those who reject all hierarchical power can use any word as a weapon to punctuate their action. Lautréamont and the illegalist anarchists were already aware of this; so were the dadaists.

The appropriator thus becomes an owner from the moment he puts the ownership of people and things in the hands of God or of some universal transcendence whose omnipotence is reflected back on him as a grace sanctifying his slightest gesture; to oppose an owner thus consecrated is to oppose God, nature, the fatherland, the people. In short, to exclude oneself from the physical and spiritual world. "We must neither govern nor be governed," writes Marcel Havrenne so neatly. For those who add an appropriate violence to his humor, there is no longer any salvation or damnation, no place in the universal order, neither with Satan, the great recuperator of the faithful, nor in any form of myth, since they are the living proof of the uselessness of all that. They were born for a life yet to be invented; insofar as they lived, it was on this hope that they finally came to grief.

Two corollaries of singularization in transcendence:

a) If ontology implies transcendence, it is clear that any ontology automatically justifies the being of the master and the hierarchical power wherein the master is reflected in degraded, more or less faithful images.

b) Over the distinction between manual and intellectual work, between practice and theory, is superimposed the distinction between work-as-real-sacrifice and the organization of work in the form of apparent sacrifice.

It would be tempting to explain fascism—among other reasons for it—as an act of faith, the auto-da-fé of a bourgeoisie haunted by the murder of God and the destruction of the great sacred spectacle, dedicating itself to the devil, to an inverted mysticism, a black mysticism with its rituals and its holocausts. Mysticism and high finance.

It should not be forgotten that hierarchical power is inconceivable without transcendence, without ideologies, without myths. Demystification itself can always be turned into a myth: it suffices to "omit," most philosophically, demystification *by acts.* Any demystification so neutralized, with the sting taken out of it, becomes painless, euthanasic, in a word, humanitarian. Except that the movement of demystification will ultimately demystify the demystifiers.

RAOUL VANEIGEM

(Concluded in the next issue.)

- What will become of the totality inherent in unitary society when it comes up against the bourgeois demolition of that society?

- Will an artificial reconstitution of unity succeed in hoodwinking the worker alienated in consumption?

- But what can be the future of totality in a fragmented society?

- What unexpected supersession of this society and its whole organization of appearance will finally bring us to a happy ending?

IF YOU DON'T ALREADY KNOW, FIND OUT IN PART TWO!

IDEOLOGIES, CLASSES AND
THE DOMINATION OF NATURE

(excerpts)

The appropriation of nature by man is precisely the *venture we have embarked on*. It is the central, indisputable project, the issue that encompasses all issues. What is always in question, at the heart of modern thought and action, is the possible use of the dominated sector of nature. The overall perspective concerning this use governs the choices among the possible alternative directions presented at each moment of the process; and also governs the rhythm and duration of productive expansion in each sector. It is the absence of an overall perspective—or rather the monopoly of a single untheorized perspective automatically produced by the present power structure's boundless economic growth—that has caused the emptiness that has been the lot of contemporary thought for forty years.

The accumulation of production and of ever-improving technological capabilities is proceeding even faster than nineteenth-century communism predicted. But we have remained at a stage of superequipped prehistory. A century of revolutionary attempts has failed: human life has not been rationalized and impassioned; the project of a classless society has not yet been achieved. We have entered a never-ending growth of material means that remains at the service of fundamentally static interests, and therefore at the service of values everyone recognizes as long dead. The spirit of the dead weighs very heavily on the technology of the living. The economic planning that reigns everywhere is insane, not so much because of its academic obsession with organizing the enrichment of the years to come as because of the rotten blood of the past that circulates through its veins and is endlessly pumped forth with each artificial pulsation of this "heart of a heartless world."

Material liberation is only a precondition for the liberation of human history and can only be judged as such. A country's choice of which kind of minimum level of development is to be given priority depends on the particular project of liberation chosen, and therefore on who makes this choice—the autonomous masses or the specialists in power. Those who accept the ideas of some type of specialist organizers regarding what is *indispensable* may well be liberated from any privation of the objects those organizers choose to produce, but they will assuredly never be liberated from the organizers themselves. The most modern and unexpected forms of hierarchy will always remain costly remakes of the old world of passivity, impotence and slavery—the antithesis of man's sovereignty over his surroundings and his history—

whatever may be the material forces abstractly possessed by the society.

Because of the fact that in present-day society the domination of nature presents itself both as an increasingly aggravated alienation and as the single great ideological justification for this social alienation, it is criticized in a one-sided, undialectical and insufficiently historical manner by some of the radical groups who are half way between the old degraded and mystified conception of the workers movement, which they have superseded, and the new form of total contestation which is yet to come (see, for example, the theories of Cardan and others in the journal *Socialisme ou Barbarie*). These groups, rightly opposing the continually more thorough reification of human labor and its modern corollary, the passive consumption of leisure activity manipulated by the ruling class, come to the point of more or less unconsciously harboring a sort of nostalgia for work in its ancient forms, for the really "human" relationships that were able to flourish in the societies of the past or even in the less developed phases of industrial society. Moreover, this attitude fits in well with the system's efforts to obtain a higher yield from existing production by doing away with both the waste and the inhumanity that characterize modern industry (in this regard see "Instructions for Taking Up Arms" in *IS* #6). But these conceptions abandon the very core of the revolutionary project, which is nothing less than the suppression of work in the ordinary sense (as well as the suppression of the proletariat) and of all the justifications of previous forms of work. It is impossible to understand the sentence in the *Communist Manifesto* that says that "the bourgeoisie has played an eminently revolutionary role in history" if one ignores the possibility, opened up to us by the domination of nature, of eliminating work in favor of a *new type of free activity*; or if one ignores the role of the bourgeoisie in the "dissolution of old ideas," that is, if one follows the unfortunate tendency of the classical workers movement to define itself positively in terms of "revolutionary ideology."

In "Basic Banalities" Vaneigem has elucidated the process of the dissolution of sacred thought and has shown how its function as analgesic, hypnotic and tranquilizer has been taken over, at a lower level, by ideology. Ideology, like penicillin, has become less effective as its use has become more widespread. As a result, the dosage has to be continually increased and the packaging made more ostentatious (one need only recall the diverse excesses of Nazism and of today's consumer propaganda). Since the disappearance of feudal society the ruling classes have been increasingly ill-served by their own ideologies: these ideologies (as petrified critical thought), after having been used by them as general weapons for seizing power, end up presenting contradictions to their particular reign. What in ideology was an unconscious lie (resulting from its having stopped at partial conclusions) becomes a systematic lie when certain of the interests it cloaked are in power and protected by a police force. The most modern example is also the most glaring: it was by taking advantage of the element of ideology present in the workers movement that the bureaucracy was able to establish its power in Russia. All the attempts to modernize an ideology—aberrant ones like fascism or consistent ones like the ideology of spectacular consumption in developed capitalism—tend toward preservation of the present, which is itself dominated by the past. A reformism of ideology in a direction hostile to the established society can never be effective because it can never get hold of the means of force-feeding thanks to which this society still commands an effective use of ideology. Revolutionary thought is necessarily on the side of the merciless critique of all ideologies—including, of course, that special ideology called "the death of ideologies" (whose title is already a confession since ideologies have always been dead thought), which is merely an empiricist ideology rejoicing over the downfall of envied rivals.

The domination of nature implies the question "For what purpose?" but this very questioning of man's praxis must concern itself with this domination, and in fact could not take place except on the basis of it. Only the crudest answer is automatically rejected: "To carry on as before, producing and consuming more and more," prolonging the reifying domination that has been intrinsic to capitalism from its beginnings (though not without "producing its own gravediggers"). It is necessary to expose the contradiction between the positive aspects of the transformation of nature—the great project of the bourgeoisie—and its petty recuperation by hierarchical power, which in all its contemporary variants remains faithful to the single model of bourgeois "civilization." In its massified form, this bourgeois model has been "socialized" for the benefit of a composite petty bourgeoisie that is taking on all the capacities for stupefaction characteristic of the old poor classes and all the signs of wealth (themselves massified) that indicate membership in the ruling class. The bureaucrats of the Eastern bloc are objectively led to follow the same pattern, and as they produce more they have less need for police in maintaining their own particular schema for the elimination of class struggle. Modern capitalism loudly proclaims a similar goal. But they're all astride the same tiger: a world in rapid transformation in which they desire the dose of immobility necessary for the perpetuation of one or another variant of hierarchical power.

The network of criticism of the present is coherent, just as is the network of apologetics. The coherence of apologetics is merely less apparent in that it must lie about, or give arbitrary values to, numerous contradictory details and variants within the established order. But if one really renounces all the variants of apologetics, one arrives at the critique that does not suffer from any guilty conscience because it is not compromised with any present ruling force. If someone thinks that a hierarchical bureaucracy can be a revolutionary power, and also agrees that mass tourism as it is globally organized by the society of the spectacle is a good thing and a pleasure, then, like Sartre, he can pay a visit to China or somewhere else. His errors, his stupidity and his lies shouldn't surprise anyone. Everyone finds their own level; other travelers, such as those who go to serve Tshombe in Katanga, are even more detestable and are paid in more real coin. The intellectual witnesses of the left, eagerly toddling wherever they are invited, bear witness to nothing so much as the abdication of a thought which for decades has been abdicating its own freedom as it oscillates between conflicting bosses. The thinkers who admire the present accomplishments of the East or the West, taken in by all the spectacular gimmicks, have obviously never thought about anything at all, as anyone can tell who has read them. The society they reflect naturally encourages us to admire its admirers. In many places they are even allowed to play their game of "Commitment," in which they opt (with or without regretful reservations) for the form of established society whose label and packaging inspires them.

Every day alienated people are shown or informed about new successes they have obtained, successes for which they have no use. This does not mean that these stages in material development are uninteresting or bad: they can be reinvested in real life, but only *along with everything else*. The victories of our day belong to star-specialists. Gagarin's exploit shows that man can *survive* farther out in space, in increasingly unfavorable conditions. But just as is the case when the joint efforts of medicine and biochemistry enable a prolonged survival in time, this statistical extension of survival is in no way linked to a qualitative improvement of life. You can survive farther away and longer, but never live more. Our task is not to celebrate such victories, but to make celebration victorious—celebration whose infinite possibilities in everyday life are potentially unleashed by these very technological advances.

Nature has to be rediscovered as a "worthy opponent." The game with nature has to be exciting: each point scored must concern us directly. The conscious construction of a moment of life is an example of our (shifting and transitory) control of our milieu and of time. Humanity's expansion into the cosmos is—at the opposite pole from the postartistic construction of individual life (though these two poles of the possible are intimately linked)—an example of an enterprise in which the present pettiness of specialist military competition comes into conflict with the objective grandeur of the project. The cosmic adventure will be extended, and thus opened up to a participation totally different from that of the specialist guinea pigs, farther and *more quickly* when the collapse of the miserly reign of specialists on this planet has opened the floodgates of an immense creativity which is presently blocked and unknown, but which is capable of leading to a geometrical progress in all human problems, supplanting the present cumulative growth restricted to an arbitrary sector of industrial production. The old schema of the contradiction between productive forces and production relations should certainly no longer be understood as a short-term death warrant for capitalist production, as if the latter were doomed to automatically stagnate and become incapable of continuing its development. This contradiction must be construed as a judgment (which remains to be executed with the appropriate weapons) against this self-regulating production's niggardly and dangerous development, in view of the grandiose *possible development* that could be based on the present economic infrastructure.

Only loaded questions are openly posed in the present society, questions that already imply certain obligatory responses. When people point out the obvious fact that the modern tradition is precisely one of innovation, they shut their eyes to the equally obvious fact that this innovation does not extend everywhere. In an era when ideology could still believe in its role, Saint-Just remarked that "in a time of innovation everything that is not new is pernicious." God's numerous successors who organize the present society of the spectacle know very well what asking too many questions can lead to. The decline of philosophy and the arts also stems from this suppression of questioning. The revolutionary elements of modern thought and art have with varying degrees of precision demanded a praxis that would be the minimum terrain necessary for their development—a praxis which is still absent. The other elements add new embellishments to the official questions, or to the futile questioning of pure speculation (the specialty of *Arguments*).

There are many ideological rooms in the House of the Father, i.e. in the old society, whose fixed reference points have been lost but whose law remains intact (God doesn't exist, but nothing is permitted). Every facility is granted to the modernisms that serve to combat the truly modern. The gang of hucksters of the unbelievable magazine *Planète*, which so impresses the school teachers, epitomizes a bizarre demagogy that profits from the gaping absence of contestation and revolutionary imagination, at least in their intellectual manifestations, over the last nearly half a century (and from the numerous obstacles still placed in the way of their resurgence today). At the same time, playing on the truism that science and technology are advancing faster and faster without anyone knowing where they are going, *Planète* harangues ordinary people with the message that henceforth everything must be changed; while at the same time taking for granted 99% of the life really lived in our era. The daze induced by the barrage of novelties can be taken advantage of to calmly reintroduce retrograde nonsense that has virtually died out in even the most primitive regions. The drugs of ideology will end their history in an apotheosis of vulgarity that even Pauwels [editor of *Planète*], for all his efforts, cannot yet imagine.

Ideology, in its various fluid forms that have replaced the solid mythical system of the past, has an increasingly large role to play as the specialist rulers need to increasingly regulate all aspects of an expanding production and consumption. Use value, indispensable still but which had already tended to become merely implicit since the predominance of an economy of producing for the market, is now explicitly manipulated (artificially created) by the planners of the modern market. It is the merit of Jacques Ellul, in his book *Propaganda* (A. Colin, 1962), which describes the unity of the various forms of conditioning, to have shown that this advertising-propaganda is not merely an unhealthy excrescence that could be prohibited, but is at the same time a remedy in a generally sick society, a remedy that makes the sickness tolerable while aggravating it. People are to a great extent accomplices of propaganda, of the reigning spectacle, because they cannot reject it without contesting the society as a whole. The single important task of contemporary thought must center upon this question of reorganizing the theoretical and material forces of contestation.

The alternative is not only between real life and a survival that has nothing to lose but its modernized chains. It is also posed within survival itself, with the constantly aggravated problems that the masters of survival are not able to solve. The risks of atomic weapons, of global overpopulation and of the increasing material impoverishment of the great majority of humanity are subjects of official alarm, even in the ordinary press. One very banal example: in an article on China (*Le Monde*, September 1962) Robert Guillain writes, without irony, on the population problem: "The Chinese leaders seem to be giving it fresh consideration and apparently want to tackle it. They are coming back to the idea of birth control, tried out in 1956 and abandoned in 1958. A national campaign has been launched against early marriages and in favor of family planning in young households." These oscillations of specialists, immediately followed by official orders, reveal the sort of interest they really have in the liberation of the people just as completely as the opportunistic religious conversions of princes in the sixteenth century (*cujus regio ejus religio*) revealed the real nature of their interest in the mythical arsenal of Christianity. A few lines further, the same journalist suggests that "the USSR is not helping China because its available resources are now being devoted to the conquest of space, which is fantastically expensive." The Russian workers have no more say in determining the quantity of surplus "available resources" produced by their labor, or in deciding whether that surplus is to be allotted to the moon rather than to China, than the Chinese peasants have in deciding whether they will have children or not. The epic of modern rulers at grips with real life, which they are led to take complete charge of, has found its best literary expression in the Ubu cycle. The only raw material that has not yet been tried out in this experimental era of ours is *freedom* of thought and behavior. [. . .]

It is necessary to distinguish, within the intelligentsia, between the tendencies toward submission and the tendencies toward refusal of the employment offered; and then, by every means, to strike a sword between these two fractions so that their total mutual opposition will illuminate the first advances of the coming social war. The careerist tendency, which fundamentally expresses the condition of all intellectual service in a class society, leads this stratum, as Harold Rosenberg remarks in his *Tradition of the New*, to expatiate on its own alienation without any action of opposition because this alienation has been made comfortable. But as the whole of modern society moves toward this comfort, which at the same time becomes more and more poisoned by boredom and anguish, the practice of sabotage can be extended to the intellectual terrain. Thus, just as in the first half of the nineteenth century revolutionary theory arose out of philosophy (out of critical reflection on philosophy, out of the crisis and death of philosophy), so now it is going to rise once again out of modern art—out of poetry—out of its supersession, out of what modern art has sought and *promised*, out of the clean sweep it has made of all the values and rules of everyday behavior.

The living values of intellectual and artistic creation are denied as much as could be by the submissive intelligentsia's entire mode of existence, yet this intelligentsia wants at the same time to embellish its social position by claiming a sort of morganatic kinship with this creation of "values." This hired intelligentsia is more or less aware of this contradiction and tries to redeem itself by an ambiguous glorification of artistic "bohemianism." The valets of reification recognize this bohemian experience as a moment of qualitative use of everyday life, which is excluded everywhere else; as a moment of richness within extreme poverty, etc. But the official version of this fairy tale must have an edifying ending: this moment of pure qualitativeness within poverty must finally arrive at ordinary "riches." Poor artists have produced masterpieces which in their time had no market value. But they are saved (their adventure with the qualitative is excused, and even turned into an edifying example) because their work, which at the time was only a by-product of their real activity, later turns out to be highly valued. Living people who struggled against reification have nevertheless ended up producing *their quota of commodities*. Thus the bourgeoisie darwinistically applauds the bohemian values that have proved fit enough to survive and enter into its quantitative paradise. Everyone agrees to consider as purely accidental the fact that it is rarely the same people who possess the products at the stage of creation and at the stage of profitable commodities.

The accelerated degradation of cultural ideology has given rise to a permanent crisis in this intellectual and artistic valorization, a crisis that dadaism brought out into the open. A dual movement has clearly characterized this end of culture: on one hand, the dissemination of false novelties automatically recycled with new packaging by autonomous spectacular mechanisms; and on the other hand, the public refusal to play along and the sabotage carried out by individuals who were clearly among those who would have been most capable of renewing "quality" cultural production (Arthur Cravan is a prototype of these people seen passing through the most radioactive zones of the cultural disaster, people who left behind them no form of commodities or memories). The conjunction of these two demoralizing forces does not cease to aggravate the malaise of the intelligentsia.

After dadaism, and in spite of the fact that the dominant culture has been able to recuperate a sort of dadaist art, it is far from certain that artistic rebellion in the next generation will continue to be recuperable into consumable works. At the same time that the most elementary spectacular conmanship can draw on an imitation post-dadaist style to produce all sorts of salable cultural objects, there exist in several modern capitalist countries centers of nonartistic bohemianism united around the notion of the end of or the absence of art, a bohemianism that explicitly no longer envisages any artistic production whatsoever. Its dissatisfaction can only radicalize with the progress of the thesis according to which "the art of the future" (the phrase itself is misleading since it implies dealing with the future in terms of present specialized categories) will no longer be valued as a commodity, since we are discovering that it is a subordinate aspect of the total transformation of our use of space, of feelings and of time. All the real experiences of free thought and behavior that succeed in taking shape in these conditions are certainly moving in our direction, toward the theoretical organization of contestation. [. . .]

In accordance with the reality presently beginning to take shape, we may consider as proletarians all people who have no possibility of altering the social space-time that society allots for their consumption (regardless of variations in their degree of affluence or of possibilities for promotion). The rulers are those who organize this space-time, or who at least have a significant margin of personal choice (even deriving, for example, from a significant survival of older forms of private property). A revolutionary movement is one that radically changes the organization of this space-time and the very manner of deciding its ongoing reorganization henceforward (and not a movement that merely changes the legal form of property or the social origin of the rulers).

Already today the vast majority everywhere consumes the odious, soul-destroying social space-time "produced" by a tiny minority. (It should be specified that this minority produces literally nothing other than this organization, whereas the "consumption" of space-time, in the sense we are using here, embraces the whole of ordinary production, in which the alienation of consumption and of all life obviously has its roots.) The ruling classes of the past at least knew how to spend in a humanly enriching way the meager slice of surplus-value they managed to wrest from a static social production grounded on general scarcity; the members of today's ruling minority have lost even this "mastery." They are nothing but consumers of power—and that, moreover, nothing but the power of miserably organizing survival. And their sole purpose in so miserably organizing this survival is to consume that power. The lord of nature, the ruler, is dissolved in the pettiness of the exercise of his power (the scandal of the quantitative). Mastery without dissolution would guarantee full employment—not of all the workers, but of all the forces of the society, of all the creative possibilities of each person, for himself and for dialogue. Where then are the real masters? At the other extremity of this absurd system. At the pole of refusal. The masters come from the negative, they are the bearers of the antihierarchical principle.

The distinction drawn here between those who organize space-time (together with their direct agents) and those who are subjected to this organization is aimed at clearly exposing the polarization that is hidden by the intentionally woven complexity of the hierarchies of function and salary, which give the impression that all the gradations are virtually imperceptible and that there are hardly any more real proletarians or real property owners at the two extremities of a social spectrum that has become highly flexible. Once this distinction is posed, other differences in status must be considered as secondary. It should not be forgotten, however, that an intellectual, or a "professional revolutionary" worker, is liable at any moment to tumble irretrievably into integration—into one niche or another in one clan or another in the camp of the ruling zombies (which is far from being harmonious or monolithic). Until real life is present for everyone, the "salt of the earth" is always susceptible to going bad. The theorists of the new contestation can neither compromise with the ruling power nor constitute themselves as a separate power without immediately ceasing to be such (their role as theorists will then be taken over by

108

others). This amounts to saying that the revolutionary intelligentsia can realize its project only by suppressing itself; that the "intellectual party" can really exist only as a party that supersedes itself, a party whose victory is at the same time its own disappearance.

THE AVANT-GARDE OF PRESENCE

(excerpts)

[. . .] The dialectic of history is such that the Situationist International's theoretical victory is already forcing its adversaries to *disguise themselves* as situationists. There are now two tendencies in close struggle against us: those who proclaim themselves situationists without having any idea what they're talking about (the varieties of Nashism) and those who, conversely, decide to adopt a few situationist ideas minus the situationists and without mentioning the SI. The increasing likelihood of the confirmation of some of the simplest and least recent of our theses leads many people to use a good part of one or another of them *without acknowledging it*. We are not, of course, concerned here with obtaining recognition and personal credit for priority. The only interest in pointing out this tendency is in order to denounce one crucial aspect of it: When these people draw on our theses in order to finally speak of some new problem (after having suppressed it as long as they could), they inevitably banalize it, eradicating its violence and its connection with the general subversion, defusing it and subjecting it to academic dissection or worse. This is the reason they must suppress any reference to the SI. [. . .]

As participation becomes more impossible, the second-rate specialists of modern art demand the participation of everyone. [. . .] We are insolently urged to "intervene" in a spectacle, an art, which concerns us *so little*. [. . .]

Free play confined within the terrain of artistic dissolution is only the recuperation of free play. In spring 1962 the press began reporting on the "happenings" produced by the New York artistic avant-garde. The happening is a sort of spectacle pushed to the extreme state of dissolution, a dadaist-style improvisation of gestures performed by a gathering of people within a closed-off space. Drugs, alcohol and eroticism are often involved. The gestures of the "actors" compose a melange of poetry, painting, dance and jazz. This form of social encounter can be considered as a limiting case of the old artistic spectacle, a hash produced by throwing together all the old artistic leftovers; and as a too aesthetically encumbered attempt to renovate the ordinary surprise party or the classic orgy. In its naïve striving to "make something happen," its absence of separate spectators and its desire to liven up the impoverished range of present human relations, the happening can even be considered as an attempt to construct a situation in isolation, *on a foundation of poverty* (material poverty, poverty of encounters, poverty inherited from the artistic spectacle, poverty of the "philosophy" that has to considerably "ideologize" the reality of these events). In contrast, the situation defined by the SI can be constructed only on a foundation of material and spiritual richness. This amounts to saying that the first ventures in constructing situations must be the work/play of the revolutionary avant-garde; people who are resigned in one or another respect to political passivity, to metaphysical despair, and even to being subjected to an artistic pure absence of creativity, are incapable of participating in them. [. . .]

People urge us to present trivial projects that would be useful and convincing (and why should we be interested in convincing them?); but if we were to oblige them they would immediately turn these projects against us, either by holding them up as proofs of our utopianism or by rushing to disseminate watered-down versions of them. In fact, those who are interested and satisfied with such partial projects can solicit them from almost anyone else, but precisely *not from us*: It is our thesis that there will not be a fundamental cultural renewal in details, but only *en bloc*. We are obviously in a good position to discover, a few years ahead of other people, all the possible gimmicks of the present extreme cultural decomposition. Since they are useful only in our enemies' spectacle, we merely make a few notes on them and file them away. After some time many of them are indeed discovered independently by someone or other and ostentatiously launched on the market. History has not yet "caught up" with the majority of them, however. Perhaps it never will with some of them. This is not simply a game, it is one more experimental verification of our perspectives. [. . .]

We are against the conventional forms of culture, even in its most modern state; but not, obviously, in preferring ignorance, neoprimitivism or the butcher's petty-bourgeois common sense. There is an anticultural attitude that favors an impossible return to the old myths. Against such a current we are of course for culture. We take our stand on the other side of culture. Not before it, but *after*. We say that it is necessary to *realize* culture by superseding it as a separate sphere; not only as a domain reserved for specialists, but above all as a domain of a specialized production that does not directly affect the construction of life—not even the life of its own specialists.

We are not completely devoid of humor; but our humor is of a rather new kind. If someone wants to know how to approach our theses, leaving aside the fine points and subtleties, the simplest and most appropriate attitude is to take us completely seriously and literally.

How are we going to bankrupt the dominant culture? In two ways—gradually at first, then suddenly. [. . .]

THE COUNTERSITUATIONIST CAMPAIGN
IN VARIOUS COUNTRIES
(excerpts)

The declaration published 25 June 1962 by the Situationist International apropos of the trial of Uwe Lausen in Munich enumerated three types of negation the situationist movement has met with so far: police, as in Germany;* silence, for which France easily holds the record; and finally widespread falsification, in which northern Europe has provided the most fertile field of study over the last year. [. . .]

In *Internationale Situationniste* #7 (pp. 53–54) we mentioned the sort of manifesto in which Jørgen Nash attacked the SI in the name of the Scandinavian section. Reckoning on the considerable geographical dispersion of the Scandinavian situationists, Nash had not even consulted with all of them before his putsch. Surprised at not being unanimously followed and at finding himself countered on the spot by the partisans of the SI majority—who immediately circulated a definitive exposure of his imposture—Nash at first feigned astonishment that things had gone to the point of a complete break with the situationists; as if the fact of launching a surprise public attack *full of lies* was compatible with carrying on a dialogue, on the basis of some sort of Nashist Scandinavian autonomy. The development of the conspiracy scarcely leaves any doubt as to his real objectives, since his new Swedish "Bauhaus," assembling two or three former Scandinavian situationists plus a mass of unknowns flocking to the feast, immediately plunged into the most shopworn forms of artistic production. [. . .] In the polemic between Nashists and situationists in Scandinavia, the Nashists resorted, in addition to all the threats and violence they thought feasible, to the systematic spreading of false information (with the active collusion of some journalists). [. . .] But all their efforts to gain time and all their petty maneuvers to prolong the confusion could not save the Nashists from appearing for what they are: foreign to the SI; much more sociable, certainly, but much less intelligent. [. . .]

We don't want to attribute some particular perversity to Nash and his associates. It seems to us that Nashism is an expression of an objective tendency resulting from the SI's ambiguous and risky policy of consenting to act *in* culture while being against the entire present organization of this culture and even against all culture as a separate sphere. (But even the most intransigent oppositional attitude cannot escape such ambiguity and risk, since it still necessarily has to coexist with the present order.) The German situationists who were excluded at the beginning of 1962 expressed an opposition comparable to that of the Nashists—though with more frankness and artistic capacity— to the extent that such opposition contains elements of a legitimately arguable position. Heimrad Prem's statement at the Göteborg Conference (see *IS* #7) dwelt on the situationist majority's reiterated refusal

111

of a large number of offers to sponsor "creations" on the conventional avant-garde artistic plane where many people wanted to involve the SI, so as to bring things back to order and the SI back into the old classification of artistic praxis. Prem expressed the desire of the situationist artists to find a satisfactory field of activity in the here and now. [. . .] The Nashists have merely gone much further in their bad faith and complete indifference to any theory and even to conventional artistic activity, preferring the grossest commercial publicity. But Prem and his friends, though comporting themselves more honorably, had themselves certainly not completely avoided concessions to the cultural market. The SI has thus for a time included a number of artists of repetition incapable of grasping the present mission of the artistic avant-garde; which is not too surprising if one takes into account both the scarcely delineated nature of our research and the notorious exhaustion of conventional art. The moment when the contradictions between them and us lead to these antagonisms marks an advance of the SI, the point where the ambiguities are forced into the open and settled clearly. The point of no return, in our relations with the partisans of a renewal of conventional art under the aegis of a situationist school, was perhaps reached with the decision adopted at Göteborg to call artistic productions of the movement "antisituationist." The contradictions expressed in Nashism are quite crude, but the development of the SI may lead to others at a higher level. [. . .]

The SI cannot be a massive organization, and it will not even accept disciples as do the conventional avant-garde groups. At this moment

---

DEFINITION

adopted by the Anvers Conference
on the motion of J.V. Martin

Nashism (French: **Nashisme**; German: **Nashismus**; Italian: **Nascismo**): Term derived from the name of Nash, an artist who seems to have lived in Denmark in the twentieth century. Principally known for his attempt to betray the revolutionary movement and theory of that time, Nash's name was detourned by that movement as a generic term applicable to all traitors in struggles against the dominant cultural and social conditions. Example: "But like all things transient and vain, Nashism soon faded away." **Nashist:** A partisan of Nash or of his doctrine. By extension, any conduct or expression evincing the aims or methods of Nashism. **Nashistique:** Popular French doublet probably derived by analogy to the English adjective **Nashistic**. **Nashisterie:** The general social milieu of Nashism. The slang term **Nashistouse** is vulgar.

of history when the task is posed, in the most unfavorable conditions, of reinventing culture and the revolutionary movement on an entirely new basis, the SI can only be a Conspiracy of Equals, a general staff that *does not want troops*. It is a matter of finding, of opening up, the "Northwest Passage" toward a new revolution that cannot tolerate masses of executants, a revolution that must surge over that central terrain which has until now been sheltered from revolutionary upheavals: the conquest of everyday life. *We will only organize the detonation*: the free explosion must escape us and any other control forever.

One of the classic weapons of the old world, perhaps the one most used against groups delving into the organization of life, is to single out and isolate a few of their participants as "stars." We have to defend ourselves against this process, which, like almost all the usual wretched choices of the present society, has an air of being "natural." Those among us who aspired to the role of stars or depended on stars had to be rejected. [. . .]¯

The same movement that would have us accept situationist executants would commit us to erroneous positions. It is in the nature of a disciple to demand certitudes, to transform real problems into stupid dogmas from which he derives his role and his intellectual security. And later, of course, to demonstrate his modernity by revolting, in the name of those simplified certitudes, against the very people who transmitted them to him. In this way over a period of time generations of submissive elites succeed one another. We intend to leave such people outside and to fight those who want to transform the SI's theoretical problematics into a mere ideology; such people are extremely handicapped and uninteresting compared with those who may not be aware of the SI but who confront their own lives. Those who on the contrary have *grasped* the direction the SI is going in can join with it because all the supersession we talk about is to be found in reality, and we have to find it together. The task of being *more extremist than the SI* falls to the SI itself; this is even the first law of its continuation.

There are already certain people who, through laziness, think they can fix our project to a perfect program, one already present, admirable and uncriticizable, in the face of which they have nothing more to do; except to declare themselves still more radical at heart, while abstaining from any activity on the grounds that everything has already been definitively said by the SI. We say that on the contrary not only do the most important aspects of the questions we have posed remain to be discovered—by the SI and by others—but also that the greater portion of what we have already discovered is not yet published due to our lack of all sorts of means; to say nothing of the still more considerable absence of means for the experiments the SI has barely begun in other domains (particularly in matters of behavior). But to speak only of editorial problems, we now think that we ourselves should rewrite the most interesting parts of what we have published so far. It is not a matter of revising certain errors or of suppressing a few deviationist seeds that have since blossomed into gross results* (e.g. Constant's technocratic concept of a situationist profession—see *IS #4*, pp. 24–25), but of correcting and improving the most important of our theses, precisely those whose development has brought us further, on the basis of the knowledge since gained thanks to them. This will require different republications, although the SI's current difficulties in publishing are far from being resolved.

Those who think that the early situationist thought is already fixed in past history, and that the time has come for violent falsification or rapt admiration of it, have not grasped the *movement* we are talking about. The SI has sown the wind. It will reap a tempest.

ALL THE KING'S MEN

The problem of language is at the heart of all struggles between the forces striving to abolish present alienation and those striving to maintain it; it is inseparable from the entire terrain of those struggles. We live within language as within polluted air. In spite of what humorists think, words do not play. Nor do they make love, as Breton thought, except in dreams. Words *work*—on behalf of the dominant organization of life. And yet they are not completely automatized; unfortunately for the theoreticians of information, words are not in themselves "informationist"; they embody forces that can upset the most careful calculations. Words coexist with power in a relationship analogous to that which proletarians (in the modern as well as the classic sense of the term) have with power. Employed *almost* constantly, exploited full time for every sense and nonsense that can be squeezed out of them, they still remain in some sense fundamentally strange and foreign.

Power presents only the falsified, official sense of words; in a manner of speaking it forces them to carry a pass, determines their place in the production process (where some of them conspicuously work overtime) and gives them their paycheck. Regarding the use of words, Lewis Carroll's Humpty Dumpty quite correctly observes, "The question is which is to be master—that's all." And he, a socially responsible employer in this respect, states that he pays overtime to those he employs excessively. We should also understand the phenomenon of the *insubordination of words*, their desertion, their open resistance, which is manifested in all modern writing (from Baudelaire to the dadaists and Joyce), as a symptom of the general revolutionary crisis of the society.

Under the control of power, language always designates something other than authentic experience. It is precisely for this reason that a total contestation is possible. The organization of language has fallen into such confusion that the communication imposed by power is exposing itself as an imposture and a dupery. An embryonic cybernetic power is vainly trying to put language under the control of the machines it controls, in such a way that information would henceforth be the only possible communication. Even on this terrain resistances are being manifested; electronic music could be seen as an attempt (obviously limited and ambiguous) to reverse the domination relation by detourning machines to the profit of language. But real opposition is much more general, much more radical. It denounces all unilateral "communication," whether in the old form of art or in the modern form of informationism. It calls for a communication that undermines all separate power. Wherever there is communication, there is no state.

Power lives off stolen goods. It creates nothing, it recuperates. If it created the meaning of words, there would be no poetry but only useful "information." Opposition would not be able to express itself in language; any refusal would be outside it, would be purely lettristic. What is poetry if not the revolutionary moment of language, inseparable as such from the revolutionary moments of history and from the history of personal life?

Power's stranglehold over language is similar to its stranglehold over the totality. Only a language that has been deprived of all immediate reference to the totality can serve as the basis for information. Information* is the poetry of power, the counterpoetry of law and order, the mediated falsification of what exists. Conversely, poetry must be understood as immediate communication within reality and as real alteration of this reality. It is nothing other than liberated language, language recovering its richness, language which breaks its rigid significations and simultaneously embraces words, music, cries, gestures, painting, mathematics, facts, acts. Poetry thus depends on the greatest wealth of possibilities in living *and changing* life at a given stage of socioeconomic structure. Needless to say, this relationship of poetry to its material base is not a unilateral subordination, but an interaction.

Rediscovering poetry may become indistinguishable from reinventing revolution, as has been demonstrated by certain phases of the Mexican, Cuban and Congolese revolutions. Outside the revolutionary periods when the masses become poets in action, the small circles of poetic adventure could be considered the only places where the totality of revolution subsists, as an unrealized but close-at-hand potentiality, like the shadow of an absent personage. What we are calling poetic adventure is difficult, dangerous and *never guaranteed* (it is, in fact, the aggregate of behaviors that are *almost impossible* in a given epoch). We can only be sure about what is no longer the poetic adventure of an era: its false, officially tolerated poetry. Thus, whereas surrealism in the heyday of its assault against the oppressive order of culture and daily life could rightly define its arsenal as "poetry without poems if necessary," it is now a matter for the SI of a poetry *necessarily* without poems. What we say about poetry has nothing to do with the retarded reactionaries of some neoversification, even one based on the least ancient of formal modernisms. Realizing poetry means nothing less than simultaneously and inseparably creating events and their language.

All in-group languages—those of informal groupings of young people; those that present avant-garde currents develop for their internal use as they grope to define themselves; those that in previous eras were conveyed by way of objective poetic production, such as *trobar clus* and *dolce stil nuovo*—all these aim at and achieve a certain direct, transparent communication, mutual recognition, accord. But such tentatives have been the work of small groups, isolated in various ways.

115

The events and festivals they have created have had to remain within the most narrow limits. One of the problems of revolution is that of federating these kinds of soviets or *communication councils* in order to initiate a direct communication everywhere that will no longer have to resort to the enemy's communication network (that is, to the language of power) and will thus be able to transform the world according to its desire.

It is a matter not of putting poetry at the service of revolution, but rather of putting revolution at the service of poetry. It is only in this way that the revolution does not betray its own project. We will not repeat the mistake of the surrealists, who put themselves at the service of the revolution right when it had ceased to exist. Bound to the memory of a partial and rapidly crushed revolution, surrealism rapidly became a reformism of the spectacle, a critique of a certain form of the reigning spectacle that was carried out from within the dominant organization of that spectacle. The surrealists seem to have overlooked the fact that every internal improvement or modernization of the spectacle is translated by power into its own encoded language, to which it alone holds the key.

Every revolution has been born in poetry, has first of all been made with the force of poetry. This is a phenomenon which continues to escape theorists of revolution—indeed, it cannot be understood if one still clings to the old conception of revolution or of poetry—but which has generally been sensed by counterrevolutionaries. Poetry, whenever it appears, frightens them; they do their best to get rid of it by means of every kind of exorcism, from auto-da-fé to pure stylistic research. The moment of real poetry, which has "all the time in the world before it," invariably wants to reorient the entire world and the entire future to its own ends. As long as it lasts its demands admit of no compromises. It brings back into play all the unsettled debts of history. Fourier and Pancho Villa, Lautréamont and the *dinamiteros* of the Asturias—whose successors are now inventing new forms of strikes—the sailors of Kronstadt and Kiel, and all those in the world who, with us or without us, are preparing to fight for the long revolution are equally the emissaries of the new poetry.

Poetry is becoming more and more clearly the empty space, the antimatter, of consumer society, since it is not consumable (in terms of the modern criteria for a consumable object: an object that is of equivalent value for each of a mass of isolated passive consumers). Poetry is nothing when it is quoted, it can only be *detourned*, brought back into play. Otherwise the study of the poetry of the past is nothing but an academic exercise. The history of poetry is only a way of running away from the poetry of history, if we understand by that phrase not the spectacular history of the rulers but rather the history of everyday life and its possible liberation; the history of each individual life and its realization.

We must leave no question as to the role of the "conservers" of old poetry, those who increase its dissemination while the state, for quite different reasons, eliminates illiteracy. These people are only a particular type of museum curator. A mass of poetry is naturally preserved in the world, but nowhere are there the places, the moments or the people to revive it, communicate it, use it. And there never can be except by way of detournement, because the understanding of past poetry has changed through the loss as well as the acquisition of knowledge; and because any time past poetry can be effectively rediscovered, its being placed in the context of particular events gives it a largely new meaning. But above all, a situation in which poetry is possible must not restore any poetic failure of the past (such failure being the inverted remains of the history of poetry, transformed into success and poetic monument). Such a situation naturally moves toward the communication of, and the possible sovereignty of, *its own poetry*.

At the same time that poetic archeology restores selections of past poetry, which are recited by specialists on LPs for the neoilliterate public created by the modern spectacle, the informationists are endeavoring to do away with all the "redundancies" of freedom in order to *simply transmit orders*. The theorists of automation are explicitly aiming at producing an automatic theoretical thought by clamping down on and eliminating the variables in life as well as in language. But bones keep turning up in their cheese! Translating machines, for example, which are beginning to ensure the planetary standardization of information along with the informationist revision of previous culture, are victims of their own preestablished programing, which inevitably misses any new meaning taken on by a word, as well as its past dialectical ambivalences. Thus the life of language—which is bound up with every advance of theoretical comprehension ("Ideas improve; the meaning of words participates in the improvement")—is expelled from the machinist field of official information. But this also means that free thought can organize itself with a secrecy that is beyond the reach of informationist police techniques. The quest for unambiguous signals and instantaneous binary classification is so clearly linked with existing power that it calls for a similar critique. Even in their most delirious formulations, the informationist theorists are no more than clumsy precursors of the future they have chosen, which is the same brave new world that the dominant forces of the present society are working toward—the reinforcement of the cybernetic state. They are the vassals of all the lords of the technocratic feudalism that is now constituting itself. There is no innocence in their buffoonery; they are the king's jesters.

The choice between informationism and poetry no longer has anything to do with the poetry of the past, just as no variant of what the classical revolutionary movement has become can anymore, anywhere, be considered as part of a real alternative to the prevailing organization of life. The same judgment leads us to announce the total disappearance of poetry in the old forms in which it was produced and consumed and to announce its return in effective and unexpected forms. Our era no longer has to *write out poetic orders*; it has to carry them out.

BASIC BANALITIES

(II)

SUMMARY OF PRECEDING SECTIONS

The vast majority of people have always devoted all their energy to SURVIVAL, thereby denying themselves any chance to LIVE. They continue to do so today as the WELFARE STATE imposes the elements of this survival in the form of technological conveniences (appliances, preserved food, prefabricated cities, Mozart for the masses).

The organization controlling the material equipment of our everyday life is such that what in itself would enable us to construct it richly plunges us instead into a poverty of abundance, making alienation all the more intolerable as each convenience promises liberation and turns out to be only one more burden. We are condemned to slavery to the means of liberation.

To be understood, this problem must be seen in the clear light of hierarchical power. But perhaps it isn't enough to say that hierarchical power has preserved humanity for thousands of years like alcohol preserves a fetus—by arresting either growth or decay. It should also be specified that hierarchical power represents the highest stage of privative appropriation, and historically is its alpha and omega. Privative appropriation itself can be defined as appropriation of things by means of appropriation of people, the struggle against natural alienation engendering social alienation.

Privative appropriation entails an ORGANIZATION OF APPEARANCE by which its radical contradictions can be dissimulated: the servants must see themselves as degraded reflections of the master, thus reinforcing, through the looking glass of an illusory freedom, everything that reinforces their submission and passivity; while the master must identify himself with the mythical and perfect servant of a god or of a transcendence which is nothing other than the sacred and abstract representation of the TOTALITY of people and things over which he wields power—a power all the more real and less contested as he is universally credited with the virtue of his renunciation. The mythical sacrifice of the director corresponds to the real sacrifice of the executant; each negates himself in the other, the strange becomes familiar and the familiar strange, each fulfills himself by being the inversion of the other. From this common alienation a harmony is born, a negative harmony whose fundamental unity lies in the notion of sacrifice. This objective (and perverted) harmony is sustained by myth—this term being used to designate the organization of appearance in unitary societies, that is, in societies where slave, tribal or feudal power is officially consecrated by a divine authority and where the sacred allows power to seize the totality.

118

The harmony originally based on the "GIFT of oneself" contains a form of relationship that was to develop, become autonomous and destroy it. This relationship is based on partial EXCHANGE (commodity, money, product, labor power . . .), the exchange of a part of oneself, which underlies the bourgeois notion of freedom. It arises as commerce and technology become preponderant within agrarian-type economies.

When the bourgeoisie seized power the unity of power was destroyed. Sacred privative appropriation became secularized in capitalist mechanisms. Freed from the grip of power, the totality once again became concrete and immediate. The era of fragmentation has been nothing but a succession of attempts to recapture an inaccessible unity, to reconstitute some ersatz sacred behind which to shelter power.

A revolutionary moment is when "everything reality presents" finds its immediate REPRESENTATION. All the rest of the time hierarchical power, increasingly deprived of its magical and mystical regalia, strives to make everyone forget that the totality (which has never been anything other than reality!) is exposing its imposture.

14

By directly attacking the mythical organization of appearance, the bourgeois revolutions, in spite of themselves, attacked the weak point not only of unitary power but of any hierarchical power whatsoever. Does this unavoidable mistake explain the guilt complex that is one of the dominant traits of bourgeois mentality? In any case, the mistake was undoubtedly inevitable.

It was a mistake because once the cloud of lies dissimulating privative appropriation was pierced, myth was shattered, leaving a vacuum that could be filled only by a delirious freedom and a splendid poetry. Orgiastic poetry, to be sure, has not yet destroyed power. Its failure is easily explained and its ambiguous signs reveal the blows struck at the same time as they heal the wounds. And yet—let us leave the historians and aesthetes to their collections—one has only to pick at the scab of memory and the cries, words and gestures of the past make the whole body of power bleed again. The whole organization of the survival of memories will not prevent them from dissolving into oblivion as they come to life; just as our survival will dissolve in the construction of our everyday life.

And it was an inevitable process: as Marx showed, the appearance of exchange-value and its symbolic representation by money opened a profound latent crisis in the heart of the unitary world. The commodity introduced into human relationships a universality (a 1000-franc note represents anything I can obtain for that sum) and an egalitarianism (equal things are exchanged). This "egalitarian universality" partially escapes both the exploiter and the exploited, but they recognize each other through it. They find themselves face to face, confronting each other no longer within the mystery of divine birth and ancestry, as was the case with the nobility, but within an intelligible transcendence, the Logos, a body of laws that can be *understood by everyone*, even if such understanding remains cloaked in mystery.

A mystery with its initiates: first of all priests struggling to maintain the Logos in the limbo of divine mysticism, but soon yielding to philosophers and then to technicians both their positions and the dignity of their sacred mission. From Plato's Republic to the Cybernetic State.

Thus, under the pressure of exchange-value and technology (generally available mediation), myth was gradually secularized. Two facts should be noted, however:

a) As the Logos frees itself from mystical unity, it affirms itself both within it and against it. Upon magical and analogical structures of behavior are superimposed rational and logical ones which negate the former while preserving them (mathematics, poetics, economics, aesthetics, psychology, etc.).

b) Each time the Logos, the "organization of intelligible appearance," becomes more autonomous, it tends to break away from the sacred and become fragmented. In this way it presents a double danger for unitary power. We have already seen that the sacred expresses power's seizure of the totality, and that anyone wanting to accede to the totality must do so through the mediation of power: the interdict against mystics, alchemists and gnostics is sufficient proof of this. This also explains why present-day power "protects" specialists (though without completely trusting them): it vaguely senses that they are the missionaries of a resacralized Logos. There are historical signs that testify to the attempts made within mystical unitary power to found a rival power asserting its unity in the name of the Logos—Christian syncretism (which makes God psychologically explainable), the Renaissance, the Reformation and the Enlightenment.

The masters who strove to maintain the unity of the Logos were well aware that only unity can stabilize power. Examined more closely, their efforts can be seen not to have been as vain as the fragmentation of the Logos in the nineteenth and twentieth centuries would seem to prove. In the general movement of atomization the Logos has been broken down into specialized techniques (physics, biology, sociology, papyrology, etc.), but at the same time the need to reestablish the totality has become more imperative. It should not be forgotten that all it would take would be an all-powerful technocratic power in order for there to be a totalitarian domination of the totality, for the Logos to succeed myth as the seizure of the totality by a future unitary (cybernetic) power. In such an event the vision of the Encyclopédistes (strictly rationalized progress stretching indefinitely into the future) would have known only a two-century postponement before being realized. This is the direction in which the Stalino-cyberneticians are preparing the future. In this perspective, peaceful coexistence should be seen as a preliminary step toward a totalitarian unity. It is time everyone realized that they are already resisting it.

15

We know the battlefield. The problem now is to prepare for battle before the pataphysician, armed with his totality without technique, and the cybernetician, armed with his technique without totality, consummate their political coitus.

From the standpoint of hierarchical power, myth could be desacralized only if the Logos, or at least its desacralizing elements, were resacralized. To attack the sacred was at the same time supposed to liberate the totality and thus destroy power (we've heard that one before!). But the power of the bourgeoisie—fragmented, impoverished, constantly contested—maintains a relative stability by relying on this ambiguity: Technology, which objectively desacralizes, subjectively appears as an instrument of liberation. Not a real liberation, which could be attained only by desacralization—that is, by the end of the spectacle—but a caricature, an imitation, an induced hallucination. What the unitary vision of the world transferred into the beyond (above), fragmentary power pro-jects ('throws forward') into a state of future well-being, of brighter tomorrows proclaimed from atop the dunghill of today—tomorrows that are nothing more than the present multiplied by the number of gadgets to be produced. From the slogan "Live in God" we have gone on to the humanistic motto "Survive until you are old," euphemistically expressed as: "Stay young at heart and you'll live a long time."

Once desacralized and fragmented, myth loses its grandeur and its spirituality. It becomes an impoverished form, retaining its former characteristics but revealing them in a concrete, harsh, tangible fashion. God doesn't run the show anymore, and until the day the Logos takes over with its arms of technology and science, the phantoms of alienation will continue to materialize and sow disorder everywhere. Watch for them: they are the first symptoms of a future order. We must start to *play* right now if the future is not to become impossible (the hypothesis of humanity destroying itself—and with it, obviously, the whole experiment of constructing everyday life). The vital objectives of a struggle for the construction of everyday life are the sensitive key points of all hierarchical power. To build one is to destroy the other. Caught in the vortex of desacralization and resacralization, we stand essentially for the negation of the following elements: the organization of appearance as a *spectacle* in which everyone denies himself; the *separation* on which private life is based, since it is there that the objective separation between owners and dispossessed is lived and reflected on every level; and *sacrifice*. These three elements are obviously interdependent, just as are their opposites: participation, communication, realization. The same applies to their context: nontotality (a bankrupt world, a controlled totality) and totality.

16

The human relationships that were formerly dissolved in divine transcendence (the totality crowned by the sacred) settled out and solidified as soon as the sacred stopped acting as a catalyst. Their materiality was revealed and, as the capricious laws of the economy succeed those of Providence, the power of men began to appear behind the power of gods. Today a multitude of roles corresponds to the mythical role everyone once played under the divine spotlight. Though their masks are now human faces, these roles still require both actors and extras to deny their real lives in accordance with the dialectic of real and mythical sacrifice. The spectacle is nothing but desacralized and fragmented myth. It forms the armor of a power (which could also be called essential mediation) that becomes vulnerable *to every blow* once it no longer succeeds in dissimulating (in the cacophony where all cries drown out each other and form an overall harmony) its nature as privative appropriation, and the greater or lesser dose of misery it allots to everyone.

Roles have become impoverished within the context of a fragmentary power eaten away by desacralization, just as the spectacle represents an impoverishment in comparison with myth. They betray its mechanisms and artifices so clumsily that power, to defend itself against popular denunciation of the spectacle, has no other alternative than to itself take the initiative in this denunciation by even more clumsily changing actors or ministers, or by organizing pogroms of supposed or prefabricated scapegoat agents (agents of Moscow, Wall Street, the Judeocracy or the Two Hundred Families). Which also means that the whole cast has been forced to become hams, that style has been replaced by manner.

Myth, as an immobile totality, encompassed all movement (consider pilgrimage, for example, as fulfillment and adventure within immobility). On the one hand, the spectacle can seize the totality only by reducing it to a fragment and to a series of fragments (psychological, sociological, biological, philological and mythological world-views), while on the other hand, it is situated at the point where the movement of desacralization converges with the efforts at resacralization. Thus it can succeed in imposing immobility only within the real movement, the movement that changes it despite its resistance. In the era of fragmentation the organization of appearance makes movement a linear succession of immobile instants (this notch-to-notch progression is perfectly exemplified by Stalinist "Dialectical Materialism"). Under what we have called "the colonization of everyday life," the only possible changes are changes of fragmentary roles. In terms of more or less inflexible conventions, one is successively citizen, head of family, sexual partner, politician, specialist, professional, producer, consumer. Yet what boss doesn't himself feel bossed? The proverb applies to everyone: You sometimes get a fuck, but you always get fucked!

The era of fragmentation has at least eliminated all doubt on one point: everyday life is the battlefield where the war between power and the totality takes place, with power using all its strength to control the totality.

What do we demand in backing the power of everyday life against hierarchical power? We demand *everything*. We are taking our stand in the generalized conflict stretching from domestic squabbles to revolutionary war, and we have gambled on the will to live. This means that we must survive as antisurvivors. Fundamentally we are concerned only with the moments when life breaks through the glaciation of survival (whether these moments are unconscious or theorized, historical—like revolution—or personal). But we must recognize that we are *also* prevented from freely following the course of such moments (except for the moment of revolution itself) not only by the general repression exerted by power, but also by the exigencies of our own struggle, our own tactics, etc. It is also important to find the means of compensating for this additional "margin of error" by widening the scope of these moments and demonstrating their qualitative significance. What prevents what we say on the construction of everyday life from being recuperated by the cultural establishment (*Arguments*, academic thinkers with paid vacations) is the fact that all situationist ideas are nothing other than faithful developments of acts attempted constantly by thousands of people to try and prevent another day from being no more than twenty-four hours of wasted time. Are we an avant-garde? If so, to be avant-garde means to move in step with reality.

17

It's not the monopoly of intelligence that we hold, but that of its use. Our position is strategic, we are at the heart of every conflict. The qualitative is our striking force. People who half understand this journal ask us for an explanatory monograph thanks to which they will be able to convince themselves that they are intelligent and cultured— that is to say, idiots. Someone who gets exasperated and chucks it in the gutter is making a more meaningful gesture. Sooner or later it will have to be understood that the words and phrases we use are still lagging behind reality. The distortion and clumsiness in the way we express ourselves (which a man of taste called, not inaccurately, "a rather irritating kind of hermetic terrorism") comes from our central position, our position on the ill-defined and shifting frontier where language captured by power (conditioning) and free language (poetry) fight out their infinitely complex war. To those who follow behind us we prefer those who reject us impatiently because our language is not yet authentic poetry—the free construction of everyday life.

Everything related to thought is related to the spectacle. Almost everyone lives in a state of terror at the possibility that they might awake to themselves, and their fear is deliberately fostered by power. Conditioning, the special poetry of power, has extended its dominion so far (all material equipment belongs to it: press, television, stereotypes, magic, tradition, economy, technology—what we call captured language) that it has almost succeeded in dissolving what Marx called the undominated sector, replacing it with another dominated one (see below our composite portrait of "the survivor"). But lived experience cannot so easily be reduced to a succession of empty configurations. Resistance to the external organization of life, to the organization of life as survival, contains more poetry than any volume of verse or prose, and the poet, in the literary sense of the word, is one who has at least understood or felt this. But such poetry is in a most dangerous situation. Certainly poetry in the situationist sense of the word is irreducible and cannot be recuperated by power (as soon as an act is recuperated it becomes a stereotype, conditioning, language of power). But it is encircled by power. Power encircles the irreducible and holds it by isolating it; yet such isolation is impracticable. The two pincers are, first, the threat of disintegration (insanity, illness, destitution, suicide), and second, remote-controlled therapeutics. The first grants death, the second grants no more than survival (empty communication, the company of family or friendship, psychoanalysis in the service of alienation, medical care, ergotherapy). Sooner or later the SI must define itself as a therapy: we are ready to defend the poetry made by all against the false poetry rigged up by power (conditioning). Doctors and psychoanalysts better get it straight too, or they may one day, along with architects and other apostles of survival, have to take the consequences for what they have done.

18

All unresolved, unsuperseded antagonisms weaken. Such antagonisms can evolve only by remaining imprisoned in previous unsuperseded forms (anticultural art in the cultural spectacle, for example). Any radical opposition that fails or is partially successful (which amounts to the same thing) gradually degenerates into reformist opposition. Fragmentary oppositions are like the teeth on cogwheels, they mesh with each other and make the machine go round, the machine of the spectacle, the machine of power.

Myth maintained all antagonisms within the archetype of Manicheanism. But what can function as an archetype in a fragmented society? In fact, the memory of previous antagonisms, presented in their obviously devalued and unaggressive form, appears today as the last attempt to bring some coherence into the organization of appearance, so great is the extent to which the spectacle has become a spectacle of confusion and equivalences. We are ready to wipe out all trace of these memories by harnassing all the energy contained in previous antagonisms for a radical struggle soon to come. All the springs blocked by power will one day burst through to form a torrent that will change the face of the world.

In a caricature of antagonisms, power urges everyone to be for or against Brigitte Bardot, the *nouveau roman*, the 4-horse Citroën, spaghetti, mescal, miniskirts, the UN, the classics, nationalization, thermonuclear war and hitchhiking. Everyone is asked their opinion about every detail in order to prevent them from having one about the totality. However clumsy this maneuver may be, it might have worked if the salesmen in charge of peddling it from door to door were not themselves waking up to their own alienation. To the passivity imposed on the dispossessed masses is added the growing passivity of the directors and actors subjected to the abstract laws of the market and the spectacle and exercising less and less real power over the world. Already signs of revolt are appearing among the actors—stars who try to escape publicity or rulers who criticize their own power; Brigitte Bardot or Fidel Castro. The tools of power are wearing out; their desire for their own freedom should be taken into account.

19

At the very moment when slave revolt threatened to overthrow the structure of power and to reveal the relationship between transcendence and the mechanism of privative appropriation, Christianity appeared with its grandiose reformism, whose central democratic demand was for the slaves to accede not to the reality of a human life—which would have been impossible without denouncing the exclusionary aspect of privative appropriation—but rather to the unreality of an existence whose source of happiness is mythical (the imitation of Christ as the price of the hereafter). What has changed? Anticipation of the hereafter has become anticipation of a brighter tomorrow; the sacrifice of real, immediate life is the price paid for the illusory freedom of an apparent life. The spectacle is the sphere where forced labor is transformed into voluntary sacrifice. Nothing is more suspect than the formula "To each according to his work" in a world where work is the blackmail of survival; to say nothing of the formula "To each according to his needs" in a world where needs are determined by power. Any construction that attempts to define itself autonomously, and thus partially, and does not take into account that it is in fact defined by the negativity in which everything is suspended, enters into the reformist project. It is trying to build on quicksand as though it were rock. Contempt and misunderstanding of the context fixed by hierarchical power can only end up reinforcing that context. On the other hand, the spontaneous acts we can see everywhere forming against power and its spectacle must be warned of all the obstacles in their path and must find a tactic taking into account the strength of the enemy and its means of recuperation. This tactic, which we are going to popularize, is *detournement*.

20

Sacrifice must be rewarded. In exchange for their real sacrifice the workers receive the instruments of their liberation (comforts, gadgets), but this liberation is purely fictitious since power controls the ways in which all the material equipment can be used; since power uses to its own ends both the instruments and those who use them. The Christian and bourgeois revolutions democratized mythical sacrifice, the "sacrifice of the master." Today there are countless initiates who receive crumbs of power for putting to public service the totality of their partial knowledge. They are no longer called "initiates" and not yet "priests of the Logos"; they are simply known as specialists.

On the level of the spectacle their power is undeniable: the contestant on "Double Your Money" and the postal clerk running on all day about all the mechanical details of his car both identify with the specialist, and we know how production managers use such identification to bring unskilled workers to heel. Essentially the true mission of the technocrats would be to unify the Logos; if only—because of one of the contradictions of fragmentary power—they weren't so absurdly compartmentalized and isolated. Each one is alienated in being out of phase with the others; he knows the whole of one fragment and knows no realization. What real control can the atomic technician, the strategist or the political specialist exercise over a nuclear weapon? What ultimate control can power hope to impose on all the gestures developing against it? The stage is so crowded that only chaos reigns as master. "Order reigns and doesn't govern" (*IS* #6).

To the extent that the specialist takes part in the development of the instruments that condition and transform the world, he is preparing the way for the *revolt of the privileged*. Until now such revolt has been called fascism. It is essentially an operatic revolt—didn't Nietzsche see Wagner as a precursor?—in which actors who have been pushed aside for a long time and see themselves as less and less free suddenly demand to play the leading roles. Clinically speaking, fascism is the hysteria of the spectacular world pushed to the point of paroxysm. In this paroxysm the spectacle momentarily ensures its unity while at the same time revealing its radical inhumanity. Through fascism and Stalinism, which constitute its romantic crises, the spectacle reveals its true nature: it is a disease.

We are poisoned by the spectacle. All the elements necessary for a detoxification (that is, for the construction of our everyday lives) are in the hands of specialists. We are thus highly interested in all these specialists, but in different ways. Some are hopeless cases: we are not, for example, going to try and show the specialists of power, the rulers, the extent of their delirium. On the other hand, we are ready to take into account the bitterness of specialists imprisoned in roles that are constricted, absurd or ignominious. We must confess, however, that our indulgence has its limits. If, in spite of all our efforts, they persist in putting their guilty conscience and their bitterness in the service of power by fabricating the conditioning that colonizes their own everyday lives; if they prefer an illusory representation in the hierarchy to true realization; if they persist in ostentatiously brandishing their specializations (their painting, their novels, their equations, their sociometry, their psychoanalysis, their ballistics); finally, if, knowing perfectly well—and soon *ignorance of this fact will be no excuse*—that only power and the SI hold the key to using their specialization, they nevertheless still choose to serve power because power, battening on their inertia, has chosen them to serve it, then fuck them! No one could be more generous. They should understand all this and above all the fact that henceforth the revolt of nonruling actors is linked to the revolt against the spectacle (see below the thesis on the SI and power).

21

The generalized anathematization of the lumpenproletariat stems from the use to which it was put by the bourgeoisie, which it served both as a regulating mechanism for power and as a source of recruits for the more dubious forces of order: cops, informers, hired thugs, artists ... Nevertheless, the lumpenproletariat embodies a remarkably radical implicit critique of the *society of work*. Its open contempt for both lackeys and bosses contains a good critique of work as alienation, a critique that has not been taken into consideration until now because the lumpenproletariat was the sector of ambiguities, but also because during the nineteenth century and the beginning of the twentieth the struggle against natural alienation and the production of well-being still appeared as valid justifications for work.

Once it became known that the abundance of consumer goods was nothing but the flip side of alienation in production, the lumpenproletariat acquired a new dimension: it liberated a contempt for organized work which, in the age of the Welfare State, is gradually taking on the proportions of a demand that only the rulers still refuse to acknowledge. In spite of the constant attempts of power to recuperate it, every experiment carried out on everyday life, that is, every attempt to construct it (an illegal activity since the destruction of feudal power, where it was limited and restricted to a minority), is concretized today through the critique of alienating work and the refusal to submit to forced labor. So much so that the new proletariat tends to define itself negatively as a "Front Against Forced Labor" bringing together all those who resist recuperation by power. This defines our field of action; it is here that we are gambling on the ruse of history against the ruse of power; it is here that we back the worker (whether steelworker or artist) who—consciously or not—rejects organized work and life, against the worker who—consciously or not—accepts working at the dictates of power. In this perspective, it is not unreasonable to foresee a transitional period during which automation and the will of the new proletariat leave work solely to specialists, reducing managers and bureaucrats to the rank of temporary slaves. In a generalized automation the "workers," instead of supervising machines, could devote their attention to watching over the cybernetic specialists, whose sole task would be to increase a production which, through a reversal of perspective, will have ceased to be the priority sector, in order to serve the priority of life over survival.

22

Unitary power strove to dissolve individual existence in a collective consciousness so that each social unit subjectively defined itself as a particle with a clearly determined weight suspended as though in oil. Everyone had to feel overwhelmed by the omnipresent evidence that everything was merely raw material in the hands of God, who used it for his own purposes, which were naturally beyond individual human comprehension. All phenomena were seen as emanations of a supreme will; any abnormal divergence signified some hidden meaning (any perturbation was merely an ascending or descending path toward harmony: the Four Reigns, the Wheel of Fortune, trials sent by the gods). One can speak of a collective consciousness in the sense that it was simultaneously for each individual and for everyone: consciousness of myth and consciousness of particular-existence-within-myth. The power of the illusion was such that authentically lived life drew its meaning from what was not authentically lived; from this stems that priestly condemnation of life, the reduction of life to pure contingency, to sordid materiality, to vain appearance and to the lowest state of a transcendence that became increasingly degraded as it escaped mythical organization.

God was the guarantor of space and time, whose coordinates defined unitary society. He was the common reference point for all men; space and time came together in him just as in him all beings became one with their destiny. In the era of fragmentation, man is torn between a time and a space that no transcendence can unify through the mediation of any centralized power. We are living in a space and time that are out of joint, deprived of any reference point or coordinate, as though we were never going to be able to come into contact with ourselves, although everything invites us to.

There is a place where you create yourself and a time in which you play yourself. The space of everyday life, that of one's true realization, is encircled by every form of conditioning. The narrow space of our true realization defines us, yet we define ourselves in the time of the spectacle. Or put another way: our consciousness is no longer consciousness of myth and of particular-*being*-in-myth, but rather consciousness of the spectacle and of particular-*role*-in-the-spectacle. (I pointed out above the relationship between all ontology and unitary power; it should be recalled here that the crisis of ontology appears with the movement toward fragmentation.) Or to put it still another way: in the space-time relation in which everyone and everything is situated, time has become the imaginary (the field of identifications); space defines us, although we define ourselves in the imaginary and although the imaginary defines us *qua* subjectivities.

Our freedom is that of an abstract temporality in which we are *named* in the language of power (these names are the roles assigned to us), with a choice left to us to find officially recognized *synonyms* for ourselves. In contrast, the space of our authentic realization (the space of our everyday life) is under the dominion of silence. There is no name to name the space of lived experience except in poetry, in language liberating itself from the domination of power.

23

By desacralizing and fragmenting myth, the bourgeoisie was led to demand first of all independence of consciousness (demands for freedom of thought, freedom of the press, freedom of research, rejection of dogma). Consciousness thus ceased being more or less consciousness-reflecting-myth. It became consciousness of successive roles played within the spectacle. What the bourgeoisie demanded above all was the freedom of actors and extras in a spectacle no longer organized by God, his cops and his priests, but by natural and economic laws, "capricious and inexorable laws" defended by a new team of cops and specialists.

God has been torn off like a useless bandage and the wound has stayed raw. The bandage may have prevented the wound from healing, but it justified suffering, it gave it a meaning well worth a few shots of morphine. Now suffering has no justification whatsoever and morphine is far from cheap. Separation has become concrete. Anyone at all can put their finger on it, and the only answer cybernetic society has to offer us is to become spectators of the gangrene and decay, spectators of survival.

The drama of consciousness to which Hegel referred is actually the consciousness of drama. Romanticism resounds like the cry of the soul torn from the body, a suffering all the more acute as each of us finds himself alone in facing the fall of the sacred totality and of all the Houses of Usher.

24

The totality is objective reality, in the movement of which subjectivity can participate only in the form of realization. Anything separate from the realization of everyday life rejoins the spectacle where survival is frozen (hibernation) and served out in slices. There can be no authentic realization except in objective reality, in the totality. All the rest is caricature. The objective realization that functions in the mechanism of the spectacle is nothing but the success of power-manipulated objects (the "objective realization in subjectivity" of famous artists, stars, celebrities of *Who's Who*). On the level of the organization of appearance, every success—and every failure—is inflated until it becomes a stereotype, and is broadcast as though it were the only possible success or failure. So far power has been the only judge, though its judgment has been subjected to various pressures. Its criteria are the only valid ones for those who accept the spectacle and are satisfied to play a role in it. But there are no more artists on that stage, there are only extras.

25

The space-time of private life was harmonized in the space-time of myth. Fourier's harmony responds to this perverted harmony. As soon as myth no longer encompasses the individual and the partial in a totality dominated by the sacred, each fragment sets itself up as a totality. The fragment set up as a totality is, in fact, the *totalitarian*. In the dissociated space-time that constitutes private life, time—made absolute in the form of abstract freedom, the freedom of the spectacle— consolidates by its very dissociation the spatial absolute of private life, its isolation and constriction. The mechanism of the alienating spectacle wields such force that private life reaches the point of being defined as that which is deprived of spectacle; the fact that one escapes roles and spectacular categories is experienced as an additional privation, as a malaise which power uses as a pretext to reduce everyday life to insignificant gestures (sitting down, washing, opening a door).

26

The spectacle that imposes its norms on lived experience itself arises out of lived experience. The time of the spectacle, lived in the form of successive roles, makes the space of authentic experience the area of objective impotence, while at the same time the objective impotence that stems from the conditioning of privative appropriation makes the spectacle the ultimate of potential freedom.

Elements born of lived experience are acknowledged only on the level of the spectacle, where they are expressed in the form of stereotypes, although such expression is constantly contested and refuted in and by lived experience. The *composite portrait of the survivors*— whom Nietzsche referred to as the "little people" or the "last men"— can be conceived only in terms of the following dialectic of possibility/ impossibility:

a) possibility on the level of the spectacle (variety of abstract roles) reinforces impossibility on the level of authentic experience;

b) impossibility (that is, limits imposed on real experience by privative appropriation) determines the field of abstract possibilities.

Survival is two-dimensional. Against such a reduction, what forces can bring out what constitutes the daily problem of all human beings: the dialectic of survival and life? Either the specific forces the SI has counted on will make possible the supersession of these contraries, reuniting space and time in the construction of everyday life; or life and survival will become locked in an antagonism growing weaker and weaker until the point of ultimate confusion and ultimate poverty is reached.

27

Lived reality is spectacularly fragmented and labeled in biological, sociological or other categories which, while being related to the communicable, never communicate anything but facts emptied of their authentically lived content. It is in this sense that hierarchical power, imprisoning everyone in the objective mechanism of privative appropriation (admission/exclusion, see section #3), is also a dictatorship over subjectivity. It is as a dictator over subjectivity that it strives, with limited chances of success, to force each individual subjectivity to become objectivized, that is, to become an object it can manipulate. This extremely interesting dialectic should be analyzed in greater detail (objective realization in subjectivity—the realization of power—and objective realization in objectivity—which enters into the praxis of constructing everyday life and destroying power).

Facts are deprived of content in the name of the communicable, in the name of an abstract universality, in the name of a perverted harmony in which everyone realizes himself in an inverted perspective. In this context the SI is in the line of contestation that runs through Sade, Fourier, Lewis Carroll, Lautréamont, surrealism, lettrism—at least in its least known currents, which were the most extreme.

Within a fragment set up as a totality, each further fragment is itself totalitarian. Sensitivity, desire, will, intelligence, good taste, the subconscious and all the categories of the ego were treated as absolutes by individualism. Today sociology is enriching the categories of psychology, but the introduction of variety into the roles merely accentuates the monotony of the identification reflex. The freedom of the "survivor" will be to assume the abstract constituent to which he has "chosen" to reduce himself. Once any real realization has been put out of the picture, all that remains is a psychosociological dramaturgy in which interiority functions as a safety-valve, as an overflow to drain off the effects one has worn for the daily exhibition. Survival becomes the ultimate stage of life organized as the mechanical reproduction of memory.

28

Until now the approach to the totality has been falsified. Power has parasitically interposed itself as an indispensable mediation between man and nature. But the relation between man and nature is based only on praxis. It is praxis which constantly breaks through the coherent veneer of lies that myth and its substitutes try to maintain. It is praxis, even alienated praxis, which maintains contact with the totality. By revealing its own fragmentary character, praxis at the same time reveals the real totality (reality): it is the totality being realized by way of its opposite, the fragment.

In the perspective of praxis, every fragment is totality. In the perspective of power, which alienates praxis, every fragment is totalitarian. This should be enough to wreck the attempts cybernetic power will make to envelop praxis in a mystique, although the seriousness of these attempts should not be underestimated.

All praxis enters into our project; it enters with its share of alienation, with the impurities of power: but we are capable of filtering them out. We will elucidate the force and purity of acts of refusal as well as the manipulative maneuvers of power, not in a Manichean perspective, but as a means of developing, through our own strategy, this combat in which everywhere, at every moment, the adversaries are seeking one another but only clashing accidentally, lost in irremediable darkness and uncertainty.

29

Everyday life has always been drained to the advantage of apparent life, but appearance, in its mythical cohesion, was powerful enough to repress any mention of everyday life. The poverty and emptiness of the spectacle, revealed by all the varieties of capitalism and all the varieties of bourgeoisie, has revealed both the existence of everyday life (a shelter life, but a shelter for what and from what?) and the poverty of everyday life. As reification and bureaucratization grow stronger, the debility of the spectacle and of everyday life is the only thing that remains clear. The conflict between the human and the inhuman has also been transferred to the plane of appearance. As soon as Marxism became an ideology, Marx's struggle against ideology in the name of the richness of life was transformed into an ideological anti-ideology, an antispectacle spectacle (just as in avant-garde culture the antispectacular spectacle is restricted to actors alone, antiartistic art being created and understood only by artists, so the relationship between this ideological anti-ideology and the function of the professional revolutionary in Leninism should be examined). Thus Manicheanism has found itself momentarily revived. Why did St. Augustine attack the Manicheans so relentlessly? It was because he recognized the danger of a myth offering only one solution, the victory of good over evil; he saw that this impossibility threatened to provoke the collapse of all mythical structures and bring into the open the contradiction between mythical and authentic life. Christianity offered the third way, the way of sacred confusion. What Christianity accomplished through the force of myth is accomplished today through the force of *things*. There can no longer be any antagonism between Soviet workers and capitalist workers or between the bomb of the Stalinist bureaucrats and the bomb of the non-Stalinist bureaucrats; there is no longer anything but unity in the chaos of reified beings.

Who is responsible? Who should be shot? We are dominated by a system, by an abstract form. Degrees of humanity and inhumanity are measured by purely quantitative variations of passivity. The quality is the same everywhere: we are all proletarianized or well on the way to becoming so. What are the traditional "revolutionaries" doing? They are eliminating certain distinctions, making sure that no proletarians are any more proletarian than all the others. But what party is working for the end of the proletariat?

The perspective of survival has become intolerable. What is weighing us down is *the weight of things in a vacuum.* That's what reification is: everyone and everything falling at an equal speed, everyone and everything stigmatized with their equal value. The reign of equal values has realized the Christian project, but it has realized it outside Christianity (as Pascal had supposed) and, above all, it has realized it over God's dead body, contrary to Pascal's expectations.

The spectacle and everyday life coexist in the reign of equal values. People and things are interchangeable. The world of reification is a world without a center, like the new prefabricated cities that are its decor. The present fades away before the promise of an eternal future that is nothing but a mechanical extension of the past. Time itself is deprived of a center. In this concentration-camp world, victims and torturers wear the same mask and only the torture is real. No new ideology can soothe the pain, neither the ideology of the totality (Logos) nor that of nihilism—which will be the two crutches of the cybernetic society. The tortures condemn all hierarchical power, however organized or dissimulated it may be. The antagonism the SI is going to revive is the oldest of all, it is radical antagonism and that is why it is taking up again and assimilating all that has been left by the insurrectionary movements and great individuals in the course of history.

30

So many other banalities could be taken up and reversed. The best things never come to an end. Before rereading the above—which even the most mediocre intelligence will be able to understand by the third attempt—the reader would be well-advised to concentrate carefully on the following text, for these notes, as fragmentary as the preceding ones, must be discussed in detail and implemented. It concerns a central question: the SI and revolutionary power.

Being aware of the crises of both mass parties and "elites," the SI must embody the supersession of both the Bolshevik Central Committee (supersession of the mass party) and of the Nietzschean project (supersession of the intelligentsia).

a) Every time a power has presented itself as directing a revolutionary upsurge, it has automatically undermined the power of the revolution. The Bolshevik C.C. defined itself simultaneously as concentration and as representation. Concentration of a power antagonistic to bourgeois power and representation of the will of the masses. This duality led it rapidly to become no more than an empty power, a power of empty representation, and consequently to rejoin, in a common form (bureaucracy), a bourgeois power that was being forced (in response to the very existence of the Bolshevik power) to follow a similar evolution. The conditions for a concentrated power and mass representation exist potentially in the SI when it states that it holds the qualitative and that its ideas are in everyone's mind. Nevertheless we refuse both concentrated power and the right of representation, conscious that we are now taking the only *public attitude* (for we cannot avoid being known to some extent in a spectacular manner) enabling those who find that they share our theoretical and practical positions to accede to revolutionary power: power without mediation, power entailing the direct action of everyone. Our guiding image could be the Durruti Column, moving from town to village, liquidating the bourgeois elements and leaving the workers to see to their own self-organization.

b) The intelligentsia is power's hall of mirrors. Contesting power, it never offers anything but passive cathartic identification to those whose every gesture gropingly expresses real contestation. The radicalism—not of theory, obviously, but of gesture—that could be glimpsed in the "Declaration of the 121,"* however, suggests some different possibilities. We are capable of precipitating this crisis, but we can do so only by entering the intelligentsia as a power against the intelligentsia. This phase—which must precede and be contained within the phase described in point a)—will put us in the perspective of the Nietzschean project. We will form a small, almost alchemical, experimental group within which the realization of the total man can be started. Nietzsche could conceive of such an undertaking only within the framework of the hierarchical principle. It is, in fact, within such a framework that we find ourselves. It is therefore of the utmost importance that we present ourselves without the slightest ambiguity (on the level of the group, the purification of the nucleus and the elimination of residues now seems to be completed). We accept the hierarchical framework in which we are placed only while impatiently working to abolish our domination over those whom we cannot avoid dominating on the basis of our criteria for mutual recognition.

c) Tactically our communication should be a diffusion emanating from a more or less hidden center. We will establish nonmaterialized networks (direct relationships, episodic ones, contacts without ties, development of embryonic relations based on sympathy and understanding, in the manner of the red agitators before the arrival of the revolutionary armies). We will claim radical gestures (actions, writings, political attitudes, works) as our own by analyzing them, and we will consider that our own acts and analyses are supported by the majority of people.

Just as God constituted the reference point of past unitary society, we are preparing to create the central reference point for a unitary society now possible. But this point cannot be fixed. As opposed to the ever-renewed confusion that cybernetic power draws from the past of inhumanity, it stands for the game that everyone will play, "the moving order of the future."

RAOUL VANEIGEM

SITUATIONIST INTERNATIONAL ANTI–PUBLIC RELATIONS SERVICE

So you agree with the SI!
You want to join the SI!

We only ask of you a little preliminary work, to verify objectively (in your own interest as well as ours) how close you are to our concerns and your ability to participate fully in our undertaking (*the SI does not want disciples*):

1. Choose for yourself a point in the theses published by the SI that you consider important and develop some arguments and possible expansions of it (minimum one page typescript; no maximum).

2. Choose for yourself, out of the same texts published by the SI, a point that can be criticized and destroy that position (same conditions).

N.B. This is not a meaningless game. The SI often proceeds like this in order to reexamine its own bases and develop new ideas. Perhaps you will chance on a point already criticized. But you might also initiate an appropriate critique of a position insufficiently questioned by us until now. Thus your critique, if it is well done, will be valid in any case; and may even be useful in putting forward something new!

NOW, THE S.I.

"Each epoch forges its own human material, and if our epoch really needed theoretical works it would itself create the forces necessary for its satisfaction."

—Rosa Luxemburg, in *Vorwärts*, 14 March 1903

Now that the situationists already have a history and their activity has carved out a very particular but undeniably central role for itself in the cultural debates of the last few years, some people reproach the SI for having succeeded and others reproach it for having failed.

In order to understand the real significance of these terms, as well as almost all the intellectual establishment's judgments concerning the SI, it is first necessary to *reverse* them. The SI's element of failure is what is commonly considered success—the artistic value that is beginning to be appreciated in us; the fact that certain of our theses have come to be sociologically or urbanistically fashionable; or simply the personal success that is virtually guaranteed any situationist as soon as he is excluded. Our element of success, which is more profound, is the fact that we have resisted the mass of compromises that have been offered us; the fact that we have not clung to our original pilot program but have proved that its main avant-garde character, in spite of some other more apparent ones, lay in the fact that *it had to lead further*, and the fact that we have thus far been refused any *recognition* within the established framework of the present order.

We have undoubtedly made many mistakes. We have often corrected or abandoned them, although it was precisely among them that were found the elements which were succeeding or for which the greatest aid was offered to bring them to success. It is easy to note the shortcomings in our first publications, the extravagant verbiage, the fantasies left over from the old artistic milieu, the holdovers from the old politics; it is, moreover, in the light of the SI's later conclusions that these earlier shortcomings are most easily criticizable. An inverse factor has naturally left less trace in our writings, but has weighed heavily on us: a nihilist abstentionism, a serious inability among many of us to think and act beyond the first stammerings of a positive dialogue. This is almost always accompanied by the most abstract and pretentious insistence on a disincarnate radicalism.

There is, however, a deviation that has threatened us more gravely than all the others: it was the risk of not differentiating ourselves clearly enough from the *modern* tendencies of explanations and proposals regarding the new society to which capitalism has brought us—

tendencies which, behind different masks, all lead to integration into this society. Since Constant's interpretation of unitary urbanism this tendency has been expressed within the SI, and it is infinitely more dangerous than the old artistic conception we have fought so much. It was more modern and therefore less apparent, and certainly had a more promising future. Our project has taken shape at the *same time* as the modern tendencies toward integration. There is thus not only a direct opposition but also an air of resemblance since the two sides are really contemporaneous. We have not paid enough attention to this aspect of things, even recently. Thus, it is not impossible to interpret Alexander Trocchi's proposals in issue #8 of this journal* as having some affinity—despite their obviously completely contrary spirit—with those poor attempts at a "psychodramatic" salvaging of decomposed art expressed for example by the ridiculous "Workshop of Free Expression" in Paris last May. But the point we have arrived at clarifies both our project and, inversely, the project of integration. All really modern nonrevolutionary ventures must now be seen and treated as our enemy number one. They are going to reinforce all existing controls.

We must not for all that abandon the extreme point of the modern world merely so as to avoid resembling it in anything, or even in order not to teach it anything that could be used against us. It is quite natural that our enemies succeed in partially using us. We are neither going to leave the present field of culture to them nor mix with them. The armchair advisors who are willing to admire and understand us from a respectful distance readily recommend to us the purity of the first attitude while they adopt the second one. We reject this suspect formalism: like the proletariat, we cannot claim to be unexploitable in the present conditions; we must simply work to make any such exploitation entail the greatest possible risk for the exploiters. The SI has taken a clear stand as an alternative to the dominant culture and particularly to its so-called avant-garde forms. The situationists consider that they must succeed to art—which is dead—and to separate philosophical reflection—whose corpse no one, despite all present efforts, will succeed in "reviving"—because the *spectacle* that is replacing this art and this thought is itself the heir of *religion*. And just as was the "critique of religion" (a critique that the present Left abandoned at the same time it abandoned all thought and action), the critique of the spectacle is today the precondition for any critique.

The path of total police control over all human activities and the path of infinite free creation of all human activities are one: it is the same path of modern discoveries. We are necessarily on the same path as our enemies—most often preceding them—but we must be there, without any confusion, *as enemies*. The best will win.

The present era can test innumerable innovations but it is incapable of putting them to use because it is chained to the fundamental conservation of an old order. In all our innovating formulations we must constantly reiterate the necessity of a revolutionary transformation of society.

The revolutionary critique of all existing conditions does not, to be sure, have a monopoly on intelligence; it only has a monopoly on its use. In the present cultural and social crisis those who do not know how to use intelligence have in fact no discernable intelligence of any kind. Stop talking to us about unused intelligence and you'll make us happy. Poor Heidegger! Poor Lukács! Poor Sartre! Poor Barthes! Poor Lefebvre! Poor Cardan! Tics, tics, and tics. Without the method for using intelligence, they have nothing but caricatural fragments of the innovating ideas that can truly comprehend the totality of our epoch in the same movement that they contest it. They are not only incapable of developing ideas, they don't even know how to skillfully plagiarize ideas developed by others. Once the specialized thinkers step out of their own domain, they can only be the dumbfounded spectators of some neighboring and equally bankrupt specialization which they were ignorant of but which has become fashionable. The former specialist of ultraleftist politics [Cardan] is awestruck at discovering, along with structuralism and social psychology, an ethnological *ideology* completely new to him: the fact that the Zuñi Indians did not have any history appears to him as a luminous explanation for his own incapacity to act in our history. (Go laugh at the first twenty-five pages of *Socialisme ou Barbarie* #36.) The specialists of thought can no longer be anything but thinkers of specialization. We don't claim to have a monopoly on the dialectics that everyone talks about; we only claim to have a temporary monopoly on its *use*.

Some people still venture to oppose our theories by gravely insisting on the necessity for practice, although those who speak at this level of methodological delirium have abundantly revealed their own inability to succeed in the slightest practice. When revolutionary theory reappears in our time and can count only on itself to propagate itself *through a new practice*, it seems to us that this is already an important beginning of practice. This theory is at the outset caught in the framework of the new educated ignorance propagated by the present society, and is much more radically cut off from the masses than it was in the nineteenth century. We naturally share its isolation, its risks, its fate.

To approach us one should therefore not already be compromised, and should know that even if we may be momentarily mistaken on many minor points, we will never admit having been mistaken in our *negative* judgment of persons. Our qualitative criteria are much too sure for us to debate them. It is thus useless to approach us if one is not theoretically and practically in agreement with our condemnations of contemporary persons or currents. Some of the thinkers who are now going to comment on and plan modern society have already commented on and *ultimately conserved* it in more archaic forms when they were, for example, Stalinists. Now, without batting an eye, they are going to reenlist, just as coolly and cheerily as before, for a second bankruptcy. Others, who fought them during the preceding phase, are now joining them in a common celebration of innovation. All the specializations of illusion can be taught and discussed by the tenured thinkers. But the situationists take their stand in the knowledge that is outside this spectacle: we are not thinkers sponsored by the state.

We have to organize a coherent encounter between the elements of critique and negation scattered around the world as acts and ideas; between those of these elements that have become perceived and comprehended and the entire life of the bearers of them; and finally, between the people or the first groups that are at this level of intellectual knowledge and practical contestation. The coordination of these researches and struggles on the most practical plane (a new international link-up) is at this moment inseparable from a coordination on the most theoretical plane (which will be expressed by several works presently being prepared by some of the situationists). For example, the present issue of this journal, in order better to explain aspects of our theses that have sometimes been presented too abstractly, gives a large place to a coherent presentation of items drawn from the ordinary daily news. The continuation of our projects will have to be expressed in fuller forms. This continuation will considerably exceed what we would have been able to undertake by ourselves.

While contemporary impotence blathers on about the belated project of "getting into the twentieth century," we think it is high time to put an end to the *dead time* that has dominated this century and to finish the Christian Era with the same stroke. Here as elsewhere, the road of excess leads to the palace of wisdom. Ours is the best effort so far toward *getting out of the twentieth century*.

QUESTIONNAIRE

1. What does the word "situationist" mean?

It denotes an activity that aims at *making* situations, as opposed to passively *recognizing* them in academic or other separate terms. This at all levels of social practice or individual history. We replace existential passivity with the construction of moments of life, and doubt with playful affirmation. So far philosophers and artists have only interpreted situations; the point now is to transform them. Since man is the product of the situations he goes through, it is essential to create human situations. Since the individual is defined by his situation, he wants the power to create situations worthy of his desires. Poetry (realized communication in concrete situations), the appropriation of nature, and complete social liberation must all merge and realize themselves in this perspective. Our time is going to replace the fixed frontier of the borderline situations that phenomenology has limited itself to describing with the practical creation of situations; it is going to continually shift this frontier with the development of our realization. We want a phenomeno-praxis. We have no doubt that this will be the first banality of the movement toward the liberation that is now possible. What is to be transformed into a situation? At different levels it could be this planet or an epoch (a civilization in Burckhardt's sense, for example) or a moment of individual life. On with the show! The values of past culture, the hopes of realizing reason in history, have no other possible future. All the rest is in decay. The term situationist in the SI's sense is the exact opposite of what is currently called a "situationist" in Portugal, which designates a partisan of the existing situation, and thus in Portugal a partisan of Salazarism.

2. Is the Situationist International a political movement?

The words "political movement" today connote the specialized activity of heads of groups and parties who derive from the organized passivity of their militants the oppressive force of their future power. The SI wants to have nothing in common with hierarchical power, no matter what form it may take. The SI is thus neither a political movement nor a sociology of political mystification. The SI aims to represent the highest degree of international revolutionary consciousness. This is why it strives to illuminate and coordinate the gestures of refusal and the signs of creativity that are defining the new contours of the proletariat, the irreducible will to freedom. Centered on the spontaneity of the masses, such an activity is incontestably political—unless one denies that the agitators themselves are political. To the extent that new radical currents appear in Japan (the extremist wing of the Zengakuren movement), in the Congo, in the Spanish underground, the SI grants them *critical* support* and thereby aids them practically. But in contrast to all the "transitional programs" of specialized politics, the SI holds to a permanent revolution of everyday life.

3. Is the SI an artistic movement?

A large part of the situationist critique of consumer society consists in showing to what extent contemporary artists, by abandoning the richness of supersession implicitly present albeit not fully realized in the 1910–1925 period, have condemned themselves to doing art as one does business. Since that time artistic movements have only been imaginary repercussions from an explosion that never took place, an explosion that threatened and still threatens the structures of the society. The SI's consciousness of this abandonment and of its contradictory implications (emptiness or a desire to return to the initial violence) makes the SI the only movement able, by incorporating the survival of art into the art of life, to speak to the project of the authentic artist. We are artists only insofar as we are no longer artists: we come to realize art.

4. Is the SI an expression of nihilism?

The SI refuses the role that would be readily granted it in the spectacle of decomposition. The supersession of nihilism is reached by way of the decomposition of the spectacle; which is precisely what the SI is working on. Whatever is elaborated and constructed outside such a perspective will collapse of its own weight without needing any help from the SI; but it is also true that everywhere in consumer society wastelands of spontaneous collapse offer to the new values a terrain of experimentation that the SI cannot do without. We can build only on the ruins of the spectacle. Moreover, the fully justified anticipation of a total destruction obliges one never to build anything except in the light of the totality.

5. Are the situationist positions utopian?

Reality is superseding utopia. There is no longer any point in projecting an imaginary bridge between the richness of present technological capacities and the poverty of their use by the rulers of every variety. We want to put the material equipment at the disposal of everyone's creativity, as the masses themselves always strive to do in the moment of revolution. It can be considered as a question of coordination or one of tactics. Everything we deal with is realizable, either immediately or in the short term, whenever our methods of research and activity begin to be put in practice.

6. Do you consider it necessary to call yourselves "situationists"?

In the existing order, where things take the place of people, any label is compromising. The one we have chosen, however, embodies its own, albeit summary, critique, in that it opposes itself to "situationism," the label others choose for us. Moreover, it will disappear when all of us have become fully situationist and are no longer proletarians struggling for the end of the proletariat. For the moment, however ridiculous a label may be, ours has the merit of trenchantly drawing a line between the previous incoherence and a new rigorousness. What thought has lacked above all over the last few decades is precisely this trenchancy.

7. What is original about the situationists considered as a distinct group?

It seems to us that three notable points justify the importance that we attribute to ourselves as an organized group of theorists and experimenters. First, we are developing for the first time, from a revolutionary perspective, a new, coherent critique of the society as it is developing *now*; this critique is deeply anchored in the culture and art of our time, which can in fact be truly grasped only by means of such a critique (this work is obviously a long way from completion). Second, we make a practice of breaking completely and definitively with all those who oblige us to do so, and in many cases with anyone else who remains in solidarity with them. Such polarization is vital in an age when the diverse forms of resignation are so subtly intertwined and interdependent. Third, we are initiating a new style of relations with our "partisans": we absolutely refuse disciples. We are interested only in participation at the highest level; and in setting autonomous people loose in the world.

8. Why don't people talk about the SI?

The SI is talked about often enough among the specialized owners of decomposing modern thought; but they write about it very little. In the broadest sense this is because we refuse the term "situationism," which would be the only pigeonhole enabling us to be introduced into the reigning spectacle, incorporated in the form of a doctrine petrified against us, in the form of an ideology in Marx's sense. It is natural that the spectacle we reject rejects us in turn. Situationists are more readily discussed as individuals in an effort to separate them from the collective contestation, although this collective contestation is the only thing that makes them "interesting" individuals. Situationists are talked about *the moment they cease to be situationists* (as with the rival varieties of "Nashism" in several countries, whose only common claim to fame is that they lyingly pretend to have some sort of relationship with the SI). The spectacle's watchdogs appropriate fragments of situationist theory without acknowledgment in order to turn it against us. It is quite natural that they get ideas from us in their struggle for the survival of the spectacle. But they have to conceal their source, not merely to protect their reputation for originality from charges of plagiarism, but because this source implies the broader, coherent context of these "ideas." Moreover, many hesitant intellectuals do not dare to speak openly of the SI because to speak of it entails taking a minimum position—saying what one rejects of it and what one accepts of it. Many of them believe, quite mistakenly, that to feign ignorance of it in the meantime will suffice to clear them of responsibility later.

9. What support do you give to the revolutionary movement?

Unfortunately there isn't one. The society certainly contains contradictions and is undergoing changes; this is what, in continually new ways, is making revolutionary activity possible and necessary. But such activity no longer exists—or does not yet exist—in the form of an organized movement. It is therefore not a question of "supporting" such a movement, but of creating it: of inseparably defining it and experimenting with it. Admitting that there is no revolutionary movement is the first precondition for developing such a movement. All the rest is a ridiculous patching up of the past.

10. Are you Marxists?

Just as much as Marx was when he said, "I am not a Marxist."

11. Is there a relation between your theories and your actual way of life?

Our theories are nothing other than the theory of our real life and of the possibilities experienced or perceived in it. As fragmented as the available terrains of activity may be for the moment, we make the most of them. We treat enemies as enemies, a first step we recommend to everyone as an accelerated apprenticeship in learning how to think. It also goes without saying that we unconditionally support all forms of liberated mores, everything that the bourgeois or bureaucratic scum call debauchery. It is obviously out of the question that we should pave the way for the revolution of everyday life with asceticism.

12. Are the situationists in the vanguard of leisure society?

Leisure society is an appearance that veils a particular type of production/consumption of social space-time. If the time of productive work in the strict sense is reduced, the reserve army of industrial life works in consumption. Everyone is successively worker and raw material in the industry of vacations, of leisure, of spectacles. Present work is the alpha and omega of present life. The organization of consumption plus the organization of leisure must exactly counterbalance the organization of work. "Free time" is a most ironic quantity in the context of the flow of a prefabricated time. Alienated work can only produce alienated leisure, for the idle (increasingly, in fact, merely semi-idle) elite as well as for the masses who are obtaining access to momentary leisure. No lead shielding can insulate either a fragment of time or the entire time of a fragment of society from the radioactivity diffused by alienated labor—if for no other reason than the fact that it is that labor which shapes the totality of products and of social life in its own image.

13. Who finances you?

We have never been able to be financed except, in a very precarious manner, by working in the present cultural economy. This employment is subject to this contradiction: we have such creative abilities that we can be virtually assured of "success" in any field; yet we have such a rigorous insistence on independence and complete consistency between our project and each of our present realizations (see our definition of antisituationist artistic production) that we are almost totally unacceptable to the dominant cultural organization, even in the most secondary activities. The state of our resources follows from these conditions. In this connection, see what we wrote in issue #8 of this journal (p. 26) on "the capital that is never lacking for Nashist enterprises" and, in contrast, *our conditions* (on the last page of this issue).*

14. How many of you are there?

A few more than the original guerrilla nucleus in the Sierra Madre, but with fewer weapons. A few less than the delegates in London in 1864 who founded the International Workingmen's Association, but with a more coherent program. As unyielding as the Greeks at Thermopylae ("Passerby, go tell them at Lacedaemon . . ."), but with a brighter future.

15. What value can you attribute to a questionnaire? To this one?

The questionnaire is manifestly a form of pseudodialogue which is becoming obsessively used in all the psychotechniques of integration into the spectacle so as to elicit people's happy acceptance of passivity under the crude guise of "participation" and pseudoactivity. We, however, by taking an incoherent, reified form of questioning as a point of departure, are able to express precise positions. In fact, these positions do not really "reply" because they don't stick to the questions; they reply by posing new questions that should *supersede* the old ones. Thus, real dialogue could begin after these responses. In the present questionnaire all the questions are *false*; our responses, however, are true.

142

RESPONSE TO A QUESTIONNAIRE FROM THE CENTER FOR SOCIO-EXPERIMENTAL ART

1. Why are the masses not concerned with art? Why does art remain the privilege of certain educated sectors of the bourgeois class?

The importance of the theme of the present questionnaire and the limited space allotted for answers oblige us to be somewhat schematic. The situationists' positions on these topics have been elaborated in more detail in the SI's journals (*Internationale Situationniste*, *Der Deutsche Gedanke* and *Situationistisk Revolution*) and in the catalogue published on the occasion of the "Destruction of RSG 6" demonstration in Denmark last June.

The masses, i.e. the nonruling classes, have no reason to feel concerned with any aspects of a culture or an organization of social life that have been developed not only without their participation or their control, but even deliberately against such participation or control. They are concerned (illusorily) only with the by-products specially designed for their consumption—the various forms of spectacular publicity and propaganda in favor of various products or behavioral models.

This does not mean, however, that art subsists merely as a "privilege" of the bourgeois class. In the past every dominant class had its *own* art—for the same reasons that a classless society will have none, will be beyond artistic practice. But the historical conditions of our time, associated with a major breakthrough in man's appropriation of nature and thus bearing the concrete project of a classless society, are such that major art in this period has necessarily been revolutionary. What has been called modern art, from its origins in the nineteenth century to its full development in the first third of the twentieth, has been an art *against* the bourgeoisie. The present crisis of art is linked to the crisis of the workers movement since the defeat of the Russian revolution and the modernization of capitalism.

Today a *fake* continuation of modern art (formal repetitions attractively packaged and publicized, completely divorced from the original combativeness of their models) along with a voracious consumption of bits and pieces of previous cultures completely divorced from their real meaning (Malraux, previously their most ludicrous salesman in the realm of "theory," is now exhibiting them in his "Culture Centers") are what actually constitute the dubious "privilege" of the new stratum of intellectual workers that proliferates with the development of the "tertiary sector" of the economy. This sector is closely connected to that of the social *spectacle*: this intellectual stratum (the requirements of whose training and employment explain both the quantita-

tive extension of education and its qualitative degradation) is both the most direct producer of the spectacle and the most direct consumer of its specifically cultural elements.

Two tendencies seem to us to typify the contemporary cultural consumption offered to this public of alienated intellectual workers:

On one hand, tentatives such as the "Visual Art Research Group" clearly tend toward the integration of the population into the dominant socioeconomic system, along the lines currently being worked toward by repressive urbanism and the theorists of cybernetic control. Through a veritable parody of the revolutionary theses on putting an end to the passivity of separated spectators and on *constructing situations*, this "Visual Art" group strives to make the spectator participate in his own misery—taking its lack of dialectics to the point of "freeing" the spectator by announcing that it is "forbidden not to participate" (tract at the Third Paris Biennial).

On the other hand, "New Realism," drawing heavily on the form of dadaism (but not its spirit), is an *apologetic* trashcan art. It fits quite well in the margin of pseudofreedom offered by a society of gadgets and waste.

But the importance of such artists remains very secondary, even in comparison with advertising. Thus, paradoxically, the "Socialist Realism" of the East, which is not art at all, nevertheless has a more decisive social function. This is because in the East power is maintained primarily by selling ideology (i.e. mystifying justifications), while in the West it is maintained by selling consumer goods. The fact that the bureaucracy has proved incapable of developing its own art, and has been forced to make a formal adaptation of the pseudoartistic vision of petty-bourgeois conformists of the last century (in spite of the inherent ineffectuality of that form), confirms the present impossibility of any art as a ruling-class "privilege."

Nevertheless, all art is "social" in the sense that it has its roots in a given society and even in spite of itself must have some relation to the prevailing conditions or to their negation. Former moments of contestation survive *fragmentarily* and lose their artistic (or postartistic) value to the precise extent they have lost the heart of contestation. With their loss of this heart they have also lost any reference to the mass of postartistic acts (of revolt and of free reconstruction of life) that already exist in the world and that are tending to replace art. This fragmentary contestation can then only withdraw to an aesthetic position and harden rapidly into a dated and ineffectual aesthetic *in a world where it is already too late for aesthetics*—as has happened with surrealism, for example. Other movements are typical of degraded bourgeois mysticism (art as substitute for religion). They reproduce—but only in the form of solitary fantasy or idealist pretension—the forces that dominate present social life both officially and in fact: noncommunication, bluff, frantic desire for novelty as such, for the rapid turnover of arbitrary and uninteresting gadgets—lettrism, for example, on which subject we remarked that "Isou, product of an era of unconsumable art, has suppressed the very idea of its consumption" and that he has "proposed the first art of solipsism" (*Internationale Situationniste #4*).

144

Finally, the very proliferation of would-be artistic movements that are essentially indistinguishable from one another can be seen as an application of modern sales techniques: marketing the same product under rival trademarks.

2. How can art be really "social"?

The time for art is over. It is now a matter of *realizing* art, of really building on every level of life everything that hitherto could only be an artistic memory or an illusion, dreamed and preserved unilaterally. Art can be realized *only by being suppressed*. However, as opposed to the present society, which suppresses it by replacing it with the automatism of an even more passive and hierarchical spectacle, we maintain that art can really be suppressed *only by being realized*.

2. (cont.) Does the political society in which you live encourage or discourage your social function as an artist?

This society has suppressed what you call the social function of the artist.

If the question refers to the function of employee in the reigning *spectacle*, it is obvious that the number of jobs to be had there expands as the spectacle does. The situationists, however, do not find this employment opportunity the least bit attractive.

If, on the other hand, we take the question as referring to the *inheriting of previous art* through new types of activity, beginning with contestation of the social totality, the society in question naturally discourages such a practice.

3. Do you think your aesthetics would be different if you lived in a socially, politically and economically different society?

Certainly. When our perspectives are realized, aesthetics (as well as its negation) will be superseded.

If we were presently living in an underdeveloped country or in one subjected to archaic forms of domination (colonialism or a Franco-type dictatorship), we would agree that an artist can to a certain extent participate as such in popular struggles. In a context of general social and cultural backwardness the social function of the artist remains real for some time yet, and a not entirely sham communication is still possible within the traditional forms.

If we were living in a country governed by a "socialist" bureaucracy, where information about cultural and other experimentation in advanced industrialized countries over the last fifty years is systematically suppressed, we would certainly support the minimum demand for dissemination of truth, including the truth about contemporary Western art. We would do this in spite of the inevitable ambiguity of such a demand, since the history of modern art, though already accessible and even glorified in the West, is nonetheless still profoundly falsified; and its importation into the Eastern bloc would first of all be exploited by hacks like Yevtushenko in their modernization of official art.

4. Do you participate in politics or not? Why?

Yes, but in only one kind: together with various other forces in the world, we are working toward the theoretical and practical organization of a new revolutionary movement.

All the considerations we are developing here constitute our inseparable reasons for going beyond the failures of previous specialized politics.

5. Does an association of artists seem necessary to you? What would be its objectives?

There are already numerous associations of artists, either without any principles or arbitrarily based on one or another extravagant absurdity—mutual aid unions, mutual congratulation societies, alliances for collective careerism. Works that on the slightest pretext are proclaimed "collective projects" are fashionable at the moment and are even put in the limelight at the pitiful Paris biennials, thus diverting attention from the real problems of the supersession of art. We regard all these associations with equal contempt and accept no contact whatsoever with this milieu.

We do believe that a coherent and disciplined association for the realization of a common program is possible on the bases worked out by the Situationist International, provided that the participants are so rigorously selected that they all have genius and more or less cease to be artists or to consider themselves as artists in the old sense of the word.

It could in fact be questioned whether the situationists are artists at all, even avant-garde ones. Not only because almost everyone in the cultural scene resists recognizing them as such (at least once the whole of the situationist program is involved) or because their interests extend far beyond the former scope of art. Their nature as artists is even more problematic on the socioeconomic level. Many situationists support themselves by rather dubious methods, ranging from historical research to poker; some are bartenders, others run puppet theaters. It is striking that of the 28 members of the Situationist International whom we have had to exclude so far, 23 personally had a socially recognized and increasingly profitable role as artists: they were known as artists in spite of their membership in the SI. But as such they were tending to reinforce the position of our enemies, who want to invent a "situationism" so as to finish with us by integrating us into the spectacle as just one more doomsday aesthetic. Yet while doing this these artists wanted to remain in the SI. This was unacceptable for us. The figures speak for themselves.

It goes without saying that any other "objectives" of any association of artists are of no interest to us, since we regard them as no longer having any point whatsoever.

6. How is the work you are presenting here related to these statements?

The enclosed work obviously cannot represent a "situationist art." In the present markedly antisituationist cultural conditions we must

146

resort to "communication containing its own critique," which we have experimented with in every accessible medium, from film to writing, and which we have theorized under the name of *detournement*. Since the Center for Socio-Experimental Art has limited its survey to the plastic arts, we have selected, from among the numerous possibilities of detournement as a means of agitation, Michèle Bernstein's anti-painting, *Victory of the Bonnot Gang*. It forms part of a series including *Victory of the Paris Commune, Victory of the Great Jacquerie of 1358, Victory of the Spanish Republicans, Victory of the Workers Councils of Budapest* and several other victories. Such paintings attempt to negate "Pop Art" (which is materially and "ideologically" characterized by *indifference* and dull complacency) by incorporating only *toy* objects and by making them meaningful in as heavy-handed a way as possible. In a sense this series resumes the painting of battles; and rectifies the history of revolts—which is not over—in a way that pleases us. It seems that each new attempt to transform the world is forced to start out with the appearance of a *new unrealism*. We hope that our remarks, both humorous and serious, will help to clarify our position on the present relationship between art and society.

For the Situationist International:
J.V. MARTIN, J. STRIJBOSCH, R. VANEIGEM, R. VIÉNET
6 December 1963

ADDRESS TO REVOLUTIONARIES OF ALGERIA AND OF ALL COUNTRIES

"Proletarian revolutions . . . pitilessly scoff at the hesitations, weaknesses and inadequacies of their first efforts, seem to throw down their adversary only to see him draw new strength from the earth and rise again formidably before them, recoil again and again before the immensity of their tasks, until a situation is finally created that makes all turning back impossible."

—Marx, *The Eighteenth Brumaire of Louis Bonaparte*

Comrades,

The disintegration of the revolutionary image presented by the international Communist movement is taking place forty years after the disintegration of the revolutionary movement itself. This time gained for the bureaucratic lie—that supplement to the permanent bourgeois lie—has been time lost for the revolution. The history of the modern world pursues its revolutionary course, but unconsciously or with false consciousness. Everywhere there are social confrontations, but nowhere is the old order liquidated, even within the very forces that contest it. Everywhere the ideologies of the old world are criticized and rejected, but nowhere is "the real movement that suppresses existing conditions" liberated from one or another "ideology" in Marx's sense: ideas that serve masters. Everywhere revolutionaries, but nowhere the revolution.

The collapse of the Ben-Bellaist image of a semirevolution in Algeria has just given a striking expression of this general discomfiture. The superficial power of Ben Bella represented the moment of rigid balance between the movement of the Algerian workers toward the management of the entire society and the bourgeois bureaucracy in the process of formation within the framework of the state. But in this official balance the revolution had nothing with which to further its objectives—it had already become a museum piece—whereas those in possession of the state controlled all power, beginning with that fundamental repressive instrument, the army, to the point of finally being able to throw off their mask, i.e. Ben Bella. Two days before the putsch, at Sidi Bel Abbès, Ben Bella added the ridiculous to the odious by declaring that Algeria was "more united than ever." Now he has ceased to lie to the people and the events speak for themselves. Ben Bella fell as he had reigned, in solitude and conspiracy, by a *palace revolution.* He was ushered out by the same forces that had ushered him in: Boumedienne's army, which had opened the road to Algiers for him in

September 1962. Ben Bella's regime ratified the revolutionary conquests that the bureaucracy was not yet able to repress: the self-management movement. The forces so well hidden behind the "Muslim Brother" Boumedienne have this clear goal: to liquidate self-management. The June 19th Declaration's mixture of Western technocratic jargon with the pathos of a reinforced Islamic moral order defines the whole policy of the new regime: "to get out of the general state of stagnation which is already manifesting itself in a lowering of productivity, a decreasing economic profitability and a disturbing withdrawal of investments" and "to keep in mind our faith, our convictions and the secular traditions and moral values of our people."

The astonishing acceleration of practical demystification must now serve to accelerate revolutionary theory. The same society of alienation, of totalitarian control (here the sociologist predominates, there the police), of spectacular consumption (here the cars and gadgets, there the words of the venerated leader) reigns everywhere, in spite of the variations in its ideological or juridical disguises. The coherence of this society cannot be understood without a total critique, illuminated by the inverse project of a liberated creativity, the project of the domination by all people over their own history at all levels. This is the demand *in acts* of all proletarian revolutions, a demand until now defeated by the specialists of power who take charge of revolutions and make them their private property.

To revive and bring into the present this *inseparable*, mutually illuminating project and critique immediately entails appropriating all the radicalism borne by the workers movement, by modern poetry and art in the West (as preface to an experimental research toward a free construction of everyday life), by the thought of the period of the supersession and realization of philosophy (Hegel, Feuerbach, Marx) and by the emancipatory struggles from the Mexico of 1910 to the Congo of today. To do this, it is first of all necessary to recognize, without holding on to any consoling illusions, the full extent of the defeat of the entire revolutionary project *in the first third of this century* and its official replacement, in every region of the world and in every aspect of life, by delusive shams and petty reforms that camouflage and preserve the old order. The domination of bureaucratic state-capitalism over the workers is the opposite of socialism—this is the truth that Trotskyism has refused to face. Socialism exists wherever the workers themselves directly manage the entire society; it therefore exists neither in Russia nor in China nor anywhere else. The Russian and Chinese revolutions were defeated from within. Today they provide the Western proletariat and the peoples of the Third World with a false model which in reality counterbalances the power of bourgeois capitalism and imperialism.

A resumption of radicality naturally entails a considerable deepening of all the old liberatory attempts. The experience of their incompletion in isolation, or their inversion into total mystification, leads to a better grasp of the coherence of the world to be transformed; and once this coherence is rediscovered, many of the partial researches developed in the recent past can be salvaged, enabled to attain their essential truth (the liberating content of psychoanalysis, for example,

149

can be neither understood nor realized outside the struggle for the abolition of all repression).* The understanding of this reversible coherence of the world—its present reality in relation to its possible reality—exposes the fallaciousness of half-measures, and the fact that there is essentially a half-measure each time the operating pattern of the dominant society—with its categories of hierarchization and specialization and corresponding habits and tastes—reconstitutes itself within the forces of negation.

Moreover, the material development of the world has accelerated. It continually accumulates more potential powers: and the specialists of the management of society, because of their very role as guardians of passivity, are forced to ignore the potential use of those powers. At the same time, this development accumulates generalized dissatisfaction and objective lethal dangers which these specialized rulers are incapable of permanently controlling. The fundamental problem of underdevelopment must be resolved on a worldwide scale, and first of all by the revolutionary overcoming of the irrational *overdevelopment* of productive forces in the framework of the various forms of rationalized capitalism. The revolutionary movements of the Third World can succeed only on the basis of a lucid contribution to global revolution. Development must not be a race to catch up with capitalist reification, but a satisfaction of all real needs as the basis for a genuine development of human faculties.

New revolutionary theory must move in step with reality, it must keep abreast with the revolutionary praxis which is starting up here and there but which yet remains partial, mutilated and without a coherent total project. Our language, which will perhaps seem fantastic, is the very language of real life. History continues to present ever more glaring confirmations of this. If in this history the familiar is not necessarily known, it is because real life itself only appears in a fantastic form, in the upside-down image imposed on it by the modern *spectacle* of the world: in the spectacle all social life, including even the representation of sham revolutions, is written in the lying language of power and filtered by its machines. The spectacle is the terrestrial heir of religion, the opium of a capitalism that has arrived at the stage of a "society of abundance" of *commodities*; it is the illusion actually consumed in "consumer society."

To the sporadic explosions of revolutionary contestation, an international organization of repression responds, operating with a global division of tasks. Each of the blocs, or of the spinoff splinters of blocs, ensures within its sphere of influence the lethargic sleep of all, the maintenance of an order that remains fundamentally the same. This permanent repression ranges from the military expedition to the more or less complete falsification practiced today by every constituted power: "The truth is revolutionary" (Gramsci) and all existing governments, even those issuing out of the most liberatory movements, are based on lies inside and out. It is precisely this repression that constitutes the most resounding verification of our hypotheses.

Revolutionary tentatives of today, because they have to break all the rules of false understanding imposed by the "peaceful coexistence" of reigning lies, begin in *isolation*, in one particular sector of the world

150

or in one particular sector of contestation. Armed with the most minimal definition of liberty, they attack only the most immediate aspect of oppression. Thus they meet with the maximum of repression and slander (they are accused of rejecting one existing order while necessarily approving of an existing variant of it) and the minimum of aid. The more difficult their victory, the more easily it is confiscated by new oppressors. The next revolutions *can find aid in the world only by attacking it in its totality.* The freedom movement of the American blacks, if it can assert itself effectively, will call into question all the contradictions of modern capitalism; it must not be sidetracked by the "black nationalism" and "black capitalism" of the Black Muslims. The workers of the United States, like those in England, engage in "wildcat strikes" against the bureaucratized unions that aim first of all at integrating them into the concentrated, semiregulated capitalist system. It is with these workers and with the students who have just won their strike at the University of California at Berkeley that a North American revolution can be made; and not with the Chinese atom bomb.

The movement drawing the Arab peoples toward unification and socialism has achieved a number of victories over classical colonialism. But it is more and more evident that it must finish with Islam, manifestly a counterrevolutionary force as are all religious ideologies; it must grant freedom to the Kurdish people; it must finish with the Palestinian pretext which justifies the dominant policy in the Arab states, since this policy insists on the destruction of Israel and thereby perpetuates itself since this destruction is impossible. The repressive forces of the state of Israel can be dissolved only by a *model of a revolutionary society realized by the Arabs.* Just as the success of a model of a revolutionary society in the world would mean the end of the largely sham confrontation between the East and the West, so would end the Arab-Israel confrontation which is a miniature version of it.

Revolutionary attempts of today are *abandoned* to repression because it is not in the interest of any existing power to support them. We *passively watch* their combat and only the illusionist babble of the UN or of the specialists of "progressive" state powers accompanies their death throes. In Santo Domingo US troops dared to intervene in a foreign country in order to back up fascist army officers against the legal government of the Kennedyist Caamaño, simply for fear that he would be overwhelmed by the people he had had to arm. What forces in the world took retaliatory measures against the American intervention? In the Congo in 1960 Belgian paratroopers, UN expeditionary forces and the Mining Association's tailor-made state [Katanga] broke the impetus of the people who thought they had won independence; they killed Lumumba and Mpolo. In 1964 Belgian paratroopers, American transport planes, and South African, European and anti-Castroist Cuban mercenaries pushed back the second insurrectional wave of the Mulelists. What practical aid was provided by "revolutionary Africa"? Wouldn't a thousand Algerian volunteers, victors of a much harder war, have been enough to prevent the fall of Stanleyville? But the armed people of Algeria had long before been replaced by a classical army on lease to Boumedienne, who had other plans.

The next revolutions are confronted with the task of *understanding themselves.* They must totally reinvent their own language and defend themselves against all the recuperations prepared for them. The Asturian miners' strike (virtually continuous since 1962) and all the other signs of opposition that herald the end of Francoism do not indicate an inevitable future for Spain, but a choice: either the holy alliance now being prepared by the Spanish Church, the monarchists, the "left Falangists" and the Stalinists to harmoniously adapt post-Franco Spain to modernized capitalism, to the Common Market; or the resumption and completion of the most radical aspects of the revolution that was defeated by Franco and his accomplices on all sides. The human relationships of socialism were realized, for a few weeks, in Barcelona in 1936.

The new revolutionary current, wherever it appears, must begin to link up the present contestatory experiences and the people who bear them. And along with unifying such groups, it must at the same time unify the *coherent basis of their project.* The first gestures of the coming revolutionary epoch embody a new content, visible and hidden, of the critique of present societies, and new forms of struggle; and also the irreducible moments of all the old revolutionary history that has remained in abeyance, moments which reappear like *ghosts.* The dominant society, which prides itself so much on its constant modernization, is going to meet its match, for it is at last beginning to produce its own modernized negation.

Long live the comrades who in 1959 burned the Koran in the streets of Baghdad!

Long live the Workers Councils of Hungary, defeated in 1956 by the so-called Red Army!

Long live the dockers of Aarhus who last year effectively boycotted racist South Africa, in spite of their union leadership and the judicial repression of the Danish social-democratic government!

Long live the "Zengakuren" student movement of Japan, which actively combats the capitalist power of imperialism and of the so-called "communist" bureaucracies!

Long live the workers' militia that defended the northeastern districts of Santo Domingo!

Long live the self-management of the Algerian peasants and workers! The option is now between the militarized bureaucratic dictatorship and the dictatorship of the "self-managed sector" *extended to all production and all aspects of social life.*

Algiers, July 1965
(circulated clandestinely)

THE DECLINE AND FALL OF THE
SPECTACLE-COMMODITY ECONOMY

From 13–16 August 1965 the blacks of Los Angeles revolted. An incident between traffic police and pedestrians developed into two days of spontaneous riots. Despite repeated reinforcements, the forces of order were unable to gain control of the streets. By the third day the blacks had armed themselves by looting accessible gun stores and so were even able to fire on police helicopters. Thousands of police and soldiers—including an entire infantry division supported by tanks— had to be thrown into the struggle in order to confine the riot to the Watts area; it then took several more days of street fighting to bring it under control. The rioters gave themselves over to widespread looting and burning of the stores in the area. Official figures testify to 32 dead (including 27 blacks), more than 800 wounded and 3000 arrested.

Reactions on all sides made things perfectly clear: the revolutionary act, by practically clarifying existing problems, always brings out an unaccustomed lucidity in the attitudes of its opponents. Police Chief William Parker, for example, refused all mediation proposed by the major black organizations, correctly asserting, "These rioters don't have any leaders." And since the blacks no longer had any leaders, it was the moment of truth for both camps. What did one of those unemployed leaders, Roy Wilkins, general secretary of the NAACP, want at that moment? He declared that the riots "should be put down with all necessary force." And the Cardinal of Los Angeles, McIntyre, who protested loudly, did not protest against the violence of the repression, which one might have supposed the cleverest tactic at a time when the Roman Catholic Church is modernizing its image; he protested most urgently against "a premeditated revolt against the rights of one's neighbor and respect for law and order," calling on Catholics to oppose the looting and "this violence without any apparent justification." And all those who went so far as to recognize the "apparent justifications" of the rage of the Los Angeles blacks—but not, to be sure, the real justification—all those "theorists" and "spokesmen" of the international Left, or rather of its nothingness, deplored the irresponsibility, the disorder, the looting (especially the fact that *arms and alcohol* were the first targets for plunder) and the 2000 fires started by the Watts gasoline throwers to light up their battle and their ball. But who has defended the rioters of Los Angeles in the terms they deserve? We will. Let us leave the economists to grieve over the 27 million dollars lost, the city planners over one of their most beautiful supermarkets gone up in smoke, and McIntyre over his slain deputy sheriff; let the sociologists bewail the absurdity and intoxication of this rebellion. The role of a revolutionary publication is not only to justify the Los Angeles insurgents, but to help uncover their *implicit reasons*, to explain theoretically the truth for which such practical action expresses the search.

In Algiers in July 1965, following Boumedienne's coup d'état, the situationists published an *Address* to the Algerians and to revolutionaries all over the world which interpreted conditions in Algeria and the rest of the world *as a whole*. Among other examples, we mentioned the movement of American blacks, stating that if it could "assert itself effectively" it would unmask the contradictions of the most advanced capitalist system. Five weeks later this effective assertion was in the streets. Theoretical criticism of modern society, in its most advanced forms, and criticism in acts of the same society already coexist: still separated but both equally advancing toward the same realities, both talking about the same thing. These two critiques explain each other; and neither is explainable without the other. Our theory of "survival" and of the "spectacle" is illuminated and verified by these actions which are so incomprehensible to American false consciousness. One day these actions will in turn be illuminated by this theory.

Until the Watts explosion, black "Civil Rights" demonstrations had been kept by their leaders within the limits of a legal system that tolerated the most appalling violence on the part of the police and the racists—as in Alabama the previous March, for example, at the time of the march on Montgomery. Even after the latter scandal, a discreet agreement between the federal government, Governor Wallace and Pastor King had led the Selma marchers on 10 March to stand back at the first request, in dignity and prayer. The confrontation expected by the demonstrators had been reduced to a mere spectacle of a potential confrontation. In that moment nonviolence reached the pitiful limit of its courage: first you expose yourself to the enemies' blows, then you push your moral grandeur to the point of sparing him the trouble of using more force. But the basic fact is that the Civil Rights movement only posed legal problems by legal means. It is logical to make an appeal to the law legally. What is irrational is to appeal legally against a blatant illegality as if this contradiction was a mere oversight that would be corrected if pointed out. It is clear that the superficial and outrageously visible illegality from which blacks still suffer in many American states has its roots in a socioeconomic contradiction that is not within the scope of existing laws; and no future *juridical* law will be able to get rid of this contradiction, in face of the more fundamental laws of the society. What the American blacks are really daring to demand is the right to really *live*. In the final analysis they want nothing less than the total subversion of this society. The problem of this necessity for subversion automatically arises the moment blacks start using subversive means. The shift to such methods takes place in their everyday lives as both the most accidental and the most objectively justified development. The issue is no longer the condition of the American blacks, but the condition of America, which merely happens to find its first expression among the blacks. This was not a *racial* conflict: the rioters left alone the whites that were in their path, attacking only the white policemen; conversely, black solidarity did not extend to black store-owners or even to black car-drivers. Even Martin Luther King had to admit in Paris last October that the riots did not fall within the limits of his specialty: "They were not race riots," he said, "they were class riots."

154

The Los Angeles rebellion was a rebellion against the commodity, against the world of the commodity in which worker-consumers are *hierarchically* subordinated to commodity values. Like the young delinquents of all the advanced countries, but more radically because they are part of a class totally without a future, a sector of the proletariat unable to believe in any significant chance of integration or promotion, the Los Angeles blacks take modern capitalist propaganda, its publicity of abundance, *literally*. They want to possess *immediately* all the objects shown and abstractly accessible because they want to *use* them. That is why they reject their exchange-value, the *commodity-reality* which is their mold, their purpose and their ultimate goal, and which has *preselected* everything. Through theft and gift they rediscover a use that immediately refutes the oppressive rationality of the commodity, revealing its relations and manufacture to be arbitrary and unnecessary. The looting of the Watts district was the most direct realization of the distorted principle, "To each according to his false needs"—needs determined and produced by the economic system that the very act of looting rejects. But since the vaunting of abundance is taken at its face value and immediately *seized upon* instead of being eternally pursued in the rat race of alienated labor and increasing but unmet social needs, real desires begin to be expressed in festival, in playful self-assertion, in the *potlatch* of destruction. People who destroy commodities show their human superiority over commodities. They stop submitting to the arbitrary forms that distortedly reflect their real needs. The flames of Watts *consummated* the system of consumption. The theft of large refrigerators by people with no electricity, or with their electricity cut off, is the best image of the lie of affluence transformed into a truth *in play*. Once it is no longer bought, the commodity lies open to criticism and alteration, whatever particular form it may take. Only when it is paid for with money is it respected as an admirable fetish, as a status symbol.

Looting is the *natural* response to the society of abundance—the society not of natural and human abundance, but of abundance of commodities. Looting, which instantly destroys the commodity as such, also discloses what the commodity ultimately implies: the army, the police and the other specialized detachments of the state's monopoly of armed violence. What is a policeman? He is the active servant of the commodity, the man in complete submission to the commodity, whose job it is to ensure that a given product of human labor remains a commodity with the magical property of having to be paid for instead of becoming a mere refrigerator or rifle—a mute, passive, insensible thing in submission to the first comer to make use of it. Over and above the indignity of depending on policemen, the blacks reject the indignity of depending on commodities. The Watts youth, having no future in market terms, grasped another *quality* of the present, and the truth of that present was so irresistible that it drew in the whole population—women, children, and even sociologists who happened to be on the scene. A young black sociologist of the district, Bobbi Hollon, had this to say to the *Herald Tribune* in October: "Before, people were ashamed to say they came from Watts. They'd mumble it. Now they say it with pride. Boys who used to go around with their shirts open to the waist, and who'd have cut you into strips in half a second, showed up here every morning at seven o'clock. They organized the distribution of food. Of course it's no use pretending the food wasn't looted. . . . All that Christian blah has been used too long against the blacks. These people could loot for ten years and they wouldn't get back half the money that these stores have stolen from them all these years. . . . Me, I'm just a little black girl." Bobbi Hollon, who has sworn never to wash from her sandals the blood that splashed on them during the rioting, adds, "The whole world is watching Watts now."

How do people make history under conditions preestablished to dissuade them from intervening in it? The Los Angeles blacks are better paid than any others in the United States, but they are also the most *separated* from that high point of flaunted affluence, California. Hollywood, the pole of the global spectacle, is in their immediate vicinity. They are promised that, with patience, they will join in America's prosperity, but they see that this prosperity is not a static sphere but rather a ladder without end. The higher they climb, the further they get from the top, because they start with a disadvantage, because they are less qualified and thus more numerous among the unemployed, and finally because the hierarchy that crushes them is not one based simply on buying power as a pure economic fact: an essential inferiority is imposed on them in every area of daily life by the customs and prejudices of a society in which all human power is based on buying power. Just as the human riches of the American blacks are hated and treated as criminal, monetary riches will never make them acceptable in America's alienated society: individual wealth will only make a *rich nigger* because blacks as a whole must *represent poverty* in a society of hierarchized wealth. Every witness noted this cry which proclaimed the fundamental meaning of the rising: "This is the black revolution and we want the world to know it!" *Freedom now* is the password of all the revolutions of history, but now for the first time it is not poverty but material abundance which must be dominated according to new laws. Dominating abundance is not just changing the way it is shared out, but *redefining its every orientation*, superficial and profound alike. This is the first step of an immense struggle, infinite in its implications.

The blacks are not isolated in their struggle, because a *new proletarian consciousness* (the consciousness of not being the master of one's own activity, of one's own life, in the slightest degree) is taking shape in America among strata which in their rejection of modern capitalism resemble the blacks. It was, in fact, precisely the first phase of the black struggle which was the signal for a more general movement of contestation that is still spreading. In December 1964 the students of Berkeley, harassed for their participation in the Civil Rights movement, initiated a strike calling in question the functioning of California's "multiversity" and consequently the entire American social system in which they are allotted such a passive role. Drinking, drug orgies and dissolute sexual mores were immediately discovered among the students—the same activities for which the blacks have long been reproached. This generation of students has since invented a new form of struggle against the dominant spectacle, the *teach-in*, a form taken up 20 October in Great Britain at the University of Edinburgh apropos of the Rhodesian crisis. This obviously imperfect and primitive form represents the *stage of the discussion of problems* that refuses to be (academically) limited in time; it strives rather to pursue the issues to their ultimate consequences and thus leads to practical activity. Also in October, tens of thousands of anti–Vietnam war demonstrators appeared in the streets of Berkeley and New York, their cries echoing those of the Watts rioters: "Get out of our district and out of Vietnam!" Many of the whites who are becoming more radical have finally gone outside the law: "courses" are given on how to defraud draft recruiting boards (*Le Monde*, 19 October 1965) and draft cards are burned in front of television cameras. In the affluent society disgust is being expressed for this affluence and *for its price*. The spectacle is being spat on by an advanced sector whose autonomous activity denies its values. The classical proletariat, to the very extent to which it had been provisionally integrated into the capitalist system, had itself failed to integrate the blacks (several Los Angeles unions refused blacks until 1959); now the blacks are the rallying point for all those who refuse the logic of this integration into capitalism, which is the ultimate limit of all the integration promised. Comfort will never be comfortable enough for those who seek what is not on the market, what in fact the market specifically eliminates. The level reached by the technology of the most privileged becomes an insult, and one more easily grasped and resented than is that most fundamental insult: reification. The Los Angeles rebellion is the first in history to justify itself with the argument that there was no air conditioning during a heat wave.

The American blacks have their own particular spectacle, their own black newspapers, magazines and stars, and if they realize this, if they vomit up this spectacle for its delusiveness, as an expression of their humiliation, it is because they see it to be a *minority* spectacle, a mere appendage of a general spectacle. They recognize that this spectacle of their consumption-to-be-desired is a colony of the white one, and thus they see through the lie of the whole economico-cultural spectacle more quickly. By wanting to participate really and immediately in affluence, which is the official value of every American, they demand the egalitarian *realization* of the American spectacle of everyday life: they demand that the half-heavenly, half-terrestrial values of this spectacle be put to the test. But it is in the nature of the spectacle that it cannot be realized either immediately or equally, *not even for the whites*. (In fact, the blacks serve the function of a perfect spectacular prod: the threat of such underprivilege spurs on the rat race.) In taking the capitalist spectacle at its face value, the blacks are already rejecting the spectacle itself. The spectacle is a drug for slaves. It is supposed not to be taken literally, but to be followed at just a few paces' distance; when this distance is abolished, the mystification becomes evident. In the United States today the whites are enslaved to the commodity while the blacks are negating it. The blacks are asking for *more than the whites*—that is the core of an insolvable problem, or rather one solvable only through the dissolution of the white social system. This is why those whites who want to escape their own servitude must first of all rally to the black revolt, not, obviously, in a solidarity based on color, but in a global rejection of the commodity and, in the final analysis, of the state. The economic and psychological distance between the blacks and the whites enables the blacks to see the white consumer for what he is, and their justified contempt for the white is in reality a contempt for any passive consumer. The whites who reject this role have no chance unless they link their struggle more and more to the struggle of the blacks, uncovering their real and coherent reasons and supporting them all the way. If such a confluence were to split apart in face of the radicalization of the struggle, the result would be the formation of a black nationalism and a confrontation between the two sides along the most traditional lines. A phase of mutual slaughter is the other possible outcome of the present situation, once resignation is no longer possible.

The attempts to build a separatist or pro-African black nationalism are dreams giving no answer to the real oppression. The American blacks have no fatherland. They are in *their own country* and they are *alienated*; so are the rest of the population, but the blacks are aware of it. In this sense they are not the most backward sector of American society, but the most advanced. They are the negation at work, "the bad aspect producing the movement that makes history by setting the struggle in motion" (*The Poverty of Philosophy*). Africa has no special monopoly on that.

The American blacks are a product of modern industry, just as are electronics, advertising or the cyclotron. And they embody its contradictions. They are the people that the spectacular paradise must simultaneously integrate and repel, with the result that the antagonism between the spectacle and human activity is totally revealed through them. The spectacle is *universal* the same way the commodity is. But since the world of the commodity is based on class conflict, the commodity is itself hierarchical. The necessity for the commodity—and hence for the spectacle, whose role is to *inform* the commodity world— to be at once universal and hierarchical leads to a universal hierarchization. But because this hierarchization must remain *unavowed*, it is expressed in the form of unavowable, because *irrational*, hierarchical value judgments in a world of *irrational rationalization*. It is this hierarchization that creates *racisms* everywhere: The English Labour government has resorted to restricting nonwhite immigration, while the industrially advanced countries of Europe are once again becoming racist as they import their subproletariat from the Mediterranean area, thus exerting a colonial exploitation within their own borders. And if Russia continues to be antisemitic, it is because it continues to be a hierarchical society in which labor must be bought and sold as a commodity. The commodity is constantly engendering new and extended forms of hierarchy, whether between the labor leader and the worker or between two car-owners with artificially distinguished models. This is the original flaw in commodity rationality, the sickness of bourgeois reason, a sickness inherited by the bureaucracy. But the repulsive absurdity of certain hierarchies, and the fact that the entire world of the commodity is directed blindly and automatically toward their protection, leads people to see—the moment they engage in a negating practice—that every hierarchy is absurd.

The rational world produced by the industrial revolution has rationally liberated individuals from their local and national limitations and linked them on a global scale; but it irrationally separates them once again, in accordance with a hidden logic that finds its expression in insane ideas and grotesque value systems. Estranged from his world, man is everywhere surrounded by strangers. The barbarian is no longer at the ends of the earth, he is *here*, made into a barbarian by his forced participation in the common hierarchical consumption. The humanism that cloaks all this is the contrary of man, the negation of his activity and his desires; it is the humanism of the commodity, the benevolence of the parasitical commodity toward the people off whom it feeds. For those who reduce people to objects, objects seem to acquire human qualities and really human manifestations appear as unconscious *animal behavior*. Thus the chief humanist of Los Angeles, William Parker, could say, "They started acting like a bunch of monkeys in a zoo."

When the "state of insurrection" was declared by the California authorities, the insurance companies recalled that they do not cover risks at that level: they guarantee nothing beyond survival. The American blacks as a whole can rest assured that if they keep quiet their *survival* is guaranteed; capitalism has become sufficiently concentrated and entrenched in the state to distribute "welfare" to the poorest. But by the simple fact that they lag *behind* in the advance of socially organized survival, the blacks pose the problems of *life*; what they demand is not to survive but to live. The blacks have nothing of their own to insure; they have to destroy all forms of private security and insurance known up to now. They appear as what they really are: the irreconcilable enemies not of the vast majority of Americans, but of the alienated way of life of the entire modern society; the most industrially advanced country only shows us the road that will be followed everywhere unless the system is overthrown.

Certain black nationalist extremists, to show why they cannot accept less than a separate state, have argued that even if American society someday concedes total civic and economic equality, it will never, on the personal level, come around to accepting interracial marriages. *It is therefore this American society which must disappear*, in America and everywhere in the world. The end of all racial prejudice, like the end of so many other prejudices related to sexual inhibitions, can only lie beyond "marriage" itself, beyond the *bourgeois family* (which has virtually collapsed among the American blacks)—the bourgeois family that prevails as much in Russia as in the United States, as a model of hierarchical relations and as the form for a stable *inheritance of power* (money or social-bureaucratic status). It is now often said that American youth, after thirty years of silence, are rising again as a force of contestation, and that the black revolt is their Spanish Civil War. This time, its "Lincoln Brigades" must understand the full significance of the struggle in which they engage and totally support it in its universal aspects. The Watts "excesses" are no more a political error in the black revolt than the armed resistance of the POUM in Barcelona in May 1937 was a betrayal of the anti-Francoist war. A rebellion against the spectacle is situated on the level of the *totality* because—even if it were only to appear in the single district of Watts—it is a protest of people against inhuman life; because it begins at the level of the *real single individual* and because community, from which the rebelling individual is separated, is the *true social nature* of man, human nature: the positive supersession of the spectacle.

December 1965

(first published in English)

THE CLASS STRUGGLES IN ALGERIA

One could almost think that the new Algerian regime has devoted itself exclusively to confirming the brief analysis that the SI made of it in the *Address to Revolutionaries* that we issued in Algiers soon after its inaugural putsch. Liquidating self-management is the entire content of Boumedienne's regime, its sole real activity; and that project began the very moment when the state, through the deployment of the military force which was the only crystalization it achieved under Ben Bella, its only solid structure, *declared its independence* vis-à-vis Algerian society. The state's other projects—the technocratic reorganization of the economy, the social and juridical extension of its power base—are beyond the capacities of the present ruling class in the real conditions of the country. The mass of undecided, who had not been enemies of Ben Bella but who were disappointed by him and who waited to judge the new regime by its actions, can see that it is ultimately doing nothing but establishing an autonomous state dictatorship and thereby declaring war on self-management. Even to formulate specific accusations against Ben Bella or to destroy him publicly seems to be beyond its power for a long time to come. The only vestige of "socialism" professed in Algeria is precisely that core of *inverted socialism*, that product of the general reaction within the workers movement itself which the defeat of the Russian revolution bequeathed as a positive model to the rest of the world, including Ben Bella's Algeria: the *big lie of the police state*. Thus the political enemy is not condemned for his real positions, but for the opposite of what he was; or else he suddenly fades into an organized silence: he never existed, either for the tribunal or for the historian. Thus Boumedienne, from the beginning one of those most responsible for the fact that Algerian self-management is only a caricature of what it needs to be, officially calls it "a caricature" in order to reorganize it authoritarianly. In the name of an essence of self-management ideologically backed by the state, Boumedienne rejects self-management's real, fledgling manifestations.

The same inversion of reality determines the Boumediennist critique of the past. What Ben Bella is reproached for having done and for having gone too far in is precisely what he did not do and what he scarcely pretended to strive for—the liberation of women or real support for the emancipation struggles in Africa, for example. The present regime lies about the past because of its own profound unity with the past. The ruling class has not changed in Algeria, it is reinforcing itself. It reproaches Ben Bella for having done poorly what he had in fact only *simulated*; for a revolutionariness that it has now ceased even simulating. The Algerian ruling class, before 19 June as well as after, is a bureaucracy in formation. It is pursuing its consolidation by partially changing the way its political power is shared out. Certain strata of this bureaucracy (military and technocratic) predominate over others (political and unionist). The basic conditions remain the weakness of the national bourgeoisie and the pressure from the poverty-stricken peasant and worker masses, a part of which took over the self-managed sector when the former (European) ruling class fled the country. The merging of the Algerian bourgeoisie with the bureaucracy in possession of the state is easier with the new ruling strata that Boumedienne represents; moreover, this evolution harmonizes better with the region of the global capitalist market to which Algeria is linked. In addition, the bureaucratic strata that ruled with Ben Bella were less capable of an open struggle against the demands of the masses. Ben Bella and the unstable social *equilibrium*, which was the temporary result of the struggle against France and the colonists, were overthrown at the same time. When they saw themselves supplanted, the previously predominant bureaucratic strata (the leaders of the FLN Federation of Greater Algiers and the General Union of Algerian Workers) hesitated, then rallied to the new regime because their solidarity with the state bureaucracy as a whole was naturally stronger than their ties to the mass of workers. The agricultural workers' union, whose congress six months before had adopted the most radical theses on self-management, was the first to come over.

Among the bureaucratic forces in the lobbies of power around Ben Bella, two groupings, enemies yet related to each other, had a special status: the Algerian Communist Party and the foreign leftists—nicknamed "*pieds-rouges*"—who placed themselves at the service of the Algerian state. They were not so much in power as pretenders to power. Poor relative of power, waiting to inherit it, this extreme-left of the bureaucracy acquired its credentials as representative of the masses *through its connection with Ben Bella*: it drew its mandate not from the masses but from Ben Bella. It dreamed of one day getting a monopoly on this power over the masses, this power that Ben Bella still shared on all sides. Since Ben Bella was personally its only access to present power and its main promise for the future, its only guarantee of being tolerated (its Sukarno), the bureaucratic extreme-left demonstrated in his defense, but in an uncertain manner. Just as it respectfully flocked around the state, it placed itself on the terrain of the state to oppose the unfavorable shift of the relation of forces within the state. Here again the Boumediennist critique of these elements, lumped together as "foreigners," in the name of a specifically Algerian socialism, is entirely false. Far from "making theory for theory's sake"

(*El Moudjahid*, 22 September 1965), the *pieds-rouges* represented an exhausted mixture of complete theoretical nullity and of unconscious or consciously hidden counterrevolutionary tendencies. Far from wanting to make adventurous utopian "experiments" in Algeria, they possessed nothing but mistakes or lies that had been *revealed as such a thousand times*. The best revolutionary ideas of the *pieds-rouges* were unsuitable not because they came from *too far away*, but because they were repeated much *too late*. It was a question not of geography, but of history.

More radical and more isolated, at the extreme left of the Ben Bella regime, Mohammed Harbi was the thinker of self-management, but only by grace of the prince, in the bureaus of power. Harbi rose to the highest point reached by Algerian revolutionary thought: up to the *idea* of self-management, but not at all up to its consistent, effective practice. He understood its notion, but not yet its being. Harbi was, paradoxically, the *governmental* theorist of self-management, or rather its court poet: soaring above practice, he eulogized self-management more than he theorized it. The *self-management state*, that logical monstrosity, had in Harbi its guilty conscience and its celebrator. Boumedienne's tanks in the streets meant a rationalization of the state, which wanted henceforth to free itself from the ridiculous paradoxes of the Ben-Bellaist equilibrium and from any guilty conscience, and simply *be a state*. It then became clear that Harbi, the unarmed prophet of self-management, had not considered self-management's *self-defense*, its defense on its own terrain, but only its defense through the *mediation* of Ben Bella. But if Harbi counted on Ben Bella alone to defend self-management, who did he count on to defend Ben Bella? The thinker of self-management was protected by Ben Bella, but who was going to protect his protector? He believed that Ben Bella, the incarnation of the state, would remain universally accepted in Algeria, although Harbi himself only accepted his "good side" (his formal recognition of self-management). But the real process advanced by way of his bad side: the forces that followed the opposite line of argument on Ben Bella were more capable of intervention. Ben Bella was not the resolution of the Algerian contradictions, he was only their temporary cover. History has shown that Harbi and all those who thought like him were mistaken. They will now have to radicalize their conceptions if they want to effectively fight the Boumediennist dictatorship and *realize* self-management.

The fall of Ben Bella is a landmark in the collapse of global illusions regarding the "underdeveloped" version of pseudosocialism. Castro remains its last star, but he, who could justifiably argue that elections were pointless because the people were armed, is already demanding that all arms be turned in, and his police are rounding them up (*Reuters*, 14 August 1965). Already his lieutenant, Guevara, has left without any explanation being given to the masses from whom these leaders had demanded a blind personal confidence. At the same time, the Algerians who are experiencing the fragility of Ben-Bellaist socialism are also discovering the value of all the so-called socialist camp's concern for their cause: the Chinese, Russian and Cuban *states*, along with Nasser, are naturally rushing to outdo each other in expressions of friendship to Boumedienne's regime. Revolutions in the underdeveloped countries will always fail miserably as long as they recognize and emulate any existing model of socialist power, since they are *all* manifestly false ones. The disintegrated official Sino-Soviet version of this socialism and the "underdeveloped" version of it admire and reinforce each other and both lead to the same outcome. The first underdevelopment we have to get beyond is the *underdevelopment of revolutionary theory* everywhere in the world.

The internal struggles of the Algerian bureaucracy, during the war and in the 1962–1965 period, took the form of clan struggles, personal rivalries, inexplicable disputes among the leaders, obscure shifts of alliances. This was a direct continuation of the conditions prevailing around Messali Hadj since before the insurrection. Not only was all theory absent, even ideology was summarily improvised and confused; everything remained centered around superficial, abstract political questions. Since 19 June another period has begun: that of the confrontation between the ruling class and the workers, and this is the real movement that creates the conditions and need for a theory. As early as 9 July, at a meeting of delegates from 2500 self-managed enterprises held at Algiers and chaired by Minister of Industry Boumaza, the delegates expressed to the latter their insistence on self-management as an inviolable principle and made a series of critiques concerning the state's role in limiting this principle. The delegates "questioned the multiplicity of overseers (prefectures, ministries, party) and denounced the state's nonpayment of debts and the heavy taxation; some delegates also brought up the problem of layoffs, the 'draconian' demands of the foreign suppliers and the paralyzing role of the customs" (*Le Monde*, 10 July 1965).

Those delegates knew what they were talking about. Since the June 19th Declaration—in which the word "self-management" is not even mentioned once—the regime has been preparing the "stabilization" of the economic situation through the strengthening of state control and the accelerated training of "cadres." It aimed to start collecting installment payments as soon as possible for the more than 100,000 lodgings occupied without permission; to recover the money "stolen from the state" in the self-managed enterprises; to reduce the wearing out of poorly maintained equipment; and to regularize all the illegal seizures carried out by the masses upon the departure of the French. Since then, in spite of the fact that self-management is the very form through which the paralyzing respect for property (private or state), which has been such an obstacle in the workers movement, can be overcome, the workers in the self-managed sector, awaiting their several months overdue wages, are continually reproached for having stolen a large part of what they have produced. The most urgent goal of the Algerian state, which already has enough soldiers and police, is to train 20,000 accountants a year.

The central struggle, veiled and open, immediately broke out between the ruling class representatives and the workers precisely over the issue of self-management. The "reassuring" declarations of Boumaza and Boumedienne didn't fool anyone. The "labor unrest" alluded to by *Le Monde* on 3 October is a euphemism for the resistance of the sole bastion of socialist revolution in Algeria—the self-managed sector—against the most recent maneuvers of the ruling bureaucratic-bourgeois coalition. The union leaders themselves could not remain silent: their official status as representatives of the workers vis-à-vis the state and their social status as left wing of the ruling class were at stake. The September articles in *Révolution et Travail*—in which real workers' demands ("when workers are reduced to poverty, self-management is violated") are mixed with expressions of the increasing alarm of the union leaders ("agreement with the June 19th Declaration's analyses," but denunciation of the technocrats and economists)—exactly reflect this situation of overlapping vertical and horizontal struggles. The increasing reference to "economic anarchy" (which always really means self-management), the judicial measures against the self-managed sector (e.g. forcing the self-managed enterprises to pay back-taxes), which the newspapers talk about less, and the restitution of the Norcolor factory to its former owner—all this shows these "labor" leaders that soon they will no longer have a place in the ruling apparatus. Already the new pretenders are there: the "scramble for power of dubious elements" that outrages *Révolution et Travail* expresses the ruling class's swing to the right. The techno-bureaucrats and the military have no possible allies but the representatives of the old traditional bourgeoisie. At the same time that the officers, in the style of South American armies, are attaining bourgeois status (everyone knows about their BMWs, duty-free and 30% discounted), a multitude of Algerian bourgeois, following in the footsteps of the Norcolor owner, are returning to the country in the expectation of recovering their property, seized "in completely illegal conditions by unscrupulous persons" (Boumaza). Added to these challenges is the rapid increase in food prices. The workers, thoroughly aware of this process, are resisting *on the spot*: the repeated strikes in the Renault factories, the strikes of the press and parcel distributors and of the telephone and insurance workers, the demonstrations of the unpaid workers of Mitidja—these are the first steps of a movement of rage which, if it asserts itself effectively, is capable of sweeping aside the whole present regime.

Incapable of mastering a single one of their problems, the rulers react with constant delirious conferences, constant torture in their prisons, and denunciations of the "slackening of morals." *El Moudjahid* (7 December 1965) attacks "the erotic sentimentalism of a young generation without political commitment" and the accurate viewpoint of those who "are tempted to reject religion as being a restraint on their taste for pleasure and on their liberation, which they take simply to mean their possibilities for pleasure, and who consider the contributions of Arab civilization as a step backward." The tone is no different from that used by the rulers in Washington or Moscow when they regretfully announce their lack of confidence in their young people. And after a few months the new regime is emulating Ben Bella in the most ludicrous manifestation of its Mohammedanism: the prohibition of alcohol.

The present opposition to the Boumediennist dictatorship is twofold: On one side, the workers are defending themselves in the enterprises (self-managed or not); they are the real contestation implied in the facts. On another side, the leftists of the FLN apparatus are trying to re-form a revolutionary apparatus. The first effort of the Organisation de la Résistance Populaire, led by Zahouane and supported by the French Stalinists, was a hollow declaration that only appeared six weeks after the coup, which analyzed neither the present regime nor the means to oppose it. Its second appeal was addressed to the Algerian police, from whom it anticipated revolutionary support. This strategy proved to be somewhat of a miscalculation since by the end of September this police had arrested Zahouane and broken up his first clandestine network (Harbi himself had already been arrested in August). The ORP is continuing its activity, beginning to collect contributions "for Ben Bella" from Algerian workers in France and winning over the majority of the student leaders. This apparatus (underground or in exile) is counting on an economico-political crisis in Algeria in the near future to reestablish its influence with the struggling Algerian workers. In this Leninist perspective it will present itself, with or without the banner of Ben Bella, as the solution for a replacement of the Boumediennist regime.

What is nevertheless going to prevent the establishment of a Bolshevik-type apparatus, striven for by so many militants? The time passed since Lenin and his failure, and the continued and evident degradation of Leninism, which is directly expressed by these leftists' allying with and fighting each other in every sort of variant: Khrushchevo-Brezhnevists, Maoists, sub-Togliattists, pure and semi-Stalinists, all the variants of Trotskyism, etc. All of them refuse, and are forced to refuse, to clearly confront the essential problem of the nature of the "socialism" (i.e. of the class power) in Russia and China, and consequently also in Algeria. Their major weakness during the struggle for power is also the major guarantee of their counterrevolutionary role if they were to accede to power. These leftists will present themselves as a natural continuation of the personalized political confusion of the preceding period; but the real class struggle in Algeria has now brought that period to a close. Their doubts about Ben Bella overlapped with their doubts on the world (and on socialism) and will continue after Ben Bella. They don't say all they know and they don't know all they say. Their social base *and their social perspective* is that bureaucratic sector which came out worst in the reshuffling of power and which wants to get back its old position. Seeing that they can no longer hope to dominate the regime, they turn toward the people in order to dominate its opposition. Nostalgic bureaucrats or would-be bureaucrats, they want to counterpose "the people" to Boumedienne, whereas Boumedienne has already revealed to the masses the real focus of opposition: state bureaucrat versus worker. But the most despicable aspect of their bolshevism is this glaring difference: the Bolshevik Party did not know the sort of bureaucratic power it was going to end up establishing, whereas these leftists have already been able to see, in the world and among themselves, that bureaucratic power which they wish to *restore* in a more or less purified form. The masses, if they have the chance to choose, will not choose this corrected version of a bureaucracy whose essential elements they have already had the opportunity of experiencing. The Algerian intellectuals who don't rally to the regime still have the choice between participating in this apparatus or seeking a direct link-up with the autonomous movement of the masses. But the whole weight of the Algerian petty bourgeoisie (storekeepers, lower functionaries, etc.) will naturally tend to support the new technocratico-military bureaucracy rather than the bureaucratic leftists.

The only road to socialism, in Algeria as everywhere else, passes through "an offensive and defensive pact with the truth," as a Hungarian intellectual put it in 1956. People in Algeria who got the SI's *Address* understood it. Wherever practical revolutionary conditions exist, no theory is too difficult. Villiers de l'Isle-Adam, a witness to the Paris Commune, noted, "For the first time one can hear the workers exchanging their opinions on problems that until now have been considered only by philosophers." The realization of philosophy, the critique and reconstruction of all the values and behavior imposed by alienated life—this is the maximum program of *generalized self-management*. The leftist militants of the bureaucratic groups, however, tell us that these theses are correct but that the time has not yet come when one can tell the masses everything. Those who argue in such a perspective never see this time as having come, and in fact they contribute toward making sure that it never does come. It is necessary to tell the masses *what they are already doing*. The specialized thinkers of revolution are the specialists of its false consciousness, who afterwards come to realize that they have done something entirely different from what they thought they were doing. This problem is aggravated here by the particular difficulties of underdeveloped countries and by the persistent theoretical weakness in the Algerian movement. Although the strictly bureaucratic fringe within the present opposition is extremely small, its very existence as a "professional leadership" is a *form* that by its weight imposes itself and determines the content of that opposition. Political alienation is always related to the state. Self-management can expect nothing from *revived bolsheviks*.

Self-management must be both the means and the end of the present struggle. It is not only what is at stake in the struggle, but also its adequate form. It is its own tool. It is itself the material it works on, and its own presupposition. It must totally recognize its own truth. The state power proposes the contradictory and absurd project of "reorganizing self-management"; it is in fact self-management that must *organize itself as a power* or disappear.

Self-management is the most modern and most important tendency to appear in the struggle of the Algerian movement, and it is also the one that is the least narrowly Algerian. Its meaning is universal. In contrast to the *Yugoslavian caricature* that Boumedienne wants to emulate, which is only a semidecentralized instrument of state control ("We have to decentralize in order better to control the self-managed enterprises," Boumedienne openly admits in *Le Monde*, 10 November 1965), a subordinate level of central administration; and in contrast to the Proudhonian mutualism of 1848, which aimed at organizing on the margins of private property, real self-management, revolutionary self-management, can be won only through the armed abolition of the titles of existing property. Its failure in Turin in 1920 was the prelude to the armed domination of Fascism. The bases of a self-managed production in Algeria were spontaneously formed—as in Spain in 1936, as in Paris in 1871 in the workshops abandoned by the Versaillese—wherever the owners had to flee following their political defeat: on *vacant property*. These takeovers are the vacation from property and oppression, the weekend of alienated life.

This self-management, by the simple fact that it exists, threatens the society's entire hierarchical organization. It must destroy all external control because all the external forces of control will never make peace with it as a living reality, but at most only with its name, with its embalmed corpse. Wherever there is self-management, there can be neither army nor police not state.

Generalized self-management, "extended to all production and all aspects of social life," would mean the end of the unemployment that affects two million Algerians, but it would also mean the end of the old society in all its aspects, the abolition of all its spiritual and material enslavements and the abolition of its masters. The present fledgling effort toward self-management can be controlled from above only because it consents to exclude below it that majority of the workers who don't participate in it or who are unemployed; and because even within its own enterprises it tolerates the formation of dominating strata of "directors" or management professionals who have worked their way up from the base or been appointed by the state. These managers are the state virus within that which tends to negate the state; they are a compromise. But the time for compromise is past, both for the state power and for the real power of the Algerian workers.

Radical self-management, the only kind that can endure and conquer, refuses any hierarchy within or outside itself; it also rejects in practice *any hierarchical separation of women* (an oppressive separation openly accepted by Proudhon's theory as well as by the backward reality of Islamic Algeria). The management committees, as well as all the delegates in the federations of self-managed enterprises, should be revocable at any moment by their base, this base obviously including all the workers, without any distinctions between permanent and seasonal ones.

The only program for the Algerian socialist elements consists in the defense of the self-managed sector, not only as it is but as it must become. This defense must therefore counter the purge carried out by the state with another purge within self-management: a purge carried out by its base against all that negates it from within. A revolutionary assault against the existing regime is only possible with a continued and radicalized self-management as its point of departure. By putting forward the program of quantitatively and qualitatively increased workers' self-management, one is calling on all the workers to directly take on the cause of self-management as their own cause. By demanding not only the defense but also the extension of self-management, *the dissolution of all specialized activity not answerable to self-management*, Algerian revolutionaries can show that this defense is the concern not only of the workers of the *temporarily self-managed* sector, but of all the workers, as the only way toward a definitive liberation. In this way they would show that they were struggling for a general liberation and not for their own future domination as specialists of revolution; that the victory of "their party" must at the same time be its end as a separate party.

As a first step, it is necessary to envisage linking up self-management delegates with each other and with the enterprise committees that are working toward self-management in the private and state sectors; to transmit and publish all information on the workers' struggles and the autonomous forms of organization that emerge out of them, and to extend and generalize these forms as the sole path for a profound contestation. At the same time, through the same clandestine relations and publications, it is necessary to develop the theory of self-management and its requirements, within the self-managed sector itself and before the masses of Algeria and the world. Self-management must become the sole solution to the mysteries of power in Algeria, and it must *know that it is that solution*.

Algiers, December 1965
(circulated clandestinely)

SOME THEORETICAL QUESTIONS TO BE TREATED WITHOUT ACADEMIC DEBATE OR SPECULATION

What can be dealt with by radical theory must be prevented from being dealt with by speculation. As the situationist analysis of reality prepares the practical realization of our project, this demand tends to have more far-reaching significance.

Knowledge is inseparable from the use that is made of it. The agitation that our irrefutable theories are beginning to foment in varying degrees in *all* the sectors of the old world is going to see to the improvement and correction of our good use of ideas and things: this is why, in the society of guaranteed abundance, we are the only ones who are not frightened by that abundance.

How to use theory is never problematical. The specialists of impotent speculation—from *Socialisme ou Barbarie* to *Planète*—are only concerned with concealing who profits from their ideology of confusion. The situationists work in the inverse perspective. They pose only the questions to which the will to subversion of the greatest number can respond. It is a matter of giving this will its maximum effectiveness.

The points to consider listed briefly below will have the interest of shedding light on the revolutionary worth of whoever deals with them, and on the importance that must be accorded to these points in the present struggle.

168

Critique of political economy — Critique of the social sciences — Critique of psychoanalysis (in particular: Freud, Reich, Marcuse) — Dialectics of decomposition and supersession in the realization of art and philosophy — Semiology, contribution to the study of an ideological system — Nature and the ideologies of nature — The role of playfulness in history — History of theories and theories of history — Nietzsche and the end of philosophy — Kierkegaard and the end of theology — Marx and Sade — The structuralists.

The romantic crisis — Preciosity — The baroque — Artistic languages — Art and everyday creativity — Critique of dadaism — Critique of surrealism — Society and pictorial perspective — Self-parodying art — Mallarmé, Joyce and Malevich — Lautréamont — Primitive arts — On poetry.

The Mexican revolution (Villa and Zapata) — The Spanish revolution — Asturias 1934 — The Vienna insurrection — The Peasant War (1525) — The Spartakist revolution — The Congolese revolution — The Jacqueries — Unknown revolutions — The English revolution — The communalist movements — The Enragés — The Fronde — Revolutionary songs (study and anthology) — Kronstadt — Bolshevism and Trotskyism — The Church and the heresies — The different currents of socialism — Socialism and underdevelopment — Cybernetics and power — The state — The origins of Islam — Theses on anarchy — Theses toward a final solution of the Christian problem — The world of the specialists — On democracy — The Internationals — On insurrection — Problems and theory of self-management — Parties and unions — On the organization of revolutionary movements — Critique of civil and penal law — Nonindustrialized societies — Theses on utopianism — Homage to Charles Fourier — Workers councils — Fascism and magical thought.

On the repetitive in everyday life — Dreams and dreamlike ambiances — Treatise on the passions — The moments and the construction of situations — Urbanism and popular construction — Manual of subversive detournement — Individual adventure and collective adventure — Intersubjectivity and coherence in revolutionary groups — Play and everyday life — Personal fantasies — On the freedom to love — Preliminary studies toward the construction of a base — Madness and entranced states of mind.

RAOUL VANEIGEM

CAPTIVE WORDS
Preface to a Situationist Dictionary

Banalities, due to what they conceal, work for the dominant organization of life. One such banality is the statement that language is not dialectical, thereby implying that all use of dialectics should be rejected. But in fact nothing is more clearly subject to dialectics than language, since it is a living reality. Thus, every critique of the old world has been made in the language of that world, yet directed against it and therefore automatically in a *different* language. Every revolutionary theory has had to invent its own terms, to destroy the dominant sense of other terms and establish new meanings in the "world of meanings" corresponding to the new embryonic reality needing to be liberated from the dominant trash heap. The same reasons that prevent our adversaries (the masters of the Dictionary) from definitively fixing language, today enable us to assert other positions which negate existing meanings. But we already know that these same reasons also prevent us from claiming any definitively legislated certitudes: a definition is always open, never definitive—ours have a historical value, they are applicable in a given period, linked to a specific historical practice.

It is impossible to get rid of a world without getting rid of the language that conceals and protects it, without laying bare its true nature. As power is the permanent lie and the "social truth," language is its permanent guarantee and the Dictionary its universal reference. Every revolutionary praxis has felt the need for a new semantic field and for expressing a new truth; from the Encyclopédistes to the Polish intellectuals' critique of Stalinist "wooden language" in 1956, this demand has continually been asserted. Because *language is the house of power*, the refuge of its police violence. Any dialogue with power is violence, suffered or provoked. When power is husbanding the use of its arms, it entrusts the guarding of the oppressive order to language. Their collaboration is in fact the most natural expression of all power.

From words to ideas is only a step, a step always taken by power and its theorists. All theories of language, from the simple-minded mysticism of Being to the supreme (oppressive) rationality of the cybernetic machine, belong to the same world: the discourse of power considered as the sole possible frame of reference, as the universal mediation. Just as the Christian God is the necessary mediation between two souls and between the soul and the self, the discourse of power establishes itself at the heart of all communication, becoming the necessary mediation between self and self. It is thus able to lay its hands on contestation, diverting it onto its own terrain, infiltrating it and controlling it from within. The critique of the dominant language, the *detournement* of it, is going to become a permanent practice of the new revolutionary theory.

Since any new interpretation is labeled *misinterpretation* by the *authorities*, the situationists are going to establish the legitimacy of misinterpretation and denounce the imposture of the interpretation given and authorized by power. Since the dictionary is the guardian of *existing* meaning, we propose to destroy it systematically. The *replacement* of the dictionary, that master reference of all inherited and tamed language, will find its adequate expression in the revolutionary infiltration of language, in that *detournement* extensively used by Marx, systematized by Lautréamont and now being put within everyone's reach by the SI.

Detournement, which Lautréamont called plagiarism, confirms the thesis, long demonstrated by modern art, of the insubordination of words, of the impossibility for power to *totally recuperate* created meanings, to fix an existing meaning once and for all; in a word, the objective impossibility of a "Newspeak." The new revolutionary theory cannot advance without redefining its fundamental concepts. "Ideas improve," says Lautréamont. "The meaning of words participates in the improvement. Plagiarism is necessary. Progress implies it. It sticks close to an author's phrase, uses his expressions, deletes a false idea, replaces it with the right one." To salvage Marx's thought it is necessary continually to make it more precise, to correct it, to reformulate it in the light of a hundred years of reinforcement of alienation and the possibilities of negating it. Marx needs to be detourned by those who are continuing on this historical path, not idiotically quoted by the thousand varieties of recuperators. On the other hand, power's own thought is becoming in our hands a weapon against power. Since its advent, the triumphant bourgeoisie has dreamed of a universal language, which the cyberneticians of today are trying to realize electronically. Descartes dreamed of a language (a forerunner of Newspeak) in which thought would follow thought with mathematical rigor: the *mathesis universalis* or perpetuity of bourgeois categories. The Encyclopédistes, dreaming (under feudal power) of "definitions so rigorous that tyranny could not tolerate them," paved the way for an eternal future power that would be the ultimate goal of history.

The insubordination of words, during the experimental phase from Rimbaud to the surrealists, has shown that the theoretical critique of the world of power is inseparable from a practice that destroys it; power's recuperation of all modern art and its transformation of it into oppressive categories of its reigning spectacle is a sad confirmation of this. "Whatever doesn't kill power is killed by it." The dadaists were the first to express their distrust in words, a distrust inseparable from the desire to "change life." Following Sade, they asserted the right to *say everything*, to liberate words and "replace the Alchemy of the Word with a real chemistry" (Breton). The *innocence* of words is henceforth consciously refuted and language is revealed as "the worst of conventions," something that should be destroyed, demystified, liberated. Dada's contemporaries did not fail to emphasize its will to destroy everything (that "demolition job," Gide worried), the danger it represented to the dominant sense. After Dada it has become impossible to believe that a word is forever bound to an idea: Dada realized all the possibilities of language and forever closed the door on art as a specialty. It definitively posed the problem of the realization of art. Surrealism was of value only insofar as it continued to pursue this exigence; in its literary productions it was *reactionary*. The realization of art—poetry in the situationist sense—means that one cannot realize oneself in a "work," but rather realizes oneself, period. Sade's inauguration of "saying everything" already implied the abolition of literature as a separate domain (where only what is literary may be said). But this abolition, consciously asserted by the dadaists after Rimbaud and Lautréamont, was not a *supersession*. There is no supersession without realization, one cannot supersede art without realizing it. In fact, there has not even been any actual abolition, since even after Joyce, Duchamp and Dada a new spectacular literature continues to thrive. This is because there can be no "saying everything" without the freedom to *do everything*. Dada had a chance for realization with the Spartakists, with the revolutionary practice of the German proletariat. Their failure made the failure of Dada inevitable. With its recuperation (including that of virtually all its original protagonists) into subsequent artistic movements, Dada has become the literary expression of the nothingness of poetic activity, the art of expressing the nothingness of everyday liberty. The ultimate expression of this art of "saying everything" deprived of any doing is the blank page. . . . Modern poetry (experimental, permutational, spatialist, surrealist or neodadaist) is the antithesis of poetry, it is the artistic project recuperated by power. It abolishes poetry without realizing it; it lives off its own continual self-destruction. "What's the point of saving language," Max Bense asks resignedly, "when there is no longer anything to say?" Confession of a specialist! Muteness or mindless chatter—the sole alternatives of the specialists of permutation. Modern thought and art, guaranteeing power and guaranteed by it, move in the realm of what Hegel called "the language of flattery." Both contribute to the eulogy of power and its products, perfecting reification and banalizing it. Asserting that "reality consists of language" or that "language can only be considered in and for itself," the specialists of language arrive at the concepts of "language-object" and "word-thing" and revel in the panegyrics of their own reification. The thing becomes the dominant model and once again the commodity finds its realization and its poets. The theory of the state, of economy, of law, of philosophy, of art, everything now has this apologetic character.

Wherever separate power replaces the autonomous action of the masses, wherever bureaucracy seizes control of all aspects of social life, it attacks language and reduces its poetry to the vulgar prose of its information. Bureaucracy appropriates language for its own use, just as it does everything else, and imposes it on the masses. Language is then supposed to communicate its messages and reflect its thought; it is the material support of its ideology. Bureaucracy ignores the fact that language is first of all a means of communication between people. Because all communication is channeled through bureaucracy, people no longer even need to talk to each other: their first duty is to play their role as *receivers* in the network of informationist communication to which the whole society is reduced, receivers of orders they must carry out.

This language's mode of existence is bureaucracy, its becoming is bureaucratization. The Bolshevik order born out of the failure of the soviet revolution imposed a whole series of more or less magical, impersonal expressions in the image of the bureaucracy in power. "Politburo," "Comintern," "Cavarmy," "Agitprop" are so many mysterious names of specialized agencies that really are mysterious, operating in the nebulous sphere of the state (or of the Party leadership) without any relation to the masses except insofar as they establish and reinforce domination. Language colonized by bureaucracy is reduced to a series of blunt, inflexible formulas in which the same nouns are always accompanied by the same adjectives and participles; the noun governs them and each time it appears they automatically fall in around it in the correct order. This "falling into step" of words reflects a more profound militarization of the whole society, its division into two basic categories: the caste of rulers and the great mass of executants. But these same words are also called on to play other roles; they are invested with the magic power to support the oppressive reality, to cloak it and present it as the truth, the only possible truth. Thus there are no more "Trotskyists" but only "Hitlero-Trotskyists"; no more Marxism but only "Marxism-Leninism"; and the opposition is automatically "reactionary" in the "Soviet regime." The rigidity with which these ritual formulas are sacralized is aimed at preserving the purity of this "substance" in the face of obviously contradictory facts. In this way the language of the masters is everything, reality nothing, or at most the shell of this language. People are required in their acts, their thoughts and their feelings to behave as if the state was that reason, justice and freedom proclaimed by the ideology; the ritual (and the police) are there to ensure conformity to this behavior (see Marcuse, *Soviet Marxism*).

The decline of radical thought considerably increases the power of words, the words of power. "Power creates nothing, it recuperates" (*IS* #8). Words forged by revolutionary critique are like partisans' weapons: abandoned on the battlefield, they fall into the hands of the counterrevolution and like prisoners of war are subjected to forced labor. Our most immediate enemies are the proponents and established functionaries of false critique. The divorce between theory and practice provides the central basis for recuperation, for the petrification of revolutionary theory into ideology, which transforms real practical demands (for whose realization the premonitory signs are already appearing in the present society) into systems of ideas, into demands of reason. The ideologues of every variety, the watchdogs of the reigning spectacle, carry out this task; the most corrosive concepts are emptied of their content and put back into circulation in the service of maintaining alienation: dadaism in reverse. They become advertising slogans (see the recent prospectus of the Club Méditerranée). Concepts of radical critique suffer the same fate as the proletariat: they are deprived of their history, cut off from their roots; they become grist for power's human thinking machines.

Our project of the liberation of words is historically comparable to the Encyclopédiste enterprise. The Enlightenment's language of "tearing apart" (to continue the Hegelian image) lacked the conscious his-

173

torical dimension; it was a real critique of the decrepit feudal world, but it was totally ignorant of what would emerge from it: none of the Encyclopédistes was a republican. It was, rather, an expression of the bourgeois thinkers' own internal tearing apart. Our language aims first of all at practice that tears apart the world, beginning with tearing apart the veils that cloak it. Whereas the Encyclopédistes sought a quantitative enumeration, the enthusiastic description of a world of objects in which the bourgeoisie and the commodity were already victorious, our dictionary translates the *qualitative* and the possible but still absent victory, the repressed of modern history (the proletariat) and *the return of the repressed*. We propose the real liberation of language because we propose to put it in a practice free of all constraints. We reject *any authority*, linguistic or otherwise: only real life *allows* a meaning and only praxis verifies it. The debate over the reality or unreality of the meaning of a word, isolated from practice, is a purely academic question. We place our dictionary in that libertarian region which is still out of the reach of power, but which is its only possible universal successor.

Language still remains the necessary mediation for the awakening of consciousness of the world of alienation (Hegel would say: the necessary alienation), the instrument of the radical theory that will eventually seize the masses because it is theirs; and only then will it find its truth. It is thus essential that we forge our own language, the language of real life, against the ideological language of power, the terrain of justification of all the categories of the old world. From now on we must prohibit the falsification or recuperation of our theories. We use specific concepts already used by the specialists, but we give them a new content, turning them against the specialists that they support and against future salaried thinkers who would be tempted to besmear situationist theory with their own shit (as Claudel did with Rimbaud and Klossowski with Sade). Future revolutions must invent their own language. Concepts of radical critique will be reexamined one by one in order to rediscover their truth. The word *alienation*, for example, one of the key concepts for the comprehension of modern society, must be disinfected after having passed through the mouth of someone like Axelos. All words have the same relation with power as does the proletariat, and like the latter they are the instrument and agent of future liberation. Poor Revel! There are no forbidden words; in language, as it will be everywhere else, *everything is permitted*. To deny ourselves the use of a word is to deny ourselves a weapon used by our adversaries.

Our dictionary will be a sort of codebook enabling one to decipher information and rend the ideological veils that cover reality. We will give possible translations that will enable people to grasp the different aspects of the society of the spectacle, and show how the slightest signs and indications contribute to maintaining it. In a sense it will be a bilingual dictionary, since each word has an "ideological" meaning for power and a real meaning which we think corresponds to real life in the present historical phase. Thus we will be able at each step to determine the various positions of words in the social war. If the problem of ideology is how to descend from the heaven of ideas to the real world, our dictionary will be a contribution to the elaboration of the new revolutionary theory where the problem is how to effect the transition from language to life. The real appropriation of the words that *work* cannot be realized outside the appropriation of work itself. The inauguration of free creative activity will at the same time be the inauguration of true communication, freed at last, and the transparency of human relations will replace the poverty of words under the old regime of opacity. Words will not cease to *work* until people do.

MUSTAPHA KHAYATI

THE ROLE OF GODARD

In cinema Godard presently represents formal pseudofreedom and the pseudocritique of manners and values—the two inseparable manifestations of all ersatz, recuperated modern art. Everyone does everything to present him as an unappreciated, misunderstood artist, shocking because of his audacity, unjustly despised; and everyone praises him, from *Elle* magazine to Aragon-the-Senile. In this way, in spite of the absence of real critiques of Godard, we see developing a sort of substitute for the famous theory of the increase of resistances in socialist regimes: the more Godard is hailed as an inspired leader of modern art, the more people rush to his defense against incredible plots. In Godard the repetition of the same clumsy stupidities is by definition breathtakingly innovative. It is beyond any attempt at explanation; the admirers consume it as confusedly and arbitrarily as Godard produced it because they recognize in it the consistent expression of a *subjectivity*. This is true, but it is a subjectivity on the level of a *concierge* educated by the mass media. Godard's "critiques" never go beyond innocuous, assimilated nightclub or *Mad* magazine humor. His flaunted culture is largely the same as that of his audience, which has read exactly the same pages in the same drugstore paperbacks. The two most famous lines from the most read poem of the most overrated Spanish poet ("Terrible five o'clock in the afternoon—the blood, I don't want to see it" in *Pierrot-le-Fou*)—this is the key to Godard's method. The most famous renegade of modern art, Aragon, in *Les Lettres Françaises* of 9 September 1965, has rendered an homage to his younger confrere which, coming from such an expert, is perfectly fitting: "Art today is Jean-Luc Godard . . . of a superhuman beauty . . . of a constantly sublime beauty. . . . There is no precedent to Godard except Lautréamont. . . . This child of genius." Even the most naïve can scarcely be taken in after such a *testimonial* from such a source.

Godard is a Swiss from Lausanne who envied the chic of the Swiss of Geneva, and then the chic of the Champs-Elysées, and his successful ascension up from the provinces is most exemplary at a time when the system is striving to usher so many "culturally deprived" people into a respectful consumption of culture—even "avant-garde" culture if nothing else will do. We are not speaking here of the overall ultimately conformist application of an art that professes to be innovative and critical. We are pointing out the directly conformist use of film by Godard.

To be sure, films, like songs, have intrinsic powers of conditioning the spectator: beauties, if you will, that are at the disposition of those who presently have the possibility of expressing themselves. Up to a point such people may make a relatively clever use of those powers. But it is a sign of the general conditions of our time that their cleverness is so limited that the extent of their ties with the dominant ways of life quickly reveals the disappointing limits of their venture. Godard is to film what Lefebvre or Morin is to social critique; each *possesses the appearance* of a certain freedom in style or subject matter (in Godard's case, a slightly free manner in comparison with the stale formulas of filmic narration). But *they have taken this very freedom from elsewhere*: from what they have been able to grasp of the advanced experiences of the era. They are the *Club Méditerranée* of modern thought (see in this issue "The Packaging of 'Free Time' "). They make use of a caricature of freedom, as marketable junk, *in place of* the authentic. This is done on all terrains, including that of formal artistic freedom of expression, which is merely one sector of the general problem of pseudocommunication. Godard's "critical" art and his admiring art critics all work to conceal the present problems of a *critique* of art—the real experience, in the SI's phrase, of a "communication containing its own critique." In the final analysis the present function of Godardism is to forestall a situationist use of the cinema.

Aragon has been for some time developing his theory of the *collage* in all modern art up to Godard. This is nothing other than an attempt to interpret *detournement* in such a way as to bring about its recuperation by the dominant culture. Laying the foundations for a Togliattist variant of French Stalinism, Garaudy and Aragon are setting up a "completely open" artistic modernism, just as they are moving "from anathema to dialogue" with the priests. Godard could become their *artistic Teilhardism*. In fact the collage, made famous by cubism in the dissolution of plastic art, is only a particular case (a destructive moment) of detournement: it is displacement, the *infidelity of the element*. Detournement, originally formulated by Lautréamont, is a return to a superior fidelity of the element. In all cases detournement is dominated by the dialectical devaluing/revaluing of the element within the development of a unifying meaning. But the collage of the merely devalued element has been widely used, well before being constituted as a Pop Art doctrine, in the modernist snobbism of the displaced object (making a spice bottle out of a chemistry flask, etc.).

This acceptance of *devaluation* is now being extended to a method of *combining neutral* and indefinitely interchangeable elements. Godard is a particularly boring example of such a use without negation, without affirmation, without quality.

176

THE IDEOLOGY OF DIALOGUE

The situationists' practice of concretely breaking with apologists for any fragment of the present order (particularly visible with regard to the *leading representatives* of the culture and politics of submission)— as well as its limiting case: the exclusion of some members of the SI— is subject to the greatest misunderstanding, although it follows quite directly from our fundamental positions. Certain commentators have propagated the most hostile interpretations of it, thereby causing concern among semi-informed people. The reality in this particular case is quite simple. Those who accept one or several variants of the prevailing false dialogue become the advocates of a new type of *free exchange* in the name of an abstract right to dialogue at any price (payable in avowed concessions to falsehood), and they reproach us for interrupting this *false dialogue*. It is, however, only in this way that we are able to be the bearers of the reality of dialogue. On the question of exclusion, we believe that through experimentation we have made an advance in determining the requirements for a nonhierarchical organization of a *common project*, which project can be sustained only by the self-discipline of individuals proving themselves in the coherence of the theories and acts through which each member strives to merit his joint responsibility with all the others. The onesidedness of Stirner's notions on the relations of the egoist with the organization that he enters or leaves at whim (though it does contain a grain of truth regarding *that aspect* of freedom) does not allow any independent basis for his passive and defenseless ghost of an "organization." Such an incoherent and undisciplined organization is at the mercy of the individual "egoist," who cynically exploits it for his own ends (and in fact the Stirnerian individual can just as well enter the most reactionary association for his own personal profit). But a free association—"a bond, not a power"—in which several individuals meet on a common basis cannot be passively subject to someone's whim. Those who wish neither to judge nor to command must be able to *reject* any person whose conduct implicates them. When the SI excludes someone, we are calling him to account not for *his* life but for *ours*, for the common project that he would falsify (for enemy purposes, or through lack of discernment). In our eyes, each remains individually free (the fact that this freedom is generally impoverished is another problem, without which there would be no need for undertakings like the SI) and by throwing back on his own an individual who has always remained autonomous we are only expressing the fact that this autonomy was not able to fulfill itself in our common project. In rejecting someone in accordance with the rules of the game that he thought he had accepted, or had pretended to accept, it is *our own resignation* that we are rejecting.

It may be helpful to elucidate these remarks with excerpts from two letters recently addressed to one of our correspondents in East Europe.

177

(*First letter.*) Our theoretical positions (on play, language, etc.) would not only risk becoming mendacious and valueless, they would today *already* be without value if we held them in coexistence with some doctrinal dogmatism, whatever it might be. All of us believe as you do that "the freedom to travel all the unaccustomed paths" must be absolute (and not only on the artistic or theoretical plane, but in all aspects of practical life). For a thousand reasons, of which the experience of the East is the most obvious, we know that an ideology in power turns any partial truth into an absolute lie. . . . We are not a *power* in society, and thus our "exclusions" only express our freedom to distinguish ourselves from the confusionism around us or even among us, which confusionism is much closer to the actual social power and partakes of all its benefits. We have never wished to prevent anyone from expressing his ideas or doing what he wants (and we have never sought to be in a practical position to exert this sort of pressure). We merely refuse *to be ourselves mixed up with* ideas and acts that run contrary to our convictions and tastes. Note that this is all the more vital in that we have hardly any freedom to express our own convictions and tastes, due to their going so sharply against the mainstream. Our "intolerance" is nothing but a very limited response to the very strict intolerance and exclusion that *we run into everywhere*, particularly among the "intellectual establishment" (considerably more intense than the hostility the surrealists had to endure), and which we scarcely find surprising. Just as we are in no degree a controlling power in society, *we refuse to become one* one day by means of some political reshuffling (we are in this regard partisans of *radical self-management*, of workers councils abolishing all separate state power or even "theoretical" power); and we are refusing to transform ourselves into any power whatsoever, even on the small scale that we would be permitted, when we refuse to enlist *disciples*, who would give us, along with the right of control and direction *over them*, a greater recognized social standing as representatives of one more artistic or political ideology. . . . One should not confuse the practical conditions of free thought here and in the East—or in Spain, for example. In countries where nothing can be openly expressed it is obviously necessary to support the right of everyone to express themselves. But in places where everyone can express themselves (though under conditions of enormous inequality) any radical thought—without of course wishing to suppress this practical freedom—must first of all clear the way for its own "unaccustomed path," must assert its own right to exist without being "recuperated" and distorted by the *order* which manifestly reigns behind this visible confusion and complexity and which ultimately possesses the *monopoly of appearance* (cf. our critique of the "spectacle" in the consumer society of commodity abundance). Finally, the reigning "tolerance" is one-way, and this on a global scale in spite of the antagonisms and complexity of the different types of exploitative societies. What the tolerant people who are in a position to express themselves tolerate, fundamentally, is the *established power* everywhere. You tell us that you live in X . . . . If you were in Paris you would see how many of these tolerant leftist intellectuals turn out to be undecided, understanding and tolerant toward the established conditions in X . . . or in Peking. What they call "the sense of history" is their Hegelian adherence *to what they read in the daily papers*.

(*Second letter.*) A radically different point of departure in fact first of all restores the *truth* of the liberatory tentatives of the past. It is necessary to break clearly with the old confusion, and thus with its open, cunning or simply unconscious partisans. We obviously have to bear the negative consequences of the attitude we have chosen. We have to acknowledge this negativity. . . . We are in complete agreement with you on the unity of the problem of the present avant-garde. We in fact initiate dialogue everywhere that *state of mind* manifests itself in a radical direction. For that state of mind is itself divided by a struggle between its truth and its organized *recuperation* by power.

INTERVIEW WITH AN IMBECILE

Even worse than the old *Observateur*, the *Nouvel Observateur* is a veritable Niagara of stupidity (6,810,000 liters per second). A considerable portion of this flow is produced by its editors, Katia Kaupp and Michel Cournot, whose writings could serve as excellent historical documents for the study of the supreme phase of spectacular decomposition: their combination of stupidity and stylistic vulgarity makes them perfect *Jean Nochers* of the left (a left which adheres to the dominant society as fundamentally as does Jean Nocher, apart from a few details concerning the "modernization" of this domination). For its launching, however, it called in some guest celebrities. Its opening issue (19 November 1964) presented a five-page interview with a star thinker. We reproduce here a few of his most extraordinary statements, the parenthetical remarks obviously being ours and not those of the *Nouvel Observateur* flunky who pretends to dialogue with the oracle.

"The young people I meet," says the imbecile, "are perhaps less hotheaded than in the past, but what I find most striking is that politically they are often at the same point as I am. My point of arrival is their point of departure. . . . And they have a whole lifetime ahead of them to build on the base that is my point of culmination." (*Obviously the young people who are not at the same point of political degradation would never be interested in seeing this imbecile; as for those who have the misfortune to be at that point, a hundred successive lifetimes "ahead of them" would never suffice to build anything on the base of his culmination, which has been revealed from every angle as an intellectual dead end.*)

"In France the 'yeah-yeah' phenomenon was used in order to turn the youth into a class of consumers." (*A perfect inversion of reality: it is because the youth of the modern capitalist countries has become a very important category of consumers that phenomena of the 'yeah-yeah' sort appear.*)

"You can only be alluding to Marxist ideology. Today I don't know of any other: bourgeois ideology stands out not by its strength but by its absence." (*Those who have read Marx know that his method is a radical critique of ideologies; but he who has only read Stalin can praise "Marxism" for having become the best of ideologies, the ideology that has had the strongest police.*)

"Socialism can be pure only *as an idea* or, perhaps, much later, if it becomes the regime of all societies. In the meantime its *incarnation* in a particular country implies that it must develop and define itself through innumerable relations with the rest of the world. Thus, in the forging of reality the purity of the idea is tainted." *(Here is a Marxist ideologue really ideologizing: ideas are pure in the heavens and become rotten when they are incarnated. Since this thinker is himself real and has affirmed the principle that any realization in the world must entail a fundamental corruption, he implicitly both admits his own degradation in his "relations with the rest of the world" and justifies it on the grounds of inevitability. From all this we can appreciate his "advanced" state of decomposition.)*

Right afterwards the imbecile quotes a Malian's statement which he greatly admires: "Our socialism is conditioned by the fact that we are a country without any outlet to the sea." *(Is it not also somewhat conditioned by the absence of an industrial proletariat in Mali? But this is just a trifling detail in the geopolitics of such a profound thinker!)*

To the idea that all the industrial societies have many traits in common, the imbecile retorts: "To say that, one would have to prove that there is a class struggle in the socialist countries, that is, that the privileges accorded certain people are becoming stratified. Now this is not at all the case. There are very real inequalities; but the money obtained by a factory manager in the USSR cannot be reinvested anywhere: it is spent and cannot be replenished or augmented in his hands to become the basis of a class power." *(A basis which lies elsewhere: in the possession of the state; the extra money received by the privileged in the USSR is not the basis of their power, but a clear expression of their power.)*

"The Soviets are shocked when one seems to believe that among them money can confer power." *(Of course, since it's the other way around!)*

"To be sure, these 'high-ranking functionaries' have numerous privileges; but to the very extent that the regime is authoritarian, there is a social instability, intermixing among different strata, demoting of leaders, a constant influx of newcomers from the base to the summit. If any conflicts were to occur in the USSR they would have the aspect of a *reformism* and not of a revolution." *(Thus the very arbitrariness serves to demonstrate the nonexistence of a ruling class in the USSR. At this level of insult to one's intelligence, one could maintain that the free-enterprise capitalism of Marx's day was also socialist since its economic laws ruined many industrialists and it sometimes happened that a worker would become a boss; hence the social instability, class intermixing, etc.)*

But the idea of a pure imbecile of this dimension would only be a "pure idea." Since such an imbecile actually exists, he must also be firmly identified with a repressive power. After the armed revolt of the Hungarian proletariat, in one of those "socialist countries" where "one would have to prove" now that class struggles could exist, this same imbecile was so set on defending the interests of the Russian bureaucracy that he took a position *to the right of Khrushchev*: "The most serious mistake was probably Khrushchev's Report [on Stalin], for the solemn public denunciation, the detailed exposure of all the crimes of a sacred personage who has represented the regime for so long, is a folly when such frankness is not made possible by a previous substantial rise in the standard of living of the population. . . . The result was to reveal the truth to masses who were not ready to receive it."

The thinker we have been talking about is Sartre; and anyone who still wants to seriously discuss the value (philosophical or political or literary—one can't separate the aspects of this hodgepodge) of such a nullity, so puffed up by the various authorities that are so satisfied with him, immediately himself loses the right to be accepted as an interlocutor by those who refuse to renounce the *potential consciousness* of our time.

THE ALGERIA OF DANIEL GUÉRIN, LIBERTARIAN

In December 1965 Daniel Guérin published, in his pamphlet *L'Algérie caporalisée?*, a curious analysis of Boumedienne's regime. According to him, nothing happened in June. Faithful to an old schema, he sees only a "Bonapartism" in power both before and after the coup d'état, struggling classically on two fronts: against the "counterrevolution of the indigenous propertied classes" and against the threatening enthusiasm of the self-management workers. And in foreign affairs he finds "the same desire on the part of both regimes for an adroit equilibrium between capitalist and socialist countries" (p. 6). "None of the declarations of the so-called 'Council of the Revolution' contains any innovations whatsoever or any hints of an original program" (p. 10). However, when he drafted his main text, dated 5 November, Guérin thought he detected some *potential* new developments—as the putschists were being pushed, as if despite themselves, to the "right"—which developments "*seem* to *foreshadow* an antisocialist policy" (p. 11, our emphasis). One might suppose that Guérin disregards the considerable differences between the two regimes because he is carried away by the equal contempt that Ben Bella and Boumedienne can inspire in a revolutionary who is a declared partisan of "libertarian socialism" and self-management. But no, not at all! He has no other revolutionary solution to recommend than the restoration of Ben Bella: "To rally a popular opposition to the colonels' regime in Algeria today without reference to Ben Bella, or while making a total political critique of Ben-Bellaism, would be an undertaking doomed to failure" (p. 17). And before 19 June the Ben Bella regime's numerous attacks on the workers, the exploits of its police and army—the same ones as today, in fact—were for Guérin only "mistakes, weaknesses and omissions" of an acceptable orientation. The king was badly advised, misinformed; never responsible. Since Guérin cannot be unaware of the open struggles of Ben Bella's regime against the masses (he himself provides

181

some excellent documentation of them, notably apropos of the Congress of Agricultural Workers) he has to reconstruct history by totally separating Ben Bella from his regime. Page 12: "The sabotage of self-management, organized, of course, without Ben Bella's knowledge." Page 2: "As we can see more clearly today, Ben Bella never had his hands free: for nearly three years he was the tool, the prisoner, the hostage of Boumedienne." In short, people thought Ben Bella was in power but his downfall has shown that he wasn't at all. This astonishing retroactive demonstration could just as well be applied to the czar, who was believed to be an autocrat before 1917. But Guérin overlooks this question: Who besides Ben Bella *made* Boumedienne, by hoisting himself into power with the aid of Boumedienne's arms? That Ben Bella later made some half-hearted and particularly clumsy attempts to get rid of his tool is another matter. It is because he was above all a bureaucrat that he was at first essentially in solidarity with, and eventually the victim of, bureaucrats more rational than he.

What then is the secret of this aberration of one of our famous leftist intellectuals, and one of the most ostensibly "libertarian" among them at that? With him it is no different than with all the others: it is the decisive influence of their common vainglorious participation in *high society*; their common tendency, even meaner than a lackey's, to be swept off their feet with joy because they have spoken with the greats of this world; and the imbecility that makes them attribute this greatness to those who have condescended to talk to them. Whether they are partisans of the self-managing masses or of police-state bureaucracies, the "leftist intellectuals" of the period from which we are just emerging always have the same rapt admiration for power and government. The closer they are to a governmental position, the more the leaders of the "underdeveloped" countries fascinate these ridiculous professors of leftist museography. In Simone de Beauvoir's memoirs, so revealing of the fundamental baseness of a whole generation of intellectuals, her narration of a dinner at the Soviet Embassy exposes a pettiness so irremediable and shameless that she isn't even aware of the avowal she is making.

So here is the secret: Guérin "knew" Ben Bella. He "listened" to him from time to time: "When I had the privilege, at the beginning of December 1963, of a brief audience at the Villa Joly in order to present to the President a report resulting from my month of traveling around the country observing the self-managed enterprises, I had the impression that he had been prejudiced against my conclusions by Ali Mahsas and the Minister of Industry and Commerce, Bachir Boumaza" (p. 7).

Guérin really is for self-management but, like Mohammed Harbi, it is in the pure form of its Spirit incarnated as a privileged hero that he prefers to meet it, recognize it and aid it with his wisdom. Daniel Guérin met the *Weltgeist* of self-management over a cup of tea, and everything else follows.

DOMENACH AGAINST ALIENATION
(excerpts)

"Alienation, that key word for a whole system of politics, of sociology, of critical thought—what does it cover? J.M. Domenach traces the astonishing itinerary of this concept of such diverse meanings from Hegel to Jacques Berque. Then he takes another look at its content. It seems to him that the moment has come to renounce this 'hospital-concept' where all the maladies of the century are lumped together, and to call into question the philosophy that developed it."

This prefatory note from the journal *Esprit* of December 1965 is not betrayed by the extraordinary impudence of Domenach's article, "To Finish With Alienation," which opens the same issue. Domenach, prince of contemporary confusionism in his important province of Christian leftism, reproaches the concept of alienation for being confused, for being used improperly, for having considerably evolved historically and for having given rise to too many "vague and outmoded" formulas. If everything that was vague was therefore outmoded, religious thought would not have survived the rationalist clarification brought into the world by bourgeois society. But in a materially divided society, vague ideas and the vague use of precise concepts necessarily serve definite forces. The history of the concept of alienation, as Domenach recounts it in a few pages, is itself a model of this vague thought that serves a precise confusionism. [. . .]

Domenach does not even want to "finish with" the concept of alienation like that philosopher depicted in *The German Ideology* who wanted to liberate man from the idea of gravity so that there would be no more drownings. Domenach wants people to stop talking about alienation so that they will become *resigned to it*. [. . .] The alienation banished from consciousness is to be replaced by the more "precise" concept of exploitation. While it is true that the general alienation in the East and the West is effectively based on the exploitation of the workers, the evolution of modern capitalism—and still more, bureaucratic ideology—have largely succeeded in masking the Marxist analyses of exploitation at the stage of free competition and in making the handling of them less precise. In contrast, these parallel evolutions have brought alienation—originally a philosophical concept—into the reality of every hour of daily life. [. . .]

To be sure, in a society that needs to spread a *mass* pseudoculture and to have its spectacular pseudointellectuals monopolize the stage, many terms are naturally rapidly vulgarized. But for the same reasons, perfectly simple and illuminating words tend to disappear: such as the word *priest*; so that Domenach and his friends come to think that no one will ever again remind them of this embarrassing vulgarity. They are mistaken. Just as the secular efforts of a Revel (*En France*) to compile a list of words to forbid, a list that mixes a few fashionable trivialities with important *contested* terms, are ridiculous because one cannot hope to *simultaneously* suppress the theoretical discoveries of our time and the interested confusion to which they give rise in order to "return" to some simplified rationalism which *never* had the efficacity the nostalgic liberals now attribute to it. [. . .]

People like Domenach, being themselves valets of power's cultural spectacle, which wants to quickly recuperate for its own use the most crucial terms of modern critical thought, will never want to admit that the truest and most important concepts of the era—alienation, dialectics, communism—are precisely marked by the organization around them of the greatest confusion and the worst misinterpretation. Vital concepts are *simultaneously* subject to the truest and the most false uses, with a multitude of intermediary confusions, because the struggle between critical reality and the apologetic spectacle leads to a struggle over words, a struggle that is more bitter the more those words are central. The *truth* of a concept is revealed not by an authoritarian purge, but by the coherence of its use in theory and in practical life. It is not important that a priest at the pulpit renounces the use of a concept that he would *never* have known *how* to use. Let us speak vulgarly since we're dealing with priests: alienation is the point of departure for everything—providing one departs from it.

THE EXPLOSION POINT OF
IDEOLOGY IN CHINA

The international association of totalitarian bureaucracies has now completely fallen apart. In the words of the *Address* published by the situationists in Algiers in July 1965, the irreversible "disintegration of the revolutionary image" that the "bureaucratic lie" counterposed to the whole of capitalist society, as its pseudonegation and actual support, has become obvious, and first of all on the terrain where official capitalism had the greatest interest in upholding the pretense of its adversary: the global confrontation between the bourgeoisie and the so-called "socialist camp." In spite of all sorts of attempts to patch it up, *that which already was not socialist has ceased to be a camp.* The disintegration of the Stalinist monolith is already manifested in the coexistence of some twenty independent "lines," from Rumania to Cuba, from Italy to the Vietnamese-Korean-Japanese bloc of parties. Russia, having this year become incapable of holding a common conference of merely all the *European* parties, prefers to forget the era when Moscow reigned over the Comintern. Thus the *Izvestia* of September 1966 blames the Chinese leaders for bringing "unprecedented" discredit on "Marxist-Leninist" ideas; and virtuously deplores the style of confrontation "in which insults are substituted for an exchange of opinions and revolutionary experiences. Those who choose this method confer an absolute value on their own experience and reveal a dogmatic and sectarian mentality in their interpretation of Marxist-Leninist theory. Such an attitude is inevitably accompanied by interference in the internal affairs of fraternal parties." In the Sino-Soviet polemic, in which each power is led to impute to its opponent every conceivable antiproletarian crime, being only obliged not to mention the *real crime* (the class power of the bureaucracy), each side can only arrive at the sobering conclusion that the other's revolutionariness was only an unexplainable mirage which, lacking any reality, has purely and simply fallen back to its old point of departure. Thus in New Delhi last February the Chinese ambassador described Brezhnev and Kosygin as "new czars of the Kremlin," while the Indian government, anti-Chinese ally of this Muscovy, simultaneously discovered that "the present masters of China have donned the imperial mantle of the Manchus." This argument against the new dynasty of the Middle Kingdom was further refined the following month in Moscow by the modernist state poet Voznesensky, who, with a "foreboding of a new Koutchoum" and his hordes, counts on "eternal Russia" to build a rampart against the Mongols who threaten to bivouac among "the Egyptian treasures of the Louvre." The accelerated decomposition of bureaucratic ideology, as evident in the countries where Stalinism has seized power as in the others where it has lost every chance of seizing it, naturally began around issues of internationalism; but this is only the *beginning* of a general and irreversible dissolution. For the bureaucracy, internationalism could be nothing but an illusory proclamation in the service of its real interests, one *ideological* justification among others, since bureaucratic society is precisely the *total inversion* of proletarian community. The bureaucracy is essentially a power based on national state possession and it must ultimately obey the logic of this reality, in accordance with the particular interests imposed by the level of development of the country in its possession. Its heroic age passed away with the ideological golden age of "socialism in a single country" that Stalin was shrewd enough to maintain by destroying the revolutions in China in 1927 and Spain in 1937. The autonomous bureaucratic revolution in China—as already shortly before in Yugoslavia—introduced into the unity of the bureaucratic world a dissolutive germ that has broken it up in less than twenty years. The general process of decomposition of bureaucratic ideology is presently attaining its supreme stage in the very country where that ideology was most necessary; where, because of the general economic backwardness, the remaining ideological pretension had to be pushed to its peak: China.

The crisis that has continually deepened in China since the spring of 1966 constitutes an unprecedented phenomenon in bureaucratic society. No doubt the ruling class of bureaucratic state-capitalism, continually and necessarily exerting terror over the exploited majority, has in Russia and East Europe often been torn apart by rivalries and antagonisms stemming from the objective difficulties it encounters, as well as from the subjectively delirious style that a totally mendacious power is led to assume. But the bureaucracy, which must be centralized due to its mode of appropriation of the economy since it must draw from itself the hierarchical guarantee to all participation in its collective appropriation of the social surplus production, has always made its purges *from the top down*. The summit of the bureaucracy has to remain fixed, for in it lies the entire legitimacy of the system. It must keep its dissensions to itself (as it always has from the time of Lenin and Trotsky). Those who hold office may be replaced or liquidated, but the office itself must always retain the same indisputable majesty. The unexplained and unanswerable repression can then normally descend to each level of the apparatus as a mere complement to what has been *instantaneously* decided at the summit. Beria must first be killed; then judged; then his faction can be hunted down; or in fact anybody can be hunted down because the power that is doing the liquidating thereby defines who and what that faction consists of and at the same time redefines itself as the sole power. This is what is not happening in China; the persistency of the declared adversaries, in spite of the fantastic raising of bids in the struggle for the totality of power, clearly shows that *the ruling class has split in two*.

A social disaster of such magnitude obviously cannot be explained, in the anecdotal style of bourgeois observers, as being the result of dissensions over foreign policy (on the contrary, the Chinese bureaucracy is quite unified in the docility with which it tolerates the insult of the crushing of Vietnam on its own doorstep). Neither could personal quarrels over succession to power have caused so much to be put at stake. When certain leaders are accused of having "kept Mao Tse-tung from power" since the end of the 1950s, everything leads one to believe that this is one of those retrospective crimes frequently fabricated during bureaucratic purges—Trotsky conducting the civil war on orders from the Mikado, Zinoviev supporting Lenin in order to work for the British Empire, etc. The man who could have taken power from someone as powerful as Mao would not have slept as long as Mao was still around to come back. Mao would thus have died that very day, and nothing would have prevented his faithful successors from attributing his death to, say, Khrushchev. If the rulers and polemicists of the bureaucratic states certainly have a much better understanding of the Chinese crisis, their statements cannot for all that be taken any more seriously, for in talking about China they have to guard against revealing too much about themselves. In the end, those susceptible to the grossest misconceptions are the leftist debris of the Western countries, who are always the willing dupes of moldy sub-Leninist propaganda. They evaluate very seriously the role in Chinese society of the continuation of allowances to the capitalists who rallied to the cause, or they rummage around in the melee trying to figure out which leader represents leftism or workers' autonomy. The most stupid among them thought there was something "cultural" about this affair, until January when the Maoist press pulled the dirty trick on them of admitting that it had been "a struggle for power from the very beginning." The only serious debate consists in examining why and how the ruling class could have split into two hostile camps; and any investigation of this question is naturally impossible for those who do not admit that the bureaucracy is a ruling class, or who ignore the specificity of this class and reduce it to the classical conditions of bourgeois power.

On the *why* of the breach within the bureaucracy, it can be said with certainty only that it was a matter in which the ruling class's very domination was at stake *since in order to settle it each side remained unyielding and neither of them hesitated to immediately risk their common class power* by jeopardizing all the existing conditions of their administration of the society. The ruling class must thus have known that it could no longer govern as before. It is certain that this conflict concerned the management of the *economy*. It is certain that the collapse of the bureaucracy's successive economic policies is the cause of the extreme acuteness of the conflict. The failure of the "Great Leap Forward" policy—mainly because of the resistance of the peasantry—not only put an end to the prospect of an ultravoluntarist takeoff of industrial production, but led to a disastrous disorganization whose effects were felt for several years. Even agricultural production has scarcely increased since 1958, and the rate of population growth remains higher than that of food supplies. It is less easy to say over exactly what economic options the ruling class split. Probably one side (consisting of the majority of the Party apparatus, the union cadres and the economists) wanted to continue, or increase more or less considerably, the production of consumer goods and to sustain the workers' efforts with economic incentives; this policy implied making some concessions to the peasants and especially to the factory workers, as well as increasing a hierarchically differentiated consumption for a good part of the bureaucracy. The other side (consisting of Mao and a large segment of the higher ranking army officers) probably wanted to resume at any price the effort to industrialize the country through an even more extreme recourse to terror and *ideological energy*, an unlimited superexploitation of the workers, and perhaps an "egalitarian" sacrifice in consumption for a considerable segment of the lower bureaucracy. Both positions are equally oriented toward maintaining the absolute domination of the bureaucracy and are calculated in terms of the necessity of erecting barriers against class struggles that threaten that domination. In any case, the urgency and vital character of this choice was so evident to everyone that both camps felt they had to run the risk of immediately aggravating the conditions in which they found themselves by the disorder of their very scission. It is quite possible that the obstinacy on both sides is justified by the fact that there is no satisfactory solution to the insurmountable problems of the Chinese bureaucracy; that the two options confronting each other were thus equally inapplicable; and yet nevertheless a choice had to be made.

As for figuring out *how* a division at the summit of the bureaucracy was able to descend from level to level—recreating at every stage remote-controlled confrontations which in turn incited or exacerbated oppositions throughout the party and the state, and finally among the masses—it is probably necessary to take into account the survival of aspects of the ancient manner of administering China by provinces tending toward semiautonomy. The Peking Maoists' denunciation in January of "independent fiefs" clearly evokes this phenomenon, and the development of the disturbances over the last few months confirms it. It is quite possible that the phenomenon of regionally autonomous bureaucratic power, which during the Russian counterrevolution was manifested only weakly and sporadically by the Leningrad organization, found firm and multiple bases in bureaucratic China, resulting in the possibility of a coexistence within the central government of clans and clienteles holding entire regions of bureaucratic power as their personal property and bargaining with each other on this basis. Bureaucratic power in China was not born out of a workers movement, but out of the military regimentation of peasants during a twenty-two year war. The Army has remained closely interknit with the Party, all of whose leaders have also been military chiefs, and it remains the principal training school of the peasant masses from which the Party selects its future cadres. It seems, moreover, that the local administrations installed in 1949 were largely based on the regions traversed by the different army regiments moving from the north to the south, leaving in their wake at every stage men who were linked to those regions by geographical origin (or by family ties: the propaganda against Liu Shao-ch'i and others has fully exposed this nepotistic factor in the consolidation of bureaucratic cliques). Such local bases of semiautonomous power within the bureaucratic administration could thus have been formed in China by a combination of the organizational structures of the conquering army with the productive forces it found to control in the conquered regions.

When the Mao faction began its public offensive against the entrenched positions of its adversaries by enlisting students and schoolchildren and putting them on the march, it was in no way for the purpose of directly initiating a "cultural" or "civilizing" remolding of the mass of workers, who were already squeezed as tightly as possible into the ideological straitjacket of the regime. The silly diatribes against Beethoven or Ming art, like the invectives against a supposed occupation or reoccupation of positions of power by a Chinese bourgeoisie that has obviously been annihilated as such, were only presented for the benefit of the peanut gallery—though not without calculating that this crude ultraleftism might strike a certain chord among the oppressed, who have, after all, some reason to suspect that there are still several obstacles in their country to the emergence of a classless society. The main purpose of this operation was to make the *regime's ideology*, which is by definition Maoist, appear in the street in the service of this faction. Since the adversaries could themselves be nothing other than officially Maoist, imposing a struggle on this terrain immediately put them in an awkward position. It forced them to make "self-critiques," the insufficiency of which, however, expressed their actual resolution to hold on to the positions they controlled. The first phase of the struggle can thus be characterized as a confrontation of the *official owners of the ideology* against the majority of the *owners of the apparatus* of the economy and the state. But the bureaucracy, in order to maintain its collective appropriation of society, needs the ideology as much as it does the administrative and repressive apparatus; thus the venture into such a separation was extremely dangerous if it was not quickly resolved. The majority of the apparatus, including Liu Shao-ch'i himself despite his shaky position in Peking, resisted obstinately. After their first attempt to block the Maoist agitation at the university level by setting up effectively anti-Maoist "work groups" among the students, that agitation spread into the streets of all the large cities and everywhere began to attack, by means of wall posters and direct action, the officials who had been designated as "capitalist-roaders"—attacks that were not without errors and excesses of zeal. These officials organized resistance wherever they could. It is likely that the first clashes between workers and "Red Guards" were in fact initiated by Party activists in the factories, under orders from the local officials of the apparatus. Soon, however, the workers, exasperated by the excesses of the Red Guards, began to intervene on their own. Whenever the Maoists spoke of "extending the Cultural Revolution" to the factories, and then to the countryside, they gave themselves the air of having *decided* on a movement which had in fact come about in spite of their plans and which throughout autumn 1966 was totally *out of their control*. The decline of industrial production; the disorganization of transportation, of irrigation and of state administration (despite Chou En-lai's efforts); the menaces that weighed on the autumn and spring harvests; the halting of all education (particularly serious in an underdeveloped country) for more than a year—all this was only the inevitable result of a struggle whose extension

189

was solely due to the resistance of that sector of the bureaucracy in power that the Maoists were trying to make back down.

The Maoists, who have no political experience with struggles in urban environments, will have had good occasion to verify Machiavelli's precept: "One should take care not to incite a rebellion in a city while flattering oneself that one can stop it or direct it at will" (*History of Florence*). After a few months of pseudocultural pseudorevolution, real class struggle has appeared in China, with the workers and peasants beginning to act for themselves. The workers cannot be unaware of what the Maoist perspective means for them; the peasants, seeing their individual plots of land threatened, have in several provinces begun to divide among themselves the land and equipment of the "People's Communes" (these latter being merely the new ideological dressing of the preexisting administrative units, generally corresponding to the old cantons). The railroad strikes, the Shanghai general strike (denounced, as in Budapest, as a favored weapon of the capitalists), the strikes of the great Wuhan industrial complex, of Canton, of Hupeh, of the metal and textile workers in Chungking, the peasants' attacks in Szechwan and Fukien—these movements came to a culmination in January, bringing China to the brink of chaos. At the same time, following in the wake of the workers who in September 1966 in Kwangsi had organized themselves as "Purple Guards" in order to fight the Red Guards, and after the anti-Maoist riots in Nanking, "armies" began to form in various provinces, such as the "August 1st Army" in Kwangtung. The national Army had to intervene everywhere in February and March in order to subdue the workers, to direct production through "military control" of the factories, and even (with the support of the militia) to control work in the countryside. The workers' struggles to maintain or increase their wages—that famous tendency toward "economism" denounced by the masters of Peking—was accepted or even encouraged by some local cadres of the apparatus in their resistance to rival Maoist bureaucrats. But the main impetus of the struggle was clearly an irresistible upsurge from the rank-and-file workers: the authoritarian dissolution in March of the "professional associations" that had formed after the first dissolution of the regime's labor unions, whose bureaucracy had been deviating from the Maoist line, is a good demonstration of this. In Shanghai that same month the *Jiefang Ribao* condemned "the feudal tendencies of these associations, which are formed not on a class basis (*i.e., not on the basis of a Maoist total monopoly of power*) but on the basis of trades and which struggle for the partial and immediate interests of the workers in those trades." This defense of the real owners of the general and permanent interests of the collectivity was also distinctly expressed on 11 February in a joint directive from the Council of State and the Military Commission of the Central Committee: "All elements who have seized or stolen arms must be arrested."

At the time when the settlement of this conflict—which has certainly cost tens of thousands of lives and involved fully equipped regiments and even warships—is being entrusted to the Chinese Army, that Army is itself divided. It has to ensure the continuation and intensification of production at a time when it is no longer in a position to ensure the unity of power in China. Moreover, its direct intervention against the peasants, considering that the Army has been recruited largely from the peasantry, would present the gravest risks. The truce sought by the Maoists in March and April, when they declared that all Party personnel were redeemable with the exception of a "handful" of traitors, and that henceforth the principal menace was "anarchism," expressed not merely the anxiety over the difficulty of reining in the liberatory desires that the Red Guard experiences had awakened among the youth; it expressed *the ruling class's essential anxiety at having arrived at the brink of its own dissolution.* The Party and the central and provincial administration were falling apart. "Labor discipline must be reestablished." "The idea of excluding and overthrowing all cadres must be unconditionally condemned" (*Red Flag*, March 1967). And already in February *New China* declared: "You smash all the officials . . . but when you have taken over some administrative body what do you have besides an empty room and some rubber stamps?" Rehabilitations and new compromises follow one another erratically. The very survival of the bureaucracy has ultimate priority, pushing its diverse political options into the background as mere means.

By spring 1967 it was evident that the "Cultural Revolution" was a disastrous failure and that this failure was certainly the most colossal of the long line of failures of the bureaucratic regime in China. In spite of the extraordinary cost of the operation none of its goals has been attained. The bureaucracy is more divided than ever. Every new power installed in the regions held by the Maoists is dividing in its turn: the "Revolutionary Triple Alliance"—Army–Party–Red Guard— has not ceased falling apart, both because of the antagonisms between these three forces (the Party, in particular, tending to remain aloof, getting involved only to sabotage) and because of the continually aggravated antagonisms within each one. It seems as difficult to patch up the old apparatus as it would be to build a new one. Most importantly, *at least two thirds of China is in no way controlled by the regime in Peking.*

Besides the governmental committees of partisans of Liu Shao-ch'i and the movements of workers' struggles that continue to assert themselves, the *Warlords* are already reappearing in the uniforms of independent "Communist" generals, treating directly with the central power and following their own policies, particularly in the peripheral regions. General Chang Kuo-hua, master of Tibet in February, after street fighting in Lhasa used armored cars against the Maoists. Three Maoist divisions were sent to "crush the revisionists." They seem to have met with only moderate success since Chang Kuo-hua still controlled the region in April. On 1 May he was received in Peking, with negotiations ending in a compromise: he was entrusted to form a Revolutionary Committee to govern Szechwan, where in April a "Revolutionary Alliance" influenced by a certain General Hung had seized power and imprisoned the Maoists; since then, in June, members of a People's Commune seized arms and attacked the Army. In Inner Mongolia the Army, under the direction of Deputy Political Commissar Liu Chiang, declared itself against Mao in February. The same thing happened in Hopeh, Honan and Manchuria. In May, General Chao Yung-shih carried out an anti-Maoist putsch in Kansu. Sinkiang, where the atomic installations are located, was neutralized by mutual agreement in March, under the authority of General Wang En-mao; the latter, however, is reputed to have attacked "Maoist revolutionaries" in June. Hupeh was in July in the hands of General Chen Tsai-tao, commander of the Wuhan district, one of the oldest industrial centers in China. In the old style of the "Sian Incident," he arrested two of the main Peking leaders who had come to negotiate with him. The Prime Minister had to go there in person, and his obtaining the release of his emissaries was announced as a "victory." At the same time 2400 factories and mines were paralyzed in that province following the armed uprising of 50,000 workers and peasants. In fact, at the beginning of summer the conflict was continuing everywhere: in June "conservative work-ers" of Honan attacked a textile mill with incendiary bombs; in July the coal miners of Fushun and the oil workers of Tahsing were on strike, the miners of Kiangsi were driving out the Maoists, there were calls for struggle against the "Chekiang Industrial Army" (described as an "anti-Marxist terrorist organization"), peasants threatened to march on Nanking and Shanghai, there was street fighting in Canton and Chungking, and the students of Kweiyang attacked the Army and seized Maoist leaders. And the government, having decided to prohibit violence "in the regions controlled by the central authorities," seems to be having a hard time of it even there. Unable to stop the disorders, it is stopping the *news* of them by expelling most of the rare foreigners in residence.

But at the beginning of August the fractures in the Army have become so dangerous that the official Peking publications are them-selves revealing that the partisans of Liu want "to set up an indepen-dent reactionary bourgeois kingdom within the Army" and that "the attacks against the dictatorship of the proletariat in China have come not only from the higher echelons, but also from the lower ones" (*People's Daily*, 5 August). Peking has gone so far as to clearly admit that at least a third of the Army has declared itself against the central government and that even a large part of the old China of eighteen provinces is out of its control. The immediate consequences of the Wuhan incident seem to have been very serious: an intervention of paratroopers from Peking, supported by gunboats ascending the Yangtze from Shanghai, was repulsed after a pitched battle; and arms from the Wuhan arsenal are reported to have been sent to the anti-Maoists of Chungking. It should be noted, moreover, that the Wuhan troops belonged to the Army group under the direct authority of Lin Piao, the only one considered completely loyal. Toward the middle of August the armed struggles have become so widespread that the Maoist government has come around to officially condemning this sort of continuation of politics by means that are turning against it; stat-ing, on the contrary, its firm conviction that it will win out by sticking to "struggle with the pen" instead of the sword. Simultaneously it announces distribution of arms to the masses in the "loyal zones." But where are such zones? Fighting has broken out again in Shanghai, which has been presented for months as one of the rare strongholds of

Maoism. In Shantung soldiers are inciting the peasants to revolt. The leaders of the Air Force are denounced as enemies of the regime. And as in the days of Sun Yat-sen, Canton, toward which the 47th Army is moving in order to reestablish order, stands out as a beacon of revolt, with the railroad and transit workers in the forefront: political prisoners have been liberated, arms destined for Vietnam have been seized from freighters in the port, and an undetermined number of individuals have been hung in the streets. Thus China is slowly sinking into a confused civil war, which is both a confrontation between diverse regions of fragmented state-bureaucratic power and a clash of workers' and peasants' demands with the conditions of exploitation that the torn bureaucratic leaderships have to maintain everywhere.

Since the Maoists have presented themselves as the champions of absolute ideology (we have seen how successfully), they have so far naturally met with the most extravagant degree of respect and approbation among Western intellectuals, who never fail to salivate to such stimuli. K.S. Karol, in the *Nouvel Observateur* of 15 February, learnedly reminds the Maoists not to forget that "the real Stalinists are not potential allies of China, but its most irreducible enemies: for them, the Cultural Revolution, with its antibureaucratic tendencies, is suggestive of Trotskyism." There were, in fact, many Trotskyists who identified with it—thereby doing themselves perfect justice! *Le Monde*, the most unreservedly Maoist paper outside China, day after day announced the imminent success of Monsieur Mao Tse-tung, finally taking the power it had been generally believed to have been his for the past eighteen years. The sinologists, virtually all Stalino-Christians—this combination can be found everywhere, but particularly among them—have resurrected the "Chinese spirit" to demonstrate the legitimacy of the new Confucius. The element of burlesque that has always been present in the attitude of moderately Stalinophile leftist bourgeois intellectuals could hardly fail to blossom out when presented with such Chinese record achievements as: This "Cultural Revolution" may well last 1000 or even 10,000 years. . . . The *Little Red Book* has finally succeeded in "making Marxism Chinese." . . . "The sound of men reciting the *Quotations* with strong, clear voices can be heard in every Army unit." . . . "Drought has nothing frightening, Mao Tse-tung Thought is our fertilizing rain." . . . "The Chief of State was judged responsible . . . for not having foreseen the about-face of General Chiang Kai-shek when the latter turned his army against the Communist troops" (*Le Monde*, 4 April 1967; this refers to the 1927 coup, which was foreseen by everyone in China but which had to be awaited passively in order to obey Stalin's orders). . . . A chorale sings the hymn entitled *One Hundred Million People Take Up Arms To Criticize the Sinister Book "How To Be a Good Communist"* (a formerly official manual by Liu Shao-ch'i). . . . The list could go on and on; we can conclude with this gem from the *People's Daily* of 31 July: "The situation of the Proletarian Cultural Revolution in China is excellent, but the class struggle is becoming more difficult."

After so much ado the historical conclusions to be drawn from this period are simple. No matter where China may go from here, the image of the last revolutionary-bureaucratic power has shattered. Its internal collapse is added to the unceasing disasters of its foreign policy: the annihilation of Indonesian Stalinism;* the break with Japanese Stalinism; the destruction of Vietnam by the United States; and finally Peking's proclamation in July that the Naxalbari "insurrection" was the beginning of a Maoist-peasant revolution throughout India (this a few days before it was dispersed by the first police intervention). By taking such a delirious position Peking broke with the majority of its own Indian partisans, that is, with the last large bureaucratic party that remained loyal to it. At the same time, China's internal crisis reflects its failure to industrialize the country and make itself a model for the underdeveloped countries.

Ideology, pushed to its extreme, *shatters*. Its absolute use is also its absolute zero: the night in which all ideological cows are black. When amidst the most total confusion bureaucrats fight each other in the name of the same dogma and everywhere denounce "the bourgeois hiding behind the red flag," *doublethink* has itself split in two. This is the joyous end of ideological lies, dying in ridicule. It is not China, it is our world that has produced this delirium. In the issue of *Internationale Situationniste* that appeared in August 1961 we rightly said that this world would become "at all levels more and more painfully ridiculous until the moment of its complete revolutionary reconstruction." The new period of proletarian critique will learn that it must no longer shelter from criticism anything that pertains to it, and that every existing ideological comfort represents a shameful defeat for it. In discovering that it is dispossessed of the false goods of its world of falsehood, it must understand that it is the specific negation of the totality of the global society; and it will discover this also in China. It is the global breaking up of the *Bureaucratic International* that is now being reproduced at the Chinese level in the fragmentation of the regime into independent provinces. Thus China is rediscovering its past, which is once again posing to it the real revolutionary tasks of the previously vanquished movement. The moment when, seemingly, "Mao is recommencing in 1967 what he was doing in 1927" (*Le Monde*, 17 February 1967) is also the moment when, for the first time since 1927, the intervention of the worker and peasant masses has surged over the entire country. As difficult as it may be for them to become conscious of their autonomous objectives and put them into practice, something has died in the total domination to which the Chinese workers were subjected. The *proletarian "Mandate of Heaven"* has expired.

16 August 1967

TWO LOCAL WARS

The Arab-Israel war was a dirty trick pulled by modern history on the good conscience of the Left, which was communing in the great spectacle of its protest against the Vietnam war. The false consciousness that saw in the NLF the champion of "socialist revolution" against American imperialism could only get entangled and collapse amidst its insurmountable contradictions when it had to decide between Israel and Nasser. Yet throughout all its ludicrous polemics it never stopped proclaiming that one or the other was completely in the right, or even that one or another of their perspectives was revolutionary.

Through its immigration into underdeveloped areas, the revolutionary struggle was subjected to a double alienation: that of an impotent Left facing an overdeveloped capitalism it was in no way capable of combating, and that of the laboring masses in the colonized countries who inherited the remains of a mutilated revolution and have had to suffer its defects. The absence of a revolutionary movement in Europe has reduced the Left to its simplest expression: a mass of spectators who swoon with rapture each time the exploited in the colonies take up arms against their masters, and who cannot help seeing these uprisings as the epitome of Revolution. At the same time, the absence from political life of the proletariat as a class-for-itself (and for us the proletariat is revolutionary or it is nothing) has allowed this Left to become the "Knight of Virtue" in a world without virtue. But when it bewails its situation and complains about the "world order" being at variance with its good intentions, and when it maintains its poor yearnings in the face of this order, it is in fact attached to this order as to its own essence, and if this order was taken away from it it would lose *everything*. The European Left shows itself so poor that, like a traveler in the desert longing for a single drop of water, all it seems to need to console itself is the meager feeling of an abstract objection. From the little with which it is satisfied one can measure the extent of its poverty. It is as alien to history as the proletariat is alien to this world; false consciousness is its natural condition, the spectacle is its element, and the apparent opposition of systems is its universal frame of reference: wherever there is a conflict it always sees Good fighting Evil, "total revolution" versus "total reaction."

The attachment of this spectator consciousness to *alien* causes remains irrational, and its virtuous protests flounder in the tortuous paths of its guilt. Most of the "Vietnam Committees" in France split up during the "Six Day War" and some of the war resistance groups in the United States also revealed *their reality*. "One cannot be at the same time for the Vietnamese and against the Jews menaced with extermination," is the cry of some. "Can you fight against the Americans in Vietnam while supporting their allied Zionist aggressors?" is the reply of others. And then they plunge into byzantine discussions . . . Sartre hasn't recovered from it yet. In fact this whole fine lot does not actually fight what it condemns, nor does it know that of which it approves. Its opposition to the American war is almost always combined with unconditional support of the Vietcong; but in any case this opposition remains spectacular for everyone. Those who were really opposed to Spanish fascism went to fight it. No one has yet gone off to fight "Yankee imperialism." The consumers of illusory participation are offered a whole range of spectacular choices: Stalino-Gaullist nationalism against the Americans (Humphrey's visit was the sole occasion the PCF has demonstrated with its remaining faithful); the sale of the *Vietnam Newsletter* or of publicity handouts from Ho Chi Minh's state; or pacifist demonstrations. Neither the Provos (before their dissolution) nor the Berlin students have been able to go beyond the narrow framework of anti-imperialist "action."

The war opposition in America has naturally been more serious since it finds itself face to face with the real enemy. For some young people, however, it means a *mechanistic* identification with the apparent enemies of their real enemies; which reinforces the confusion of a working class already subjected to the worst brutalization and mystification, and contributes to maintaining it in that "reactionary" state of mind from which one draws arguments against it.

Guevara's critique seems to us more important since it has its roots in real struggles, but it falls short by default. Che is certainly one of the last consequent Leninists of our time. But like Epimenides, he seems to have slept for the last fifty years to be able to believe that there is still a "progressive bloc" which is unaccountably "failing." This bureaucratic and romantic revolutionary only sees in imperialism the highest stage of capitalism, struggling against a society that is socialist in spite of its imperfections.

The USSR's embarrassingly evident deficiencies are coming to seem more and more "natural." As for China, according to an official declaration it remains "ready to accept all national sacrifices to support North Vietnam against the USA (*SI note: in lieu of supporting the workers of Hong Kong*) and constitutes the most solid and secure *rear guard* for the Vietnamese people in their struggle against imperialism." In fact, no one doubts that if the last Vietnamese were killed, Mao's bureaucratic China would still be intact. (According to *Izvestia*, China and the United States have already concluded a mutual nonintervention pact.)

Neither the manichean consciousness of the virtuous Left nor the bureaucracy are capable of seeing the profound unity of today's world. Dialectics is their common enemy. As for revolutionary criticism, it begins beyond good and evil; it takes its roots in history and operates on the totality of the existing world. In no case can it applaud a belligerent *state* or support the bureaucracy of an exploiting state in formation. It must first of all lay bare the *truth* of present struggles by putting them back into their historical context, and unmask the hidden ends of the forces *officially* in conflict. The arm of critique is the prelude to the critique by arms.

The peaceful coexistence of bourgeois and bureaucratic lies ended up prevailing over the lie of their confrontation; the balance of terror was broken in Cuba in 1962 with the rout of the Russians. Since that time American imperialism has been the unchallenged master of the world. And it can remain so only by aggression since it has no chance of seducing the disinherited, who are more easily attracted by the Sino-Soviet model. State-capitalism is the natural tendency of colonized societies where the state is generally formed before the historical classes. The total elimination of its capital and its commodities from the world market is the deadly threat that haunts the American propertied class and its free-enterprise economy; this is the key to its aggressive rage.

Since the great crisis of 1929, state intervention has been more and more conspicuous in market mechanisms; the economy can no longer function steadily without massive expenditures by the state, the main "consumer" of all noncommercial production (especially that of the armament industries). This does not save it from remaining in a state of permanent crisis and in constant need of expanding its public sector at the expense of its private sector. A relentless logic pushes the system toward increasingly state-controlled capitalism, generating severe social conflicts.

The profound crisis of the American system lies in its inability to produce sufficient profits on the social scale. It must therefore achieve *abroad* what it cannot do at home, namely increase the amount of profit in proportion to the amount of existing capital. The propertied class, which also more or less possesses the state, relies on its imperialist enterprises to realize this insane dream. For this class, state-capitalism means death just as much as does *communism*; that is why it is essentially incapable of seeing any difference between them.

The artificial functioning of the monopolistic economy as a "war economy" ensures, for the moment, that the ruling-class policy is willingly supported by the workers, who enjoy full employment and a spectacular abundance: "At the moment, the proportion of labor employed in jobs connected with national defense amounts to 5.2% of the total American labor force, compared with 3.9% two years ago. . . . The number of civil jobs in the national defense sector has increased from 3,000,000 to 4,100,000 over the last two years." (*Le Monde*, 17 September 1967.) Meanwhile, market capitalism vaguely feels that by extending its territorial control it will achieve an accelerated expansion capable of balancing the ever-increasing demands of non-profit-making production. The ferocious defense of regions of the "free" world where its interests are often trifling (in 1959 American investments in South Vietnam did not exceed 50 million dollars) is part of a long-term strategy that hopes eventually to be able to write off military expenditures as mere business expenses in ensuring the United States not only a market but also the monopolistic control of the means of production of the greater part of the world. But everything works against this project. On one hand, the internal contradictions of private capitalism: particular interests conflict with the general interest of the propertied class as a whole, as with groups that make short-term profits from state contracts (notably arms manufacturers), or monopolistic enterprises that are reluctant to invest in underdeveloped countries, where productivity is very low in spite of cheap labor, preferring instead the "advanced" part of the world (especially Europe, which is still more profitable than saturated America). On the other hand, it clashes with the immediate interests of the disinherited masses, whose first move can only be to eliminate the indigenous strata that exploit them—which are the only strata able to ensure the United States any infiltration whatsoever.

According to Rostow, the "growth" specialist of the State Department, Vietnam is for the moment only the first testbed of this vast strategy, which to ensure its exploitative peace must start with a war of destruction that can hardly succeed. The aggressiveness of American imperialism is thus in no way the aberration of a bad administration, but a necessity for the class relations of private capitalism, which, if not overthrown by a revolutionary movement, unrelentingly evolves toward a technocratic state-capitalism. It is in this general framework of a still undominated global economy that the history of the alienated struggles of our time must be situated.

The destruction of the old "Asiatic" structures by colonial penetration gave rise to a new urban stratum while increasing the pauperization of a large portion of the superexploited peasantry. The conjuncture of these two forces constituted the driving force of the Vietnamese movement. Among the urban strata (petty bourgeois and even bourgeois) were formed the first nationalist nuclei and the skeleton of what was to be, from 1930 on, the Indochinese Communist Party. Its adherence to Bolshevik ideology (in its Stalinist version), which led it to graft an essentially agrarian program on to the purely nationalist one, enabled the ICP to become the principal director of the anticolonial struggle and to marshal the great mass of peasants who had spontaneously risen. The "peasant soviets" of 1931 were the first manifestation of this movement. But by linking its fate to that of the Third International, the ICP subjected itself to all the vicissitudes of Stalinist diplomacy and to the fluctuations of the national and state interests of the Russian bureaucracy. After the Seventh Comintern Congress (August 1935) "the struggle against French imperialism" vanished from the program and was soon replaced by a struggle against the powerful Trotskyist party. "As for the Trotskyists, no alliances, no concessions; they must be unmasked for what they are: the agents of fascism" (Report of Ho Chi Minh to the Comintern, July 1939). The Hitler-Stalin Pact and the banning of the CP in France and its colonies allowed the ICP to change its line: "Our party finds it a question of life or death . . . to struggle against the imperialist war and the French policy of piracy and massacre (*i.e. against Nazi Germany—SI*) . . . but we will at the same time combat the aggressive aims of Japanese fascism."

Toward the end of World War II, with the effective help of the Americans, the Vietminh was in control of the greater part of the country and was recognized by France as the sole representative of Indochina. It was at this point that Ho preferred "to sniff a little French shit rather than eat Chinese shit for a lifetime" and signed, to make the task of his colleague-masters easier, the monstrous compromise of 1946, which recognized Vietnam as both a "free state" and as "belonging to the Indochinese Federation of the French Union." This compromise enabled France to reconquer part of the country and, at the same time the Stalinists lost their share of bourgeois power in France, to wage a war that lasted eight years, at the end of which the Vietminh gave up the South to the most retrograde strata and their American protectors and definitively won the North for itself. After systematically eliminating the remaining revolutionary elements (the last Trotskyist leader, Ta Tu Thau, was assassinated by 1946) the Vietminh bureaucracy imposed its totalitarian power on the peasantry and started the industrialization of the country within a state-capitalist framework. The bettering of the lot of the peasants, following their conquests during the long liberation struggle, was, in line with bureaucratic logic, subordinated to the interests of the rising state: the

198

goal was to be greater productivity, with the state remaining the uncontested master of that production. The authoritarian implementation of agrarian reform gave rise in 1956 to violent insurrections and bloody repression (above all in Ho Chi Minh's own native province). The peasants who had carried the bureaucracy to power were to be its first victims. For several years afterwards the bureaucracy tried to smother the memory of this "serious mistake" in an "orgy of self-criticism."

But the same Geneva agreements enabled the Diem clique to set up, south of the 17th parallel, a bureaucratic, feudal and theocratic state in the service of the landowners and compradore bourgeoisie. Within a few years this state was to nullify, by a few suitable "agrarian reforms," everything the peasantry had won. The peasants of the South, some of whom had never laid down their arms, were to fall back in the grip of oppression and superexploitation. This is the second Vietnam war. The mass of the insurgent peasants, taking up arms once more against their old enemies, also followed once again their old leaders. The National Liberation Front succeeded the Vietminh, inheriting both its qualities and its grave defects. By making itself the champion of national struggle and peasant war, the NLF won over the countryside from the very first and made it the main seat of the armed resistance. Its successive victories over the official army provoked the increasingly massive intervention of the Americans, to the point of reducing the conflict to an open colonial war, with the Vietnamese pitted against an invading army. Its determination in the struggle, its clearly antifeudal program and its unitary perspectives remain the principal qualities of the movement. But in no way does the NLF's struggle go beyond the classical framework of national liberation struggles. Its program remains based on a compromise among a vast coalition of classes, dominated by the overriding goal of wiping out the American aggression. It is no accident that it rejects the title "Vietcong" (i.e. Vietnamese communists) and insists on its national character. Its structures are those of a state in formation: in the zones under its control it already levies taxes and institutes compulsory military service.

These minimal qualities in the struggle and the social objectives that they express remain totally absent in the confrontation between Israel and the Arabs. The specific contradictions of Zionism and of splintered Arab society add to the general confusion.

Since its origins the Zionist movement has been the contrary of the revolutionary solution to what used to be called the *Jewish question*. A direct product of European capitalism, it did not aim at the overthrow of a society that needed to persecute Jews, but at the creation of a Jewish national entity that would be protected from the antisemitic aberrations of decadent capitalism; it aimed not at the abolition of injustice, but at its transfer. The original sin of Zionism is that it has always acted as if Palestine were a desert island. The revolutionary workers movement saw the answer to the Jewish question in proletarian community, that is, in the destruction of capitalism and "its religion, Judaism"; the emancipation of the Jews could not take place apart from the emancipation of man. Zionism started from the opposite hypothesis. As a matter of fact, the counterrevolutionary development of the last half century proved it right, but in the same way as the development of European capitalism proved right the reformist theses of Bernstein. The success of Zionism and its corollary, the creation of the state of Israel, is merely a miserable by-product of the triumph of world counterrevolution. To "socialism in a single country" came the echo "justice for a single people" and "equality in a single kibbutz." It was with Rothschild capital that the colonization of Palestine was organized and with European surplus-value that the first kibbutzim were set up. The Jews recreated *for themselves* all the fanaticism and segregation of which they had been victims. Those who had suffered mere toleration in their society were to struggle to become *in another country* owners disposing of the right to tolerate others. The kibbutz was not a revolutionary supersession of Palestinian "feudalism," but a mutualist formula for the self-defense of Jewish worker-settlers *against the capitalist exploitative tendencies of the Jewish Agency.* Because it was the main Jewish owner of Palestine, the Zionist Organization defined itself as the sole representative of the superior interests of the "Jewish Nation." If it eventually allowed a certain element of self-management, it is because it was sure that this would be based on the systematic rejection of the Arab peasant.

As for the Histadrut, it was since its inception in 1920 subjected to the authority of world Zionism, that is, to the direct opposite of workers' emancipation. Arab workers were statutorily excluded from it and its activity often consisted of forbidding Jewish businesses to employ them.

The development of triangular struggles between the Arabs, the Zionists and the British was to be turned to the profit of the Zionists. Thanks to the active patronage of the Americans (since the end of World War II) and the blessing of Stalin (who saw Israel as the first "socialist" bastion in the Middle East, but also as a way to rid himself of some annoying Jews), it did not take long before the Herzlian dream was realized and the Jewish state was arbitrarily proclaimed. The recuperation of all "progressive" forms of social organization and their integration within the Zionist ideal allowed even the most "revolutionary" to work in good conscience for the building of the bourgeois, militaristic, rabbinical state that modern Israel has become. The prolonged sleep of proletarian internationalism once more brought forth a monster. The basic injustice against the Palestinian Arabs came back to roost with the Jews themselves: the State of the Chosen People was nothing but one more class society in which all the anomalies of the old societies were recreated (hierarchical divisions, tribal opposition between the Ashkenazi and the Sephardim, racist persecution of the Arab minority, etc.). The labor union organization assumed its normal function of integrating workers into a capitalist economy, an economy of which it itself has become the main owner. It employs more workers than the state itself. It presently constitutes the bridgehead of the imperialist expansion of the new Israeli capitalism. ("Solel Boneh," an important building branch of the Histadrut, invested 180 million dollars in Africa and Asia from 1960–1966 and currently employs 12,000 African workers.)

And just as this state could never have seen the light of day without the direct intervention of Anglo-American imperialism and the massive aid of Jewish finance capital, it cannot balance its *artificial economy* today without the aid of the same forces that created it. (The annual balance of payments deficit is 600 million dollars, that is, more for each Israeli inhabitant than the average earnings of an Arab worker.) Since the settling of the first immigrant colonies, the Jews have formed a modern, European-style society alongside the economically and socially backward Arab society; the proclamation of the state of Israel only completed this process by the pure and simple expulsion of the backward elements. Israel forms by its very existence the bastion of Europe in the heart of an Afro-Asian world. Thus it has become doubly *alien*: to the Arab population, permanently reduced to the status of refugees or of colonized minority; and to the Jewish population, which had for a moment seen in it the earthly realization of all egalitarian ideologies.

But this is due not only to the contradictions of Israeli society; from the outset this situation has been constantly maintained and aggravated by the surrounding Arab societies, which have so far proved incapable of any contribution toward an effective solution.

Throughout the British Mandate period [1920–1948] the Arab resistance in Palestine was completely dominated by the propertied class: the Arab ruling classes and their British protectors. The Sykes-Picot Agreement had put an end to all the hopes of nascent Arab nationalism and subjected the skillfully carved up area to a foreign domination that is far from being over. The same strata that ensured the servitude of the Arab masses to the Ottoman Empire turned to the service of the British occupation and became accomplices of Zionist colonization (by the sale, at very inflated prices, of their land). The backwardness of Arab society did not yet allow for the emergence of new and more advanced leaderships, and the spontaneous popular upheavals found each time the same recuperators: the "bourgeois-feudal" notables and their commodity: national unity.

The armed insurgence of 1936–1939 and the six-month general strike (the longest in history) were decided and carried out in spite of opposition from the leadership of all the "nationalist" parties. They were widespread and spontaneously organized; this forced the ruling class to join them so as to take over the leadership of the movement. But this was in order to put a check on it, to lead it to the conference table and to reactionary compromises. Only the victory of that uprising in its ultimate consequences could have destroyed both the British Mandate and the Zionist aim of setting up a Jewish state. Its failure heralded the disasters to come and ultimately the defeat of 1948.

This latter defeat tolled the knell for the "bourgeois-feudality" as the leading class of the Arab movement. It was the opportunity for the petty bourgeoisie to come to power and constitute, with the officers of the defeated army, the driving force of the present movement. Its program was simple: unity, a kind of socialist ideology, and the liberation of Palestine (the Return). The Tripartite aggression of 1956 provided it with the best opportunity to consolidate itself as a dominant class and to find a leader-program in the person of Nasser, put forward for the collective admiration of the completely dispossessed Arab masses. He was their religion and their opium. But the new exploiting class had its own interests and autonomous goals. The rallying cries that produced the popularity of the bureaucratic military regime of Egypt were already bad in themselves; in addition, the regime was incapable of carrying them out. Arab unity and the destruction of Israel (invoked successively as the liquidation of the usurper state or as the pure and simple driving of the Israeli population into the sea) were the core of this propaganda-ideology.

What ushered in the decline of the Arab petty bourgeoisie and its bureaucratic power was first of all its own internal contradictions and the superficiality of its options (Nasser, the Baath Party, Kassem and the so-called "Communist" parties have never ceased fighting each other and compromising and allying with the most dubious forces).

Twenty years after the first Palestinian war, this new stratum has just demonstrated its complete incapacity to resolve the Palestinian problem. It has lived by delirious bluff, for it was only able to survive by permanently raising the specter of Israel, being utterly incapable of effecting any radical solution whatsoever to the innumerable internal problems. The Palestinian problem remains the key to the Arab power struggles. It is everyone's central reference point and all conflicts hinge on it. It is the basis of the objective solidarity of *all* the Arab regimes. It produces the "Holy Alliance" between Nasser and Hussein, Faisal and Boumedienne, Aref and the Baath.

The latest war has dissipated all these illusions. The absolute rigidity of "Arab ideology" was pulverized on contact with an effective reality that was just as hard but also permanent. Those who spoke of waging a war neither wanted it nor prepared for it, and those who spoke only of defending themselves actually prepared the offensive. Each of the two camps followed their respective propensities: the Arab bureaucracy that for lying and demagogy, the masters of Israel that for imperialist expansion. It is as a negative element that the Six Day War has had a prime importance: it has revealed all the secret weaknesses and defects of what was presented as the "Arab Revolution." The "powerful" military bureaucracy of Egypt crumbled to dust in two days, disclosing all at once the secret *reality* of its achievements: the fact that the axis around which all the socioeconomic transformations took place—the Army—has remained fundamentally the same. On one hand, it claimed to be changing everything in Egypt (and even in the Arab world as a whole), and on the other, it did everything to avoid any transformation in itself, in its values or its habits. Nasser's Egypt is still dominated by pre-Nasser forces; its bureaucracy is a conglomeration without coherence or class consciousness, united only by exploitation and the division of the social surplus-value.

As for the politicomilitary apparatus that governs Baathist Syria, it is entrenching itself more and more in the extremism of its ideology. But its phraseology takes in no one anymore (except Pablo!): everyone knows that it did not fight and that it gave up the front without resistance because it preferred to keep its best troops in Damascus for its own defense. Those who consumed 65% of the Syrian budget to defend the territory have definitively unmasked their own cynical lies.

Finally, the war has shown, to those who still needed showing, that a Holy Alliance with someone like Hussein can only lead to disaster. The Arab Legion [Jordanian Army] withdrew on the first day and the Palestinian population, which has suffered for twenty years under its police terror, found itself without arms or organization in the face of the Israeli occupation forces. Since 1948 the Hashemite throne had shared the colonization of the Palestinians with the Zionist state. By deserting the West Bank it gave the Israelis the police files on all the Palestinian revolutionary elements. But the Palestinians have always known that there was no great difference between the two colonizations, and the blatancy of the new occupation at least makes the terrain of resistance clearer.

As for Israel, it has become everything that the Arabs had accused it of before the war: an imperialist state behaving like the most classic occupation forces (police terror, dynamiting of houses, permanent martial law, etc.). Internally a collective hysteria, led by the rabbis, is developing around the "ironclad right of Israel to its Biblical borders." The war put a stop to the whole movement of internal struggles generated by the contradictions of this artificial society (in 1966 there were several dozen riots, and there were no fewer than 277 strikes in 1965 alone) and provoked unanimous support for the objectives of the ruling class and its most extremist ideology. It also served to shore up all the Arab regimes not involved in the armed struggle. Boumedienne could thus, from 3000 miles away, enter the chorus of political braggadocio and have his name applauded by the Algerian crowd before which he had not even dared to appear the day before; and finally obtain the support of a totally Stalinized ORP ("for his anti-imperialist policy"). Faisal, for a few million dollars, obtained Egypt's withdrawal from North Yemen and the strengthening of his throne. Etc., etc.

As always, war, when not civil, only freezes the process of social revolution. In North Vietnam it has brought about the peasantry's support, never before given, for the bureaucracy that exploits it. In Israel it has killed off for a long time any opposition to Zionism; and in the Arab countries it is reinforcing—temporarily—the most reactionary strata. In no way can revolutionary currents find anything there with which to identify. Their task is at the other pole of the present movement since it must be its absolute negation.

It is obviously impossible to seek, at the moment, a *revolutionary* solution to the Vietnam war. It is first of all necessary to put an end to the American aggression in order to allow the real social struggle in Vietnam to develop in a *natural* way; that is to say, to allow the Vietnamese workers and peasants to rediscover their enemies at home: the bureaucracy of the North and all the propertied and ruling strata of the South. The withdrawal of the Americans will mean that the Stalinist bureaucracy will immediately seize control of the whole country: this is the unavoidable conclusion. Because the invaders cannot indefinitely sustain their aggression; ever since Talleyrand it has been a commonplace that one can do anything with a bayonet except sit on it. The point, therefore, is not to give unconditional (or even conditional) support to the Vietcong, but to struggle consistently and without any concessions against American imperialism. The most effective role is presently being played by those American revolutionaries who are advocating and practicing insubordination and draft resistance on a very large scale (compared to which the resistance to the Algerian war in France was child's play). The Vietnam war is rooted in America and it is from there that it must be rooted out.

Unlike the American war, the Palestinian question has no immediately evident solution. No short-term solution is feasible. The Arab regimes can only crumble under the weight of their contradictions and Israel will be more and more the prisoner of its colonial logic. All the compromises that the great powers try to piece together are bound to be counterrevolutionary in one way or another. The hybrid status quo—neither peace nor war—will probably prevail for a long period, during which the Arab regimes will meet with the same fate as their predecessors of 1948 (and probably at first to the profit of the openly reactionary forces). Arab society, which has produced all sorts of dominant classes caricaturing all the classes of history, must now produce the forces that will bring about its total subversion. The so-called national bourgeoisie and the Arab bureaucracy have inherited all the defects of those two classes without ever having known the historical realizations those classes achieved in other societies. The future Arab revolutionary forces which must arise from the ruins of the June 1967 defeat must know that they have nothing in common with any of the existing Arab regimes and nothing to respect among the established powers that dominate the present world. They will find their model in themselves and in the repressed experiences of revolutionary history. The Palestinian question is too serious to be left to the states, that is, to the colonels. It is too close to the two basic questions of modern revolution—*internationalism* and *the state*—for any existing force to be able to provide an adequate solution. Only an Arab revolutionary movement that is resolutely internationalist and antistate can both dissolve the state of Israel and have on its side that state's exploited masses. And only through the same process will it be able to dissolve all the existing Arab states and create Arab unity through the power of the Councils.

OUR GOALS AND METHODS IN
THE STRASBOURG SCANDAL

The various expressions of stupor and indignation in response to the situationist pamphlet *On the Poverty of Student Life*, which was published at the expense of the Strasbourg chapter of the French National Student Union (UNEF), although having the salutary effect of causing the theses in the pamphlet itself to be rather widely read, have inevitably given rise to numerous misconceptions in the reportage and commentaries on the SI's role in the affair. In response to all kinds of illusions fostered by the press, by university officials and even by a certain number of unthinking students, we are now going to specify exactly what the conditions of our intervention were and recount the goals we were pursuing with the methods that we considered consistent with them.

Even more erroneous than the exaggerations of the press or of certain opposing lawyers concerning the amount of money the SI supposedly took the opportunity of pillaging from the treasury of the pitiful student union is the absurd notion, often expressed in the journalistic accounts, according to which the SI sunk so low as to campaign among the Strasbourg students in order to persuade them of the validity of our perspectives and to get a bureau elected on such a program. We neither did this nor attempted the slightest infiltration of the UNEF by secretly slipping SI partisans into it. One has only to read us to realize that we have no interest in such goals and do not use such methods. The fact is that a few Strasbourg students came to us in the summer of 1966 and informed us that six of their friends—and not they themselves—had just been elected as officers of the Bureau of the local Students Association (AFGES), without any program whatsoever and in spite of their being widely known in the UNEF as extremists in complete disagreement with all the variants of that decomposing body, and even determined to destroy it. The fact that they were elected (quite legally) clearly showed the complete apathy of the mass of students and the complete impotence of the Association's remaining bureaucrats. These latter no doubt figured that the "extremist" Bureau would be incapable of finding any adequate way to express its negative intentions. Conversely, this was the fear of the students who came to see us; and it was mainly for this reason that they had felt they themselves shouldn't take part in this "Bureau": for only a coup of some scope, and not some merely humorous exploitation of their position, could save its members from the air of compromise that such a pitiful role immediately entails. To add to the complexity of the problem, while the students who spoke with us were familiar with the SI's positions and declared themselves in general agreement with them, those who were in the Bureau were for the most part ignorant of them, and counted mainly on the students we were seeing to determine the activity that would best correspond to their subversive intentions.

At this stage we limited ourselves to suggesting that all of them write and publish a general critique of the student movement and of the society, such a project having at least the advantage of forcing them to clarify in common what was still unclear to them. In addition, we stressed that their legal access to money and credit was the most useful aspect of the ridiculous authority that had so imprudently been allowed to them, and that a nonconformist use of these resources would certainly have the advantage of shocking many people and thus drawing attention to the nonconformist aspects of the content of their text. These comrades agreed with our recommendations. In the development of this project they remained in contact with the SI, particularly through Mustapha Khayati.

The discussion and the first drafts undertaken collectively by those we had met with and the members of the AFGES Bureau—who had all resolved to see the matter through—brought about an important modification of the plan. Everyone agreed on the basis of the critique to be made, and specifically on the main points as Khayati had outlined them, but they found they were incapable of effecting a satisfactory formulation, especially in the short time remaining before the beginning of the term. This inability should not be seen as the result of any serious lack of talent or experience, but was simply the consequence of the extreme *heterogeneity* of the group, both within and outside the Bureau. Their initial coming together on the most vague bases prepared them very poorly to collectively articulate a theory they had not really appropriated together. In addition, personal antagonisms and mistrust arose among them as the project progressed; the common concern that the coup attain the most far-reaching and incisive effect was all that still held them together. In such circumstances, Khayati ended up drafting the greater part of the text, which was periodically discussed and approved among the group of students at Strasbourg and by the situationists in Paris—the only (few) significant changes being made by the latter.

Various preliminary actions announced the appearance of the pamphlet. On 26 October the cybernetician Moles (see *IS #9*, page 44), having finally attained a professorial chair in social psychology in order to devote himself to the programing of young cadres, was driven from it in the opening minutes of his opening lecture by tomatoes hurled at him by a dozen students. (Moles was given the same treatment in March at the Musée des Arts Décoratifs in Paris, where this certified robot was to lecture on the control of the masses by means of urbanism; this latter refutation was carried out by some thirty young anarchists belonging to groups that want to bring revolutionary criticism to bear on all modern issues.) Shortly after this inaugural class— which was at least as unprecedented in the annals of the university as Moles himself—the AFGES began publicizing the pamphlet by pasting up André Bertrand's comic strip, *The Return of the Durruti Column*, a document that had the merit of stating in no uncertain terms what his comrades were planning on doing with their positions: "The general crisis of the old union apparatuses and leftist bureaucracies was felt everywhere, especially among the students, where activism had for a long time had no other outlet than the most sordid self-sacrifice to stale ideologies and the most unrealistic ambitions. The last squad of professionals who elected our heroes didn't even have the excuse of mystification. They placed their hopes for a new lease on life in a group that didn't hide its intentions of scuttling this archaic militantism once and for all."

The pamphlet was distributed point-blank to the notables at the official opening ceremony of the university; simultaneously, the AFGES Bureau made it known that its only "student" program was the immediate dissolution of that Association, and convoked a special general assembly to vote on that question. This perspective immediately horrified many people. "This may be the first concrete manifestation of a revolt aiming quite openly at the destruction of society," wrote a local newspaper (*Dernières Nouvelles*, 4 December 1966). And *L'Aurore* of 26 November: "The Situationist International, an organization with a handful of members in the chief capitals of Europe, anarchists play-ing at revolution, talk of 'seizing power'—not in order to keep it, but to sow disorder and destroy even their own authority." And even in Turin the *Gazetta del Popolo* of the same date expressed excessive concern: "It must be considered, however, whether repressive measures ... might not risk provoking disturbances. ... In Paris and other university cities in France the Situationist International, galvanized by the triumph of its adherents in Strasbourg, is preparing to launch a major offensive to take control of the student organizations." At this point we had to take into consideration a new decisive factor: the situationists had to defend themselves from being *recuperated* as a "news item" or an intellectual fad. The pamphlet had ended up being transformed into an SI text: we had not felt that we could refuse to aid these comrades in their desire to strike a blow against the system, and it was unfortunately *not possible for this aid to have been less than it was*. This involvement of the SI gave us, for the duration of the project, a function of de facto leadership which we in no case wanted to prolong beyond this limited joint action: as anyone can well imagine, the pitiful *student milieu* is of no interest to us. Here as in any other situation, we simply had to act in such a way as to make the new social critique that is presently taking shape reappear by means of the practice without concessions that is its exclusive basis. It was the unorganized character of the group of Strasbourg students which had created the necessity for the direct situationist intervention and at the same time prevented even the carrying out of an orderly dialogue, which alone could have ensured a minimal equality in de-cision-making. The debate that normally characterizes a joint action undertaken by independent groups had scarcely any reality in this agglomeration of individuals who showed more and more that they were united in their approval of the SI and separated in every other regard.

It goes without saying that such a deficiency in no way constituted for us a recommendation for the *ensemble* of this group of students, who seemed more or less interested in joining the SI as a sort of easy way of avoiding having to express themselves autonomously. Their lack of homogeneity was also revealed, to a degree we had not been able to foresee, on an unexpected issue: at the last minute several of them hesitated before the forthright distribution of the text at the university's opening ceremony. Khayati had to show these people that one must not try to make scandals half way, nor hope, in the midst of such an act in which one has already implicated oneself, that one will become less implicated by toning down the repercussions of the coup; that on the contrary, the success of a scandal is the only relative safe-guard for those who have deliberately triggered it. Even more unac-ceptable than this last-minute hesitation on such a basic tactical point was the possibility that some of these individuals, who had so little confidence even in each other, would at some point come to make state-ments in our name. Khayati was thus charged by the SI to have the AFGES Bureau declare that none of them was a situationist. This they did in their communiqué of 29 November: "None of the members of our Bureau belongs to the Situationist International, a movement which for some time has published a journal of the same name, but we declare ourselves in complete solidarity with its analyses and perspectives." On the basis of this declared *autonomy*, the SI then addressed a letter to André Schneider, president of the AFGES, and Vayr-Piova, vice-president, to affirm its total solidarity with what they had done. The SI's solidarity with them has been maintained ever since, both by our refusal to dialogue with those who tried to approach us while manifesting a certain envious hostility toward the Bureau members (some even having the stupidity to denounce their action to the SI as being "spectacular"!) and by our financial assistance and public support during the subsequent repression (see the declaration signed by 79 Strasbourg students at the beginning of April in solidarity with Vayr-Piova, who had been expelled from the university; a penalty that was rescinded a few months later). Schneider and Vayr-Piova stood firm in the face of penalties and threats; this firmness, however, was not maintained to the same degree in their attitude toward the SI.

The judicial repression immediately initiated in Strasbourg—and which has since been followed by a series of proceedings in the same vein that are still going on—concentrated on the supposed illegality of the AFGES Bureau, which was, upon the publication of the situationist pamphlet, suddenly considered as a mere "de facto Bureau" usurping the union representation of the students. This repression was all the more necessary since the holy alliance of the bourgeois, the Stalinists and the priests, formed in opposition to the AFGES, enjoyed an "authority" even smaller than that of the Bureau among the city's 18,000 students. It began with the court order of 13 December, which sequestered the Association's offices and administration and prohibited the general assembly that the Bureau had convoked for the 16th for the purpose of voting on the dissolution of the AFGES. This ruling (resulting from the mistaken belief that a majority of the students were likely to support the Bureau's position if they had the opportunity to vote on it), by freezing the development of events, meant that our comrades—whose only perspective was to destroy their own position of leadership without delay—were obliged to continue their resistance until the end of January. The Bureau's best practice until then had been their treatment of the mass of journalists who were flocking to get interviews: they refused most of them and insultingly boycotted those who represented the worst institutions (French Television, *Planète*); thus one segment of the press was induced to give a more exact account of the scandal and to reproduce the AFGES communiqués less inaccurately. Since the fight was now taking place on the terrain of administrative measures and since the legal AFGES Bureau was still in control of the local section of the National Student Mutual, the Bureau struck back by deciding on 11 January, and by implementing this decision the next day, to close the "University Psychological Aid Center" (BAPU), which depended financially on the Mutual, "considering that the BAPUs are the manifestation in the student milieu of a repressive psychiatry's parapolice control, whose clear function is to maintain . . . the passivity of all exploited sectors . . . , considering that the existence of a BAPU in Strasbourg is a disgrace and a threat to all the students of this university who are determined to think freely." At the national level, the UNEF was forced by the revolt of its Strasbourg chapter—which had previously been held up as a model—to recognize its own general bankruptcy. Although it obviously did not go so far as to defend the old illusions of unionist liberty that were so blatantly denied its opponents by the authorities, the UNEF nevertheless could not sanction the judicial expulsion of the Strasbourg Bureau. A Strasbourg delegation was thus present at the general assembly of the UNEF held in Paris on 14 January, and at the opening of the meeting demanded a preliminary vote on its motion to *dissolve the entire UNEF*, "considering that the UNEF declared itself a union uniting the vanguard of youth (Charter of Grenoble, 1946) at a time when workers unionism had long since been defeated and turned into a tool for the self-regulation of modern capitalism, working to integrate the working class into the commodity system, . . . considering that the vanguardist pretension of the UNEF is constantly belied by its subreformist slogans and practice, . . . considering that student unionism is a pure and simple farce and that it is urgent to put an end to it." This motion concluded by calling on "all revolutionary students of the world . . . to prepare along with all the exploited people of their countries a relentless struggle against all aspects of the old world, with the aim of contributing toward the advent of the international power of the workers councils." Only two associations, those of Nantes and of the convalescent-home students, voted with Strasbourg to deal with this preliminary motion before hearing the report of the national leadership (it should be noted, however, that in the preceding weeks the young UNEF bureaucrats had succeeded in deposing two other Association bureaus that had been spontaneously in favor of the AFGES position, those of Bordeaux and Clermont-Ferrand). The Strasbourg delegation consequently walked out on a debate where it had nothing more to say.

The final exit of the AFGES Bureau was not to be so noble, however. At this time three situationists [the "Garnautins"] had just been excluded for having jointly perpetrated—and been forced to admit before the SI—several slanderous lies directed against Khayati, whom they had hoped would himself be excluded as a result of this clever scheme (see the 22 January tract *Warning! Three Provocateurs*). Their exclusion had no relation with the Strasbourg scandal—in it as in everything else they had ostensibly agreed with the conclusions reached in SI discussions—but two of them happened to be from the Strasbourg region. In addition, as we mentioned above, certain of the Strasbourg students had begun to be irritated by the fact that the SI had not rewarded them for their shortcomings by *recruiting* them. The excluded liars sought out an uncritical public among them and counted on covering up their previous lies and their admission of them by piling new lies on top of them. Thus all those who had been *rejected* joined forces in the mystical pretension of going beyond the practice that had condemned them. They began to believe the newspapers and even to expand on them. They saw themselves as masses who had really "seized power" in a sort of Strasbourg Commune. They told themselves that they hadn't been treated the way a revolutionary proletariat deserves to be treated. They assured themselves that their historic action had superseded all previous theories: forgetting that the only discernable "action" in an affair of this sort was, at most, *the drafting of a text*, they collectively compensated for this deficiency by inflating their illusions. This amounted to nothing more ambitious than dreaming together for a few weeks while continually upping the dose of constantly reiterated falsifications. The dozen Strasbourg students who had effectively supported the scandal split into two equal parts. This supplementary problem thus acted as a *touchstone*. We naturally made no *promises* to those who remained "partisans of the SI" and we clearly stated that we would not make any: it was simply up to them to be, unconditionally, partisans of the truth. Vayr-Piova and some others became partisans of falsehood with the excluded "Garnautins" (although certainly without knowledge of several excessive blunders in Frey's and Garnault's recent fabrications, but nevertheless being aware of quite a few of them). André Schneider, whose support the liars hoped to obtain since he held the title of AFGES president, was overwhelmed with false tales from all of them, and was weak enough to believe them without further investigation and to countersign one of their declarations. But after only a few days, independently becoming aware of a number of indisputable lies that these people thought it natural to tell their initiates in order to save their miserable cause, Schneider immediately decided that he should publicly acknowledge the mistake of his first course: with his tract *Memories from the House of the Dead* he denounced those who had deceived him and led him to share the responsibility for a false accusation against the SI. The return of Schneider, whose character the liars had underestimated and who had thus been privileged to witness the full extent of their collective manipulation of embarrassing facts, struck a definitive blow in Strasbourg itself against the excluded and their accomplices, who had already been discredited everywhere else. In their spite these wretches, who the week before had gone to so much trouble to win over Schneider in order to add to the credibility of their venture, proclaimed him a notoriously feeble-minded person who had simply succumbed to "the prestige of the SI." (More and more often, recently, in the most diverse discussions, liars end up in this way unwittingly identifying "the prestige of the SI" with *the simple fact of telling the truth*—an amalgam that certainly does us honor.) Before three months had gone by, the association of Frey and consorts with Vayr-Piova and all those who were willing to maintain a keenly solicited adhesion (at one time there were as many as eight or nine of them) was to reveal its sad reality: based on infantile lies by individuals who considered each other to be clumsy liars, it was the very picture, involuntarily parodic, of a type of "collective action" that should never be engaged in; and with the type of people who should never be associated with! They went so far as to conduct a ludicrous *electoral campaign* before the students of Strasbourg. Dozens of pages of pedantic scraps of misremembered situationist ideas and phrases were, with a total unawareness of the absurdity, run off with the sole aim of *keeping the "power" of the Strasbourg chapter of the MNEF*, microbureaucratic fiefdom of Vayr-Piova, who was eligible for reelection 13 April. As successful in this venture as in their previous maneuvers, they were defeated by people as stupid as they were—Stalinists and Christians who were more naturally partial to electoralism, and who also enjoyed the bonus of being able to denounce their deplorable rivals as "false situationists." In the tract *The SI Told You So*, put out the next day, André Schneider and his comrades were easily able to show how this unsuccessful attempt to exploit the *remains* of the scandal of five months before for promotional purposes revealed itself as the complete renunciation of the spirit and the declared perspectives of that scandal. Finally Vayr-Piova, in a communiqué distributed 20 April, stated: "I find it amusing to be at last denounced as a 'nonsituationist'—something I have openly proclaimed since the SI set itself up as an official power." This is a representative sample of a vast and already forgotten literature. That the SI has become *an official power*—this is one of those theses typical of Vayr-Piova or Frey, which can be examined by those who are interested in the question; and after doing this they will know what to think of the intelligence of such theoreticians. But this aside, the fact that Vayr-Piova proclaims—"openly," or even perhaps "secretly" in a "proclamation" reserved for the most discreet accomplices in his lies, for example?—that he has not belonged to the SI since whenever was the date of our transformation into an "official power"—this is a *boldfaced lie*. Everyone who knows him knows that Vayr-Piova has *never* had the opportunity to claim to be anything but a "nonsituationist" (see what we wrote above concerning the AFGES communiqué of 29 November).

The most favorable results of this whole affair naturally go beyond this new and opportunely much-publicized example of our refusal to enlist anything that a neomilitantism in search of glorious subordination might throw our way. No less negligible is that aspect of the result that forced the official recognition of the irreparable decomposition of the UNEF, a decomposition that was even more advanced than its pitiful appearance suggested: the *coup de grâce* was still echoing in July at its 56th Congress in Lyon, in the course of which the sad president Vandenburie had to confess: "The unity of the UNEF has long since ended. Each association lives (*SI note: this term is pretentiously inaccurate*) autonomously, without paying any attention to the directives of the National Committee. The growing gap between the base and the governing bodies has reached a state of serious degradation. The history of the proceedings of the UNEF has been nothing but a series of crises. . . . Reorganization and a revival of action have not been possible." Equally comical were some side-effects stirred up among the academics who felt that this was another current issue to petition about. As can be well imagined, we considered the position published by the forty professors and assistants of the Faculty of Arts at Strasbourg, which denounced the *false students* behind this "tempest in a teacup" about false problems "without the shadow of a solution," to be more logical and socially rational (as was, for that matter, Judge Llabador's summing up) than that wheedling attempt at approval circulated in February by a few decrepit modernist-institutionalists gnawing their meager bones at the professorial chairs of "Social Sciences" at Nanterre (impudent Touraine, loyal Lefebvre, pro-Chinese Baudrillart, cunning Lourau).

In fact, we want ideas to become *dangerous* again. We cannot be accepted with the spinelessness of a false eclectic interest, as if we were Sartres, Althussers, Aragons or Godards. Let us note the wise words of a certain Professor Lhuillier, reported in the 21 December *Nouvel Observateur*: "I am for freedom of thought. But if there are any Situationists in the room, I want them to get out right now." While not entirely denying the effect that the dissemination of a few basic truths may have had in slightly accelerating the movement that is impelling the lagging French youth toward an awakening awareness of an impending more general crisis in the society, we think that the distribution of *On the Poverty of Student Life* has been a much more significant factor of clarification in some other countries where such a process is already much more clearly under way. In the afterword of their edition of Khayati's text, the English situationists wrote: "The most highly developed critique of modern life has been made in one of the least highly developed modern countries—in a country which has not yet reached the point where the complete disintegration of all values becomes patently obvious and engenders the corresponding forces of radical rejection. In the French context, situationist theory has anticipated the social forces by which it will be realized." The theses of *On the Poverty of Student Life* have been much more truly understood in the United States and England (the strike at the London School of Economics in March caused a certain stir, the *Times* commentator unhappily seeing in it a return of the class struggle he had thought was over with). To a lesser degree this is also the case in Holland—where the SI's critique, reinforcing a much harsher critique by events themselves, was not without effect on the recent dissolution of the "Provo" movement—and in the Scandinavian countries. The struggles of the West Berlin students this year have picked up something of the critique, though in a still very confused way.

But revolutionary youth naturally has no other course than to join with the mass of workers who, starting from the experience of the new conditions of exploitation, are going to take up once again the struggle for the domination of their world, for the suppression of work. When young people begin to know the current theoretical form of this real movement that is everywhere spontaneously bursting forth from the soil of modern society, this is only a *moment* of the progression by which this unified theoretical critique, which identifies itself with an adequate *practical unification*, strives to break the silence and the general organization of separation. It is only in this sense that we find the result satisfactory. We obviously exclude from these young people that alienated semiprivileged fraction molded by the university: this sector is the natural base for an admiring consumption of a fantasized situationist theory considered as the latest spectacular fashion. We will continue to disappoint and refute this kind of approbation. Sooner or later it will be understood that the SI must be judged not on the superficially scandalous aspects of certain manifestations through which it appears, but on its *essentially scandalous* central truth.

THE SITUATIONISTS
AND THE NEW FORMS OF ACTION
AGAINST POLITICS AND ART

Up to now our subversion has mainly drawn on the forms and categories inherited from past revolutionary struggles, mainly those of the
last century. I propose that we round out our contestatory expression
with means that dispense with any reference to the past. I mean by
this not that we should abandon the forms within which we have
waged battle on the traditional terrain of the supersession of philosophy, the realization of art and the abolition of politics; but that we
should extend the work of the journal onto terrains it does not yet
reach.

A great many proletarians are aware that they have no power over
their lives; they know it, but they don't express it in the language of
socialism and of previous revolutions.

Let us spit in passing on those students who have become militants
in the tiny would-be mass parties, who sometimes have the nerve to
claim that the workers are incapable of reading *Internationale Situationniste*, that its paper is too slick to be put in their lunchbags and
that its price doesn't take into account their low standard of living.
The most consistent of them thus distribute the mimeographed image
they have of the consciousness of a class in which they fervently seek
their stereotype Joe Worker. They forget, among other things, that
when workers read revolutionary literature in the past they had to
pay relatively more than for a theater ticket; and that when they once
again develop an interest in it they won't hesitate to spend two or
three times what it costs for an issue of *Planète*. But what these de-
tracters of typography forget most of all is that the rare individuals
who read their bulletins are precisely those who already have the
minimal background necessary to understand us right away, and that
what they write is completely unreadable for anyone else. Some of
them, ignoring the immense readership of bathroom graffiti, particularly in cafés, have thought that by using a parody of gradeschool
writing, printed on paper pasted on gutters like notices of apartments
for rent, they could make the form correspond to the content of their
slogans; and in this at least they have succeeded. All this serves to
clarify what must not be done.

What we have to do is link up the theoretical critique of modern
society with the critique of it in acts. By detourning the very propo-
sitions of the spectacle, we can explain on the spot the implications of
present and future revolts.

I propose that we pursue:

1. *Experimentation in the detournement of romantic photo-comics*
as well as of "pornographic" photos, and that we bluntly impose their
real truth by restoring real dialogues by adding or altering speech

bubbles. This operation will bring to the surface the subversive bubbles that are spontaneously, but more or less consciously, formed and then dissolved in the imaginations of those who look at these photos. In the same spirit, it is also possible to detourn *any* advertising billboards—particularly those in subway corridors, which form remarkable sequences—by pasting over pre-prepared placards.

2. *The promotion of guerrilla tactics in the mass media*: an important form of contestation, not only at the stage of urban guerrilla warfare, but even before it. The trail was blazed by those Argentinians who took over the control station of an electric newspaper and broadcast their own directives and slogans. It is still possible to take advantage of the fact that radio and television stations are not yet guarded by troops. On a more modest level, it is known that any ham radio operator can at little expense jam, if not broadcast, on a local level; and that the small size of the necessary equipment permits a great mobility, thus easily enabling one to slip away before one's position is trigonometrically located. A group of CP dissidents in Denmark had their own pirate radio station a few years ago. Counterfeit issues of one or another periodical can add to the confusion of the enemy. This list of examples is vague and limited for obvious reasons.

The illegality of such actions makes a sustained engagement on this terrain impossible for any organization that has not chosen to go underground, because it would otherwise entail the formation within it of a *specialized organization*, which cannot be effectual without compartmentalization and thus hierarchy, etc. Without, in a word, finding oneself on the slippery path toward terrorism.* We can more appropriately envision propaganda by deed, which is a very different matter. Our ideas are in everybody's mind, as is well known, and any group without any relation to us, or a few individuals coming together for a specific purpose, can improvise and improve on tactics experimented with elsewhere by others. This type of unconcerted action cannot be expected to bring about any decisive upheaval, but it can usefully serve to accentuate the coming awakening of consciousness. In any case, there's no need to get hung up on the idea of illegality. Most actions in this domain can be done without breaking any existing law. But the fear of such interventions will make newspaper editors paranoid about their typesetters, radio managers paranoid about their technicians, etc., at least until more specific repressive legislation has been worked out and enacted.

3. *The development of situationist comics.* Comic strips are the only truly popular literature of our century. Cretins marked by years at school have not been able to resist writing dissertations on them; but they'll get little pleasure out of reading ours. No doubt they'll buy them just to burn them. In our task of "making shame more shameful still," it is easy to see how easy it would be, for example, to transform "13 rue de l'Espoir [hope]" into "1 blvd. du Désespoir [despair]" merely by adding in a few elements; or balloons can simply be changed. In contrast to Pop Art, which breaks comics up into fragments, this method aims at restoring to comics their content and importance.

4. *The production of situationist films.* The cinema, which is the newest and undoubtedly most utilizable means of expression of our

time, has marked time for nearly three quarters of a century. To sum it up, we can say that it effectively became the "seventh art" so dear to film buffs, film clubs and parents' associations. For our purposes this age is over (Ince, Stroheim, the one and only *L'âge d'or*, *Citizen Kane* and *Mr. Arkadin*, the lettrist films), even if there remain a few traditional narrative masterpieces to be unearthed in the film archives or on the shelves of foreign distributors. We should appropriate the first stammerings of this new language; and above all its most consummate and modern examples, those which have escaped artistic ideology even more than American 'B' movies: newsreels, previews, and above all, filmed ads.

Although it has obviously been in the service of the commodity and the spectacle, filmed advertising, in its extreme freedom of technical means, has laid the foundations for what Eisenstein had an inkling of when he talked of filming *The Critique of Political Economy* or *The German Ideology*.

I am confident that I could film *The Decline and Fall of the Spectacle-Commodity Economy* in a way that would be immediately understandable to the proletarians of Watts who are ignorant of the concepts implied in that title. And this adaptation to a new form will undoubtedly contribute to deepening and intensifying the "written" expression of the same problems; which we could verify, for example, by making a film called *Incitement to Murder and Debauchery* before drafting its equivalent in the journal, *Correctives to the Consciousness of a Class That Will Be the Last*. Among other possibilities, the cinema lends itself particularly well to studying the present as a historical problem, to dismantling the processes of reification. To be sure, historical reality can be apprehended, known and filmed only in the course of a complicated process of mediations enabling consciousness to recognize one moment in another, its goal and its action in destiny, its destiny in its goal and action, and its own essence in this necessity. This mediation would be difficult if the empirical existence of facts themselves was not already a mediated existence, which only takes on an appearance of immediateness because and to the extent that consciousness of the mediation is lacking and that the facts have been uprooted from the network of their determining circumstances, placed in an artificial isolation and poorly strung together again in the montage of classical cinema. It is precisely this mediation which has been lacking, and inevitably so, in presituationist cinema, which has limited itself to "objective" forms or re-presentation of politico-moral concepts, whenever it has not been merely academic-type narrative with all its hypocrisies. If what I have just written were filmed, it would become much less complicated. This is all banalities. But Godard, the most famous Swiss Maoist, will never be able to understand them. He might well, as is his usual practice, recuperate the above—pick out a word from it or an idea like that concerning filmed advertisements—but he will never be capable of anything but brandishing little novelties picked up elsewhere: images or star words of the era, which definitely have a resonance, but one he can't grasp (Bonnot, worker, Marx, made in USA, Pierrot le Fou, Debord, poetry, etc.). He really is a child of Mao and Coca-Cola.

The cinema enables one to express anything, just like an article, a book, a leaflet or a poster. This is why we should henceforth require that each situationist be as capable of making a film as of writing an article (cf. "Anti–Public Relations," *IS* #8). Nothing is too beautiful for the blacks of Watts.

RENÉ VIÉNET

TO HAVE AS GOAL PRACTICAL TRUTH

In attempting to present to the new revolutionary forces a model of theoretico-practical coherence, the SI can and must at any moment sanction, by exclusion or break, the failings, insufficiencies and compromises of those making of it—or recognizing in it—the most advanced experimental stage of their common project. If the insurgent generation, determined to found a new society, manifests an alertness, based on indisputable first principles, to smash every *attempt* at recuperation, this is not at all out of a taste for purity, but out of a simple reflex of self-defense. In organizations prefiguring in their essential features the type of social organization to come, the least of requirements consists in not tolerating those people whom power is able to tolerate quite well.

In its positive aspect, the "exclusion" and "break" response raises the question of membership in the SI and of alliance with autonomous groups and individuals. In its "Minimum Definition of Revolutionary Organizations" the 7th Conference stressed among other things the following point: "A revolutionary organization refuses to reproduce within itself any of the hierarchical conditions of the dominant world. The only limit to participating in its total democracy is that each member must have recognized and appropriated the coherence of its critique. This coherence must be both in the critical theory proper and in the relationship between this theory and practical activity. The organization radically criticizes every ideology as separate power of ideas and as ideas of separate power."

The coherence of the critique and the critique of incoherence are one and the same movement, condemned to decay and rigidify into ideology the moment separation is introduced between different groups of a federation, between different members of an organization or between the theory and practice of one of its members. In the total struggle in which we are engaged, to yield an inch on the front of coherence is to allow separation to gain the upper hand all the way down the line. This is what spurs us to the greatest vigilance: to never take our coherence for granted, to remain alert to the dangers that threaten it in the fundamental unity of individual and collective behavior, to anticipate and avoid these dangers.

That a secret fraction [the Garnautins] was able to form among us, but also that it was rapidly exposed, sufficiently indicates our rigor and our lack of rigor in transparency in intersubjective relations. Put another way, this means that the SI's influence stems essentially from this: it is capable of *setting an example*, both negatively, by showing its weaknesses and correcting them, and positively, by deriving new exigencies from these corrections. We have often reiterated the importance of our not being mistaken in judging individuals; we have to prove this continually and thereby at the same time make it more impossible for people to be mistaken about us. And what goes for individuals goes for groups as well.

We recall the words of Socrates to one of the young men he was talking to: "Speak a little so I can see what sort of person you are." We are in a position to avoid this kind of Socrates and this kind of young man if the exemplary character of our activity ensures the radiating force of our presence in and against the reigning spectacle. To the mafiosi of recuperation and to the smalltime jerks who are going to agree to present us as a directing group, we should counterpose the antihierarchical example of permanent radicalization—we must not dissimulate any part of our experiences; we must establish, through the dissemination of our methods, critical theses and agitational tactics, the greatest transparency concerning the collective project of liberating everyday life.

The SI should act like an axis which, receiving its movement from the revolutionary impulses of the entire world, precipitates in a unitary manner the radical turn of events. In contrast to the backward sectors that persistently strive for tactical unity above all else (common, national and popular fronts), the SI and allied autonomous organizations will meet each other only in the search for organic unity, considering that tactical unity is effective only where organic unity is possible. Group or individual, everyone must live in pace with the radicalization of events in order to radicalize them in turn. Revolutionary coherence is nothing else.

We are certainly still far from such a harmony of progression, but we are just as certainly working toward it. The movement from first principles to their realization involves groups and individuals, and thus their possible retardations. Only transparency in real participation cuts short the menace that weighs on coherence: the transformation of retardation into separation. Everything that still separates us from the realization of the situationist project is only the result of the hostility of the old world we live in; but the awareness of these separations already contains their resolution.

Now, it is precisely in the struggle against separations that retardation appears in various degrees; it is there that unconsciousness of retardation obscures consciousness of separations, thereby introducing incoherence. When consciousness rots, ideology oozes out. We have seen Kotányi keep the results of his analyses to himself, communicating them drop by drop with the niggardly superiority of a water clock over time; and others (the most recently excluded) keeping to themselves their deficiencies in all respects, making like a peacock while lacking the tail. Mystical wait-and-see-ism and egalitarian ecumenicalism had the same odor. Vanish, grotesque charlatans of incurable malaises!

The notion of retardation pertains to the ludic mode, it is connected with the notion of "game leader." Just as dissimulation of retardation or of experiences recreates the notion of prestige, tends to transform the game leader into a chief and engenders stereotyped behavior (roles, with all their neurotic outgrowths, their contorted attitudes, their inhumanity), so transparency enables us to enter the common project with the calculated innocence of [Fourier's] phalansterian players, emulating each other ("composite" passion), varying their activities ("butterfly" passion) and striving for the most advanced radicality ("cabalist" passion). But lightheartedness must be based on conscious, "heavy" relationships. It implies lucidity regarding everyone's abilities.

We don't want to know anything about abilities apart from the revolutionary use that can be made of them, a use that acquires its sense in everyday life. The problem is not that some comrades live, think, fuck, shoot or talk better than others, but that no comrade should live, think, fuck, shoot or talk so poorly that he comes to dissimulate his retardations, to play the oppressed minority and demand, in the very name of the surplus-value he grants to the others because of his own insufficiencies, a democracy of impotence in which he would obviously affirm his mastery. In other words, every revolutionary must at the very least have the passion to defend his most precious attribute: his passion for individual realization, his desire to liberate his own everyday life.

If someone gives up engaging the totality of his abilities—and consequently their development—in the fight for his creativity, his dreams, his passions, thereby giving up himself, he has thereby immediately debarred himself from speaking in his own name, and all the more so from speaking in the name of a group embodying the chances for the realization of all individuals. The exclusion or break only concretizes publicly—with the logic of transparency he lacked—his taste for sacrifice, his choice of the inauthentic.

On questions of membership or alliance, the *example* of real participation in the revolutionary project is the deciding factor. Consciousness of retardations, struggle against separations, passion to attain greater coherence—this is what must constitute the basis of an objective confidence among us, as well as between the SI and autonomous groups and federations. There is every reason to hope that our allies will rival us in the radicalization of revolutionary conditions, just as we expect those who will join us to do so. Everything allows us to suppose that at a certain point in the extension of revolutionary consciousness each group will have attained such a coherence that the game-leading level of all the participants and the negligibility of retardations will enable individuals to vary their options and change organizations according to their passional affinities. But the momentary preeminence of the SI is a fact that must also be taken into account: a gratifying disgrace, like the ambiguous smile of the Cheshire Cat of invisible revolutions.

Because the International has today a theoretical and practical wealth at its disposal that only increases once it is shared, appropriated and renewed by revolutionary elements (up to the point when the

SI and the autonomous groups in turn disappear into the revolutionary richness), it must welcome only those wanting to take part in it who fully know what they are doing; that is, anyone who has demonstrated that in speaking and acting for himself, he speaks and acts in the name of many, whether by creating through the poetry of his praxis (leaflet, riot, film, agitation, book) a regroupment of subversive forces, or by his turning out to be the only one to maintain coherence in the process of the radicalization of a group. The advisability of his entry into the SI then becomes a tactical question to be debated: either the group is strong enough to cede one of its game leaders, or its failure is such that the game leaders are the only ones to have a say in the matter, or the game leader, due to unavoidable objective circumstances, has not succeeded in forming a group.

Wherever the new proletariat experiments with its emancipation, autonomy in revolutionary coherence is the first step toward generalized self-management. The lucidity that we are striving to maintain concerning ourselves and the world teaches us that in organizational practice there's no such thing as too much precision or alertness. On the question of freedom, an error of detail is already a truth of state.

RAOUL VANEIGEM

CONTRIBUTIONS TOWARD RECTIFYING PUBLIC OPINION CONCERNING REVOLUTION IN THE UNDERDEVELOPED COUNTRIES

1

The eminently revolutionary role of the bourgeoisie consists in having introduced the economy into history in a decisive and irreversible way. Faithful master of this economy, the bourgeoisie has since its appearance been the effective—though at times unconscious—master of "universal history." For the first time universal history ceased to be some metaphysical fantasy or some act of the *Weltgeist* and became a material fact as concrete as the trivial existence of each individual. Since the emergence of commodity production, nothing in the world escapes the implacable development of this neo-Fate, the invisible economic rationality: *the logic of the commodity*. Totalitarian and imperialist in essence, it demands the entire planet as its terrain and the whole of mankind as its servants. Wherever the *commodity* is present there are only slaves.

2

To the bourgeoisie's oppressive coherence in keeping humanity in *prehistory*, the revolutionary movement—a direct and unintended product of bourgeois capitalist domination—has for more than a century counterposed the project of a liberatory coherence, the work of each and everyone, the free, conscious intervention in the creation of *history*: the real abolition of all class division and the suppression of the economy.

3

Wherever it has penetrated—that is, almost everywhere in the world—the virus of the commodity never stops toppling the most ossified socioeconomic structures, allowing millions of human beings to discover through poverty and violence the historical time of the economy. Wherever it penetrates it spreads its destructive principle, dissolves the vestiges of the past and pushes all antagonisms to their extreme. In a word, it hastens social revolution. All the walls of China crumble in its path, and scarcely has it established itself in India when everything around it disintegrates and agrarian revolutions explode in Bombay, in Bengal and in Madras: the precapitalist zones of the world accede to bourgeois modernity, but without its material basis. There also, as in the case of the proletariat, the forces that the bourgeoisie has contributed toward liberating, or even creating, are now going to turn against the bourgeoisie and its native servants: the revolution of the underdeveloped is becoming one of the main chapters of modern history.

4

If the problem of revolution in the underdeveloped countries poses itself in a particular way, this is due to the very development of history: In these countries the general economic backwardness—fostered by colonial domination and the social strata that support it—and the underdevelopment of productive forces have impeded the development of socioeconomic structures that would have made immediately practicable the revolutionary theory elaborated in the advanced capitalist societies for more than a century. All these countries, at the time they enter the struggle, lack heavy industry, and the proletariat is far from being the majority class. It is the poor peasantry that assumes that function.

5

The various national liberation movements appeared well after the rout of the workers movement resulting from the defeat of the Russian revolution, which right from its victory turned into a counterrevolution in the service of a bureaucracy claiming to be communist. They have thus suffered—either consciously or with false consciousness—from all the defects and weaknesses of that generalized counterrevolution; and with the general backwardness added to this, they have been unable to overcome any of the limits imposed on the defeated revolutionary movement. And it is precisely because of this defeat that the colonized and semicolonized countries have had to fight imperialism by themselves. But because they have fought only imperialism and on only a part of the total revolutionary terrain, they have only *partially* driven it out. The oppressive regimes that have installed themselves wherever national liberation revolutions believed themselves victorious are only one of the guises by which the *return of the repressed* takes place.

6

No matter what forces have participated in them, and regardless of the radicalism of their leaderships, the national liberation movements have *always* led the ex-colonial societies to *modern forms of the state* and to pretensions of modernity in the economy. In China, father-image of underdeveloped revolutionaries, the peasants' struggle against American, European and Japanese imperialism ended up, because of the defeat of the Chinese workers movement in 1925–1927, bringing to power a bureaucracy on the Russian model. The Stalino-Leninist dogmatism with which this bureaucracy gilds its ideology—recently reduced to Mao's red catechism—is nothing but the lie, or at best the false consciousness, that accompanies its counterrevolutionary practice.

7

Fanonism and Castro-Guevaraism are the false consciousness through which the peasantry carries out the immense task of ridding precapitalist society of its semifeudal and colonialist leftovers and acceding to a national dignity previously trampled on by colonists and retrograde dominant classes. Ben-Bellaism, Nasserism, Titoism and Maoism are the ideologies that announce the end of these movements and their privative appropriation by the petty-bourgeois or military urban strata: the reconstitution of exploitative society, but this time with new masters and based on new socioeconomic structures. Wherever the peasantry has fought victoriously and brought to power the social strata that marshaled and directed its struggle, it has been the first to suffer their violence and to pay the enormous cost of their domination. Modern bureaucracy, like that of antiquity (in China, for example), builds its power and prosperity on the superexploitation of the peasants: ideology changes nothing in the matter. In China or Cuba, Egypt or Algeria, everywhere it plays the same role and assumes the same functions.

8

In the process of capital accumulation, *the bureaucracy is the realization of that of which the bourgeoisie was only the concept.* What the bourgeoisie has done for centuries, "through blood and mud," the bureaucracy wants to achieve consciously and "rationally" in a few decades. But the bureaucracy cannot accumulate capital without accumulating lies: that which constituted the *original sin* of capitalist wealth is sinisterly baptized "socialist primitive accumulation." Everything that the underdeveloped bureaucracies present as or imagine to be socialism is nothing but a realized *neomercantilism*. "The bourgeois state minus the bourgeoisie" (Lenin) cannot go beyond the historical tasks of the bourgeoisie, and the most advanced industrial country shows to the less developed ones the *image* of their own development to come. Once in power, the Bolshevik bureaucracy could find nothing better to propose to the revolutionary Russian proletariat than to "follow the lessons of German state-capitalism." All the so-called "socialist" powers are at most underdeveloped imitations of the bureaucracy that dominated and defeated the revolutionary movement in Europe. What the bureaucracy can do or is forced to do will neither emancipate the laboring masses nor substantially improve their social condition, because that depends not only on the productive forces but also on *their appropriation by the producers*. In any case, what the bureaucracy will not fail to do is create the material conditions to realize both. Has the bourgeoisie ever done less?

9

In the peasant-bureaucratic revolutions only the bureaucracy aims consciously and lucidly at power. The seizure of power is the historical moment when the bureaucracy lays hold of the state and declares its independence vis-à-vis the revolutionary masses before even having eliminated the vestiges of colonialism and achieving effective independence from foreign powers. Upon entering the state, the new class suppresses all autonomy of the masses by ostensibly suppressing its own autonomy and devoting itself to the service of the masses. Exclusive owner of the entire society, it declares itself the exclusive representative of the society's superior interests. In so doing, the bureaucratic state is the Hegelian State realized. Its separation from society sanctions at the same time the society's separation into antagonistic classes: the momentary union of the bureaucracy and the peasantry is only the fantastic illusion through which both accomplish the immense historical tasks of the absent bourgeoisie. The bureaucratic power built on the ruins of precapitalist colonial society is not the abolition of class antagonisms; it merely substitutes new classes, new conditions of oppression and new forms of struggle for the old ones.

10

The only people who are underdeveloped are those who see a positive value in the power of their masters. The rush to catch up with capitalist reification remains the best road to reinforced underdevelopment. The question of economic development is inseparable from the question of who is the real owner of the economy, the real master of labor power; all the rest is specialists' babble.

11

So far revolutions in the underdeveloped countries have only tried to imitate Bolshevism in various ways; from now on the point is to dissolve it in the *power of the soviets*.

MUSTAPHA KHAYATI

MINIMUM DEFINITION OF
REVOLUTIONARY ORGANIZATIONS

Since the only purpose of a revolutionary organization is the abolition of all existing classes in a way that does not bring about a new division of society, we consider any organization revolutionary which *consistently and effectively* works toward the international realization of the absolute power of the workers councils, as prefigured in the experience of the proletarian revolutions of this century.

Such an organization makes a unitary critique of the world, or is nothing. By unitary critique we mean a comprehensive critique of all geographical areas where various forms of separate socioeconomic powers exist, as well as a comprehensive critique of all aspects of life.

Such an organization sees the beginning and end of its program in the complete decolonization of everyday life. It thus aims not at the masses' self-management of the *existing world*, but at its uninterrupted transformation. It embodies the radical critique of *political economy*, the supersession of the commodity and of wage labor.

Such an organization refuses to reproduce within itself any of the hierarchical conditions of the dominant world. The only limit to participating in its total democracy is that each member must have recognized and appropriated the *coherence of its critique*. This coherence must be both in the critical theory proper and in the relationship between this theory and practical activity. The organization radically criticizes every *ideology* as *separate power* of ideas and as *ideas of separate power*. It is thus at the same time the negation of any remnants of religion, and of the prevailing social *spectacle* which, from news media to mass culture, monopolizes communication between people around their unilateral reception of images of their alienated activity. The organization dissolves any "revolutionary ideology," unmasking it as a sign of the failure of the revolutionary project, as the private property of new specialists of power, as one more fraudulent *representation* setting itself above real proletarianized life.

Since the *ultimate criterion* of the modern revolutionary organization is its totalness, such an organization is ultimately a critique of politics. It must explicitly aim to dissolve itself as a separate organization at its moment of victory.

Adopted by the 7th Conference of the SI, July 1966.

SIX POSTSCRIPTS TO THE PREVIOUS ISSUE

(excerpts)

It seems to us that the insurrections of the blacks in Newark and Detroit have indisputably confirmed our 1965 analysis of the Watts revolt: in particular, the participation of numerous whites in the looting demonstrates that in its deepest sense Watts really was "a revolt against the commodity" and the first summary response to "commodity abundance." On the other hand, the danger of the *leadership* that is trying to constitute itself over the movement is now taking more definite shape: the Newark Conference has adopted the essential features of the Black Muslim program of black capitalism. Carmichael and the other "Black Power" stars are walking the tightrope between the vague, *undefined* extremism necessary to establish themselves at the head of the black masses (Mao, Castro, power to the blacks and we don't even have to say what we're going to do about the 9/10 of the population who are white) and the *actual* unavowed paltry *reformism* of a black "third party" which would auction off its swing vote in the American political marketplace and which would eventually create, in the person of Carmichael and his colleagues, an "elite" like those that emerged out of the other American minorities (Poles, Italians, etc.), an elite that has so far never developed among the blacks.

In Algeria, too, Boumedienne has unfortunately proved the correctness of our theses on his regime. Self-management is dead. We have no doubt we will see it return under more favorable conditions. But for the moment no revolutionary network has succeeded in forming on the basis of the offensive resistance of the self-managed sector; and our own direct efforts toward this goal have been enormously insufficient. [. . .]

Daniel Guérin wrote to us to say that our note about him was unfair and that he wanted to explain himself. We met him. He had to admit that we gave a correct account of his theses on Algeria, which are at the opposite pole from ours. He complained only of having been presented as a sort of agent of Ben Bella. We stated that our note in no way suggests such an idea. Guérin explained his admiration for Ben Bella by psychological arguments whose sincerity we don't question: He had found Ben Bella very likable, particularly after thirty years of disappointments with his other North African militant anticolonialist friends who have generally ended up becoming government officials. Ben Bella remained a man of the people, that was his good side. He became President of the Republic, that was his failing. Guérin already found Ben Bella's Algeria "miraculous" and reproached us for demanding a succession of additional miracles. We replied that such a succession was precisely our conception of revolution; that any single "miracle" that remains miraculous—isolated, exceptional—will quickly disappear. We proposed to Guérin that he publish a text in response to our article; but he considered that his oral explanation was sufficient. [. . .]

THE BEGINNING OF AN ERA

"These Germans will make a political revolution in *our* lifetime? My friend, that is just wishful thinking," wrote Arnold Ruge to Marx in March 1844; and four years later that revolution had come. As an amusing example of a type of historical unconsciousness constantly produced by similar causes and always contradicted by similar results, Ruge's unfortunate statement was quoted as an epigraph in *The Society of the Spectacle*, which appeared December 1967; and six months later came the occupations movement, the greatest revolutionary moment in France since the Paris Commune.

The largest general strike that ever stopped the economy of an advanced industrial country, and the first *wildcat general strike* in history; revolutionary occupations and first steps toward direct democracy; the increasingly complete withering of state power for nearly two weeks; the complete verification of the revolutionary theory of our time and even here and there the beginning of its partial realization; the most important experience of the modern proletarian movement that is in the process of constituting itself in its *fully developed* form in all countries, and the model it must now go beyond—this is what the French May 1968 movement was essentially, and this in itself is *already* its essential victory.

Further on we will go into the movement's weaknesses and deficiencies, which were the natural consequences of ignorance, improvisation and the dead weight of the past exerting themselves precisely where this movement best asserted itself; the consequences, above all, of the *separations* that all the joint forces for the preservation of the capitalist order narrowly succeeded in defending, with the politico-union bureaucratic machines exerting themselves to this end more intensely and effectively than the police at this moment of life or death for the system. But let us first enumerate the evident characteristics at the *heart* of the occupations movement, where it was freest to translate its content into words and acts. There it proclaimed its goals *much more explicitly* than any other spontaneous revolutionary movement in history; and those goals were much more radical and up-to-date than were ever expressed in the programs of the revolutionary organizations of the past, even at their best moments.

The occupations movement was the sudden return of the proletariat as a historical class, a proletariat *enlarged* to include a majority of the wage laborers of modern society and still tending toward the actual suppression of classes and wage labor. The movement was a rediscovery of collective and individual history, an awareness of the possibility of intervening in history, an awareness of participating in an irreversible event ("Nothing will ever be the same again"); people looked back in amusement at the *strange* existence they had led a week before, at their outlived survival. It was a *generalized critique* of all alienations, of all ideologies and of the entire old organization of real life; it was the passion for generalization and unification. In such a process property was negated, everyone finding themselves at home everywhere. The *recognized desire* for dialogue, for completely free expression, and the taste for real community found their terrain in the buildings transformed into open meeting places and in the common struggle. The telephones (which were among the few technical means still functioning) and the wandering of so many emissaries and travelers through Paris and throughout the entire country, between the occupied buildings, the factories and the assemblies, manifested this real practice of communication. The occupations movement was obviously a rejection of alienated labor; it was a festival, a game, a real presence of people and of time. And it was a rejection of all authority, all specialization, all hierarchical dispossession; a rejection of the state and thus of the parties and unions, a rejection of sociologists and professors, of medicine and repressive morality. All those awakened by the lightning chain-reaction of the movement (one of the graffiti, perhaps the most beautiful, simply said, *"Quick"*) thoroughly despised their former conditions of existence and therefore those who had worked to keep them there, from the television stars to the urbanists. Many people's Stalinist illusions, in various diluted forms from Castro to Sartre, were torn apart, and all the rival and interdependent lies of an era crumbled. International solidarity spontaneously reappeared: numerous foreign workers flung themselves into the struggle and many European revolutionaries rushed to France. The extensive participation of women in all aspects of struggle was an unmistakable sign of its revolutionary depth. The liberation of mores took a big step forward. The movement was also a critique, still partially illusory, of the commodity (in its inept sociological disguise as "consumer society"), and already a *rejection* of art that did not yet know itself as the historical *negation* of art (a rejection expressed in the poor abstract slogan, "Power to the imagination," which did not know the means to put this power into practice, to reinvent everything; and which, lacking power, lacked imagination). Hatred of *recuperators* was expressed everywhere, though it did not yet reach the theoretico-practical knowledge of how to get rid of them: the neoartists, the political neoleaders, the neospectators of the very movement that contradicted them. If the critique in acts of the spectacle of nonlife was not yet the revolutionary supersession of these recuperators, this was because the "spontaneously councilist" tendency of the May uprising was ahead of almost all the concrete means, including theoretical and organizational consciousness, that will enable it to transform itself into a power by being the only power.

Let us spit in passing on the trivializing commentaries and false testimonies by sociologists, retired Marxists and all the doctrinaires of the old preserved ultraleftism or of the servile ultramodernism of spectacular society; no one who *lived* this movement can deny that it contained everything we have said.

In March 1966, in *Internationale Situationniste* #10 (p. 77), we wrote, "What might appear to be audacious speculation in several of our assertions, we advance with the assurance that the future will bring their overwhelming and undeniable historical confirmation." It couldn't have been said better.

Naturally we had prophesied nothing. We had simply pointed out what was *already present*: the material preconditions for a new society had long since been produced; the old class society had maintained itself *everywhere* by considerably modernizing its oppression, while developing its contradictions ever more *abundantly*; the previously vanquished proletarian movement was returning for a second, more conscious and more total assault. Many people, of course, were already aware of these facts, so clearly demonstrated by history and by the present, and some people even stated them; but they did so abstractly and thus in a vacuum, without any echo, without any possibility of intervention. The merit of the situationists was simply to have recognized and pointed out the new focuses of revolt in modern society (focuses which do not at all exclude the old ones, but on the contrary bring them back to light): urbanism, the spectacle, ideology, etc. Because this task was carried out radically, it was able to stir up, or at least considerably reinforce, certain practical acts of revolt. If our enterprise struck a certain chord it was because the critique *without concessions* was scarcely to be found among the leftisms of the preceding period. If many people *did* what we *wrote*, it was because we essentially wrote the negative that had been lived by us and by so many others before us. What thus came to the light of consciousness in the spring of 1968 was nothing other than what had been sleeping in the night of the "spectacular society," whose spectacles showed nothing but an eternal positive façade. But we had "cohabited with the negative" in accordance with the program we formulated in 1962 (see *IS* #7, p. 10). We are not going into our "merits" in order to be applauded, but for the benefit of others who are going to act in similar ways.

All those who shut their eyes to this "critique in the melee" only saw, in the immovable force of modern domination, the reflection of their own renunciation. Their antiutopian "realism" was no more real than a police station or the Sorbonne were more real buildings before than after their transformation by arsonists or "Katangans."* When the subterranean phantoms of total revolution rose and extended their force over the entire country, it was then all the forces of the old world that appeared as ghostly illusions dissipated in the daylight. Quite simply, after thirty years of poverty that in the history of revolutions amounted to no more than a month, came this month of May that recapitulated thirty years.

To transform our desires into reality is a precise task, precisely the contrary of the task of the intellectual prostitution that grafts its illusions of permanence onto any reality that happens to exist. Take Lefebvre, for example, whom we already quoted in the preceding issue of this journal (October 1967) because in his book *Positions contre les technocrates* (Gonthier) he ventured a categorical conclusion whose scientific validity was revealed scarcely more than six months later: "The situationists . . . propose not a concrete utopia, but an abstract one. Do they really imagine that one fine day or one decisive evening people will look at each other and say, 'Enough! We're fed up with work and boredom! Let's put an end to them!' and that they will then proceed into the eternal Festival and the creation of situations? Although this happened once, at the dawn of 18 March 1871, this combination of circumstances will not occur again." A certain intellectual influence has been attributed to Lefebvre for certain of the SI's radical theses that he surreptitiously copied (see in this issue the reproduction of our 1963 tract *Into the Trashcan of History*),* but he reserved the truth of that critique for the past, even though it was born out of the *present* more than out of his academic reflections on the past. He warned against the illusion that any present struggle could ever again achieve those results. Don't jump to the conclusion that Henri Lefebvre is the only former thinker the events have made a complete fool of: those who avoided committing themselves to such ludicrous declarations nevertheless had the same convictions. Overcome by their shock in May, all the *researchers of historical nothingness* have admitted that no one had in any way foreseen what occurred. We must acknowledge a sort of exception to this in the case of all the sects of "resurrected Bolsheviks," of whom it is fair to say that for the last thirty years they have not for one instant ceased heralding the imminence of the revolution *of 1917*. But they too were badly mistaken: this was not at all 1917 and they were not even exactly Lenin. As for the remains of the old non-Trotskyist ultraleft, they still needed at least a major economic crisis. They made any revolutionary moment contingent on its return, and saw nothing coming. Now that they have recognized a revolutionary crisis in May they therefore have to prove that in the spring of 1968 there was some *invisible* economic crisis. They are earnestly working on this problem without fear of ridicule, producing diagrams of increases in prices and unemployment. For them the economic crisis is thus no longer that terribly conspicuous objective reality that was so extensively experienced and described up through 1929, but rather a sort of eucharistic presence that is one of the foundations of their religion.

Just as it would be necessary to reissue the entire collection of *IS* journals in order to show how greatly all these people were mistaken *before* May, so it would require a thick volume to go through all the stupidities and semiadmissions they have produced since then. We will limit ourselves to citing the picturesque journalist Gaussen, who felt that he could reassure the readers of *Le Monde* on 9 December 1966 that the few situationist maniacs who perpetrated the Strasbourg scandal had "a messianic confidence in the revolutionary capacity of the masses and in their aptitude for freedom." Since then Frédéric Gaussen's aptitude for freedom has not progressed one millimeter, but we find him in the same paper, 29 January 1969, panic-stricken at finding everywhere "the feeling that revolutionary aspirations are universal." "Highschoolers in Rome, students in Berlin, 'enragés' in Madrid, 'Lenin's orphans' in Prague, radical dissidents in Belgrade, all are attacking the same world, the Old World . . ." And Gaussen, using almost the same words as before, now attributes to all those revolutionary masses the same "quasimystical belief in the creative spontaneity of the masses."

We don't want to dwell in triumph on the discomfiture of all our intellectual adversaries; not that this "triumph," which is in fact simply that of the modern revolutionary movement, is not quite significant, but because the subject is so monotonous and because the reappearance of history, the reappearance of direct class struggle recognizing *present-day* revolutionary goals, has pronounced such a clear verdict on the whole period that came to an end in May* (previously it was the subversion of the existing society that seemed unlikely; now it is its continuation). Instead of going over what is already verified, it is henceforth more important to pose the new problems; to *criticize the May movement* and embark on the practice of the new era.

In all other countries the recent and up to now confused quest for a radical critique of modern capitalism (private or bureaucratic) had not yet broken out of the narrow base it had in the student milieu. In complete contrast, whatever the government, the newspapers and the ideologists of modernist sociology pretend to believe, *the May movement was not a student movement*. It was a revolutionary proletarian movement rising again after a half century of suppression and generally *deprived* of everything. Its unfortunate paradox was that it was able to concretely express itself and take shape only on the very unfavorable *terrain* of a student revolt: the streets held by the rioters around the Latin Quarter and the largely university buildings occupied in the same area. Instead of lingering over the laughable historical parody of Leninist or Maoist-Stalinist students disguising themselves as proletarians and as the leading vanguard of the proletariat, it must be realized that it was, on the contrary, the most advanced segment of the workers, unorganized and separated by all the forms of repression, that was *disguised as students* in the reassuring imagery of the unions and the spectacular news. The May movement was not some political theory looking for workers to carry it out; it was the acting proletariat seeking its theoretical consciousness.

The *sabotage* of the university by a few groups of young and notoriously *antistudent* revolutionaries at Nantes and Nanterre (we are referring here to the "Enragés" and not, of course, to the majority of the "March 22nd Movement" who later imitated their actions) presented the *opportunity* to develop forms of direct struggle that workers, mainly young ones, had already in their dissatisfaction initiated in the early months of 1968 (at Caen and Redon, for example). But this circumstance was in no way fundamental and could do the movement no harm. What was harmful was the fact that the unions were eventually able to control the *wildcat strike* that had been launched against their will and despite all their maneuvers. They accepted the strike they had been unable to prevent, which is the usual tactic of a union faced with a wildcat; but this time they had to accept one on a national scale. And by accepting this "unofficial" general strike they remained accepted by it. They remained in possession of the factory gates, simultaneously *isolating* the vast majority of the workers *from the real movement* and each plant from all the others. Thus the most unitary action and the most *radical* critique-in-action ever seen was at the same time a sum of isolations and a pageant of banal, officially approved demands. Just as the unions had to let the general strike

229

spread *little by little*, winding up in virtual unanimity, so they strove to liquidate the strike little by little, using the terrorism of falsification and their monopoly of communication to coerce the workers in each separate enterprise to accept the crumbs they had *all* collectively rejected on 27 May. The revolutionary strike was thus reduced to a *cold war* balance of power between the union bureaucracies and the workers. The unions *recognized* the strike on the condition that the strike tacitly recognize, by its practical passivity, *that it would lead nowhere*. The unions did not "miss an opportunity" to act revolutionarily, because from the Stalinists to the bourgeoisified reformists there is nothing revolutionary about them. And if they did not even act to bring about *substantial reforms*, it was because the situation was too dangerously revolutionary to play around with, even to try to exploit it to their own advantage. They very obviously wanted it to be brought to a stop immediately, at any cost. In this exceptional moment the Stalinists—admirably imitated in this hypocrisy by the semileftist sociologists (cf. Coudray in *La Brèche*, Editions du Seuil, 1968)—though usually of such a contrary opinion, suddenly feigned an extraordinary respect for the competence of the workers, for their wise "decision," presented with the most fantastic cynicism as having been clearly debated, voted in full knowledge of the facts and absolutely unequivocal: for once the workers supposedly knew what they wanted because "they did not want a revolution"! But all the obstacles and muzzles and lies that the panic-stricken bureaucrats resorted to in the face of this supposed *unwillingness* of the workers constitutes the best proof of their real will, unarmed but dangerous. It is only by forgetting the historical totality of the movement of modern society that one can blather on in this circular positivism, which thinks it sees a rationality everywhere in the existing order because it raises its "science" to the point of successively considering that order from the side of the demand and the side of the response. Thus the same Coudray notes, "If you have these unions, a raise of 5% is the most you can get, and if 5% is what you want, these unions suffice." Leaving aside the question of their intentions in relation to their real life and their interests, what all these gentlemen lack at the very least is dialectics.

The workers, who as always and everywhere naturally had quite enough good reasons for being dissatisfied, started the wildcat strike because they sensed the *revolutionary situation* created by the new forms of sabotage in the universities and the government's successive mistakes in reacting to them. They were obviously as indifferent as we were to the forms and reforms of the university system; but certainly not to the critique of advanced capitalism's culture, environment and everyday life, a critique that spread so quickly upon the first rip in that university veil.

By launching the wildcat strike the workers *gave the lie to the liars* who spoke in their name. In most of the factories they proved incapable of really speaking on their own behalf and of *saying what they wanted*. But in order to say what they want it is first necessary for the workers to create, through their own autonomous action, the concrete conditions that enable them to speak and act, conditions that now exist *nowhere*. The absence, almost everywhere, of such dialogue, of such linking up, as well as the lack of theoretical knowledge of the autonomous goals of proletarian class struggle (these two factors being able to develop only together), prevented the workers from *expropriating the expropriators of their real life*. Thus the advanced nucleus of workers, around which the next revolutionary proletarian organization will take shape, came to the Latin Quarter as a *poor relative* of a "student reformism" that was itself a largely artificial product of pseudoinformation or of the illusionism of the little leftist sects. This advanced nucleus included young blue-collar workers; white-collar workers from the occupied offices; delinquents and unemployed; rebellious high-schoolers, who were often those working-class youth that modern capitalism recruits for the cut-rate education designed to prepare them for a role in developed industry (*"Stalinists, your children are with us!"* was one of the slogans); "lost intellectuals"; and "Katangans."

The fact that a significant fraction of French students took part in the movement, particularly in Paris, is obvious; but this cannot be invoked as fundamentally characterizing the movement, or even as one of its main aspects. Out of 150,000 Parisian *students* at most 10–20 thousand were present during the least difficult times of the demonstrations, and only a few thousand during the violent street confrontations. The sole moment of the crisis involving students alone—admittedly one of the decisive moments for its extension—was the spontaneous uprising of the Latin Quarter on 3 May following the arrest of the leftist leaders in the Sorbonne. On the day after the occupation of the Sorbonne nearly half the participants in its general assemblies, at a time when those assemblies had clearly taken on an insurgent role, were still students worried about the conditions for their exams and hoping for some university reform in their favor. Probably a slight majority of the *student* participants recognized that the question of power was posed, but they usually did so as naïve clientele of the little leftist parties, as spectators of old Leninist schemas or even of the Far Eastern exoticism of Maoist Stalinism. The base of these little leftist groups was indeed almost exclusively confined to the student milieu; and the *poverty* that was sustained there was clearly evident in virtually all the leaflets issuing from that milieu: nothingness of all the Kravetzes, stupidity of all the Péninous. Even the best statements of the workers who came to the Sorbonne during the first days were often stupidly received with a pedantic and condescending attitude by these students who fantasized themselves as PhDs in revolution, although they were ready to salivate and applaud at the stimulus of the clumsiest manipulator proclaiming some stupidity while invoking "the working class." Nevertheless, the very fact that these groups manage to recruit a certain number of students is already a symptom of the malaise in present-day society: these little groups are the theatrical expression of a real yet vague revolt that is bargain-shopping for its answers. Finally, the fact that a small fraction of students really supported all the radical demands of May is another indication of the depth of the movement; and remains to their credit.

Although several thousand students, as individuals, were able through their experience of 1968 to break more or less completely with the position assigned to them in the society, the mass of students were not transformed by it. This was not in virtue of the pseudo-Marxist platitude that considers the student's social *background* (bourgeois or petty-bourgeois in the great majority of cases) as the determining factor, but rather because of his social destiny: the student's *becoming* is the truth of his being. He is mass-produced and conditioned for an upper, middle or lower position in the organization of modern industrial production. Moreover, the student is being dishonest when he affects to be scandalized at "discovering" this logic of his education, which has always been proclaimed openly. It is evident that the economic uncertainties of his optimum employment, and especially the dubious desirability of the "privileges" present society can offer him, have played a role in his bewilderment and revolt. But it is precisely because of this that the student is such a perfect customer, eagerly seeking his quality brand in the ideology of one or another of the little bureaucratic groups. The student who dreams of himself as a Bolshevik or a swaggering Stalinist (i.e. a Maoist) is playing both sides: Simply as a result of his studies he reckons on obtaining some modest position managing some small sector of the society as a cadre of capitalism, should a change in power never arrive to fulfill his wishes. And in case his dream of such a power change were to become a reality, he sees himself in an even more glorious managerial role and a higher rank as a "scientifically" warranted political cadre. These groups' dreams of domination are often clumsily revealed in the contempt their fanatics have the nerve to express toward certain aspects of workers' demands, which they often term "mere bread and butter issues." In this impotence that would be better advised to keep silent one can already glimpse the disdain with which these leftists would like to be able to respond to any future discontent among these same workers if these self-appointed specialists in the general interests of the proletariat ever managed to get their little hands on state power and police; as in Kronstadt, as in Peking. But leaving aside this perspective of these germ-carriers of sovereign bureaucracies, nothing serious can be recognized in the sociologico-journalistic oppositions between rebellious students, who are supposedly rejecting "consumer society," and the workers, who are supposedly still eager to participate in it. The consumption in question is only that of commodities. It is a hierarchical consumption and it is increasing for everyone, but it is at the same time becoming more and more hierarchical. The decline and falsification of use-value are present for everyone, though to differing degrees, in the modern commodity. Everyone experiences this consumption of both spectacular *and* real commodities in a fundamental poverty "because it is not itself beyond privation, but is only enriched privation" (*The Society of the Spectacle*). The workers also spend their lives consuming the spectacle, passivity, the lies of ideologies and commodities. But they have fewer illusions than anyone about the concrete conditions imposed on them, about the price they have to pay, every moment of their lives, for the *production* of all that.

For all these reasons the students considered as a social stratum— a stratum itself also in crisis—were in May 1968 nothing but the *rear guard* of the whole movement.

The deficiency of almost all the students who expressed revolutionary intentions was, considering all their free time which they *could have* devoted to elucidating the problems of revolution, certainly deplorable, but quite secondary. The deficiency of the vast majority of workers, constantly leashed and gagged, was in contrast quite excusable, but decisive. The situationists' description and analysis of the *principal moments* of the crisis have been set forth in René Viénet's book *Enragés and Situationists in the Occupations Movement* (Gallimard, 1968). We will merely summarize here the main points related in that book, which was written in Brussels during the last three weeks of July on the basis of then-existing documentation, but of which, it seems to us, no conclusion needs to be modified.

From January to March the Enragés group of Nanterre (whose tactics were later taken up and carried on in April by the March 22nd Movement) successfully undertook the sabotage of classes and university departments. The Paris University Council's bungling and too-late repression, together with two successive shutdowns of the Nanterre Faculty, led to the spontaneous student riot in the Latin Quarter on 3 May. The university was paralyzed by the police and the strike. There was fighting in the streets for a week, and the young workers joined in it; while the Stalinists discredited themselves each day by incredible slanders, the leaders of SNESup and the little leftist groups exposed their lack of imagination and rigor, and the government replied successively and always at the wrong moment with force and inept concessions. On the night of 10 May the uprising that took over the neighborhood around Rue Gay-Lussac, set up sixty barricades and held it for more than eight hours aroused the entire country and forced the government into a major capitulation: it withdrew the police forces from the Latin Quarter and reopened the Sorbonne that it could no longer keep running. From 13–17 May the movement irresistibly advanced to the point of becoming a general revolutionary crisis, with the 16th probably being the crucial day, the day the factories began to declare themselves for a wildcat strike. The single-day general strike decreed for the 13th by the big bureaucratic organizations, with the aim of bringing the movement to a rapid end and if possible turning it to their own advantage, was in fact only a beginning: the workers and students of Nantes attacked the prefecture and those who occupied the Sorbonne opened it up to the workers. The Sorbonne immediately became a *"club populaire"* that made the language and demands of the clubs of 1848 seem timid by comparison. On the 14th the workers of Sud-Aviation at Nantes occupied their factory and locked up their managers. Their example was followed by two or three enterprises on the 15th and by several more after the 16th, the day the rank and file imposed the Renault strike at Billancourt. Virtually all the enterprises in the country were soon to follow;* and virtually all institutions, ideas and habits were to be contested in the succeeding days. The government and the Stalinists made feverish efforts to bring the crisis to a halt by breaking up its main power: they came to an agreement on wage concessions that they hoped would be sufficient to lead to an immediate return to work. On the 27th the rank and file everywhere rejected these "Grenelle Accords." The regime, which a month of Stalinist devotion had not been able to save, saw itself on the brink of destruction. On the 29th the Stalinists themselves had to recognize the likelihood of the collapse of Gaullism and reluctantly prepared, along with the rest of the left, to inherit its dangerous legacy: a social revolution having to be disarmed or crushed. If, in the face of the panic of the bourgeoisie and the wearing thin of the Stalinist braking force, de Gaulle had retired, the new regime would only have been a weakened but *officialized* version of the preceding *de facto* alliance: the Stalinists would have defended a Mendès-Waldeck government, for example, with bourgeois militias, party activists and fragments of the army. They would have tried to play the role not of Kerensky, but rather that of Noske. De Gaulle, more steadfast than the staff of his administration, relieved the Stalinists by announcing on the 30th that he would strive to maintain himself in power by any means necessary; that is to say, by calling out the army and initiating a civil war in order to hold or reconquer Paris. "The Stalinists, delighted, were very careful not to call for a continuation of the strike until the fall of the regime. They immediately rallied around the Gaullist elections, regardless of what it might cost them. In such conditions, the immediate alternative was either the autonomous self-affirmation of the proletariat or the complete defeat of the movement; councilist revolution or the Grenelle Accords. The revolutionary movement could not settle with the PCF without first having got rid of de Gaulle. The form of workers' power that could have developed in a post-Gaullist phase of the crisis, finding itself blocked both by the old reaffirmed state and by the PCF, no longer had any chance to hold back its onrushing defeat." (Viénet, *op. cit.*) The movement began to ebb, although the workers for one or more weeks stubbornly persisted in the strike that all their unions urged them to stop. Of course the bourgeoisie had not disappeared in France; it had merely been dumbstruck with terror. On 30 May it reemerged, along with the conformist petty bourgeoisie, to demonstrate its support for the state. But this state, already so well defended by the bureaucratic left, could not be brought down against its will as long as the workers had not eliminated the power base of those bureaucrats by imposing the form of their own autonomous power. The workers left the state this freedom and naturally had to endure the consequences. The majority of them had not recognized the total significance of their own movement; and nobody could do it in their place.

If, in a single large factory, between 16 May and 30 May, a general assembly had constituted itself as a *council* holding all powers of decision and execution, expelling the bureaucrats, organizing its self-defense and calling on the strikers of all the enterprises to link up with it, this last qualitative step could have immediately brought the movement to the *final struggle*, the struggle whose general outlines have all been historically traced by this movement. A very large number of enterprises would have followed the course thus discovered. This factory could immediately have taken the place of the dubious and in every sense eccentric Sorbonne of the first days, and have become the real center of the occupations movement: genuine *delegates* from the numerous councils that already virtually existed in some of the occupied buildings, and from all the councils that could have imposed themselves in all the branches of industry, would have rallied around this base. Such an assembly could then have proclaimed the expropriation of all capital, *including that of the state*; announced that all the country's means of production were henceforth the collective property of the proletariat organized in direct democracy; and appealed directly (by finally seizing some of the means of telecommunication, for example) to the workers of the entire world to support this revolution. Some people will say that such a hypothesis is utopian. We answer: it is precisely because the occupations movement was objectively at several moments *only an hour away* from such a result that it spread such terror, visible to everyone at the time in the impotence of the state and the panic of the so-called Communist Party, and since then in the conspiracy of silence concerning its gravity. This silence has been so total that millions of witnesses, recaptured by the "social organization of appearance" that presents this period to them as a short-lived madness of youth (maybe even merely student youth), must ask themselves if a society is not itself mad if it could *allow* such a stupefying aberration to occur.

In such an eventuality, civil war would naturally have been inevitable. If armed confrontation had no longer hinged on what the government feared or pretended to fear concerning the possible evil designs of the "Communist" Party, but had objectively faced the consolidation of a direct, industrially based proletarian power (of course we are speaking here of a total power and not of some "workers' power" limited to some sort of pseudocontrol of the production of their own alienation), then armed counterrevolution would certainly have been launched immediately. But it would not have been certain of winning. Some of the troops would obviously have mutinied; the workers would have figured out how to get weapons, and they certainly would not have built any more barricades—which were no doubt a good form of *political* expression at the beginning of the movement, but obviously ridiculous *strategically*. (And all the people like Malraux who claim afterwards that tanks could have taken Rue Gay-Lussac much more quickly than the state troopers did are certainly right on that point; but could they have afforded the *political* expense of such a victory? In any case, the state held its forces back and did not risk it; and it is certainly not because of its humanism that it swallowed this humiliation.) Foreign intervention would have inevitably followed, whatever some ideologues may think (it is possible to have read Hegel and Clausewitz and still be nothing more than a Glucksmann), probably beginning with NATO forces, but with the direct or indirect support of the Warsaw Pact. But then everything would once again have hinged on the European proletariat: double or nothing.

Since the defeat of the occupations movement, both those who participated in it and those who had to endure it have often asked the question: "Was it a revolution?" The general use in the press and in daily conversation of the cowardly neutral phrase, "the events," is nothing but a way of evading answering or even formulating this question. Such a question must be placed in its true historical light. In this context the journalists' and governments' superficial references to the "success" or "failure" of a revolution mean nothing for the simple reason that since the bourgeois revolutions *no revolution has yet succeeded*: not one has abolished classes. Proletarian revolution has so far not been victorious anywhere, but the practical process through which its project manifests itself has already created at least ten revolutionary moments of an extreme historical importance that can appropriately be termed revolutions. In none of these moments was the *total content* of proletarian revolution fully developed; but in each case there was a fundamental interruption of the ruling socioeconomic order and the appearance of new forms and conceptions of real life: variegated phenomena that can be understood and evaluated only in their overall significance, which significance cannot itself be separated from its possible historical future. Of all the partial criteria for judging whether a period of disruption of state power deserves the name of revolution or not, the worst is certainly that which considers whether the political regime in power fell or survived. This criterion, much invoked after May by the Gaullist thinkers, is the same one that enables the daily news to term as a revolution the latest military *putsch* in Brazil or Ghana or Iraq . . . But the revolution of 1905 did not bring down the czarist regime, it only obtained a few temporary concessions from it. The Spanish revolution of 1936 did not formally suppress the existing political power: it arose, in fact, out of a proletarian uprising initiated in order to defend that Republic against Franco. And the Hungarian revolution of 1956 did not abolish Nagy's liberal-bureaucratic government. Among other regrettable limitations, the Hungarian movement had many aspects of a national uprising against foreign domination; and this characteristic of national resistance, though less important in the Commune, nevertheless played a certain role in the latter's origins. The Commune supplanted Thiers's power only within the limits of Paris. And the St. Petersburg Soviet of 1905 never even took control of the capital. All the crises cited here as examples, though incomplete in their practical achievements and even in their perspectives, nevertheless produced enough radical innovations and put their societies severely enough in check to be legitimately termed revolutions. As for judging revolutions by the amount of bloodshed they lead to, this romantic vision is not even worth discussing. Some incontestable revolutions have manifested themselves through clashes involving very little bloodshed—including even the Paris Commune, which was to end in a massacre—while on the other hand numerous civil confrontations have caused thousands of deaths without in any way being revolutions. It is generally not revolutions that are bloody, but the reaction's subsequent repression of them. The question of the number of deaths during the May movement has given rise to a polemic that the temporarily reassured defenders of order keep coming back to. The official version is that there were only five deaths, all of them instant, including one policeman. All those who affirm this add themselves that this was an unexpectedly low number. Adding considerably to its improbability is the fact that it has never been admitted that any of the very numerous seriously wounded people could have died in the following days: this extraordinary good luck was certainly not due to rapid medical assistance, particularly on the night of the Gay-Lussac uprising. But if an easy coverup in underestimating the number of deaths was very useful *at the time* for a government up against the wall, it remained useful *afterwards* for different reasons. But on the whole, the retrospective proofs of the revolutionariness of the occupations movement are as striking as those that its very *existence* threw in the face of the world at the time: The proof that it had established its own new legitimacy is that the regime reestablished in June has never, in its striving to restore internal state security, dared to prosecute those responsible for overtly illegal actions, those who had partially divested it of its authority and even of its buildings. But the clearest proof, for those who know the history of our century, is still this: everything that the Stalinists did ceaselessly and at every stage in order to oppose the movement confirms the presence of revolution.

While the Stalinists, as always, represented antiworker bureaucracy in its purest form, the little leftist bureaucratic embryos were straddling the fence. They all openly accommodated the actual bureaucracies, as much out of calculation as out of ideology (except for the March 22nd Movement, which limited itself to accommodating the manipulators who had infiltrated it: JCR, Maoists, etc.). They could envisage nothing more than "pushing to the left"—but only in terms of their own defective schemas—both a spontaneous movement that was much more extremist than they were and bureaucratic apparatuses that could not possibly make any concessions to leftism in such an obviously revolutionary situation. Pseudostrategical illusions flourished: Some leftists believed that the occupation of one or another ministry on the night of 24 May would have ensured the victory of the movement (but other leftists maneuvered to prevent such an "excess," which did not enter into their own blueprint for victory). Others, prior to their more modest dream of maintaining a cleaned up and "responsible" administration of the university buildings in order to hold a "Summer University," believed that those buildings would become bases for urban guerrilla warfare (all of them, however, fell after the workers' strike without being defended; and even the Sorbonne at the very time when it was the momentary center of an expanding movement could, on the crucial night of 16 May when all the doors were open and there were hardly any people there, have been retaken in less than an hour by a CRS raid). Not wanting to see that the movement had already gone beyond a political change in the state, or in what terms the real stakes were posed (a total, *coherent* awakening of consciousness in the enterprises), the little leftist groups certainly worked against that perspective by abundantly disseminating moth-eaten illusions and by everywhere presenting bad examples of the bureaucratic conduct that all the revolutionary workers were rejecting in disgust; and finally, by the most pathetic parodying of all the forms of past revolutions, from parliamentarianism to Zapata-style guerrilla war, without their poor dramatics having the slightest relation to reality. Fervent admirers of the errors of a vanished revolutionary past, the backward ideologists of the little leftist parties were naturally very ill-prepared to understand a *modern* movement. The March 22nd Movement, the eclectic aggregate of these ideologies enriched with some pieced-together modern incoherence, combined almost all the ideological defects of the past

237

with the defects of a naïve confusionism. Recuperators were installed in the leadership of the very people who expressed their fear of "recuperation," which was for them a vague and almost mystical peril since they lacked the slightest knowledge of elementary truths about recuperation or organization, or on the difference between a delegate and an irresponsible "spokesman"—a spokesman [Cohn-Bendit] who was the *de facto* leader, since the main effective power of the March 22nd Movement stemmed from its communication with reporters. Its laughable celebrities came before the spotlights to announce to the press that they were taking care not to become celebrities.*

The "Action Committees," which were spontaneously formed just about everywhere, were on the ambiguous borderline between direct democracy and infiltrated and recuperated confusionism. This contradiction created internal divisions in almost all of them. But there was an even clearer division between the two main types of organization that went by the same label. On one hand, there were committees formed on a *local* basis (neighborhood or enterprise ACs, occupation committees of certain buildings that had fallen into the hands of the revolutionary movement) or set up in order to carry out some specialized task whose practical necessity was obvious, notably the internationalist extension of the movement (Italian AC, North African AC, etc.). On the other hand, there was a proliferation of *professional* committees: attempts to revive the old unionism, but usually for the benefit of semiprivileged sectors and thus with a clearly corporatist character; these committees served as tribunes for separate specialists who wanted to join the movement while maintaining their separate specialized positions, or even to derive some favorable publicity from it ("Congress of Cinema Workers," Writers Union, English Institute AC, etc.). The methods of these two types of AC were even more clearly opposed than their goals. In the former, decisions were executory and prefigured the revolutionary power of the councils; in the latter, they were abstract wishes and parodied the pressure groups of state power.

The occupied buildings, when they were not under the authority of "loyal union managers," and to the extent that they did not remain isolated as exclusive pseudofeudal possessions of their usual university users, constituted one of the strongest points of the movement (for example, the Sorbonne during the first days, the buildings opened up to the workers and young slum-dwellers by the "students" of Nantes, the INSA taken over by the revolutionary workers of Lyon, and the Institut Pédagogique National). The very logic of these occupations could have led to the best developments: it should be noted, moreover, how a movement that remained paradoxically timid at the prospect of *requisitioning* commodities did not have the slightest misgivings about having already appropriated a part of the state's fixed capital.

If this example was ultimately prevented from spreading to the factories, it should also be said that the style created by many of these occupations left much to be desired. Almost everywhere the persistence of old routines hindered people from seeing the full scope of the situation and the means it offered for the action in progress. For example, *Informations, Correspondance Ouvrières* #77 (January 1969) objects to Viénet's book—which had mentioned their presence at Censier—by declaring that the workers who had been with ICO for a long time "did not 'set up quarters' at the Sorbonne or at Censier or anywhere else; all were engaged in the strike at their own workplaces" and "in the assemblies and in the streets." "They never considered maintaining any sort of 'permanent center' in the university buildings, much less constituting themselves as a 'workers coordinating committee' or a 'council,' even if it were for 'maintaining the occupations' " (ICO considering this latter as tantamount to "participating in parallel organizations that would end up substituting themselves for the worker"). Further on, *ICO* adds that their group nevertheless held "two meetings a week" there because "rooms were freely available at the university departments, particularly at Censier, which was calmer." Thus the scruples of the ICO workers (whom we are willing to assume to be quite capable as long as they modestly limit themselves to striking at their own workplaces or in the nearby streets) led them to see in one of the most original aspects of the crisis nothing but the possibility of switching from their usual café hangout by borrowing free rooms in a quiet university department. With the same complacency they also admit that a number of their comrades "soon stopped coming to ICO meetings because they did not find any response there to their desire to 'do something'." Thus, for these workers, "doing something" has automatically become a shameful inclination to substitute oneself for "the worker"—for a sort of being-in-himself worker who, by definition, would exist only in his own factory, where for example the Stalinists would force him to keep silent, and where ICO would have to wait for all the workers to purely liberate themselves *on the spot* (otherwise wouldn't they risk substituting themselves for this still mute real worker?). Such an ideological acceptance of dispersion defies the essential need whose vital urgency was felt by so many workers in May: the need for coordination and communication of struggles and ideas, starting from bases of free encounter outside their union-policed factories. But *ICO* has never, in fact, either before or since May, consistently followed out its metaphysical reasoning. It exists, as a mimeographed publication through which a few dozen workers resign themselves to "substituting" their analyses for those that might spontaneously be made by the several hundred other workers who read it without having participated in writing it. Their issue #78 in February informs us that "in one year the circulation of *ICO* has risen from 600 to 1000 copies." But the *Council for Maintaining the Occupations* [CMDO], for example, which seems to shock the virtue of *ICO* by the mere fact that it occupied the Institut Pédagogique National, was able (to say nothing of its other activities or publications at the time) to get 100,000 copies of various of its texts printed for free, through an immediate agreement reached with the strikers of the IPN press at Montrouge. The vast majority of these texts were distributed to other striking workers; and so far no one has tried to show that the content of these texts could in the slightest way threaten to substitute itself for the decisions of any worker. And the strikers' participation in the linkups established by the CMDO in and outside Paris never contradicted their presence at their own workplaces (nor, to be sure, in the streets). Moreover, the striking typesetters who were members of the CMDO much preferred working elsewhere where there were machines available rather than remaining passive in "their" usual workplaces.

If the purists of worker inaction certainly missed opportunities to speak and make up for all the times they have been forced into a silence which has become a sort of proud habit among them, the presence of a mass of neobolshevik manipulators was much more harmful. But the worst thing was still the extreme *lack of homogeneity* of the assembly, which in the first days of the Sorbonne occupation found itself, without having either wished it or understood it clearly, in the position of an exemplary center of a movement that was drawing in the factories. This lack of social homogeneity stemmed first of all from the overwhelming numerical preponderance of students, in spite of the good intentions of many of them, a preponderance which was made even worse by a rather high proportion of visitors with merely touristic motivations. This was the objective base that made possible the most gross maneuvers on the part of people like Péninou and Krivine. The ambiguity of the participants added to the essential ambiguity of the acts of an improvised assembly which by force of circumstances had come to *represent* (in all senses of the word, including the worst) the councilist perspective for the entire country. This assembly made decisions both for the Sorbonne (and even there in a poor and mystified manner: it never even succeeded in mastering its own functioning) and for the whole society in crisis: it wanted and proclaimed, in clumsy but sincere terms, a union with the workers and the negation of the old world. While pointing out its faults, let us not forget how much it was *listened to*. The same issue #77 of *ICO* reproaches the situationists for having sought in that assembly an exemplary act that would "enter into legend" and for having set up some heroes "on the podium of history." We don't believe we have ever built up anybody as a star on a historical tribune, but we also think that the superior irony affected by these lofty workerists falls flat: it *was* a historical tribune.

With the defeat of the revolution, the sociotechnical mechanisms of false consciousness were naturally reestablished, virtually intact: when the spectacle clashes with its pure negation, no reformism can succeed in winning an increase, not even of 7%, in the spectacle's concessions to reality. To demonstrate this to even the most casual observer it would suffice to examine the some *300 books* on May that have appeared in France alone in the year following the occupations movement. It is not the number of books in itself that merits being scoffed at or blamed, as certain people obsessed with the perils of recuperation have felt obliged to declare (people who, however, have little to worry about on that score since they generally don't possess much that could attract the greed of recuperators). The fact that so many books have been published mainly expresses the fact that the historical importance of the movement has been deeply sensed, in spite of all the incomprehension and interested denials. What is criticizable is the simple fact that out of three hundred books there are scarcely ten that are worth reading: a few accounts or analyses that don't follow laughable ideologies, and a few collections of unfalsified documents. The misinformation and falsification prevalent everywhere are particularly evident in almost all the accounts of the situationists' activities.

240

Leaving aside those books that limit themselves to remaining silent on this question, or to a few absurd imputations, we can distinguish three main styles of falsification. The first pattern consists in limiting the SI's action to Strasbourg, eighteen months before, as a first, remote triggering of a crisis from which it would later seem to have disappeared (this is also the position of the Cohn-Bendits' book, which even manages not to say a word about the existence of the Nanterre "Enragés" group). The second pattern, presenting a positive lie and no longer merely a lie by omission, asserts, in spite of all indications to the contrary, that the situationists accepted some sort of contact with the March 22nd Movement; and many even go so far as to make us an integral part of it. Finally, the third pattern presents us as an autonomous group of irresponsible maniacs springing up by surprise, perhaps even armed, at the Sorbonne and elsewhere in order to stir up disorder and shout extravagant demands.

It is difficult, however, to deny a certain continuity in the situationists' action from 1967–1968. It seems, in fact, that this very continuity was felt as an annoyance by those who through their quantity of ostentatious interviews or recruitments strove to be recognized as having had a role of leader of the movement, a role the SI has always rejected for itself: their stupid ambition leads some of these people to hide certain facts that they are somewhat more aware of than are others. Situationist theory had a significant role in the origins of the generalized critique that produced the first incidents of the May crisis and that developed along with that crisis. This was not only due to our intervention against Strasbourg University. Two or three thousand copies each of Vaneigem's and Debord's books, for example, had already been circulated in the months preceding May, particularly in Paris, and an unusual proportion of them had been read by revolutionary workers (according to certain indications it also appears that these two books were *the most frequently stolen* from bookstores in 1968, at least relative to their circulation). By way of the Enragés group, the SI can flatter itself with not having been without importance in the very origin of the Nanterre agitation, which was to have such far-reaching effects. Finally, we don't think we stayed too far behind the great spontaneous movement of the masses that dominated the country in May 1968, both in what we did at the Sorbonne and in the various forms of action later carried out by the Council for Maintaining the Occupations. In addition to the SI itself and to a good number of individuals who acknowledged its theses and acted accordingly, many others defended situationist perspectives, whether unconsciously or as a result of direct influence, because those perspectives were to a large extent objectively implied by this era of revolutionary crisis. Those who doubt this need only *read the walls* (those without this direct experience can refer to the collection of photographs published by Walter Lewino, *L'Imagination au pouvoir*, Losfeld, 1968).

It can thus be said that the systematic minimization of the SI is merely a detail corresponding to the current—and, from the dominant viewpoint, natural—minimization of the whole occupations movement. But the sort of jealousy felt by certain leftists, which strongly contributes to this minimization, is completely off base. Even the most leftist of the little groups have no grounds for setting themselves up as rivals to the SI, because the SI is not a group of their type, competing on their terrain of militantism or claiming like they do to be leading the revolutionary movement in the name of the "correct" interpretation of one or another petrified truth derived from Marxism or anarchism. To see the question in this way is to forget that, in contrast to these abstract repetitions in which old conclusions that happen still to be valid in class struggles are inextricably mixed in with a mass of conflicting errors and frauds, the SI had above all brought a *new spirit* into the theoretical debates on society, culture and life. This spirit was assuredly revolutionary. It entered to a certain extent into a relation with the real revolutionary movement that was recommencing. And it was precisely to the extent that this movement also had a new character that it turned out to *resemble* the SI and partially appropriated its theses; and not at all by way of a traditional political process of recruiting members or followers. The largely new character of this practical movement is easily discernable in this very *influence* the SI exerted, an influence completely divorced from any directing role. All the leftist tendencies—including the March 22nd Movement, which included in its hodgepodge Leninism, Chinese Stalinism, anarchism and even a dash of misunderstood "situationism"—relied very explicitly on a long past of struggles, examples and doctrines published and discussed a hundred times. It is true that these struggles and publications had been smothered by Stalinist reaction and neglected by bourgeois intellectuals. But they were nevertheless infinitely more accessible than the SI's new positions, which had never had any means to make themselves known except our own recent publications and activities. If the SI's few known documents found such an audience it was obviously because a part of the advanced practical critique recognized itself in this language. We thus now find ourselves in a rather good position to say what May was essentially, even in its latent aspects; to make conscious the unconscious tendencies of the occupations movement. Others lyingly say that there was nothing to understand in this absurd outbreak; or they describe, through the filter of their ideology, only a few older and less important aspects of the movement as if they were the whole of it; or they simply draw from it new topics for their academic "argumentation" that feeds on itself. They have the support of major newspapers and influential connections, of sociology and mass-market circulation. We don't have any of that and we draw our right to speak only from ourselves. Yet what they say about May will inevitably fade in indifference and be forgotten; and what we say about it will remain, will finally be believed and will be taken up again.

The influence of situationist theory can be read not only on the walls, but in the diversely exemplary actions of the revolutionaries of Nantes and the Enragés of Nanterre. In the press at the beginning of 1968 one can see the indignation that was aroused by the new forms of action initiated or systematized by the Enragés, those "campus hooligans" who one day decided that "everything disputable must be disputed" and ended up shaking up the whole university.

In fact, those who at that time met and formed the *Enragés Group*

242

had no preconceived idea of agitation. These "students" were only there as a matter of form in order to get *grants*. It simply happened that broken-down streets and slums were less odious to them than concrete buildings, thickheaded self-satisfied students and smooth-tongued modernist professors. In the former terrain they saw some vestiges of humanity, whereas they found only poverty, boredom and lies in the cultural soup where Lefebvre and his honesty, Touraine and his end of class struggle, Bourricaud and his strongarms and Lourau and his future were all splashing about in unison. Furthermore, they were acquainted with the situationist theses and they knew that these thinkers of the university ghetto also knew about them and derived their modernism from them. They decided that everyone should know about this, and set about unmasking the lies, with the expectation of finding other playgrounds later on: they reckoned that once the liars and the students were routed and the university was destroyed, chance would weave them other encounters on another scale and that then "fortune and misfortune would take their shape."

Their avowed pasts (predominantly anarchist, but also surrealist and in one case Trotskyist) immediately worried those they first confronted: the old leftist sects, Trotskyists of the CLER, Daniel Cohn-Bendit and other anarchist students, all wrangling over the lack of future of the UNEF and the function of psychologists. By making numerous exclusions without useless leniency they insured themselves against the success they rapidly encountered among some twenty-odd *students*: this also insured them against weak-minded adherents on the lookout for a situationism without situationists in which they could express all their obsessions and miseries. In these conditions the group which sometimes had as many as fifteen members more often comprised a mere half dozen agitators. Which turned out to be enough.

If the methods used by the Enragés—particularly the sabotage of lectures—are commonplace today in both universities and high schools, at the time they profoundly scandalized leftists as well as good students; the former sometimes even organized squads to protect the professors from a hail of insults and rotten oranges. The generalization of the use of deserved insults and of graffiti, the call for an unconditional boycott of exams, the distribution of leaflets on university premises, and finally the simple daily scandal of their existence drew upon the Enragés the first attempt at repression: Riesel and Bigorgne were summoned before the dean on 25 January; Cheval was expelled from the campus at the beginning of February; Bigorgne was expelled from the university grounds later that same month, eventually to be excluded altogether from French universities for five years at the beginning of April. Meanwhile the leftist groups began a more narrowly political agitation.

The old apes of the intellectual reservation, lost in the muddled presentation of their "thought," only belatedly started to get worried. But they were soon forced to drop their masks and make fools of themselves, as when Morin, green with spite amidst the hooting of students, screamed, "The other day you consigned me to the trashcan of history . . ." (Interruption: "How did you get back out?") "I prefer to be on the side of the trashcans rather than on the side of those who handle them, and in any case I prefer to be on the side of the trashcans rather than on the side of the crematories!" Or Touraine, foaming at the mouth and howling: "I've had enough of these anarchists and more than enough of these situationists! Right now I am in command here, and if one day you are, I will go somewhere else where people know what it means to work!" A year later these profound perceptions were further developed in articles by Raymond Aron and Étiemble protesting the impossibility of working under the rising tide of leftist totalitarianism and red fascism. From 26 January to 22 March violent class disruptions were almost constant. The Enragés participated in this continuous agitation while working on several projects that proved abortive, including the publication of a pamphlet projected for the beginning of May and the invasion and looting of the administration building with the aid of some revolutionaries from Nantes at the beginning of March. But even before having seen that much, Dean Grappin, speaking at a press conference on 28 March, denounced "a group of irresponsible students who for several months have been disrupting classes and examinations and practicing guerrilla methods in the University. . . . These students are not connected with any known political organization. They constitute an explosive element in a very sensitive milieu." As for the pamphlet, the Enragés' printer did not progress as fast as the revolution. After the crisis they had to abandon the idea of publishing this text, which would have seemed intended to demonstrate retrospectively their prophetic accuracy.

All this explains the interest the Enragés took in the evening of 22 March, however dubious they already were about the other protesters. While Cohn-Bendit, already a star in the Nanterre skies, was debating with the less decided, ten Enragés alone installed themselves in the Faculty Council room, where they were only joined 22 minutes later by the future "March 22nd Movement." Viénet's book describes how and why they withdrew from this farce.* In addition, they saw that the police were not coming and that with such people they could not carry out the only objective they had planned for the night: the complete destruction of the exam files. In the early hours of the 23rd they decided to exclude five of their number who had refused to leave the room out of fear that they would be "cutting themselves off from the masses" of students!

It is certainly piquant to find that the origin of the May movement involved a settling of accounts with the two-faced thinkers of the old *Arguments* gang. But in attacking this ugly cohort of state-appointed subversive thinkers, the Enragés were doing more than settling an old quarrel: they already spoke as an *occupations movement* struggling for everyone's real occupation of all the sectors of a social life governed by lies. And by writing "Take your desires for reality" on the concrete walls, they were already destroying the recuperative ideology of the "Power to the imagination" that was pretentiously launched by the March 22nd Movement. They had desires, while the others had no imagination.

The Enragés scarcely returned to Nanterre in April. The vague fancies of direct democracy ostentatiously proclaimed by the March 22nd Movement obviously could not be realized in such bad company, and they refused in advance the small place that would readily have been granted them as extremist entertainers to the left of the laughable "Culture and Creativity Commission." On the other hand, the taking up of some of their agitational techniques by the Nanterre students, even if with a muddled anti-imperialism perspective, meant that the debate was beginning to be placed on the terrain the Enragés had wanted to establish. This was also demonstrated by the Parisian students' 3 May attack on the police in response to the university administration's latest blunder. The Enragés' violent warning leaflet, *Gut Rage*, distributed on 6 May chimed so perfectly with the real movement that the only people it outraged were the Leninists it denounced; in two days of street fighting the rioters had discovered its relevance. The Enragés' autonomous activity culminated as consistently as it had begun. They were treated *as situationists* even before entering the SI, since the leftist recuperators picked up on some of their ideas while imagining that they could conceal the existence of their source through lavish performances in front of the reporters whom the Enragés had naturally rebuffed. The very term "Enragés," by which Riesel had given an unforgettable touch to the occupations movement, was later for a while given a spectacular "Cohn-Bendist" meaning.

The rapid succession of street struggles in the first two weeks of May had immediately brought together the members of the SI, the Enragés and a few other comrades. Their accord was formalized on 14 May, the day after the occupation of the Sorbonne, when they federated as an "Enragés-SI Committee" which began that very day to publish texts thus signed. In the following days we carried out a more widespread autonomous expression of situationist theses within the movement; but this was not in order to lay down particular principles in accordance with which we would have claimed to shape or guide the real movement: in saying what we thought, we said *who* we were, while so many others were disguising themselves in order to explain that it was necessary to follow the correct line of their central committee. That evening the Sorbonne general assembly, which was effectively open to the workers, undertook to organize its own power, and René Riesel, who had expressed the most radical positions on the very organization of the Sorbonne and on the total extension of the struggle that had begun, was elected to the first Occupation Committee. On the 15th the situationists present in Paris addressed a circular to persons elsewhere in France and in other countries: *To the members of the SI and to the comrades who have declared themselves in agreement with our theses*. This text briefly analyzed the process that was going on and its possible developments, in order of decreasing probability: exhaustion of the movement if it remained limited "to the students before the antibureaucratic agitation has extended more deeply into the worker milieu"; repression; or finally, "social revolution?" It also contained an account of our activity until then and called for immediate action "to publicize, support and extend the agitation." We proposed as immediate themes in France: "the occupation of the factories" (we had just learned of the Sud-Aviation occupation that had taken place the night before); "the formation of workers councils; the definitive shutdown of the universities; and the complete critique of all forms of alienation." It should be noted that this was the first time since the SI was formed that we ever asked anyone, however close they were to our positions, to do anything. All the more reason why our circular did not remain without response, particularly in the cities where the May movement was asserting itself most strongly. On the evening of the 16th the SI dispatched a second circular recounting the developments of the day and anticipating "a major confrontation." The general strike interrupted this series, which was taken up in another form after 20 May by the emissaries that the CMDO sent throughout France and to various other countries.

Viénet's book describes in detail how the majority of the members of the Sorbonne Occupation Committee, which was reelected *en bloc* by the general assembly on the evening of the 15th, soon after slunk away, yielding to the maneuvers and attempts at intimidation of an informal bureaucracy (UNEF, MAU, JCR, etc.) that was striving to underhandedly recapture the Sorbonne. The Enragés and situationists thus found themselves with the responsibility for the Occupation Committee on 16 and 17 May. The general assembly of the 17th having finally neither approved the acts by which this Committee had carried out its mandate, nor even disapproved them (the manipulators having prevented any vote in the assembly), we immediately declared that we were leaving that played-out Sorbonne. All those who had grouped themselves around this Occupation Committee departed with us: they were to constitute the core of the Council for Maintaining the Occupations. It is worth pointing out that the second Occupation Committee, elected after our departure, maintained its glorious bureaucratic existence without any changes until the return of the police in June. *Never again was there any question of the assembly daily electing revocable delegates.* This Committee of professionals soon even went so far as to suppress the general assemblies altogether, which from their point of view were only a cause of trouble and a waste of time. In contrast, the situationists can sum up their action in the Sorbonne with the single formula: "All power to the general assembly." It is thus amusing to hear people now talking about *situationist power* in the Sorbonne, when the reality of this "power" was to constantly insist on direct democracy there and everywhere, to constantly denounce the recuperators and bureaucrats, and to demand that the general assembly take on its own responsibilities *by making decisions* and by making all its decisions executory.

By its consistent attitude our Occupation Committee had aroused the general indignation of the leftist manipulators and bureaucrats. If we had defended the principles and methods of direct democracy in the Sorbonne, we nevertheless had no illusions as to the social composition and general level of consciousness of that assembly: we were quite aware of the paradox of delegates being more resolute in their desire for direct democracy than their mandators, and we saw that it could not last. But we were more than anything striving to put the not inconsiderable means with which the possession of the Sorbonne provided us at the service of the wildcat strike that had just started. Thus the Occupation Committee issued a brief declaration at 3:00 p.m. on the 16th calling for "the immediate occupation of all the factories in

France and the formation of workers councils." All the other reproaches against us were almost nothing in comparison to the scandal provoked everywhere—except among the "rank-and-file occupiers"—by this "reckless" commitment of the Sorbonne. Yet at that very moment two or three factories were occupied, some of the NMPP truckdrivers were trying to block the distribution of newspapers and (as we were to learn two hours later) several Renault shops were successfully beginning to stop work. In the name of what, we wonder, could unauthorized individuals claim the right to manage the Sorbonne if they did not support the workers' right to seize all the property in the country? It seems to us that the Sorbonne, by declaring itself for such occupations, was making its last response that still remained at the level of the movement that the factories were fortunately to carry on, that is to say, at the level of the response the factories themselves had made to the first limited struggles in the Latin Quarter. This appeal certainly did not run counter to the intentions of the majority of people who were at the Sorbonne and who did so much to spread it. Moreover, as the factory occupations spread, even the leftist bureaucrats changed their minds and expressed their support of a *fait accompli* on which they had not dared to take a stand the day before, though they did not give up their hostility to the idea of councils. The occupations movement did not really need the approval of the Sorbonne in order to spread to other factories. But beyond the fact that at that moment every hour counted in linking up all the factories with the action initiated by a few of them, while the unions were stalling everywhere in order to prevent a general work stoppage; and the fact that we knew that such an appeal, coming from the Sorbonne Occupation Committee, would immediately be widely disseminated, even by radio—beyond this, it seemed to us above all important to show the *maximum* toward which the struggle that was beginning should aim right away. But the factories did not go so far as to form councils, and the strikers who began to come to the Sorbonne certainly did not discover any model there.

It seems likely that this appeal contributed here and there to opening up perspectives of radical struggle. In any case, it certainly figured among the events of that day that awakened the greatest fears. At 7:00 in the evening the Prime Minister issued an official statement declaring that "in view of the various attempts announced or initiated by extremist groups to provoke a generalized agitation," the government would do everything possible to maintain "public peace" and the republican order, since "university reform is turning into a mere pretext for plunging the country into disorder." At the same time, 10,000 state trooper reservists were called up. "University reform" was indeed merely a pretext, even for the government, which masked its retreat in the face of the Latin Quarter riot behind this suddenly discovered respectable necessity.

The Council for Maintaining the Occupations, which at first occupied the IPN on Rue d'Ulm, did its best during the remainder of the crisis, to which, from the moment the strike became general and came to a defensive standstill, none of the then-existing organized revolutionary groups any longer had the means to make a notable contribution. Bringing together the situationists, the Enragés and some thirty to sixty other councilist revolutionaries (of whom less than a tenth could be considered students), the CMDO established a large number of link-ups both within and outside France, making a special effort, toward the end of the movement, to communicate its significance to revolutionaries of other countries, who could not fail to be inspired by it. It published a number of posters and texts—around 200,000 copies of each in some cases—of which the most important were "Report on the Occupation of the Sorbonne" (19 May), "For the Power of the Workers Councils" (22 May) and "Address to All Workers" (30 May). The CMDO, which had been neither directed nor organized by anyone for the future, "decided to dissolve itself on 15 June. . . . The CMDO had not sought to obtain anything *for itself*, not even any sort of recruitment in view of a permanent existence. Its participants did not separate their personal goals from the general goals of the movement. They were independent individuals who had grouped together for a struggle on determined bases at a˙specific moment; and who again became independent after it." (Viénet, *op. cit.*) The Council for Maintaining the Occupations had been "a bond, not a power."

Some people have reproached us, during May and since then, for having criticized everybody and for thus having presented the situationists' activity as the only acceptable one. This is not true. We approved the mass movement in all its depth and the remarkable initiatives of tens of thousands of individuals. We approved of the conduct of several revolutionary groups that we knew of in Nantes and Lyon, as well as the acts of all those who were in contact with the CMDO. The documents quoted in Viénet's book clearly demonstrate that in addition we *partially* approved of a number of statements issuing from some of the Action Committees.* It is certain that many groups or committees that were unknown to us during the crisis would have had our approval if we had been aware of them—and it is even more obvious that in being unaware of them we could in no way have criticized them. On the other hand, in regard to the little leftist parties or the March 22nd Movement, or people like Barjonet or Lapassade, it would indeed be surprising if anyone expected some polite approbation from us, considering our previous positions and the activity of these people during May.

Neither have we claimed that certain forms of action that characterized the occupations movement—with the possible exception of the use of critical comic strips—had a directly situationist origin. On the contrary, we see the origin of all these forms in "wildcat" *workers' struggles*; and for several years our journals have pointed them out as they developed and specified where they came from. Workers were the first to attack a newspaper building to protest against the falsification of news concerning them (Liège, 1961); to burn cars (Merlebach, 1962); to begin writing on the walls the formulas of the new revolution ("Here freedom ends," on a wall of the Rhodiaceta factory, 1967). On the other hand, we can point out, as a clear prelude to the Enragés' activity at Nanterre, the fact that on 26 October 1966 in Strasbourg a university professor was for the first time attacked and driven from his podium: that was the lot to which the situationists subjected the cybernetician

248

Abraham Moles at his inaugural lecture.

All the texts issued by the situationists during the occupations movement show that we never spread any illusions as to the chances for a complete success of the movement. We knew that this objectively possible and necessary revolutionary movement had begun from a subjectively very low level: spontaneous and fragmented, ignorant of its own past and of all its goals, it was reemerging after a half century of repression and in the face of its still firmly entrenched bureaucratic and bourgeois vanquishers. A lasting revolutionary victory was in our eyes only a very slight possibility between 17 and 30 May. But from the moment this chance existed, we showed it to be the *maximum* that had come to be at stake as soon as the crisis reached a certain point, and as something certainly worth risking. From our point of view the movement was already a great historic victory, regardless of where it might go from there, and we thought that *even half* of what had already happened would already have been a very significant result.

Nobody can deny that the SI, in contrast in this regard, too, to all the leftist groups, refused to make any propaganda for itself. The CMDO did not raise any "situationist banner" and none of our texts of the period mentioned the SI except in the one instance when we responded to the impudent invitation for a common front issued by Barjonet the day after the Charléty meeting. And amidst all the brand-name initials of groups pretending to a leadership role, not a single inscription mentioning the SI was to be found on the walls of Paris, even though our partisans were undoubtedly the best and most prolific writers of graffiti.

It seems to us—and we present this conclusion first of all to the comrades of other countries that will experience crises of this nature—that these examples show what can be done in the first stage of reappearance of the revolutionary proletarian movement by a few basically coherent individuals. In May there were only ten or twelve situationists and Enragés in Paris and none in the rest of France. But the fortunate conjunction of spontaneous revolutionary improvisation with a sort of aura of sympathy that existed around the SI made possible the coordination of a rather widespread action, not only in Paris but in several large cities, as if there had been a preexisting nationwide organization. Even more far-reaching than this spontaneous organization, a sort of vague, mysterious situationist menace was felt and denounced in many places; those who embodied this menace were some hundreds or even thousands of individuals whom the bureaucrats and moderates called situationists or, more often, referred to by the popular abbreviation that appeared during this period, *situs*. We consider it an honor that this term "situ," which seems to have originated as a pejorative term among certain student milieus in the provinces, served not only to designate the most extremist participants in the occupations movement, but also tended to evoke an image of a vandal, a thief or a hoodlum.

We do not think we avoided making mistakes. It is again for the benefit of comrades who may later find themselves in similar situations that we enumerate them here.

On Rue Gay-Lussac, where we came together in small spontaneously assembled groups, each of these groups met several dozen acquaintances or people who merely knew us by sight and came to talk with us. Then everyone, in the wonderful disorder found in that "liberated neighborhood," split up toward one or another "front line" or battle preparation long before the inevitable police attack. As a result, not only did all those people remain more or less isolated, but even our own groups were unable to keep in contact with each other most of the time. It was a serious mistake on our part not to have immediately asked everyone to remain grouped together. In less than an hour a group acting in this way would have inevitably snowballed and gathered together everyone we knew among the barricade fighters—among whom each of us ran into more friends than one chances to meet in Paris in a whole year. In this way we could have formed a band of two or three hundred people who knew each other and acted together, which was precisely what was most lacking in that dispersed fight. Of course, the vastly unequal forces—there were more than three times as many police surrounding the area as rioters, to say nothing of their superior armament—would have doomed this struggle to failure in any case. But such a group would have made possible a certain freedom of maneuver, either by counterattacking at some spot or by extending the barricades to the east of Rue Mouffetard (an area rather poorly controlled by the police until very late) in order to open a path of retreat for all those who were caught in the dragnet (several hundred escaped only by chance, thanks to the precarious refuge of the Ecole Normale Supérieure).

In and with the Sorbonne Occupation Committee we did virtually everything we could have done, considering the conditions and hurriedness of the moment. We cannot be reproached for not having done more to alter the architecture of that dismal edifice, which we didn't even have the time to scout out. It is true that a chapel remained there (closed), but our posters—and also Riesel in his statement in the general assembly on 14 May—had appealed to the occupiers to destroy it as soon as possible. As for "Radio Sorbonne," it had no transmitter so we cannot be blamed for not having used it. It goes without saying that we neither considered nor prepared for setting the building on fire on 17 May, as was rumored at that time following some obscure slanders on the part of certain leftist groups: the date alone suffices to show how ill-advised such a project would have been. Neither did we spread ourselves thin in routine details, however useful we may recognize them to have been. It is thus a pure fantasy when Jean Maitron states, "The Sorbonne restaurant and cooking . . . remained under the control of the 'situationists' until June. There were very few students among them, but many unemployed youth." (La Sorbonne par elle-même, Editions Ouvrières, 1968, p. 114.) We must, however, reproach ourselves for this error: from 16 May, 5:00 p.m. on, the comrades in charge of sending the leaflets and declarations of the Occupation Committee to be printed replaced the signature "Occupation Committee of the Sorbonne" with "Occupation Committee of the Autonomous and Popular Sorbonne University" and no one thought anything about it. This was certainly a regression of some importance because in our eyes the Sorbonne was of interest only as *a building seized by the revolutionary movement,* and this signature gave the impression that we could have recognized that place as still having some legitimacy as a *university,* albeit "autonomous and popular"—something we despise in any case and which was all the more unfortunate to seem to accept at such a time. A less important slip was made on 17 May when a leaflet composed by rank-and-file workers who had come from the Renault factory was circulated with the signature "Occupation Committee." The Occupation Committee was quite right to provide these workers with means of expression without any censorship, but it should have been specified that this text was written by them and merely *printed* by the Occupation Committee; and all the more so as these workers, while calling for a continuation of the "marches on Renault," still accepted the unions' mystifying argument according to which the factory gates should be kept closed so that the police could not derive from their being open a pretext or an advantage for an attack.

The CMDO forgot to add to each of its publications the note, "Printed by striking workers," which certainly would have been exemplary and in perfect accord with the theories those publications expressed, and which would have been an excellent reply to the usual union printshop label. A more serious error: while an excellent use was made of telephones, we completely overlooked the possibility of using the *teletype machines,* which would have enabled us to get in touch with a number of occupied buildings and factories in France and to transmit information throughout Europe. We particularly neglected the network of astronomical observatories, which was accessible to us at least by way of the occupied Meudon Observatory.

But everything considered, we do not see how the SI's activities during the May movement could merit any significant blame.

Let us now enumerate the main *results* of the occupations movement so far. In France this movement was defeated, but in no way *crushed.* This is probably its most notable point and the one that presents the greatest practical interest. Probably never before has such a severe social crisis ended without a repression debilitating the revolutionary current for a substantial period—a sort of seemingly inevitable price that had to be paid for each moment of radical historical experience. Although of course numerous foreigners were administratively expelled from the country and several hundred rioters were convicted in the following months for "common law" misdemeanors, there was no political repression properly speaking. (More than a third of the members of the CMDO had been arrested in the various confrontations, but none of them were caught in this later roundup, their retreat at the end of June having been very well carried out.) All the political leaders who were not able to escape arrest at the end of the crisis were set free after a few weeks and not one of them was brought to trial. The government was forced to accept this new retreat merely to obtain a semblance of a calm reopening of the universities and a *semblance of exams* in fall 1968; this important concession was obtained as early as August by the mere pressure of the Medical Students Action Committee.

The depth of the revolutionary crisis has seriously thrown off balance "what was frontally attacked ... the *well-functioning* capitalist economy" (Viénet), not so much, of course, because of the wage increases, which the economy can easily bear, nor even because of the total paralysis of production for several weeks, but primarily because the French bourgeoisie *has lost confidence in the stability of the country.* This—in conjunction with other aspects of the present international monetary crisis—led to the massive exodus of capital and the crisis of the franc as early as November 1968 (the French reserves of foreign currency dropped from 30 billion francs in May 1968 to 18 billion one year later). After the *delayed* devaluation of 8 August 1969 *Le Monde* began to notice that "the franc, like the General, 'died' in May."

The "Gaullist" regime was nothing but a trivial detail in this general calling into question of modern capitalism. Nevertheless, de Gaulle's power also received a mortal blow in May. We have previously shown how it was objectively easy for de Gaulle to reestablish himself in June, since the real struggle had already been lost elsewhere. But in spite of his reinstatement, de Gaulle, as the leader of the state that had *survived* the occupations movement, was unable to wipe out the blemish of having been the leader of the state that had been *subjected* to the scandal of such a movement's existence. De Gaulle, who in his personal style only served as a cover for anything that might occur—specifically, for the normal modernization of capitalist society—had claimed to reign by prestige. In May his prestige was subjected to a definitive humiliation that was subjectively felt by him as well as objectively expressed by the ruling class and the voters who always support that class. The French bourgeoisie is now searching for a more rational form of political power, less capricious and dreamy, more intelligent in defending it from the new threats whose emergence so dumbfounded it. De Gaulle wanted to wipe out the persistent nightmare, "the last phantoms of May," by winning on 27 April 1969 the referendum announced on 24 May 1968 but canceled that very night by a riot. He sensed that his tottering "stable power" had not recovered its equilibrium and he imprudently insisted on being quickly reassured by a factitious rite of reaffirmation of his cause. The demonstrators' slogans on 13 May 1968 [e.g. "Ten years is enough"] turned out to be right: de Gaulle's reign did not endure to its eleventh anniversary; not, of course, due to the bureaucratic or pseudoreformist opposition, but because after the Gay-Lussac uprising everyone realized that Rue Gay-Lussac opened on to all the factories of France.

A generalized disorder, calling in question the very foundations of all institutions, has taken hold of most of the university departments and especially the high schools. If the state, limiting itself to the most vital sectors, succeeded in largely reestablishing the functioning of the scientific disciplines and the elite professional schools, elsewhere the 1968–1969 academic year has been a complete loss and diplomas have been devalued, though they are still far from being despised by the mass of students. Such a situation is in the long run incompatible with the normal functioning of an advanced industrial country, triggering a fall into underdevelopment by creating a qualitative bottleneck in secondary education. Even if the extremist current has in reality only retained a narrow base in the student milieu, this seems to be enough to maintain a process of continual deterioration: the occupation and sacking of the rectorate of the Sorbonne at the end of January, and a number of serious incidents since then, have shown that merely maintaining some sort of pseudoeducation constitutes a subject of considerable concern for the forces of order.

In the factories, where the workers have learned how to make wildcat strikes and where there is an implantation of radical groups more or less consciously opposed to the unions, the sporadic agitation has, despite the efforts of the bureaucrats, led to numerous partial strikes that easily paralyze the increasingly concentrated enterprises in which the different operations become increasingly interdependent. These tremors do not allow anyone to forget that the ground under the enterprises has not become solid again, and that in May the *modern* forms of exploitation revealed both the complete interrelatedness of their means and their new fragility.

With the deterioration of the old orthodox Stalinism (discernable even in the CGT's losses in recent union elections), it is now the turn of the little leftist parties to wear themselves out with bungling maneuvers: almost all of them would have liked to *mechanically* recommence the May process in order to recommence their errors there. They easily infiltrated what remained of the Action Committees, and those Action Committees have not failed to fade away. The little leftist parties are themselves splitting into numerous hostile tendencies, each one holding firm to some stupidity that prides itself on excluding all the stupidities of its rivals. The radical elements have become more numerous since May, but are still scattered—above all in the factories. Because they have not yet been capable of organizing a genuinely autonomous practice, the coherence they have to acquire is still distorted and obscured by old illusions, or verbosity, or sometimes even by an unhealthy unilateral "pro-situationist" admiration. Their only path, which is obviously going to be long and difficult, has nevertheless been mapped out: the formation of *councilist* organizations of revolutionary workers, federating with each other on the sole basis of total democracy and total critique. Their first theoretical task will be to combat and refute in practice the last form of ideology the old world will set against them: *councilist ideology*. At the end of the crisis the Toulouse-based *Révolution Internationale* group expressed a preliminary gross form of this ideology, quite simply proposing (we don't know, moreover, to whom) that workers councils should be *elected above* the general assemblies, whose only task would thus be to ratify the acts of this wise revolutionary neoleadership. This Lenino-Yugoslavian monstrosity, since adopted by Lambert's "Trotskyist Organization," is almost as bizarre nowadays as the Gaullists' use of the phrase "direct democracy" when they were infatuated with referendary "dialogue." The next revolution will recognize as councils only sovereign rank-and-file general assemblies, in the enterprises and the neighborhoods, whose delegates are always subject to recall and derive their power only from those assemblies. A councilist organization will never defend any other goal: it must translate into acts a dialectic that supersedes the frozen and one-sided poles of spontaneism and of openly or covertly bureaucratized organization. It must be an organization advancing *revolutionarily* toward the revolution of the councils; an organization that neither disperses at the first moment of declared struggle nor institutionalizes itself.

This perspective is not limited to France, it is international. The total meaning of the occupations movement must be understood everywhere. Already in 1968 its example touched off, or pushed to higher levels, severe disorders throughout Europe and in America and Japan. The most remarkable immediate consequences of May were the bloody revolt of the Mexican students, which was broken in its relative isolation, and the Yugoslavian students' movement against the bureaucracy and for proletarian self-management, which partially drew in the workers and put Tito's regime in great danger. What finally came to the rescue of the latter, more than the concessions proclaimed by the ruling class, was the Russian intervention in Czechoslovakia, which allowed the Yugoslavian regime to rally the country around itself by brandishing the menace of an invasion by a foreign bureaucracy. The hand of the new International is beginning to be denounced by the police of several countries, who believe they have discovered the directives of French revolutionaries in Mexico during summer 1968 and in the anti-Russian demonstration in Prague on 28 March 1969; and the Franco government explicitly justified its recourse to a state of emergency at the beginning of this year by referring to the risk that the university agitation would evolve into a general crisis of the French type. England has been experiencing wildcat strikes for a long time, and one of the main goals of the Labour government is obviously to succeed in prohibiting them; but it was unquestionably this first experience of a general wildcat strike that led Wilson to strive with such urgency and determination to obtain repressive legislation against this type of strike this year. This careerist didn't hesitate to risk his career, and even the very unity of the Labour party-union bureaucracy, on the "Barbara Castle project," for if the unions are the direct enemies of wildcat strikes, they are nevertheless afraid of themselves losing all importance by losing all control over the workers once the right to intervene against the real forms of class struggle is left solely to the state, without having to pass through their own mediation. On 1 May the antiunion strike of 100,000 dockers, printers and metal workers against the threat of this law was the first political strike in England since 1926: it is most fitting that this form of struggle has reappeared against a Labour government.

Wilson had to lose face by giving up his dearest project and handing back to the union police the task of repressing the 95% of work stoppages in England now caused by wildcat strikes. In August the victory of the eight-week wildcat strike of the Port Talbot blast furnace workers "has proved that the TUC leadership was not armed for this role" (*Le Monde*, 30 August 1969).

It is easy to recognize throughout the world the new tone with which a radical critique is pronouncing its declaration of war on the old society—from the graffiti on the walls of England and Italy to the extremist Mexican group *Caos*, which during the summer of 1968 called for the sabotage of the Olympics and of "the society of spectacular consumption"; from the acts and publications of the *Acratas* in Madrid to the shout of a Wall Street demonstration (AFP, 12 April), "Stop the Show," in that American society whose "decline and fall" we already pointed out in 1965, and whose very officials now admit that it is "a sick society."

In Italy the SI was able to make a certain contribution to the revolutionary current as early as the end of 1967, when the occupation of the University of Turin served as the starting point for a vast movement; both by way of the publication of some basic texts—badly translated by publishers Feltrinelli and De Donato, but nevertheless rapidly sold out—and by way of the radical action of a few individuals, although the present Italian section of the SI was formally constituted only in January 1969. The slow evolution of the Italian crisis over the last twenty-two months—which has thus become known as "the creeping May"—first got itself bogged down in 1968 in the forming of a "Student Movement" much more backward even than in France, as well as being isolated—with virtually the sole exemplary exception being the joint occupation of the city hall of Orgosolo, Sardinia, by students, shepherds and workers. The workers' struggles themselves began slowly, but grew more serious in 1969 in spite of the efforts of the Stalinist party and the unions, who worked to fragment the threat by allowing one-day national strikes by category or one-day general strikes by province. At the beginning of April the Battipaglia insurrection, followed by the prison revolts of Turin, Milan and Genoa, pushed the crisis to a higher level and reduced even more the bureaucrats' margin of maneuver. In Battipaglia the workers kept control of the town for twenty-four hours after the police opened fire, seizing arms, laying siege to the police holed up in their barracks and demanding their surrender, and obstructing roads and trains. Even after the massive reinforcements of state troopers had regained control of the town and communications routes, an embryo of a council still existed in Battipaglia, claiming to replace the town government and expressing the inhabitants' direct power over their own affairs. If the demonstrations in support of Battipaglia throughout Italy were regimented by the bureaucrats and remained platonic, the revolutionary elements of Milan at least succeeded in violently attacking the bureaucrats and the police and ravaging the downtown area of the city. On this occasion the Italian situationists took up the French methods in the most appropriate manner.

In the following months the "wildcat" movements at Fiat and among the workers of the North have demonstrated, more clearly than has the complete collapse of the government, how close Italy is to a *modern* revolutionary crisis. The turn taken in August by the wildcat strikes at Pirelli in Milan and Fiat in Turin point to the imminence of a total confrontation.

The reader will easily understand the main reason we have dealt here both with the question of the general significance of the new revolutionary movement and with the question of their relation with the theses of the SI. Until recently, even those who readily recognized an interest in some points of our theory regretted that we ourselves made the whole truth of that theory contingent upon the return of social revolution, which they considered an incredible "hypothesis." Conversely, various activists with no real contact with reality, but taking pride in their eternal allergy to any relevant theory, posed the stupid question: "What is the SI's practical activity?" Lacking the slightest comprehension of the dialectical process through which the real movement meets "its own unknown theory," they all wanted to disregard what they believed to be an *unarmed critique*. Now this critique is arming itself. The "sunburst that in one flash reveals the features of the new world" was seen in France in that month of May, with the intermingled red and black flags of workers' democracy. The followup will come everywhere. And if we have to a certain extent marked the return of this movement with our name, it is not in order to hold on to any of it or to derive any authority from it. From now on we are sure of a satisfactory consummation of our activities: the SI will be superseded.

REFORM AND COUNTERREFORM
IN BUREAUCRATIC POWER

It could almost be said that the history of the last twenty years has set itself the sole task of refuting Trotsky's analyses concerning the bureaucracy. Victim of a sort of "class subjectivism," Trotsky refused throughout his life to recognize in Stalinist practice anything but a temporary deviation of a usurping *stratum*, a "Thermidorian reaction." As an ideologue of the Bolshevik revolution, he was unable to become a theorist of proletarian revolution at the time of the Stalinist restoration. By refusing to recognize the bureaucracy in power for what it *is*, namely a *new exploiting class*, this Hegel of the revolution betrayed deprived himself of the possibility of making a genuine critique of it. The theoretical and practical impotence of Trotskyism (in all its variants) is largely attributable to this original sin of the master.

In *Enragés and Situationists in the Occupations Movement* (p. 20) we said, a month before the Russian invasion: "The bureaucratic appropriation of society is inseparable from a totalitarian possession of the state and from the exclusive reign of its ideology. The present rights of free expression and association and the absence of censorship pose this short-term alternative in Czechoslovakia: either a repression, which would reveal the sham character of these concessions; or a proletarian assault against the bureaucratic ownership of the state and the economy, which ownership would be unmasked as soon as the dominant ideology was deprived for any length of time of its omnipresent police. The outcome of such a conflict is of the greatest concern for the Russian bureaucracy, whose very survival would be called into question by a victory of the Czech workers." Now it's settled: the first alternative was effected by the intervention of "Soviet" tanks. The basis of Moscow's absolute domination over the "socialist" countries was this golden rule proclaimed and practiced by the Russian bureaucracy: "Socialism is not to go further than our army." Wherever that army has been the main force installing "Communist" parties in power, it has the last word each time its former protégés manifest any leanings toward independence that might endanger the totalitarian bureaucratic domination. The Russian socioeconomic system has been from the beginning the *ideal type* for the new bureaucratic regimes. But fidelity to this archetype has often conflicted with the specific requirements of the particular dominated societies; since the dominant class interests of each satellite bureaucracy do not necessarily coincide with those of the Russian bureaucracy, interbureaucratic relations have always contained underlying conflicts. Caught between the hammer and the anvil, the satellite bureaucracies always end up clinging to the hammer as soon as proletarian forces demonstrate their desire for autonomy. In Poland or Hungary, as recently in Czechoslovakia, the national bureaucratic "revolt" never goes beyond replacing one bureaucrat with another.

As the first industrialized state conquered by Stalinism, Czechoslovakia has over the last twenty years occupied a "privileged" position in the international system of exploitation set up by the Russians after 1949, in the framework of the "socialist division of labor" directed by the Comecon. The naked totalitarianism of the Stalin era meant that upon their coming to power the Czech Stalinists could do nothing but servilely imitate the "universal socialist system." But in contrast to the other bureaucratic countries where there was a real need for economic development and industrialization, the level of productive forces in Czechoslovakia was in complete contradiction with the objectives of the economic program of the new regime. After fifteen years of irrational bureaucratic management the Czech economy was on the brink of catastrophe; the reform of this economy then became a matter of life and death for the ruling class. This was the root of the "Prague Spring" and the adventurous liberalization attempted by the bureaucracy. But before going into the analysis of this "bureaucratic reform," let us orient ourselves by examining its origins in the purely Stalinist (or Novotnyist) period.

After the [1948] Prague coup, the integration of Czechoslovakia into the Eastern bloc's almost totally self-contained economic system made it the main victim of Russian domination. Since it was the most developed country it had to bear the costs of industrializing its neighbors, themselves yoked under a policy of superexploitation. After 1950 the totalitarian planning, with its emphasis on metallurgical and engineering industries, introduced a serious imbalance into the functioning of the economy which has steadily grown worse. In 1966 investment in Czech heavy industry reached 47%, the highest rate in the world. This was because Czechoslovakia had to provide—at ridiculously low prices that did not even cover the costs of production and the wear and tear of the machinery—raw materials (in five years the USSR used up fifty years' worth of reserves from the Jachymov uranium deposits in Bohemia) and manufactured goods (machines, armaments, etc.) to the USSR, the other "socialist" countries, and later to the "Third World" countries coveted by the Russians. "Production for production's sake" was the ideology that accompanied this enterprise, the costs of which the workers were the first to bear. As early as 1953, in the wake of a monetary reform, the workers of Pilsen, seeing their wages decreasing and prices rising, revolted and were immediately repressed. The consequences of this economic policy were essentially: the Czech economy's increasing dependence on Soviet supplies of raw materials and fuel; an orientation toward foreign interests; a sharp decline in the standard of living following a decline in real wages; and finally a decline in the national income after 1960 (its growth rate fell from an average of 8.5% from 1950–1960 to 0.7% in 1962). In 1963, for the first time in the history of a "socialist" country, the national income fell rather than rose. This was the alarm signal for the new reform. Ota Sik estimated that investment would have to be quadrupled in order to attain in 1968 the same national income growth as in 1958. From 1963 on it began to be officially admitted that "the national economy of Czechoslovakia is going through a period of serious structural imbalance, with limited inflationary tendencies appearing in all sectors of life and society, notably in foreign trade, the home market and investments" (*Czechoslovakian Foreign Trade*, October 1968).

Voices began to be heard insisting on the urgency of transforming the economy. Professor Ota Sik and his team began preparing their reform plan, which was to be more or less adopted after 1965 by the upper echelons of the state. The new Ota Sik plan made a rather daring critique of the functioning of the economy over the preceding years. It questioned the Russian tutelage and proposed that the economy should be freed from rigid central planning and opened to the world market. To do this it was necessary to go beyond simple reproduction of capital, put an end to the system of "production for production's sake" (denounced as an antisocialist crime after having been glorified as a fundamental principle of socialism), reduce the cost of production and raise the productivity index, which had gone from 7.7% in 1960 to 3.1% in 1962 and had fallen even further in the following years.

This plan, a model of technocratic reform, began to be implemented in 1965 and took full effect from 1967 on. It required a clean break with the administrative methods that had crushed all initiative: giving the producers an "interest" in the results of their work, granting autonomy to the different enterprises, rewarding successes, penalizing failures, encouraging through appropriate technical measures the development of profitable industries and enterprises, and putting the market back on its feet by bringing prices in line with the world market. Resisted by the hidebound administrative cadres, this program was applied only in small doses. The Novotnyist bureaucracy began to see the dangerous implications of such a venture. The temporary rise in prices, which was not matched by a corresponding rise in wages, enabled this backward stratum to denounce the project in the eyes of the workers. Novotny himself presented himself as the defender of working-class interests and openly criticized the new measures at a workers meeting in 1967. But the "liberal" wing, aware of the real interests of the bureaucratic regime in Czechoslovakia and sure of the

258

support of the population, joined battle. As a journalist of *Kulturni Tvorba* (5 January 1967) put it, "For the people, the new economic system has become synonymous with the need for change"—*total change*. This was the first link in a chain of developments that would necessarily lead to far-reaching social and political changes. The conservative bureaucracy, having no real support to rely on, could only admit its failings and gradually bow out of the political scene: any resistance on its part would have rapidly led to an explosion analogous to that of Budapest in 1956. The June 1967 Fourth Congress of Writers (though writers along with filmmakers had already been allowed a certain margin of freedom in the aesthetic practice of their profession) turned into a veritable public indictment of the regime. With their last strength the "conservatives" reacted by excluding a certain number of radical intellectuals from the Party and by putting their journal under direct ministerial control.

But the winds of revolt were blowing harder and harder, and nothing could any longer stem the popular enthusiasm for transforming the prevailing conditions of Czech life. A student demonstration protesting against an electricity shutdown, after being strongly repressed, turned into a meeting leveling accusations against the regime. One of the first discoveries of this meeting, which was to become the watchword of the whole subsequent movement of contestation, was the absolute insistence on *telling the truth*, stressing "the incredible contradictions between what is said and what is actually done." In a system based on the permanent lying of ideology such a demand becomes quite simply revolutionary; and the intellectuals did not fail to develop its implications to the limit. In the bureaucratic systems, where nothing must escape the party-state totalitarianism, a protest against the slightest detail of life necessarily leads to calling in question the *totality* of existing conditions, to the protest of man against the whole of his inhuman life. Even if it was limited to the Prague University campus, the student demonstration concerned all the alienated aspects of Czech life, which was denounced as unacceptable in the course of the meeting.

The neobureaucracy then took over the leadership of the movement and tried to contain it within the narrow framework of its reforms. In January 1968 an "Action Program" was adopted, marking the rise of the Dubček team and the removal of Novotny. In addition to Ota Sik's economic plan, now definitively adopted and integrated into this new program, a certain number of political measures were proudly proclaimed by the new leadership. Almost all the formal "freedoms" of bourgeois regimes were guaranteed. This policy, totally unprecedented for a bureaucratic regime, shows how much was at stake and how serious the situation was. The radical elements, taking advantage of these bureaucratic concessions, were to reveal their real purpose as "*objectively necessary*" measures for safeguarding bureaucratic domination. Smrkovsky, the most liberal among the newly promoted members, naïvely expressed the truth of the bureaucratic liberalism: "Knowing that even in a socialist society evolution takes place through constant conflicts of interest in the economic, social and political domains, we should seek a system of *political guidance* that permits the

259

settling of all social conflicts and avoids the necessity for extraordinary administrative interventions." But the new bureaucracy did not realize that by renouncing those "extraordinary interventions," which in reality constitute its only *normal* manner of governing, it would be leaving its regime open to a pitiless radical critique. The freedom of association and of cultural and political expression produced a veritable orgy of critical truth. The notion that the Party's "leading role" should be "naturally and spontaneously recognized, even at the rank-and-file level, based on the ability of its Communist functionaries to work and command" (Action Program) was disparaged everywhere, and new demands for autonomous workers' organizations began to be raised. At the end of spring 1968 the Dubček bureaucracy was giving the ridiculous impression of wanting to have its cake and eat it too. It reaffirmed its intention of maintaining its political monopoly: "If anticommunist elements attempt to attack this historic fact (*i.e. the right of the Party to lead*), the Party will mobilize all the forces of the people and of the socialist state in order to drive back and extinguish this adventurist attempt" (Resolution of the Central Committee, June 1968). But once the bureaucratic reform had opened participation in decision-making to the majority of the Party, how could the great majority outside the Party not also want to decide things for themselves? When those at the top of the state play the fiddle, how can they expect those at the bottom not to start dancing?

From this point on the revolutionary tendencies began to turn their critique toward denunciation of the liberal formalism and its ideology. Until then democracy had been, so to speak, "imposed on the masses" in the same way the dictatorship had been imposed on them, that is, by barring them from any real participation. Everyone knew that Novotny had come to power as a partisan of liberalization; and that a "Gomulka-type regression" constantly threatened the Dubček movement. A society is not transformed by changing its political apparatus, but by overthrowing it from top to bottom. Thus people came to the point of criticizing the Bolshevik conception of the party as leader of the working class, and to demanding an autonomous organization of the proletariat; which would spell a rapid death for the bureaucracy. This is because for the bureaucracy the proletariat must exist only as an *imaginary* force; the bureaucracy reduces it—or tries to reduce it— to the point of being nothing but an appearance, but it wants this appearance to exist and to believe in its own existence. The bureaucracy bases its power on its formal ideology, but its *formal* goals become its actual content and it thus everywhere enters into conflict with *real* goals. Wherever it has seized the state and the economy, wherever the general interest of the state becomes an interest apart and consequently a *real* interest, the bureaucracy enters into conflict with the proletariat just as every consequence conflicts with the existence of the bureaucracy's own presuppositions.

But the opposition movement following upon the bureaucratic reform only went half way. It did not have time to follow out all its practical implications. The relentless theoretical critique of "bureaucratic dictatorship" and Stalinist totalitarianism had scarcely begun to be taken up autonomously by the vast majority of the population

260

when the neobureaucracy reacted by brandishing the Russian threat, which had already been present from May on. It can be said that the great weakness of the Czechoslovakian movement was that the working class scarcely intervened as an autonomous and decisive force. The themes of "self-management" and "workers councils" included in Ota Sik's technocratic reform did not go beyond the bureaucratic perspective of a Yugoslavian-style "democratic management"; this is true even of the counterproject, obviously drafted by unionists, presented on 29 June 1968 by the Wilhelm Pieck factory. The critique of Leninism, presented by "certain philosophers" as being "already a deformation of Marxism since it inherently contains the logic of Stalinism," was not, as the *Rouge* dimwits would have it, "an absurd notion because it ultimately amounts to denying the leading role of the proletariat" (!), but the highest point of theoretical critique attained in a bureaucratic country. Dutschke himself was ridiculed by the revolutionary Czech students and his "anarcho-Maoism" scornfully rejected as "absurd, laughable and not even deserving the attention of a fifteen-year-old." All this criticism, which obviously could only lead to the *practical calling into question of the class power of the bureaucracy*, was tolerated and even sometimes encouraged by the Dubček regime as long as the latter could *recuperate* it as a legitimate denunciation of "Stalino-Novotnyist errors." The bureaucracy does denounce its own crimes, but always as having been committed by *others*; it suffices for it to detach a part of itself, to elevate it into an autonomous entity and to attribute to it all the antiproletarian crimes (since the most ancient times, sacrifice has been bureaucracy's favored method for perpetuating its power). In Czechoslovakia, as in Poland and Hungary, nationalism has been the best argument for winning the population's support of the ruling class. The clearer the Russian threat became, the more Dubček's bureaucratic power was reinforced; his sole desire would have been for the Warsaw Pact forces to remain indefinitely at the borders. But sooner or later the Czech proletariat would have discovered through struggle that the point is not to know what any given bureaucrat, or even the bureaucracy as a whole, momentarily represents as its goal, but to know what the bureaucracy really is, what it, *in conformity with its own nature*, will be historically forced to do. And the proletariat would have taken appropriate action.

It was the fear of such a discovery that haunted the Russian bureaucracy and its satellites. Picture a Russian (or East German) bureaucrat in the midst of this "ideological" panic, how his brain—as sick as his power—is tortured, confused, stunned by these cries of independence, of workers councils, of "bureaucratic dictatorship," by the conspiracy of workers and intellectuals and their threat to defend their conquests arms in hand; and you will understand how in this clamorous confusion of truth and freedom, of plots and revolution, the Russian bureaucracy could cry out to its Czech counterpart: "Better a fearful end than a fear without end!"

If ever an event had cast its shadow before it long before it happened, it was, for those who know how to read modern history, the Russian intervention in Czechoslovakia. It was long contemplated and, in spite of all its international repercussions, virtually inevitable. In bringing into question the omnipotence of bureaucratic power, Dubček's adventurous—though necessary—effort began to imperil this same power wherever it was to be found, and thus became intolerable. Six hundred thousand soldiers (almost as many as the Americans in Vietnam) were sent to put a brutal stop to it. Thus when the "antisocialist" and "counterrevolutionary" forces, continually conjured up and exorcised by all the bureaucrats, finally appeared, they appeared not under the portrait of Beneš or armed by "revanchist Germans," but in the uniform of the "Red" Army.

A remarkable popular resistance was carried on for seven days— *"the magnificent seven"*—mobilizing virtually the entire population against the invaders. Paradoxically, clearly revolutionary methods of struggle were taken up for the defense of a reformist bureaucracy. But what was not realized in the course of the movement could certainly not be realized under the occupation: the Russian troops, having enabled the Dubčekists to brake the revolutionary process as much as possible while they were at the borders, also enabled them to control the whole resistance movement after 21 August. They played exactly the same role as the American troops do in North Vietnam: the role of ensuring the masses' unanimous support of the bureaucracy that exploits them.

The first reflex of the people of Prague, however, was to defend not the Palace of the Republic, but the radio station, which was considered the symbol of their main conquest: truth of information against organized falsehood. And what had been the nightmare of all the Warsaw Pact bureaucracies—the press and the radio—was to continue to haunt them for another entire week. The Czechoslovakian experience has shown the extraordinary possibilities of struggle that a consistent and organized revolutionary movement will one day have at its disposal. Equipment provided by the Warsaw Pact (in anticipation of a possible imperialist invasion of Czechoslovakia!) was used by the Czech journalists to set up 35 clandestine broadcasting stations linked with 80 emergency backup stations. The Soviet propaganda—so necessary for an occupation army—was thus totally undermined; and the population was able to know just about everything that was happening in the country and to follow the directives of the liberal bureaucrats or of the radical elements that controlled certain stations. For example, in response to a radio appeal aimed at sabotaging the operations of the Russian police, Prague was transformed into a veritable "labyrinth-city": all the streets lost their names, all the houses lost their numbers and were covered with inscriptions in the best style of May 1968 Paris. Defying all the police, Prague became a home of freedom, an example of the revolutionary detournement of repressive urbanism. Due to exceptional proletarian organization, *all* the newspapers were able to be freely printed and distributed under the noses of the Russians who asininely guarded the newspaper offices. Several factories were transformed into printing works turning out thousands of papers and leaflets—including a counterfeit issue of *Pravda* in Russian. The 14th Party Congress was able to meet secretly for three days under the protection of the workers of "Auto-Praha." It was this conference that sabotaged "Operation Kádár" and forced the Russians to negotiate with Dubček. But by using both their troops and the internal contradictions of the Czechoslovakian bureaucracy, the Russians were eventually able to transform the liberal team into a sort of disguised Vichy-type government. Husak, who was thinking of his own future, was the principal agent responsible for canceling the 14th Congress (on the pretext of the absence of the Slovak delegates, who had in fact apparently stayed away on his recommendation). The day after the "Moscow Accords" he declared, "We can accept this accord, which will enable *sensible men* (our emphasis) to lead the people out of the present impasse in such a way that they will have no call to feel ashamed in the future."

The Czech proletariat, when it becomes revolutionary, will not be ashamed of its mistake in having trusted Husak, Dubček or Smrkovsky. It already knows that it can count only on its own forces; and that one after the other Dubček and Smrkovsky will betray it just as the neobureaucracy collectively betrayed it by yielding to Moscow and falling in line with its totalitarian policy. The emotional attachment to one or another celebrity is a vestige of the miserable era of the proletariat, a vestige of the old world. The November strikes and the suicides somewhat slowed down the process of "normalization," which was not brought to completion until April 1969. By reestablishing itself in its true form, the bureaucratic power became more effectively combated. The illusions all melted away one after the other and the Czechoslovakian masses' attachment to the reformist bureaucracy disappeared. By rehabilitating the "collaborators" the reformists lost their last chance for any future popular support. The workers' and students' revolutionary consciousness deepened as the repression became more severe. The return to the methods and "narrow, stupid mentality of the fifties" is already provoking violent reactions on the part of the workers and students, whose diverse forms of linking up constitute the main anxiety common to Dubček, his successor and their masters. The workers are proclaiming their "inalienable right to respond to any extreme measures" with their "own extreme countermeasures" (motion by the workers of the CKD to the Minister of Defense, 22 April 1969). The restoration of Stalinism has shown once and for all the illusory character of any bureaucratic reformism and the congenital impossibility for the bureaucracy to "liberalize" its management of society. Its pretense of a "socialism with a human face" is nothing but the introduction of a few "bourgeois" concessions into its totalitarian world; and even these concessions immediately threaten its existence. The only possible *humanization* of "bureaucratic socialism" is its suppression by the revolutionary proletariat, not by a mere "political revolution," but by the total subversion of existing conditions and the practical dissolution of the Bureaucratic International.

The riots of 21 August 1969 have revealed to what extent *ordinary Stalinism* has been reestablished in Czechoslovakia, and also to what extent it is threatened by the proletarian critique: ten deaths, 2000 arrests and the threats of expelling or prosecuting the puppet Dubček have not stopped the *national slowdown strike* through which the Czech workers are endangering the survival of the economic system of their indigenous and Russian exploiters.

The Russian intervention was able to slow down the objective process of change in Czechoslovakia, but it has been dearly paid for by international Stalinism. The bureaucratic powers of Cuba and Hanoi, directly dependent on the "Soviet" state, could only applaud their masters' intervention—to the great embarrassment of their Trotskyist and surrealist admirers and the high-minded souls of the left. Castro, with a singular cynicism, justified the military intervention at great length as being necessitated by threats of a restoration of capitalism; thereby unmasking the nature of his own "socialism." Hanoi and the bureaucratic Arab powers, themselves the victims of foreign occupation, push their absurd logic to the point of supporting an analogous aggression because in this case it is carried out by their self-styled protectors.

As for those members of the Bureaucratic International that shed tears over Czechoslovakia, they all do so for their own *national* reasons. The "Czechoslovakian affair," coming right after the heavy shock suffered by the French CP in the May revolutionary crisis, dealt the latter another serious blow; now divided into archaeo-, neo- and orthodox-Stalinist fractions, it is torn between fidelity to Moscow and its own interest on the bourgeois political chessboard. If the Italian CP was bolder in its denunciation, the reason was to be found in the rising crisis in Italy and above all in the direct blow struck against its "Togliattism." The nationalist bureaucracies of Yugoslavia and Rumania found in the intervention an opportunity to consolidate their class domination, regaining the support of populations that can see nothing but the Russian threat—a threat more imaginary than real. Stalinism, which has already tolerated Titoism and Maoism as other images of itself, will always tolerate one or another sort of "Rumanian independence" as long as it does not directly threaten its "socialist model" faithfully reproduced everywhere. There is no point in going into the Sino-Albanian critique of "Russian imperialism": in the logic of their "anti-imperialist" delirium, the Chinese in turn reproach the Russians for not intervening in Czechoslovakia like they did in Hungary (see *Peking News*, 13 August 1968) and then denounce the "odious aggression" perpetrated by "the Brezhnev-Kosygin fascist clique."

"The international association of totalitarian bureaucracies has now completely fallen apart," we wrote in *IS* #11. The Czechoslovakian crisis has only confirmed the advanced decomposition of Stalinism. Stalinism would never have been able to play such a great role in the crushing of the workers movement *everywhere* if the Russian totalitarian bureaucratic model had not been closely related both to the bureaucratization of the old *reformist* movement (German Social Democracy and the Second International) and to the increasingly bureaucratic organization of modern capitalist production. But now, after more than forty years of counterrevolutionary history, the revolution is being reborn everywhere, striking terror into the hearts of the masters of the East as well as those of the West, attacking them both in their differences and in their deep affinity. The courageous isolated protests voiced in Moscow after 21 August herald the revolution that will not fail to break out soon *in Russia itself.* The revolutionary movement now knows its real enemies, and none of the alienations produced by the two capitalisms—private-bourgeois or state-bureaucratic—can any longer escape its critique. Facing the immense tasks that lie before it, the movement will no longer waste its time fighting phantoms or supporting illusions.

HOW NOT TO UNDERSTAND
SITUATIONIST BOOKS

(excerpts)

If the SI's action had not recently led to some publicly scandalous and threatening consequences, it is certain that no French publication would have reviewed our recent books. François Châtelet ingenuously admits as much in the 3 January 1968 *Nouvel Observateur:* "One's first impulse when confronted with such works is purely and simply to exclude them, to leave this absolutist point of view in the absolute, in the unrelative, in the unstated." But having left us in the unstated, the organizers of this conspiracy of silence have within a few years seen this strange "absolute" fall on their heads and turn out to be not so very distinct from *present history,* from which they were absolutely separated. All their efforts were unable to prevent this "old mole" from making his way toward daylight. [. . .]

And so it is that publications in France have felt obliged to devote several dozen articles to discussing our books; and nearly as many have appeared in the foreign press, the latter being somewhat more honest and informed. Some have even contained praises, which there is no point going into here. [. . .] In order to avoid tedious repetition, we will limit ourselves to examining three typical attitudes, each one manifesting itself in relation to one of our books: the attitudes of an academic Marxist, a psychoanalyst and an ultraleftist militant.

During the early 1950s Claude Lefort was a revolutionary and one of the principal theorists of the journal *Socialisme ou Barbarie*—regarding which we stated in *IS* #10 that it had sunk to run-of-the-mill academic speculation on the level of *Arguments* and that it was bound to disappear: which it confirmed by folding a month or two later. By that time Lefort had already been separated from it for years, having been in the forefront of the opposition to any form of revolutionary organization, which he denounced as inevitably doomed to bureaucratization. Since this distressing discovery he has consoled himself by taking up an ordinary academic career and writing in *La Quinzaine Littéraire.* In the 1 February 1968 issue of that periodical this very knowledgeable but domesticated man makes a critique of *The Society of the Spectacle.* He begins by recognizing some merits in it. The book's use of Marxian methodology, and even of detournement, has not escaped him, though he doesn't go so far as to recognize also its use of Hegel. But the book nevertheless seems academically unacceptable to him for the following reason: "Debord adds thesis upon thesis but he does not advance; he endlessly repeats the same idea: that the real is inverted in ideology, that ideology, changed in its essence in the spectacle, passes itself off for the real, that it is necessary to overthrow ideology in order to bring the real back into its own. It makes little difference what particular topics he treats, this idea is reflected in all the others; it is only due to his exhaustion that he has stopped at the 221st thesis." Debord readily admits that he found, at the 221st thesis, that he had said quite enough, and accomplished exactly what he had aimed at: an "endless" description of what the *spectacle* is and how it can be overthrown. The fact that "this idea is reflected in all the others" is precisely what we consider the characteristic of a *dialectical book*. Such a book does not have to "advance," like some doctoral dissertation on Machiavelli, toward the approval of a jury and the attainment of a diploma. (And as Marx puts it in the Afterword to the second German edition of *Capital*, regarding the way the dialectical "method of presentation" may be viewed, "This reflecting may make it seem as if we had before us a mere *a priori* construction.") *The Society of the Spectacle* does not hide its *a priori* engagement, it does not attempt to derive its conclusions from academic argumentation; it is written only to show the *concrete* coherent field of application of a thesis that already exists at the outset, having issued from the investigation that revolutionary criticism has made of modern capitalism. In our opinion, it is basically *a book that lacked nothing but one or more revolutions*. Which were not long in coming. But Lefort, having lost all interest in this kind of theory and practice, finds that this book is in itself a closed world: "One would have expected this book to be a violent attack against its adversaries, but in fact this ostentatious discourse had no other aim than showing off. Admittedly it has its beauty. The style is flawless. Since any question that does not have an automatic response has been banished from the very first lines, one would search in vain for any fault." The misinterpretation is total: Lefort sees a sort of Mallarméan purity in a book which, as a *negative* of spectacular society (in which also, but in an inverse manner, any question that does not have an automatic response is banished at every moment), ultimately seeks nothing other than to *overthrow* the existing *relation of forces* in the factories and the streets.

After this overall rejection of the book, Lefort still wants to play the Marxist regarding a detail in order to remind us that this is his specialty, the reason he gets assignments from intellectual periodicals. Here he begins to falsify in order to give himself the opportunity of introducing a pedantic reminder of what is well known. He solemnly announces that Debord has changed "the commodity into the spectacle," which transformation is "full of consequences." He ponderously summarizes what Marx says on the commodity, then falsely charges Debord with having said that "the production of the phantasmagoria governs that of commodities," whereas in fact *the very contrary* is clearly stated in *The Society of the Spectacle*, notably in the second chapter where the spectacle is defined as simply a *moment* of the development of commodity production. [. . .]

We sink lower still with André Stéphane's *Univers contestationnaire* (Payot, 1969), the thirteenth chapter of which is a critique of Vaneigem's *Treatise on Living for the Young Generations*. The publisher announces that "Stéphane" is the pseudonym of "two psychoanalysts."

Judging by their colossal ineptitude and parody of "orthodox Freudianism," they could just as well have been twenty-two, or the work could have been done by a computer programmed for psychoanalysis. Since the authors are psychoanalysts, Vaneigem is naturally insane. He is paranoid, this is why he so perfectly expressed in advance the May movement and various distressing tendencies of the entire society. It's really only a matter of fantasies, delirium, rejection of the objective world and of the oedipal problem, fusional narcissism, exhibitionism, sadistic impulses, etc. They crown their edifice of imbecilities by professing to admire the book "as a work of art." But this book has fallen into bad hands: the May movement horrified our psychiatrists by its blind violence, its inhuman terrorism, its nihilist cruelty and its explicit goal of destroying civilization and perhaps even the planet. When they hear the word "festival" they reach for their electrodes; they insist that one get back to the serious, never doubting for a single moment that they themselves are excellent representatives of the seriousness of psychoanalysis and of social life and that they can write about all that without making people laugh. Even the people who had the foolishness to be the *customers* of this Laurel and Hardy of mental medicine told them that after May they felt less depressed and dissociated. [. . .] For these psychoanalysts there is no doubt that this May movement, which they analyze with such perspicacity, was a movement of *students alone* (these police dogs of the detection of the irrational have not for one moment found it *abnormal* and unexplainable that a mere outburst of student vandalism was able to paralyze the economy and the state in a large industrial country). Moreover, according to them all students are rich, living in comfort and abundance, without any discernable rational reason for discontent: they enjoy virtually all the benefits of a happy society which has never been less repressive. Our psychoanalysts thus conclude that this socioeconomic happiness, evidently enjoyed by *all* the May rebels, has revealed the inner, existential misery of people who had an "infantile desire" for the absolute, people whose immaturity makes them incapable of profiting from the "benefits" of modern society, thus demonstrating "an incapacity of libidinal expression in the external world due to internal conflicts." [. . .]

At the end of 1966 Rector Bayen of Strasbourg declared to the press that *we should be dealt with by psychiatrists*. In the following year he saw the abolition of the "University Psychological Aid Centers" of Strasbourg and Nantes, and eighteen months later the crumbling of his whole fine university world along with a great number of his hierarchical superiors. Finally, though a bit late, the psychiatrists with which we were threatened have arrived, and made this critique of Vaneigem. They have probably disappointed those who were hoping for a final solution of the situationist problem.

René Viénet's book has not had the honors of psychiatry, but has been criticized in an article in issue #2 of *Révolution Internationale* [obsolete address omitted], the organ of an ultraleftist group that is anti-Trotskyist and non-Bordighist, but scarcely disengaged from Leninism: it is still aiming at reconstituting the wise leadership of a true "party of the proletariat," which promises, however, to remain democratic once it manages to come into existence. This group's ideas are a bit too musty for it to be of interest to discuss them here. Since we are dealing with people who have revolutionary intentions, we will merely point out a few of their specific *falsifications*. Such falsification is in our opinion *much more inconsistent* with the activity of a revolutionary organization than the mere assertion of erroneous theories, which can always be discussed and corrected. Moreover, those who think they have to falsify texts in order to defend their theses admit *ipso facto* that their theses are otherwise undefendable.

The critic says he is disappointed with the book, "especially since the several months' period of writing time should have made possible something better." In fact, although the book only appeared at the end of October 1968, it is clearly indicated in the introduction (p. 8) that it was completed 26 July. It was then immediately sent to the publisher, after which no alterations were made apart from the addition of two short notes (pp. 20 and 209) explicitly dated October, concerning post-July developments in Czechoslovakia and Mexico.

Our critic reproaches the book for "yielding to current fashion"— that is, in fact, to our own style, since it adopted the same sort of presentation as the previous *IS* journals—because it includes photos and comics; and he reproaches the situationists for being contemptuous of "the great infantile mass of workers" by aiming to *divert* them as do the capitalist press and cinema. He sternly notes that "it is above all the action of the Enragés and situationists that is described"; only to add immediately: "which, moreover, is stated in the title." Viénet proposed to draw up right away a report on our activities in the May period, accompanied with our analyses and some documents, considering that this would constitute a valuable documentation for understanding May, particularly for those who will have to act in future crises of the same type (and it is with the same purpose that we have further taken up these questions in this issue). This experience may seem useful to some and negligible to others, depending on how they think and *what they really are*. But what is certain is that without this book this precise documentation would have been unknown (or known fragmentarily and falsely) by many people. The title says clearly enough what it's about.

Without going so far as to insinuate that there is the slightest false detail in this report, our critic is of the opinion that Viénet has given too large a place to our action, that we have imagined it to have been "preponderant." He writes that, "reduced to its correct proportions, the place occupied by the situationists was certainly inferior to that of numerous other groups, or in any case not superior." We don't really know where this "certainty" of his comparison comes from, as if it were a matter of weighing the total amount of paving stones that each group threw in the same direction at the same building. The CRS and even the Maoists certainly had a greater "place" in the crisis than we had, a greater weight. The question is *in what direction* the force of one or another grouping was exerted. If we restrict ourselves to the *revolutionary* current, a great number of unorganized workers obviously had a weight so determinative that no group can even be compared with them; but this tendency did not become the conscious master of its own action. If—since our critic seems more interested in a sort of race among the "groups" (and perhaps he is thinking of *his*?)—we restrict ourselves to groups holding clearly revolutionary positions, we know very well that they were not so "numerous"! And in this case one would have to specify *which groups* one is referring to and *what they did*, instead of leaving everything in a mysterious vagueness, merely deciding that the specific action of the SI, in relation to these unknown groups, was "certainly inferior," and then—what is a bit different—"not superior."

In reality, *RI* reproaches the situationists for having said, for years, that a *new* setting out of the revolutionary proletarian movement was to be expected from a modern critique of the new conditions of oppression and the new contradictions those conditions were bringing to light. For *RI* fundamentally there is nothing new in capitalism, nor therefore in the critique of it; the occupations movement presented nothing new; the concepts of "spectacle" or of "survival," the critique of the commodity attaining a stage of abundant production, etc., are only empty words. It can be seen that these three series of postulates are all interlinked.

If the situationists were merely fanatics of intellectual innovation, *Révolution Internationale*, which knows everything about proletarian revolution since 1920 or 1930, would attach no importance to them. What our critic objects to is that we showed at the same time that this *newness* in capitalism, and consequently the new developments in its negation, *also link up with* the old truth of the previously vanquished proletarian revolution. This is most annoying to *RI* because it wants to possess this old truth *without any newness mixed in*; the fact that this newness arises in reality as well as in the SI's or others' theory is of no significance to *RI*. Here begins the falsification. *RI* excerpts a few sentences from pages 13 and 14 of Viénet's book, where he recapitulates these basic banalities of the unaccomplished revolution, and adds a bunch of marginal notes like a professor's red ink corrections: "It's really wonderful that the SI 'readily' affirms what all workers and revolutionaries already knew"; "what a marvelous discovery!"; "obviously"; etc. But the excerpts from these two pages are, if we may say so, rather artfully selected. One of them, for example, is quoted exactly as follows: "the SI knew well (. . .) that the emancipation of the workers still clashed everywhere with bureaucratic organizations." What are the words deleted by this opportune parenthesis? Here is the exact sentence: "The SI knew well, *as did so many workers with no means of expressing it*, that the emancipation of the workers still clashed everywhere with bureaucratic organizations." *RI*'s method is as obvious as the existence of class struggle, which this group seems to imagine itself the exclusive owner of—the class struggle to which Viénet was explicitly referring in response to "so many commentators" having the means of expressing themselves in books and newspapers who "agreed that the movement was unforeseeable."

And, always so as to deny that the SI has said in advance any truth on the proximity of a new period of the revolutionary movement, *RI*, which does not at all want this period to be new, asks ironically how the SI can claim to have foreseen this crisis; and why it didn't appear

until exactly *fifty* years after the defeat of the Russian revolution—
"Why not thirty or seventy?" The answer is very simple. Even leaving
aside the fact that the SI followed rather closely the rise of certain
elements of the crisis (in Strasbourg, Turin and Nanterre, for example),
we predicted not the date, but the content.

The *Révolution Internationale* group may very well be in total disagreement with us when it comes to judging the content of the occupations movement, as it is more generally at variance with the comprehension of its era and therefore with the forms of practical action
that other revolutionaries have already begun to appropriate. But if
we scorn the *Révolution Internationale* group and want no contact
with it, it is not because of the content of its somewhat musty theoretical science, but because of the petty-bureaucratic *style* it is naturally led to adopt in order to defend that content. Thus the form and
content of its perspectives are in accord with each other, both dating
from the same sad years.

But modern history has also created the eyes that know how to read
us.

PRELIMINARIES ON THE COUNCILS
AND COUNCILIST ORGANIZATION

"The Workers and Peasants Government has decreed that Kronstadt and the rebelling ships must immediately submit to the authority of the Soviet Republic. I therefore order all who have raised
their hands against the socialist fatherland to lay down their arms
at once. Recalcitrants are to be disarmed and turned over to the
Soviet authorities. The commissars and other members of the government who have been arrested are to be liberated at once. Only
those who surrender unconditionally can expect mercy from the
Soviet Republic.

"I am simultaneously giving orders to prepare for the suppression of the rebellion and the subjugation of the sailors by armed
force. All responsibility for the harm that may be suffered by the
peaceful population will rest entirely on the heads of the White
Guard mutineers. This warning is final."

—Trotsky, Kamenev, *Ultimatum to Kronstadt*

"We have only one answer to all that: *All power to the soviets!*
Take your hands off them—your hands that are red with the blood
of the martyrs of freedom who fought the White Guards, the landowners and the bourgeoisie!"

—*Kronstadt Izvestia #6*

For the fifty years since the Leninists reduced communism to electri-
fication, since the Bolshevik counterrevolution erected the *Soviet State*
over the dead body of the power of the soviets, and since soviet has
ceased to mean *council*, revolutions have not ceased to hurl the Kron-

stadt demand in the faces of the masters of the Kremlin: *"All power to the soviets and not to the parties."* The remarkable persistence of the *real tendency* toward *workers councils* throughout this half century of attempts and repeated suppressions of the modern proletarian movement now imposes the councils on the new revolutionary current as the sole form of antistate dictatorship of the proletariat, as the sole tribunal that will be able to pass judgment on the old world and carry out the sentence itself.

The council notion must be more precisely delineated, not only by refuting the gross falsifications propagated by social democracy, the Russian bureaucracy, Titoism and even Ben-Bellaism, but above all by recognizing the insufficiencies in the fledgling practical experiences of the power of the councils that have briefly appeared so far; as well, of course, as the insufficiencies in councilist revolutionaries' very conceptions. The council's *ultimate tendency* appears negatively in the limits and illusions which have marked its first manifestations and which have caused its defeat quite as much as has the immediate and uncompromising struggle that is naturally waged against it by the ruling class. The council aims at being the form of the *practical unification* of proletarians in the process of appropriating the material and intellectual means of changing all existing conditions and making themselves the masters of their history. It can and must be the organization in acts of historical consciousness. But in fact it has nowhere yet succeeded in overcoming the separation embodied in *specialized* political organizations and the forms of ideological false consciousness that they produce and defend. Moreover, although it is quite natural that the councils that have been major agents of a revolutionary moment have generally been *councils of delegates*, since it is such councils which coordinate and federate the decisions of local councils, it nevertheless appears that the general assemblies of the rank and file have almost always been considered as mere assemblies of electors, so that the first level of the "council" is thus situated above them. Here already lies a principle of separation, which can only be surmounted by making the local general assemblies of all the proletarians in revolution *the council itself,* from which any delegation must derive its power at every moment.

Leaving aside the precouncilist features of the Paris Commune that fired Marx with enthusiasm ("the finally discovered political form through which the economic emancipation of labor could be realized")— features which, moreover, can be seen more in the organization of the Central Committee of the National Guard, which was composed of delegates of the Parisian proletariat in arms, than in the elected Commune—the famous St. Petersburg "Council of Workers' Deputies" was the first fledgling manifestation of an organization of the proletariat in a revolutionary moment. According to the figures given by Trotsky in *1905,* 200,000 workers had sent their delegates to the St. Petersburg Soviet; but its influence extended far beyond its immediate area, with many other councils in Russia drawing inspiration from its deliberations and decisions. It directly grouped the workers from more than one hundred fifty enterprises, besides welcoming representatives from sixteen unions that had rallied to it. Its first nucleus was formed on

13 October, and by the 17th the soviet had established an Executive Committee over itself which Trotsky says "served it as a ministry." Out of a total of 562 delegates, the Executive Committee comprised only 31 members, of which 22 were actually workers delegated by the entirety of the workers in their enterprises and 9 represented three revolutionary parties (Mensheviks, Bolsheviks and Social Revolutionaries); however, "the representatives of the parties had only consultative status and were not entitled to vote." It can be granted that the rank-and-file assemblies were faithfully represented by their revocable delegates, but the latter had obviously abdicated a large part of their power, in a very *parliamentary* way, into the hands of an Executive Committee where the "technical advisors" of the political parties had an enormous influence.

How did this soviet originate? It seems that this form of organization was discovered by certain politically aware elements among the ordinary workers, who for the most part themselves belonged to one or another socialist fraction. Trotsky seems to be quite unjustified in writing that "one of the two social-democratic organizations in St. Petersburg took the initiative of creating an autonomous revolutionary workers' administration" (moreover, that "one of the two" organizations that immediately recognized the significance of this workers' initiative was precisely the Mensheviks). But the general strike of October 1905 in fact originated first of all in Moscow on 19 September, when the typographers of the Sytine printing works went on strike, notably because they wanted punctuation marks to be counted among the 1000 characters that constituted their unit of payment. Fifty printing works followed them out, and on 25 September the Moscow printers formed a council. On *3 October* "the assembly of workers' deputies from the printers, mechanics, carpenters, tobacco workers and other guilds adopted the resolution to set up a general council (soviet) of Moscow workers" (Trotsky, *op. cit.*). It can thus be seen that this form appeared spontaneously at the beginning of the strike movement. And this movement, which began to fall back in the following days, was to surge forward again up to the great historic crisis when on 7 October the railroad workers, beginning in Moscow, spontaneously began to stop the railway traffic.

The councils movement in Turin, in March and April 1920, originated among the highly concentrated proletariat of the Fiat factories. Between August and September 1919 new elections for an "internal commission"—a sort of collaborationist factory committee set up by a collective convention in 1906 for the purpose of better integrating the workers—suddenly provided the opportunity, amid the social crisis that was then sweeping Italy, for a complete transformation of the role of these "commissioners." They began to federate among themselves as direct representatives of the workers. In October 1919 30,000 workers were represented at an assembly of "executive committees of factory councils," which resembled more an assembly of shop stewards (with one commissioner elected by each workshop) than an organization of councils in the strict sense. But the example acted as a catalyst and the movement radicalized, supported by a fraction of the Socialist Party (including Gramsci) that was in the majority in Turin and by the Piedmont anarchists (see Pier Carlo Masini's pamphlet, *Anarchici e comunisti nel movimento dei Consigli a Torino*). The movement was combated by the majority of the Socialist Party and by the unions. On 15 March 1920 the councils began a strike *combined with occupation of the factories* and *resumed production* under their own control. By 14 April the strike was general in Piedmont; in the following days it affected much of northern Italy, particularly the railroad workers and dockers. The government had to use warships to land troops at Genoa to march on Turin. While the councilist program was later to be approved by the Congress of the Italian Anarchist Union when it met at Bologna on 1 July, the Socialist Party and the unions succeeded in sabotaging the strike by keeping it in isolation: when Turin was besieged by 20,000 soldiers and police, the party newspaper *Avanti* refused to print the appeal of the Turin socialist section (see Masini). The strike, which would clearly have made possible a victorious insurrection in the whole country, was vanquished on 24 April. What happened next is well known.

In spite of certain remarkably advanced features of this rarely cited experience (numerous leftists believe that factory occupations took place for the first time in France in 1936), it should be noted that it contains serious ambiguities, even among its partisans and theorists. Gramsci wrote in *Ordine Nuovo* (second year, #4): "We conceive the factory council as the historical beginning of a process that must necessarily lead to the foundation of the workers' state." For their part, the councilist anarchists were sparing in their criticism of unionism and claimed that the councils would give it a renewed impetus.

However, the manifesto launched by the Turin councilists on 27 March 1920, "To the Workers and Peasants of All Italy," calling for a general congress of the councils (which did not take place), formulates some essential points of the council program: "The struggle for conquest must be fought with arms of conquest, and no longer only with those of defense (*SI note*: this is aimed at the unions, "organisms of resistance . . . crystallized in a bureaucratic form"). A new organization must be developed as a direct antagonist of the organs of the bosses' government; for that task it must spring up spontaneously in the workplace and unite all the workers, because all of them, as producers, are subjected to an authority that is alien (*estranea*) to them, and must liberate themselves from it. . . . This is the beginning of freedom for you: the beginning of a social formation that by rapidly and universally extending itself will put you in a position to eliminate the exploiter and the middleman from the economic field and to become yourselves the masters—the masters of your machines, of your work, of your life . . ."

The majority of the Workers and Soldiers Councils in the Germany of 1918–1919 were more crudely dominated by the Social-Democratic bureaucracy or were victims of its maneuvers. They tolerated Ebert's "socialist" government, whose main support came from the General Staff and the Freikorps. The "Hamburg seven points" (concerning the immediate liquidation of the old Army), presented by Dorrenbach and passed with a large majority by the Congress of Soldiers Councils that opened 16 December in Berlin, were not implemented by the "People's

Commissars." The councils tolerated this defiance, and the legislative elections that had been quickly set for 19 January; and then the attack launched against Dorrenbach's sailors, and then the crushing of the Spartakist insurrection on the very eve of those elections. In 1956 the Central Workers Council of Greater Budapest, constituted on 14 November and declaring itself determined to defend socialism, demanded "the withdrawal of all political parties from the factories" while at the same time pronouncing itself in favor of Nagy's return to power and free elections within a short time. It is true that this was during the time it was continuing the general strike even though the Russian troops had already crushed the armed resistance. But even before the second Russian intervention the Hungarian councils had asked for parliamentary elections: that is to say, they themselves were seeking to return to a dual-power situation at a time when they were in fact, in the face of the Russians, the only actual power in Hungary.

Consciousness of what the power of the councils is and *must be* arises from the very practice of that power. But at an *impeded* stage of that power it may be very different from what one or another isolated member of a council, or even an entire council, thinks. *Ideology* opposes the truth in acts whose field is the system of the councils; and this ideology manifests itself not only in the form of hostile ideologies, or in the form of ideologies *about the councils* devised by political forces that want to subjugate them, but also in the form of an ideology *in favor of* the power of the councils, which restrains and reifies their total theory and practice. Ultimately a pure *councilism* would itself necessarily be an enemy of the reality of the councils. There is a risk that such an ideology, more or less consistently formulated, will be borne by revolutionary organizations that are in principle in favor of the power of the councils. This power, which is itself *the organization of revolutionary society* and whose coherence is objectively defined by the practical necessities of this historical task grasped as a whole, can in no case escape the practical problem posed by *specialist organizations* which, whether enemies of the councils or more or less genuinely in favor of them, will inevitably interfere in their functioning. The masses organized in councils must be aware of this problem and overcome it. Here councilist theory and the existence of authentically councilist organizations have a great importance. In them already appear certain essential points that will be at stake in the councils and in their own interaction with the councils.

All revolutionary history shows the part played in the failure of the councils by the emergence of a councilist ideology. The ease with which the spontaneous organization of the proletariat in struggle wins its first victories is often the prelude to a second phase in which counter-revolution works from the inside, in which the movement lets go of its reality in order to follow the illusion that is its defeat. Councilism is the new youth of the old world.

Social democrats and Bolsheviks are in agreement in wishing to see in the councils only an auxiliary body of the party and the state. In 1902 Kautsky, worried because the unions were becoming discredited in the eyes of the workers, wanted workers in certain branches of industry to elect "delegates who would form a sort of parliament designed to regulate the work and keep watch over the bureaucratic administration" (*The Social Revolution*). The idea of a hierarchized system of workers' representation culminating in a parliament was to be implemented most convincingly by Ebert, Noske and Scheidemann. The way this type of councilism treats the councils was definitively demonstrated—for anyone who doesn't have shit for brains—as long ago as 9 November 1918, when the Social Democrats combated the spontaneous organization of the councils on its own ground by founding in the *Vorwärts* offices a "Council of the Workers and Soldiers of Berlin" consisting of 12 loyal factory workers, functionaries and Social-Democratic leaders.

Bolshevik councilism has neither Kautsky's naïveté nor Ebert's crudeness. It springs from the most radical base, "All power to the soviets," and lands on its feet on the other side of Kronstadt. In *The Immediate Tasks of the Soviet Government* (April 1918) Lenin adds enzymes to Kautsky's detergent: "Even in the most democratic capitalist republics in the world, the poor never regard the bourgeois parliament as 'their' institution. . . . It is the closeness of the Soviets to the 'people,' to the working people, that creates the special forms of recall and other means of control from below which must be most zealously developed now. For example, the Councils of Public Education, as periodical conferences of Soviet electors and their delegates convoked to discuss and control the activities of the Soviet authorities in this field, deserve our full sympathy and support. Nothing could be sillier than to transform the Soviets into something congealed and self-contained. The more resolutely we have to stand for a ruthlessly firm government, for the dictatorship of individuals *in specific processes of work*, in specific aspects of *purely executive* functions, the more varied must be the forms and methods of control from below in order to counteract every shadow of a possibility of distorting the principles of Soviet government, in order tirelessly and repeatedly to weed out bureaucracy." For Lenin, then, the councils, like charitable institutions, should become pressure groups correcting the inevitable bureaucratization of the state's political and economic functions, respectively handled by the Party and the unions. The councils are the social component that, like Descartes's soul, has to be hooked on somewhere.

Gramsci himself merely cleanses Lenin in a bath of democratic niceties: "The factory commissioners are the only true social (economic and political) representatives of the working class because they are elected under universal suffrage by all the workers in the workplace itself. At the different levels of their hierarchy, the commissioners represent the union of all the workers such as it is realized in the production units (work gang, factory department, union of factories in an industry, union of establishments in a city, union of production units of mechanical and agricultural industries in a district, a province, a region, the nation, the world), whose councils and system of councils represent power and the management of society." (Article in *Ordine Nuovo*.) Since the councils have been reduced to economicosocial fragments preparing the way for a "future Soviet Republic," it goes without saying that the Party, that "Modern Prince," appears as the indispensable political mediation, as the preexisting *deus ex mach-*

ina taking care to ensure its future existence: "The Communist Party is the instrument and historical form of the process of internal liberation thanks to which the workers, from being executants become initiators, from being masses become *leaders* and *guides*, from being muscles are transformed into minds and wills" (*Ordine Nuovo*, 1919). The tune may change but the song of councilism remains the same: Councils, Party, State. To treat the councils fragmentarily (economic power, social power, political power), as does the councilist cretinism of the *Révolution Internationale* group of Toulouse, is like thinking that by clenching your ass you'll only be buggered half way.

After 1918 Austro-Marxism also constructed a councilist ideology of its own, along the lines of the slow reformist evolution that it advocated. Max Adler, for example, in his book *Democracy and Workers Councils*, recognizes the council as the instrument of workers' self-education, as the possible end of the separation between order-givers and order-takers, as the constituting of a *homogenous people* that could realize socialist democracy. But he also recognizes that the fact that councils of workers hold some power in no way guarantees that they have a coherent revolutionary aim: for that, the worker members of the councils must explicitly want to transform the society and realize socialism. Since Adler is a theorist of *legalized dual power*, that is, of an absurdity that will inevitably be incapable of lasting as it gradually approaches revolutionary consciousness and prudently prepares a revolution for later on, he is denied the single really fundamental element of the proletariat's self-education: revolution itself. To replace this irreplaceable terrain of proletarian homogenization and this sole mode of selection *for the very formation of the councils* as well as for the formation of ideas and coherent modes of activity in the councils, Adler comes to the point of imagining that there is no other remedy than this incredibly asinine rule: "The right to vote in workers council elections must depend on membership in a socialist organization."

Leaving aside the social-democratic or Bolshevik ideologies *about* the councils, which from Berlin to Kronstadt always had a Noske or a Trotsky too many, councilist ideology itself, as manifested in past *councilist organizations* and in some present ones, has always had several general assemblies and imperative mandates too few. All the councils that have existed until now, with the exception of the *agrarian collectives of Aragon, saw themselves* as simply "democratically elected councils"; even when the highest moments of their practice, when all decisions were made by sovereign general assemblies mandating revocable delegates, contradicted this limitation.

Only historical practice, through which the working class must discover and realize all its possibilities, will indicate the precise organizational forms of council power. On the other hand, it is the immediate task of revolutionaries to determine the fundamental principles of the *councilist organizations* that are going to arise in every country. By formulating some hypotheses and recalling the fundamental requirements of the revolutionary movement, this article—which should be followed by some others—is intended to initiate a *real, egalitarian* debate. The only people who will be excluded from it are those who refuse to pose it in these terms, those who in the name of some sub-anarchist spontaneism declare themselves opponents of any form of organization, and who only reproduce the defects and confusion of the old movement—mystics of nonorganization, workers discouraged by having been mixed up with Trotskyist sects too long, students imprisoned in their impoverishment who are incapable of escaping from bolshevik organizational schemas. The situationists are obviously partisans of organization—the existence of the *situationist organization* testifies to that. Those who announce their agreement with our theses while crediting the SI with a vague spontaneism simply don't know how to read.

Organization is indispensable precisely because it isn't everything and doesn't enable everything to be saved or won. Contrary to what butcher Noske said (in *Von Kiel bis Kapp*) about the events of 6 January 1919, the masses did not fail to become "masters of Berlin on noon that day" because they had "fine talkers" instead of "determined leaders," but because the factory councils' form of autonomous organization had not yet attained a sufficient level of autonomy for them to be able to do without "determined leaders" and separate organizations to handle their link-ups. The shameful example of Barcelona in May 1937 is another proof of this: the fact that arms were brought out so quickly in response to the Stalinist provocation says a lot for the Catalonian masses' immense capacities for autonomy; but the fact that the order to *surrender* issued by the anarchist ministers was so quickly obeyed demonstrates how much autonomy for victory *they still lacked*. Tomorrow again it will be the workers' degree of autonomy that will decide our fate.

The councilist organizations that will be formed will therefore not fail to recognize and appropriate, as indeed a minimum, the "Minimum Definition of Revolutionary Organizations" adopted by the 7th Conference of the SI (see *IS* #11). Since their task will be to work toward the power of the councils, which is incompatible with any other form of power, they will be aware that an *abstract* agreement with this definition definitively condemns them to nonexistence; this is why their real agreement will be practically demonstrated in the nonhierarchical relations within their groups or sections; in the relations between these groups and with other autonomous groups or organizations; in the development of revolutionary theory and the unitary critique of the ruling society; and in the ongoing critique of their own practice. Refusing the old partitioning of the workers movement into separate organizations, parties and unions, they will affirm their unitary program and practice. Despite all the beautiful history of the councils, all the councilist organizations of the past that have played a significant role in class struggles have sanctioned separation into political, economic and social sectors. One of the few old parties worth analysis, the *Kommunistische Arbeiter Partei Deutschlands* (KAPD, German Communist Workers Party) adopted the councils as its program, but by assigning itself as its only essential tasks propaganda and theoretical discussion—"the political education of the masses"—it left the role of federating the revolutionary factory organizations to the *Allgemeine Arbeiter Union Deutschlands* (AAUD, General Workers Union of Germany), a schema not far from traditional syndicalism. Even though the KAPD rejected the Leninist idea of the mass party, along with the parliamentarianism and syndicalism of the KPD (*Kommunistische Partei Deutschlands*—German Communist Party), and preferred to group together politically conscious workers, it nevertheless remained tied to the old hierarchical model of the vanguard party: professionals of Revolution and salaried propagandists. The rejection of this model, principally the rejection of a political organization separated from the revolutionary factory organizations, led in 1920 to the secession of some of the AAUD members, who then formed the AAUD-E (the 'E' for *Einheitsorganisation*—Unified Organization). By the very working of its internal democracy the new unitary organization was to accomplish the educative work that had until then devolved on the KAPD, and it simultaneously assigned itself the task of coordinating struggles: the factory organizations that it federated were supposed to transform themselves into councils at the revolutionary moment and take over the management of the society. There, too, the modern watchword of workers councils was still mixed with messianic memories of the old revolutionary syndicalism: the factory organizations would magically become councils when all the workers took part in them.

All that led where it would. After the crushing of the 1921 insurrection and the repression of the movement, the workers, discouraged by the waning prospect of revolution, in large numbers left the factory organizations, which deteriorated as they ceased to be organs of a real struggle. The AAUD was another name for the KAPD, and the AAUD-E saw revolution recede as fast as its membership declined. They were no longer anything but bearers of a *councilist ideology* more and more cut off from reality.

The KAPD's terrorist evolution and the AAUD's later involvement in "bread and butter" issues led to the split between the factory organization and its party in 1929. In 1931 the corpses of the AAUD and the AAUD-E pathetically and without any explicit, sound bases merged against the rise of Nazism. The revolutionary elements of the two organizations regrouped to form the KAUD (*Kommunistische Arbeiter Union Deutschlands*—German Communist Workers Union). A self-consciously minority organization, the KAUD was also the only one in the whole movement for the councils in Germany that did not claim to take upon itself the future economic (economicopolitical in the case of the AAUD-E) organization of society. It called on the workers to form autonomous groups and to themselves handle the link-ups between those groups. But in Germany the KAUD came much too late; by 1931 the revolutionary movement had been dead for almost ten years.

If only to make them cry, let us remind the retarded devotees of the anarcho-Marxist feud that the CNT-FAI—with its dead weight of anarchist ideology, but also with its greater practice of liberatory imagination—was akin to the Marxist KAPD-AAUD in its organizational arrangements. In the same way as the German Communist Workers Party, the Iberian Anarchist Federation aimed to be the *political* organization of the conscious Spanish workers, while its AAUD, the CNT, was to take charge of the management of the future society. The FAI militants, the elite of the proletariat, propagated the anarchist idea among the masses; the CNT did the practical work of organizing the workers in its unions. There were two essential differences, however, the ideological one of which was to bear the fruit one could have expected of it: first, the FAI did not want to take power but contented itself with influencing all the CNT's policies; second, the CNT *really* represented the Spanish working class. Adopted on 1 May 1936 at the CNT congress at Saragossa, two months before the revolutionary explosion, one of the most beautiful programs ever put forward by a revolutionary organization was partially put into practice by the anarchosyndicalist masses, while their leaders foundered in ministerialism and class-collaboration. With the pimps of the masses, García Oliver, Secundo Blanco, etc., and the brothel madam Montseny, the antistate libertarian movement, which had already tolerated the anarcho-trenchist* Prince Kropotkin, finally attained the historical consummation of its ideological absolutism: government anarchists. In the *last* historical battle it was to wage, anarchism was to see all the ideological sauce that comprised its being fall back into its face: State, Freedom, Individual and other musty ingredients with capital letters; while the libertarian militiamen, workers and peasants were saving its honor, making *the greatest practical contribution* to the international proletarian movement, burning the churches, fighting on all fronts against the bourgeoisie, fascism and Stalinism, and beginning to *realize communist society*.

Some organizations exist today that cunningly pretend not to. By this means they are conveniently able to avoid bothering with the slightest clarification of the bases on which they assemble any assortment of people (while magically labeling them all "workers"); to give their semimembers no account of the *informal leadership* that holds the controls; to say anything at all and particularly to condemn in *amalgam* any other possible organization and to automatically anathematize any theoretical expression. Thus the *Informations, Correspondance Ouvrières* group writes in a recent bulletin (*ICO* #84, August 1969): "The councils are the transformation of strike committees under the influence of the situation itself and in response to the very necessities of the struggle, within the very dialectic of that struggle. Any other attempt, at any moment in a struggle, to express the necessity of creating workers councils reveals a councilist ideology such as can be seen in diverse forms in certain unions, in the PSU or among the situationists. The very concept of council excludes any ideology." These individuals obviously know nothing about ideology—theirs is distinguished from more fully developed ideologies only by a spineless eclecticism. But they have heard (perhaps from Marx, perhaps only from the SI) that ideology has become a bad thing. They take advantage of this to try to have it believed that any theoretical work—which they avoid like sin—is an ideology, among the situationists exactly as in the PSU. But their valiant recourse to the "dialectic" and the "concept" which they have now added to their vocabulary in no way saves them from an imbecilic ideology of which the above quotation alone is evidence enough. If one idealistically relies on the council "concept" or, what is even more euphoric, on the practical inactivity of ICO, to "exclude all ideology" in the real councils, one must expect the worst: we have seen that historical experience justifies no optimism of this kind. The supersession of the primitive council form can only come from struggles becoming more conscious, and from struggles for *more consciousness*. ICO's mechanistic image of the strike committee's perfect automatic response to "necessities," which presents the council as automatically coming into existence at the appropriate time *provided that one makes sure not to talk about it*, completely ignores the experience of the revolutions of our century, which shows that "the situation itself" is just as ready to liquidate the councils, or to enable them to be manipulated and recuperated, as it is to give rise to them.

Let us leave this contemplative ideology, this extreme caricature of the natural sciences which would have us observe the emergence of a proletarian revolution almost as if it were a solar eruption. Councilist organizations will be formed, though they must be quite the contrary of general staffs that would cause the councils to rise up on order. In spite of the new period of open social crisis we have entered since the occupations movement, and the proliferation of encouraging situations here and there, from Italy to the USSR, it is quite likely that genuine councilist organizations will still take a long time to form and that other important revolutionary moments will occur before such organizations are in a position to intervene in them at a significant level. One must not play with councilist organization by setting up or supporting premature parodies of it. But the councils will certainly have greater chances of maintaining themselves as sole power if they contain conscious councilists and if there is a real appropriation of councilist theory.

In contrast to the council as permanent *basic unit* (ceaselessly setting up and modifying councils of delegates emanating from itself), as the assembly in which all the workers of an enterprise (workshop and factory councils) and all the inhabitants of an urban district rallying to the revolution (street councils, neighborhood councils) must participate, a councilist organization, in order to guarantee its coherence and the authentic working of its internal democracy, must *choose its members* in accordance with what they explicitly want and what they actually can do. As for the councils, their coherence is guaranteed by the single fact that they are *the* power; that they eliminate all other power and decide everything. This practical experience is the terrain where people acquire the comprehension of their own action, where they "realize philosophy." It goes without saying that their majorities also run the risk of making many momentary mistakes and not having the time or the means to rectify them. But they are aware that their own fate is the real product of their own decisions, and that their very existence will inevitably be annihilated by the consequences of any mistakes they don't correct.

Within councilist organizations real equality of everyone in making decisions and carrying them out will not be an empty slogan, an abstract demand. Of course, not all the members of an organization will have the same talents (it is obvious, for example, that a worker will invariably write better than a student). But because in its aggregate the organization will have all the necessary talents, no hierarchy of individual talents will come to undermine its democracy. It is neither membership in a councilist organization nor the proclamation of an ideal equality that will enable all its members to be beautiful and intelligent and to live well; but only their real aptitudes for becoming more beautiful and more intelligent and for living better, freely developing in the only game that's worth the pleasure: the destruction of the old world.

In the social movements that are going to spread, the councilists will refuse to let themselves be elected onto strike committees. On the contrary, their task will be to act in such a way as to promote the rank-and-file self-organization of the workers into general assemblies that decide how the struggle is carried out. It will be necessary to begin to understand that the absurd call for a "central strike committee" advanced by some naïve individuals during the occupations movement would, had it succeeded, have sabotaged the movement toward the autonomy of the masses even more quickly, since almost all the strike committees were controlled by the Stalinists.

Given that it is not for us to forge a plan for all time, and that one step forward by the real movement of the councils will be worth more than a dozen councilist programs, it is difficult to state precise hypotheses regarding the relation of councilist organizations with the councils in the revolutionary moment. The councilist organization—which knows itself to be *separated* from the proletariat—must cease to exist as a separate organization in the moment that abolishes separations; and it will have to do this even if the complete freedom of association guaranteed by the power of the councils allows various parties and organizations that are enemies of this power to survive. It may be doubted, however, that it is feasible to immediately dissolve all councilist organizations the very *moment* the councils first appear, as Pannekoek wished. The councilists will speak as councilists within the council, and will not have to make an exemplary dissolution of their organizations only to regroup them on the side and play at pressure groups in the general assembly. In this way it will be easier and more legitimate for them to combat and denounce the inevitable presence of bureaucrats, spies and old scabs who will infiltrate here and there. They will also have to struggle against fake councils or fundamentally reactionary ones (e.g. police councils) which will not fail to appear. They will act in such a way that the unified power of the councils does not recognize these bodies or their delegates. Because the infiltration of other organizations is exactly the contrary of the ends they are pursuing, and because they refuse any incoherence within themselves, councilist organizations will prohibit any dual membership. As we have said, all the workers of a factory must take part in the council, or at least all those who accept the rules of its game. The solution to the problem of whether to accept participation in the council by "those who yesterday had to be thrown out of the factory at gunpoint" (Barth) will be found only in practice.

Ultimately, the councilist organization will stand or fall solely by the coherence of its theory and action and by its struggle for the complete elimination of all power remaining external to the councils or trying to make itself independent of them. But in order to simplify the discussion right off by refusing even to take into consideration a mass of councilist pseudo-organizations that may be simulated by students or obsessive professional militants, let us say that it does not seem to us that an organization can be recognized as councilist if it is not comprised of at least 2/3 workers. As this proportion might pass for a concession, let us add that it seems to us indispensable to correct it with this rider: in all delegations to central conferences at which decisions may be taken that have not previously been provided for by imperative mandates, workers must make up 3/4 of the participants. In sum, the inverse proportion of the first congresses of the "Russian Social-Democratic Workers Party."

It is known that we have no inclination toward workerism of any form whatsoever. Our above considerations refer to workers who have "become dialecticians," as they will have to become *en masse* in the exercise of the power of the councils. But on the one hand, the workers continue to be the *central* force capable of halting the existing functioning of society and the *indispensable* force for reinventing all its bases. On the other hand, although the councilist organization obviously must not separate other categories of wage-earners, notably intellectuals, from itself, it is in any case important that the dubious importance the latter may assume should be severely restricted: not only by verifying, by considering all aspects of their lives, if they are really councilist revolutionaries, but also by seeing to it that there are as few of them as possible in the organization.

The councilist organization will not consent to speak on equal terms with other organizations unless they are consistent partisans of proletarian autonomy; just as the councils will have to rid themselves not only of the grip of parties and unions, but also of any tendency aiming to accord them a recognized place and negotiate with them as one power with another. The councils are the only power or they are nothing. The means of their victory are already their victory. With the lever of the councils *and* the fulcrum of a total negation of the spectacle-commodity society, the Earth can be raised.

The victory of the councils is not the end of the revolution, but the beginning of it.

RENÉ RIESEL

NOTICE TO THE CIVILIZED CONCERNING
GENERALIZED SELF-MANAGEMENT

"Never sacrifice present good for the good to come. Enjoy the moment. Avoid any matrimonial or other association that does not satisfy your passions from the very beginning. Why should you work for the good to come when it will exceed your desires anyway and you will have in the Combined Order only one displeasure, that of not being able to double the length of days in order to accommodate the immense range of enjoyments available to you?"

—Charles Fourier, *Notice to the Civilized
Concerning the Next Social Metamorphosis*

1

While not going all the way, the occupations movement has given rise to a confused popular awareness of the necessity of a supersession. The imminence of a total upheaval, felt by everyone, must now discover its practice: the passage to generalized self-management by the establishment of workers councils. The point of arrival to which the revolutionary upsurge has brought consciousness is now going to become a point of departure.

2

History is answering the question Lloyd George posed to the workers, a question which has since been taken up in chorus by all the servants of the old world: "You want to destroy our social organization, but what will you put in its place?" We know the answer thanks to the profusion of little Lloyd Georges who advocate the state dictatorship of a proletariat of their choice, counting on the working class to organize itself in councils in order to dissolve the existing dictatorship and elect another.

3

Each time the proletariat takes the risk of changing the world it rediscovers the total memory of history. The establishing of a society of councils—until now intermingled with the history of its crushing in different periods—reveals the reality of its past possibilities through the possibility of its immediate realization. This has been made evident to all the workers since May, when Stalinism and its Trotskyist residues showed by their aggressive weakness their inability to crush a council movement if one had appeared, and by their force of inertia their ability still to impede the emergence of one. Without really manifesting itself, a movement toward councils was implicitly present in the resultant of two contradictory forces: the internal logic of the occupations and the repressive logic of the parties and unions. Those who still open their Lenin to find out what is to be done are only rummaging in the trashcan of history.

4

Many people intuitively rejected any organization not directly emanating from the proletariat negating itself as proletariat, and this feeling was inseparable from the feeling that an everyday life without dead time was possible at last. In this sense the notion of workers councils is the first principle of generalized self-management.

5

May marked an essential phase in the long revolution: the individual history of millions of people, each day seeking an authentic life, linking up with the historical movement of the proletariat in struggle against the whole *system* of alienations. This spontaneous unity of action, which was the passional motive power of the occupations movement, can only develop its theory and practice unitarily. What was in everyone's heart is going to be in everyone's head. Having felt that they "could no longer live like before, not even a little better than before," many people are inclined to prolong the memory of this exemplary moment of life and the briefly experienced hope of a great possibility—to prolong them in a line of force which, to become revolutionary, lacks only a greater lucidity on the *historical construction of free individual relations*, on generalized self-management.

6

Only the proletariat, by negating itself, gives clear shape to the project of generalized self-management, because it bears it within itself objectively and subjectively. This is why the first specifics will come from the unity of its combat in everyday life and on the front of history; and from the consciousness that all demands are realizable right away, but only by the proletariat itself. In this sense the importance of a revolutionary organization will henceforth be measured by its ability to hasten its own disappearance in the reality of the society of the councils.

7

Workers councils constitute a new type of social organization through which the proletariat puts an end to the proletarianization of everyone. Generalized self-management is simply the totality in accordance with which the councils unitarily inaugurate a style of life based on permanent individual and collective emancipation.

8

It is clear from all these theses that the project of generalized self-management requires as many specifics as there are desires in each revolutionary, and as many revolutionaries as there are people dissatisfied with their everyday life. The spectacle-commodity society produces both the conditions that repress subjectivity and—contradictorily, through the refusal it provokes—the positivity of subjectivity; just as the formation of the councils, similarly arising out of the struggle against overall oppression, produces the conditions for a permanent realization of subjectivity without any limits but its own impatience to make history. Thus generalized self-management is tied to the capacity of the councils to realize the imagination historically.

9

Outside generalized self-management, workers councils lose their sense. Anyone who speaks of the councils as economic or social bodies, anyone who does not place them at the center of the revolution of everyday life with the practice this entails, must be treated as a future bureaucrat and thus as a present enemy.

10

One of Fourier's great merits is to have shown the necessity to realize immediately—and for us this means from the inception of generalized insurrection—the objective conditions for individual emancipation. For everyone the beginning of the revolutionary moment must mark an *immediate rise in the pleasure of living*; the consciously experienced entry into the totality.

11

The accelerating rate at which reformism, with its tricontinental bellyache, is leaving behind ridiculous leftist droppings—all those little Maoist, Trotskyist and Guevaraist piles—proves by its smell what the Right, and in particular the socialists and Stalinists, have long sensed: partial demands are essentially contrary to a total change. But attempting to cut off the hydra heads of reformism one by one is futile. Better to overthrow the old ruse of history once and for all: this would seem to be the final solution to the problem of recuperators. This implies a strategy that sparks the general conflagration by means of insurrectional moments at ever-closer intervals; and a tactic of qualitative progression in which necessarily partial actions each entail, as their necessary and sufficient condition, the liquidation of the world of the commodity. It is time to begin the *positive sabotage* of spectacle-commodity society. As long as our mass tactics stick to the law of immediate pleasure there will be no need to worry about the outcome.

12

It is easy to mention here, merely as suggestive examples, a few possibilities which will quickly be surpassed by the practice of liberated workers: On every occasion—openly during strikes, more or less clandestinely during work—*initiate the reign of freeness* by giving away factory and warehouse goods to friends and revolutionaries, by making gift objects (radio transmitters, toys, weapons, clothes, ornaments, machines for various purposes), by organizing "giveaway" strikes in department stores; *break the laws of exchange and begin the end of wage labor* by collectively appropriating products of work and collectively using machines for personal and revolutionary purposes; *depreciate the function of money* by spreading payment strikes (rent, taxes, installment payments, transportation fares, etc.); *encourage everyone's creativity* by starting up provisioning and production sectors exclusively under workers' control, even if this can only be done intermittently, while regarding this experimentation as necessarily groping and subject to improvement; *wipe out hierarchies and the spirit of sacrifice* by treating bosses and union bureaucrats as they deserve and by rejecting militantism; *act unitarily everywhere against all separations*; *draw out theory from all practice and vice versa* by composing leaflets, posters, songs, etc.

13

The proletariat has already shown that it knows how to respond to the oppressive complexity of capitalist and "socialist" states by the simplicity of organization carried out *directly* by and for everyone. In our time questions of survival are posed only on the condition that they never be solved; in contrast, the problems of the history to be lived are clearly posed through the project of the workers councils, as both positivity and negativity; namely, as basic element of a unitary passional and industrial society, and as antistate.

14

Because they exercise no power separate from the decisions of their members, the councils tolerate no power other than their own. Encouraging antistate actions everywhere should thus not be understood to imply a premature creation of councils which would lack absolute power over their own areas, would be separated from generalized self-management and inevitably emptied of content and ripe for every kind of ideology. The only lucid forces that can presently respond to the history that *has* been made with the history *to be made* will be the revolutionary organizations that are developing, in the project of the councils, an equal awareness of the adversary to be combated and the allies to be supported. An important aspect of such a struggle is manifesting itself before our eyes with the appearance of a *dual power*. In factories, offices, streets, houses, barracks and schools a new reality is taking shape: contempt for bosses, regardless of their label, their pose or their rhetoric. From now on this contempt must be pushed to its logical conclusion by demonstrating, through the concerted action of workers, that the bosses are not only contemptible but also useless, and that even from their own utilitarian point of view they can be liquidated with impunity.

15

Recent history will soon come to be seen, by rulers as well as revolutionaries, in terms of an alternative that concerns them both: generalized self-management or insurrectional chaos; new society of abundance or social disintegration, pillage, terrorism and repression. The struggle within dual power is already inseparable from such a choice. Our coherence requires that the paralysis and destruction of all modes of government not be distinct from the construction of councils. If the adversary has even the slightest prudence it should realize that only an organization of new everyday relationships can prevent the spread of what an American police specialist has already called "our nightmare": small insurgent commandos bursting out of subway entrances, shooting from rooftops, taking advantage of the mobility and infinite resources of urban guerrilla warfare to fell the police, liquidate the servants of authority, stir up riots and destroy the economy. But we don't have to save the rulers in spite of themselves. It will be enough to prepare the councils and ensure their self-defense by every means. In one of Lope de Vega's plays some villagers, driven beyond endurance by the exactions of a royal functionary, put him to death. When they are brought before the magistrate and charged to name the guilty party, all respond with the name of their village, "Fuenteovejuna." This "Fuenteovejuna" tactic, used by many Asturian miners against pro-company engineers, has the drawback of smacking too much of terrorism and the *watrinage* tradition. Generalized self-management will be our "Fuenteovejuna." It is no longer enough for collective action to discourage repression (imagine the powerlessness of the forces of order if during an occupations movement bank employees appropriated the funds); it must at the same time encourage progression toward a greater revolutionary coherence. The councils represent order in the face of the decomposition of the state, whose form is being contested by the rise of regional nationalisms and whose basic principle is being contested by social demands. To the pseudoproblems they see posed by this decomposition, the police can respond only by estimating the number of deaths. Only the councils offer a definitive answer. What prevents looting? The organization of distribution and the end of the commodity. What prevents sabotage of production? The appropriation of the machines by collective creativity. What prevents explosions of anger and violence? The end of the proletariat through the collective construction of everyday life. There is no other justification for our struggle than the immediate satisfaction of this project—than what satisfies us immediately.

16

Generalized self-management has only one basis, one motive force: the exhilaration of universal freedom. This is quite enough to enable us right now to infer the rigor that will be necessary for its elaboration. Such rigor must henceforth characterize revolutionary councilist organizations; conversely, their practice will already contain the experience of direct democracy. This will enable us to concretize certain formulas more rigorously. A principle like "All power to the general assembly," for example, also implies that whatever escapes the direct control of the autonomous assembly will recreate, in mediated forms, all the autonomous varieties of oppression. Through its representatives, the whole assembly with all its tendencies must be present at the moment of decision. Even though the destruction of the state basically rules out a repetition of the "Supreme Soviet" farce, it is still necessary to take care that organization is simple enough to preclude the possibility of any neobureaucracy arising. But the abundance of telecommunications techniques—which might at first sight appear as a pretext for the continuation or return of specialists—is precisely what makes possible the constant control of delegates by the base, the immediate confirmation, correction or repudiation of their decisions at all levels. Telex, computers, television, etc., are thus the inalienable possession of the primary assemblies. They make it possible for the assemblies to be simultaneously aware of events everywhere. In the composition of a council (there will no doubt be neighborhood, city, regional and international councils) it will be a good idea for the assembly to elect and control: an *equipping section* for the purpose of collecting requests for supplies, determining the possibilities of production and coordinating these two sectors; an *information section* charged with keeping in constant touch with the experiences of other councils; a *coordination section* whose task it will be (to the extent permitted by the necessities of the struggle) to enrich personal relationships, to radicalize the Fourierist project, to take care of requirements of passional satisfaction, to equip individual desires, to furnish whatever is necessary for experiments and adventures, to harmonize playful possibilities of organizing necessary tasks (cleaning, babysitting, education, cooking contests, etc.); and a *self-defense section*. Each section is responsible to the full assembly; delegates regularly meet and report on their activities and are revocable and subject to vertical and horizontal rotation.

17

The logic of the commodity system, sustained by alienated practice, must be answered with the practice immediately implied by the social logic of desires. The first revolutionary measures will necessarily relate to reducing labor time and to the greatest possible reduction of forced labor. It will be a good idea for the councils to distinguish between *priority sectors* (food, transportation, telecommunications, metallurgy, construction, clothing, electronics, printing, armament, medicine, comfort, and in general whatever material equipment is necessary for the permanent transformation of historical conditions); *reconversion sectors*, whose workers consider that they can detourn them to revolutionary uses; and *parasitical sectors*, whose assemblies decide purely and simply to suppress them. The workers of the eliminated sectors (administration, agencies, spectacular industries, purely exchange-value industries) will obviously prefer to put in three or four hours a week at some work they have freely chosen from among the priority sectors rather than eight hours a day at their old workplace. The councils will experiment with attractive forms of carrying out necessary tasks, not in order to dissimulate their unpleasant aspects, but in order to compensate for that unpleasantness with a playful organization of it, and as far as possible to eliminate such tasks in favor of creativity (in accordance with the principle "Work no, pleasure yes"). As the transformation of the world comes to be identical with the construction of life, necessary labor will disappear in the pleasure of history for itself.

18

To state that the councilist organization of distribution and production prevents looting and the destruction of machinery and goods is still to remain within a purely negative, antistate perspective. The councils, as organization of the new society, will eliminate the element of separation still present in this negativity by means of a *collective politics of desires.* Wage labor can be ended the moment the councils are set up, the precise moment when the "equipment and provisions" section of each council organizes production and distribution in accordance with the desires of the plenary assembly. At that point, in tribute to the best Bolshevik prediction, urinals can be made out of gold and sterling silver, and dubbed "lenins."

19

Generalized self-management implies the extension of the councils. At first, work areas will be taken over by the workers concerned, grouped in councils. In order to rid these first councils of their corporative aspect, the workers will as soon as possible open them to their friends, to people living in the same neighborhood and to volunteers coming in from the parasitical sectors, so that they rapidly take the form of local councils (units of more or less the same size, perhaps 8000 to 10,000 people?)—parts of the Commune.

20

The internal extension of the councils must be matched by their geographical extension. It is necessary to maintain vigilantly the most complete radicality of the liberated zones, without Fourier's illusion as to the contageousness of the first communes, but also without underestimating the seductiveness of any authentic experience of emancipation once the intervening veils of falsification have been swept aside. The councils' self-defense thus illustrates the formula: "Armed truth is revolutionary."

21

Generalized self-management will soon have its own *code of possibilities,* designed to liquidate repressive legislation and its millenial domination. Perhaps it will appear during a period of dual power, before the judicial machinery and the penal system scum have been annihilated. The new rights of man—everyone's right to live as he pleases, to build his own house, to participate in all assemblies, to arm himself, to live as a nomad, to publish what he thinks (to each his own wall-newspaper), to love without restraints; the right to meet, the right to the material equipment necessary for the realization of desires, the right to creativity, the right to the conquest of nature, the end of commodity time, the end of history in itself, the realization of art and the imagination, etc.—await their antilegislators.

RAOUL VANEIGEM

THE CONQUEST OF SPACE
IN THE TIME OF POWER

1

Science in the service of capital, the commodity and the spectacle is nothing other than capitalized knowledge, fetishism of idea and method, alienated image of human thought. Pseudogreatness of man, its passive knowledge of a mediocre reality is the magical justification of a race of slaves.

2

It has been a long time since the power of knowledge has been transformed into the knowledge of power. Contemporary science, experimental heir of the religion of the Middle Ages, fulfills the same functions in relation to class society: it compensates people's daily stupidity with its eternal specialist intelligence. Science sings in numerals of the grandeur of the human race, but science is nothing other than the organized sum of man's limitations and alienations.

3

Just as industry, which was intended to free people from work through machinery, has so far done nothing but alienate them in the work of the machines, so science, which was intended to free people historically and rationally from nature, has done nothing but alienate them in an irrational and antihistorical society. Mercenary of separate thought, science works for survival and therefore cannot conceive of life except as a mechanical or moral formula. It does not conceive of man as subject, nor of human thought as action, and it is for this reason that it is ignorant of history as deliberate activity and makes people "patient(s)" in its hospitals.

4

Founded on the essential deceptiveness of its function, science can do nothing but lie to itself. And its pretentious mercenaries have preserved from their ancestor priests the taste and necessity for mystery. A dynamic element in the justification of states, the scientific profession jealously guards its corporative laws and the "Machina ex Deo" secrets that make it a despicable sect. It is hardly surprising, for example, that doctors—those repairmen of labor-power—have illegible handwriting: it is part of the police code of monopolized survival.

5

But if the *historical* and *ideological* identification of science with temporal powers clearly shows that it is a servant of states, and therefore fools no one, it was necessary to wait until our day to see the last separations disappear between class society and a science that professed to be neutral and "at the service of humanity." The present impossibility of scientific research and application without enormous means has effectively placed the spectacularly concentrated knowledge in the hands of power and has steered it toward statist objectives. There is no longer any science that is not in the service of the economy, the military and ideology; and the science of ideology reveals its other side, the ideology of science.

6

Power, which cannot tolerate a vacuum, has never forgiven celestial regions for being open terrains left open to the imagination. Since the origin of class society the unreal source of separate power has always been placed in the skies. When the state justified itself religiously, heaven was included in the *time* of religion; now that the state wishes to justify itself scientifically, the sky is in the *space* of science. From Galileo to Werner von Braun, it is nothing but a question of state ideology. Religion wished to preserve its time, therefore no one was to tamper with its space. Faced with the impossibility of prolonging its time, power must make its space boundless.

7

If the heart transplant is still a miserable artisan technique that does not make people forget science's chemical and nuclear massacres, the "Conquest of the Cosmos" is the greatest spectacular expression of scientific oppression. The space scientist is to the smalltime doctor what Interpol is to the policeman on the beat.

8

The heaven formerly promised by priests in black cassocks is now really being seized by white-uniformed astronauts. Sexless superbureaucratized neuters, the first men to go beyond the atmosphere are the stars of a spectacle that hangs over our heads day and night, that can conquer temperature and distance and that oppresses us from above like the cosmic dust of God. As an example of survival in its highest manifestation, the astronauts make an unintentional critique of the Earth: condemned to an orbital trajectory—in order to avoid dying from cold and hunger—they submissively ("technically") accept the boredom and poverty of being satellites. Inhabitants of an urbanism of necessity in their cabins, prisoners of scientific gadgetry, they exemplify *in vitro* the plight of their contemporaries: in spite of their distance they do not escape the designs of power. Flying billboards, the astronauts float in space or leap about on the moon in order to make people march to the time of work.

9

And if the Christian astronauts of the West and the bureaucratic cosmonauts of the East amuse themselves with metaphysics and secular morals (Gagarin "did not see God" and Borman prayed for the little Earth), it is in obedience to their spatial "assignment," which must be the essence of their religion; as with Exupéry the saint, who spoke the lowest imbecilities from high altitudes, but whose essence lay in his threefold role of militarist, patriot and idiot.

10

The conquest of space is part of the planetary hope of an economic system which, saturated with commodities, spectacles and power, ejaculates into space when it arrives at the end of the noose of its terrestrial contradictions. A new America, space must serve the states as a new territory for wars and colonies—a new territory to which to send producer-consumers and thus enable the system to break out of the planet's limitations. Province of accumulation, space is destined to become an accumulation of provinces—for which laws, treaties and international tribunals already exist. A new Yalta, the dividing up of space shows the inability of the capitalists and bureaucrats to resolve their antagonisms and struggles here on Earth.

11

But the revolutionary old mole, which is now gnawing at the bases of the system, will destroy the barriers that separate science from the generalized knowledge of historical man. No more ideas of separate power, no more power of separate ideas. Generalized self-management of the permanent transformation of the world by the masses will make science a basic banality, and no longer a truth of state.

12

Man will enter into space to make the universe the playground of the last revolt: that which will go against the limitations imposed by nature. And having smashed the walls that separate people from science today, the conquest of space will no longer be an economic or military "promotional" gimmick, but the blossoming of human freedoms and realizations, attained by a race of gods. We will enter into space not as employees of an astronautic administration or as "volunteers" of a state project, but as masters without slaves reviewing their domains: the entire universe pillaged for the workers councils.

EDUARDO ROTHE

THE LATEST EXCLUSIONS

(excerpts)

On 21 December 1967 Timothy Clark, Christopher Gray and Donald Nicholson-Smith were excluded from the SI just as they were getting ready to publish a journal in England and begin a group activity there. (Charles Radcliffe had resigned for personal reasons a couple months before.)

The divergences, which had been nonexistent or at least unnoticed in all other regards, suddenly appeared not in regard to their activity in England but on the question of the SI's relations and possible action in the United States. Vaneigem had gone to New York in November as the delegate of all the situationists and carried out his mandate precisely, notably in discussions with the comrades with whom in everyone's opinion—including that of the British—we had the most developed contacts, and who have since formed our American section. Vaneigem refused to meet a certain Ben Morea, publisher of the bulletin *Black Mask*, with whom our American comrades were in conflict on virtually every question concerning revolutionary action and whose intellectual honesty they even challenged. Vaneigem had, moreover, already been obliged to break off a conversation with a certain Hoffman, who was eulogistically expounding to him a *mystical* interpretation of his text "Basic Banalities" and who was at that time the main collaborator in Morea's publications: the enormity of this fact naturally led Vaneigem no longer even to want to discuss our other more general divergences with Morea.* Everything seemed quite clear upon his return to Europe. But Morea wrote to the London situationists to complain of having been misrepresented to Vaneigem. Upon the insistence of the English comrades, who were concerned about fully clarifying the matter in the unlikely case that Morea himself was under some misapprehension, we wrote a collective letter detailing all the facts of the situation. The English agreed, however, that this would be the last response we would send him. Morea wrote once again to all of us saying that what we had written concerned false pretexts and that the real dispute lay elsewhere; he insulted our New York friends and this time questioned Vaneigem's testimony. *In spite of their express commitment*, the English responded again to Morea, saying that they no longer understood what was going on and that "someone" must be lying. They had more and more indulgence toward Morea and more and more mistrust of our American friends; and even of Vaneigem, though refusing to admit it. We called on the three English to rectify this outrageous, publicly aired vacillation by immediately breaking with the falsifier and his mystical acolyte. They accepted this demand in principle, but equivocated and finally refused to implement it. We then had to break with them. In three weeks this discussion had given

293

rise to two meetings in Paris and London and to the exchange of a dozen long letters. Our patience had been rather excessive, but what had at first seemed to be merely a surprising slowness in reasoning increasingly began to appear as a conscious, inexplicable obstruction. Up to the moment of their exclusion, however, the discussion had never concerned anything but the details described here and the questions of method it so strangely raised regarding the SI's solidarity and general criteria for breaking (for the English never denied that Morea was involved with a mystical idiot). Gray later passed through New York and sadly recounted to whoever would listen that his stillborn group had concerned itself directly with America in order to save the revolutionary project there from a detrimental incomprehension on the part of the continental European situationists (and of the Americans themselves). The English comrades themselves had not felt sufficiently appreciated. They hadn't dared to say so, but they had suffered from a lack of interest on the part of the Continentals in *what they were going to do*. They were left isolated in their country—all surrounded by water. A more "theoretical" reason emerged *after the discussion*: England being much closer to a revolutionary crisis than the Continent, the "Continental" theorists were supposedly moved by spite at seeing that "their" theories would be realized somewhere else. The value of this historical law of Anglo-American revolutionism was demonstrated only five months later. [. . .]

Gray has since published a rag called *King Mob* which passes, quite wrongly, for being slightly pro-situationist, in which one can read eulogies to the eternal Morea. Since Morea is all that Gray has left, Gray and his acolytes have gone so far as to *conceal* certain of Morea's current writings that would be too embarrassing to reveal to the people in their entourage who they want to continue to respect their idol. And they advance the amusing argument that Morea supposedly had the merit of transferring certain radical positions "from the situationist salon" to street fighting—they say this a year after the occupations movement! Gray also tried to reestablish contact with us, but surreptitiously, through the intermediary of a certain Allan Green, who pretended not to know him but was unmasked at the second meeting. Fine work, and as cleverly conducted as might have been expected! The "unique" Garnautins must be turning over in their university graves in envy of such a worthy successor.

It will be noted that for nearly two years there have been no other exclusions. We must admit that this notable success is not entirely due to the real elevation of consciousness and coherent radicality of individuals in the present revolutionary period. It is also due to the fact that the SI, applying with increasing rigor its previous decisions on the preliminary examination of those wanting to join it, has during the same period refused some fifty or sixty requests for admission: which has spared us an equal number of exclusions.

MAITRON THE HISTORIAN

(excerpts)

[The article opens by describing how the "libertarian" historian Jean Maitron, in collaboration with a notorious Stalinist, put out a book on May 1968 containing, in addition to numerous erroneous assertions on the SI's activities, reproductions of CMDO texts that were knowingly falsified—critiques of the Stalinists deleted with no indication of the omissions, completely fabricated passages sympathetic to the CGT added, etc.]

[. . .] On 24 October the SI wrote Maitron a letter that pointed out, with supporting proofs, the most gross falsifications concerning us in his book and demanded "a written apology." In two weeks he hadn't replied. Riesel and Viénet then went to his residence, insulted him as he merited, and in order to stress their point, smashed a soup tureen which according to this historian was "an heirloom."

We thus showed this person that his specific dishonesty would not pass unobserved, and could even expose him to being disagreeably insulted; which may make others pause to reflect before committing similar falsifications. [. . .]

[The article then goes on to describe how this incident is soon afterwards ridiculously inflated in several public accounts—that his typewriter was smashed, that his home was "ransacked" by "several" situationists, giving the impression that he was lucky to escape alive, etc.]

But beyond the comical aspects of this incident—*Révolution Prolétarienne* of December 1968 rages about the "fascism" of our "massive trashing" and even calls for "counterviolence" against us—there is an important issue here. In our opinion, the number one objective for the revolutionary movement that is presently taking shape—even more important and urgent than elaborating a consistent theoretical critique or linking up with democratic rank-and-file committees in the factories or paralyzing the universities—is giving practical support for an *insistence on truth and nonfalsification*. This is the *precondition* and the *beginning* of all the rest. Whoever falsifies must be discredited, boycotted, spit on. When it is a matter of *systems of falsification* (as in the case of Stalinist bureaucrats or of bourgeois) it is obviously those systems that must be destroyed by a large-scale social and political struggle. But this very struggle must create its own conditions: when one is dealing with individuals or groups aiming to establish themselves anywhere in the revolutionary current,* one must *not let them get away with anything*. By maintaining this insistence, the movement will fundamentally smash all the conditions of falsification that accompanied and brought about its disappearance for half a century. As we see it, all revolutionaries must now recognize it as their immediate task to denounce and *discourage*, by all means and whatever the price, those who continue to falsify. [. . .]

To reply in advance to those who will still say that the situationists always insult everyone to the same degree* and blame everything in the absolute, we will mention two books that devote a considerable space to our documents or to analysis of our action in May: *Le projet révolutionnaire* by Richard Gombin (Ed. Mouton, 1969) and *The French Student Uprising* by Alain Schnapp and P. Vidal-Naquet (Seuil, 1969). While we are in disagreement with the methods and ideas of these authors, as well as with virtually all of their interpretations and even on certain facts, we readily recognize that these books are put together honestly, that they accurately cite authentic versions of documents; and therefore that they contribute material that will be useful toward writing the history of the occupations movement.

THE ELITE AND THE BACKWARD

(excerpts)

The situationists are undoubtedly very criticizable. So far, unfortunately, almost no one has made any of these critiques—that is, the intelligent and precise critiques, made without bad faith, that revolutionaries could make and will one day easily be able to make regarding many of our theses and many aspects of our real activity. But the way in which many present-day revolutionaries advance inept objections or accusations, as if to repress the problem with the miserable reflexes acquired during the former period of their defeats and nonexistence, only reveals a persistent leftist sectarian poverty, or even miserable *ulterior motives*.

Let us say first of all that just as we find it quite natural that bourgeois, bureaucrats and intellectual recuperators hate us, we recognize that revolutionaries—if there are any—who claim to be opposed on principle to any form of organization on a precise platform, entailing the practical coresponsibility of its participants, naturally condemn us completely since we manifestly have a contrary opinion and practice. But all the others? It is a clear demonstration of dishonesty and *an implicit avowal of aims of domination* to accuse the SI of constituting a dominating organization when we have gone to great lengths to make it *almost impossible* to become a member of the SI* (which seems to us to destroy at the roots any concrete risk of our becoming a "leadership" vis-à-vis even the slightest fraction of the masses); and considering, in addition, that it is quite clear that we have never *traded on* our "intellectual prestige," either by frequenting any bourgeois or intellectual circles (much less by accepting any of their "honors" or remunerations), or by competing with all the leftist sects for the control or admiration of the miserable student public, or by trying to exert the slightest secret influence, *or even the slightest direct or indirect presence*, in the autonomous revolutionary organizations whose existence we and a few others have predicted, and which are now beginning to form. Those who have never accomplished anything apparently feel they have to attribute the scandalous fact that we have been able to accomplish something to imaginary goals *and means*. In reality it is because we shock certain people by refusing contact with them, or even their requests for admission to the SI, that we are accused of being an "elite" and of aspiring to dominate those whom we don't even want to know! But what "elitist" role are we supposed to have reserved for ourselves? A theoretical one? We have said that the workers *must become dialecticians* and themselves take care of all their theoretical and practical problems. Those who are concerned with running their own affairs need only appropriate our *methods* instead of lapping up the latest rumors *about* us and they will become that much more independent from us. [. . .]

CINEMA AND REVOLUTION

In *Le Monde* of 8 July 1969 the Berlin Film Festival correspondent J.P. Picaper is awestruck by the fact that "in *The Gay Science* (an ORTF–Radio Stuttgart production, banned in France) Godard has pushed his praiseworthy self-critique to the point of projecting sequences shot in the dark or even of leaving the spectator for an almost unbearable length of time before a blank screen." Without seeking more precisely what constitutes "an almost unbearable length of time" for this critic, we can see that Godard's work, following the latest fashions as always, is culminating in a destructive style just as belatedly plagiarized and pointless as all the rest, this negation having been expressed in the cinema long before* Godard had ever begun the long series of pretentious pseudoinnovations that aroused such enthusiasm among students in the previous period. The same journalist reports that Godard, through one of the characters in his short entitled *Love*, confesses that "the revolution cannot be put in images" because "the cinema is the art of lying." The cinema has no more been an "art of lying" than has any of the rest of art, which was dead in its totality long before Godard, who has not *even* been a modern artist, that is, who has not even been capable of the slightest personal originality. This Maoist liar is in this way winding up his bluff by trying to arouse admiration for his brilliant discovery of a noncinema cinema, while denouncing a sort of ontological lie in which he has participated, but no more so than have many others. In fact, Godard was immediately *outmoded* by the May 1968 movement, recog manufacturer of a superficial pseudocritical ar trashcans of the past (see "The Role of Godar point Godard's career as a filmmaker was esser personally insulted and ridiculed on several o aries who happened to cross his path. The cine olutionary communication is not intrinsically m

Godard or Jacopetti has touched it, any more than all political analysis is doomed to duplicity just because Stalinists have written. Currently several new filmmakers in various countries are trying to utilize films as instruments of a revolutionary critique, and some of them will partially succeed in this. However, the limitations in their very grasp of present revolutionary requirements, as well as in their aesthetic conceptions, will in our opinion prevent them for some time still from going as far as is necessary. We consider that at the moment only the situationists' positions and methods, as formulated by René Viénet in our previous issue, are adequate for a directly revolutionary use of cinema—although of course political and economic conditions still present obstacles to the realization of such films.

It is known that Eisenstein wanted to make a film of *Capital*. Considering his formal conceptions and political submissiveness, it can be doubted if his film would have been faithful to Marx's text. But for our part, we are sure we can do better. For example, as soon as it becomes possible, Guy Debord will himself make a cinematic adaptation of *The Society of the Spectacle* that will certainly not fall short of his book.

THE ORGANIZATION QUESTION
FOR THE S.I.

1. Everything the SI has been known for until now belongs to a period that is fortunately over. (More precisely, it can be said that that was our "second period," if the 1957–1962 activity that centered around the supersession of art is counted as the first.)

2. The new revolutionary tendencies of present-day society, however weak and confused they may still be, are no longer restricted to a marginal underground: this year they are appearing in the streets.

3. At the same time, the SI has emerged from silence. It must now strategically exploit this breakthrough. We cannot prevent the term "situationist" from becoming fashionable here and there. We must act in such a way that this (natural) phenomenon works more for us than against us. To me, "what works for us" is not distinct from what serves to unify and radicalize scattered struggles. This is the SI's task as an organization. Apart from this, the term "situationist" could be used vaguely to designate a certain period of critical thought (which it is already no mean feat to have initiated), but one in which everyone is responsible only for what he does personally, without any reference to organizational community. But as long as this community exists, have to distinguish itself from whoever talks about it without rt of it.

4. Regarding the necessary tasks we have previously set for ourselves, we should now concentrate less on theoretical elaboration (which should nonetheless be continued) and more on the communication of theory, on the practical link-up with whatever new gestures of contestation appear (by quickly increasing our possibilities for intervention, criticism, exemplary support).

5. The movement that is hesitantly beginning is the beginning of our victory (that is, the victory of what we have been supporting and pointing out for many years). But we must not "capitalize" on this victory (with each new affirmation of a moment of revolutionary critique, at whatever level, any advanced coherent organization must know how to lose itself in revolutionary society). In present and forthcoming subversive currents there is much to criticize. It would be very inelegant for us to make this necessary critique while leaving the SI above it all.

6. The SI must now prove its effectiveness in a subsequent stage of revolutionary activity—or else disappear.

7. In order to have any chance of attaining this effectiveness, we must recognize and state several truths about the SI. These were obviously already true before; but in the present stage in which this "truth is verifying itself" it has become urgent to make it more precise.

8. We have never considered the SI as a goal, but as a moment of a historical activity; the force of circumstances is now leading us to prove it. The SI's "coherence" is the relationship, striving toward coherence, between all our formulated theses and between these theses and our action; as well as our solidarity in those cases where the group is responsible for the action of one of its members (this collective responsibility holds regarding many issues, but not all). It cannot be some sort of mastery guaranteed to someone who would be reputed to have so thoroughly appropriated our theoretical bases that he would automatically derive from them a perfectly exemplary line of conduct. It cannot be a demand for (much less a pretension of) an equal excellence of everyone in all questions or operations.

9. Coherence is acquired and verified by egalitarian participation in the entirety of a common practice, which simultaneously reveals shortcomings and provides remedies. This practice requires formal meetings to arrive at decisions, transmission of all information and examination of all observed lapses.

10. This practice presently demands more participants in the SI, drawn from among those who declare their accord and demonstrate their abilities. The small number of members, rather unjustly selected until now, has been the cause and consequence of a ridiculous overvaluation "officially" accorded to everyone merely by virtue of the fact that they were SI members, even though many of them never demonstrated the slightest real capabilities (consider the exclusions that occurred last

year, whether of the Garnautins or the English). Such a pseudoqualitative numerical limitation both encourages stupidities and exaggeratedly magnifies the importance of each particular stupidity.

11. Externally, a direct product of this selective illusion has been the mythological recognition of autonomous pseudogroups, gloriously situated at the level of the SI when in fact they were only feeble admirers of it (and thus inevitably soon to become dishonest vilifiers of it). It seems to me that we cannot recognize any group as autonomous unless it is engaged in autonomous practical work; nor can we recognize such a group as durably successful unless it is engaged in united action with the workers (without, of course, falling short of our "Minimum Definition of Revolutionary Organizations"). All kinds of recent experiences have shown the recuperated confusionism of the term "anarchist," and it seems to me that we must oppose it everywhere.

12. I think that we should allow SI members to constitute distinct tendencies oriented around differing preoccupations or tactical options, as long as our general bases are not put in question. Similarly, we must move toward a complete practical autonomy of national groups as soon as they are able really to constitute themselves.

13. In contrast to the habits of the excluded members who in 1966 pretended to attain—inactively—a total realization of transparency and friendship in the SI (to the point that one almost felt guilty for pointing out how boring their company was), and who as a corollary secretly developed the most idiotic jealousies, lies unworthy of a grade-school kid and conspiracies as ignominious as they were irrational, we must accept only historical relationships among us (critical confidence, knowledge of each member's possibilities or limits), but on the basis of the fundamental loyalty required by the revolutionary project that has been defining itself for over a century.

14. We have no right to be mistaken in breaking with people. We will have to continue to be more or less frequently mistaken in admitting people. The exclusions have almost never marked any theoretical progress in the SI: we have not derived from these occasions any more precise definition of what is unacceptable (the surprising thing about the Garnautin affair was that it was an exception to this rule). The exclusions have almost always been responses to objective threats that existing conditions hold in store for our action. There is a danger of this recurring at higher levels. All sorts of "Nashisms" could reconstitute themselves: we must simply be in a position to destroy them.

15. In order to make the form of this debate consistent with what I see as its content, I propose that this text be communicated to certain comrades close to the SI or capable of taking part in it, and that we solicit their opinion on this question.

GUY DEBORD
April 1968

300

Note added August 1969:

These notes of April 1968 were a contribution to a debate on organization that we were about to engage in. Two or three weeks later the occupations movement, which was obviously more pleasant and instructive than this debate, forced us to postpone it.

The last point alone had been immediately approved by the SI comrades. Thus this text, which certainly had nothing secret about it, was not even a strictly internal document. Toward the end of 1968, however, we discovered that truncated and undated versions of it had been circulated by some leftist groups, with what purpose I don't know. The SI consequently decided that the authentic version should be published in this journal.

When the SI was able to resume the discussion on organization in fall 1968, the situationists adopted these theses, which had been confirmed by the rapid march of events in the intervening period. Conversely, the SI proved capable of acting in May in a manner that suitably fulfilled the requirements that these theses had formulated for the immediate future.

Since this text is now receiving a wider circulation, I think I should clarify one point in order to avoid any misunderstanding regarding the relative openness demanded for the SI. I was not proposing any concession to "united action" with the semiradical currents that are already beginning to take shape; and certainly not any abandonment of our rigor in choosing members of the SI and in limiting their number. I criticized a bad, abstract use of this rigor, which could lead to the contrary of what we want. The admiring or subsequently hostile excesses of all those who speak of us from the viewpoint of excessively impassioned spectators should not be able to find a justification in a corresponding "situ-vaunting" on our part that would promote the belief that the situationists are wondrous beings who have all actually appropriated in their lives everything they have articulated—or merely agreed with—in the matter of revolutionary theory and program. Since May we have seen the magnitude and urgency this problem has assumed.

The situationists do not have any monopoly to defend, nor any reward to expect. A task that suited us was undertaken and carried out through good and bad and, on the whole, correctly, with the means available to us. The present development of the subjective conditions of revolution should lead toward defining a strategy that, starting from different conditions, will be as good as that followed by the SI in more difficult times.

G.D.

Miscellaneous
SI Publications
(1960–1969)

PRELIMINARIES TOWARD DEFINING
A UNITARY REVOLUTIONARY PROGRAM

I — Capitalism: A Society Without Culture

1

Culture can be defined as the ensemble of means through which a society thinks of itself and shows itself to itself, and thus decides on all aspects of the use of its available surplus-value; that is to say, it is the organization of everything over and beyond the immediate necessities of the society's reproduction.

All forms of capitalist society today are in the final analysis based on the generalized and—at the level of the masses—stable division between directors and executants: those who give orders and those who carry them out. Transposed onto the plane of culture, this means the separation between "understanding" and "doing," the inability to organize (on the basis of permanent exploitation) the continuously accelerating domination of nature toward any goal whatsoever.

For the capitalist class, dominating production entails monopolizing the understanding of productive activity, of work. To achieve this, work is on the one hand more and more parcelized, i.e. rendered incomprehensible to those who do it; and on the other hand, it is reconstituted as a unity by specialized agencies. But these agencies are themselves subordinated to the real directorate, which alone possesses the theoretical comprehension of the whole since it dictates the direction of production in accordance with its general directives. However, this comprehension and these objectives are themselves subjected to a certain arbitrariness since they are cut off from practice and even from all realistic knowledge, which it is in no one's interest to transmit.

The total social activity is thus split into three levels: the workshop, the office and the directorate. Culture, in the sense of active and practical comprehension of society, is likewise cut apart into these three moments. Their unity is in fact only reconstituted (partially and clandestinely) by people's constant transgression of the separate sectors in which they are regimented by the system.

2

The formative mechanism of culture thus amounts to a reification of human activities which fixates the living and models the transmission of experience from one generation to another on the transmission of commodities; a reification which strives to ensure the past's domination over the future.

Such cultural functioning enters into contradiction with capitalism's constant need to obtain people's adherence and to enlist their creative activity, within the narrow limits within which it imprisons them. In short, the capitalist order can survive only by ceaselessly fabricating a new past for itself. This can be seen particularly clearly in the cultural sector proper, whose publicity is based on the periodic launching of pseudoinnovations.

3

Work thus tends to be reduced to pure execution and thereby made absurd. As technology evolves, its application is trivialized; work is simplified and becomes more and more absurd.

But this absurdity extends to the offices and laboratories: the ultimate determinations of their activity come from outside them, from the political sphere of the running of the whole of society.

On the other hand, as the activity of the offices and laboratories is integrated into the overall functioning of capitalism, the necessity to fully exploit this activity requires the introduction into it of the capitalist division of labor, that is, of parcelization and hierarchization. The logical problem of scientific synthesis then intersects with the social problem of centralization. The result of these changes is, contrary to appearances, a general lack of culture at all levels of knowledge: scientific synthesis is no longer carried out, science no longer comprehends itself. Science is no longer a real and practical clarification of people's relation with the world; it has destroyed the old representations without being able to provide new ones. The world as unified totality becomes indecipherable; only some specialists possess a few fragments of rationality, fragments which they themselves are incapable of communicating even to each other.

4

This state of things gives rise to a certain number of conflicts. There is a conflict between, on the one hand, technics, the natural tendency of the development of material processes (and largely even the natural tendency of the development of the sciences); and on the other, the technology which is an application of these technics in strict accordance with the requirements of exploiting the workers and thwarting their resistance. There is also a conflict between capitalist imperatives and people's elementary needs. Thus the contradiction between present nuclear practices and a still generally prevalent taste for living is echoed even in the moralizing protests of certain physicists. The alterations that man can now bring about in his own nature (ranging from plastic surgery to controlled genetic mutations) also demand a society controlled by itself, the abolition of all specialized directors.

Everywhere the vastness of the new possibilities poses the urgent alternative: revolutionary solution or science-fiction barbarism. The compromise represented by the present society is contingent on the preservation of a status quo which is in fact everywhere constantly out of its control.

5

Present culture as a whole can be characterized as alienated in the sense that every activity, every moment of life, every idea, every type of behavior, has a meaning only outside itself, in an elsewhere which, being no longer in heaven, is only the more maddening to try and locate: a utopia, in the literal sense of the word, dominates the life of the modern world.

6

Having from the workshop to the laboratory emptied productive activity of all meaning for itself, capitalism strives to place the meaning of life in leisure activities and to reorient productive activity on that basis. Since production is hell in the prevailing moral schema, real life must be found in consumption, in the use of goods.

But for the most part these goods have no use except to satisfy a few private needs that have been hypertrophied to meet the requirements of the market. Capitalist consumption imposes a general reduction of desires by its regular satisfaction of artificial needs, which remain needs without ever having been desires—authentic desires being constrained to remain unfulfilled (or compensated in the form of spectacles). The consumer is in reality morally and psychologically consumed by the market. But above all, these goods have no social use because the social horizon does not extend beyond the factory; outside the factory everything is organized as a desert (dormitory towns, freeways, parking lots . . .)—the terrain of consumption.

However, the society constituted in the factory has the exclusive domination over this desert. The real use of goods is simply as status symbols which, in accordance with an inevitable tendency of the industrial commodity, have at the same time become obligatory for everyone. The factory is symbolically reflected in leisure activities, though with enough room for variation to allow for the compensation of a few frustrations. The world of consumption is in reality the world of the mutual spectacularization of everyone, the world of everyone's separation, estrangement and nonparticipation. The directorial sphere also strictly directs this spectacle, which is composed automatically and miserably in accordance with imperatives external to the society, imperatives to which absurd values are attributed (and the directors themselves, as living people, can also be considered as victims of this automatic directorial machine).

7

Outside of work, the spectacle is the dominant mode through which people relate to each other. It is only through the spectacle that people acquire a (falsified) knowledge of certain general aspects of social life, from scientific or technological achievements to prevailing types of conduct and orchestrated meetings of international statesmen. The relation between authors and spectators is only a transposition of the fundamental relation between directors and executants. It answers perfectly to the needs of a reified and alienated culture: the spectacle-spectator relation is in itself a staunch bearer of the capitalist order. The ambiguity of all "revolutionary art" lies in the fact that the revolutionary aspect of any particular spectacle is always contradicted and offset by the reactionary element present in all spectacles.

This is why the improvement of capitalist society means to a great degree the improvement of the mechanism of spectacularization. This is obviously a complex mechanism, for if it must be most essentially the propagator of the capitalist order, it nevertheless must not appear to the public as the delirium of capitalism; it must involve the public by incorporating elements of representation that correspond—in fragments—to social rationality. It must sidetrack the desires whose satisfaction is forbidden by the ruling order. For example, modern mass tourism presents cities and landscapes not in order to satisfy authentic desires to live in such human or geographical milieus; it presents them as pure, rapid, superficial spectacles (spectacles from which one can gain prestige by reminiscing about). Similarly, striptease is the most obvious form of the degradation of eroticism into a mere spectacle.

8

The evolution and the conservation of art have been governed by these lines of force. At one pole, art is purely and simply recuperated by capitalism as a means of conditioning the population. At the other pole, capitalism grants art a perpetual privileged concession: that of pure creative activity, an alibi for the alienation of all other activities (which thus makes it the most expensive and prestigious status symbol). But at the same time, this sphere reserved for "free creative activity" is the only one in which the question of what we do with life and the question of communication are posed practically and in all their fullness. Here, in art, lies the basis of the antagonisms between partisans and adversaries of the officially dictated reasons for living. The established meaninglessness and separation give rise to the general crisis of traditional artistic means—a crisis linked to the experience of alternative ways of living or to the demand for such experience. Revolutionary artists are those who call for intervention; and who have themselves intervened in the spectacle to disrupt and destroy it.

II — Culture and Revolutionary Politics

1

The revolutionary movement can be nothing less than the struggle of the proletariat for the actual domination and deliberate transformation of all aspects of social life—beginning with the management of production and work by the workers directly deciding everything. Such a change immediately implies a radical transformation of the nature of work and the development of a new technology tending to ensure the workers' domination over the machines.

This radical transformation of the meaning of work will lead to a number of consequences, the main one of which is undoubtedly the shifting of the center of interest of life from passive leisure to the new type of productive activity. This does not mean that overnight all productive activities will become in themselves passionately interesting. But to work toward making them so, by a general and ongoing reconversion of the ends as well as the means of industrial work, will in any case be the minimum passion of a free society.

All activities will tend to blend the life previously separated between leisure and work into a single but infinitely diversified flow. Production and consumption will merge and be superseded in the creative use of the goods of the society.

2

Such a program proposes to people no reason to live other than their own construction of their own lives. This presupposes not only that people be objectively freed from real needs (hunger, etc.), but above all that they begin to develop real desires in place of the present compensations; that they refuse all forms of behavior dictated by others and continually reinvent their own unique fulfillment; that they no longer consider life to be the maintaining of a certain stability, but that they aspire to the unlimited enrichment of their acts.

3

Such demands today are not based on some sort of utopianism. They are based first of all on the struggle of the proletariat at all levels, and on all the forms of explicit refusal or profound indifference that the unstable ruling society constantly has to combat with every means. They are also based on the lesson of the essential defeat of all attempts at less radical changes. Finally, they are based on the extremist strivings and actions appearing today among certain sectors of youth (in spite of all efforts at disciplining and repressing them) and in a few artistic milieus.

But this basis also has a utopian aspect: the invention and experimentation of solutions to present problems without being preoccupied with whether or not the conditions for their realization are immediately present (it should be noted that this utopian sort of experimentation now plays a key role in modern science). This temporary, historical utopianism is legitimate; and it is necessary because it serves to incubate the projection of desires without which free life would be empty of content. It is inseparable from the necessity to dissolve the present ideology of everyday life, and therefore the bonds of everyday oppression, so that the revolutionary class can disabusedly discover present and future possibilities of freedom.

Utopian practice makes sense, however, only if it is closely linked to the practice of revolutionary struggle. The latter, in its turn, cannot do without such utopianism without being condemned to sterility. The seekers of an experimental culture cannot hope to realize it without the triumph of the revolutionary movement, while the latter cannot itself establish authentic revolutionary conditions without resuming the efforts of the cultural avant-garde toward the critique of everyday life and its free reconstruction.

Revolutionary politics thus has as its content the totality of the problems of the society. It has as its form the experimental practice of a free life through organized struggle against the capitalist order. The revolutionary movement must thus itself become an experimental movement. Henceforth, wherever it exists, it must develop and resolve as profoundly as possible the problems of a revolutionary microsociety. This comprehensive politics culminates in the moment of revolutionary action, when the masses abruptly intervene to make history and discover their action as direct experience and as festival. At such moments they undertake a conscious and collective construction of everyday life which, one day, will no longer be stopped by anything.

PIERRE CANJUERS,* GUY DEBORD

20 July 1960

FOR A REVOLUTIONARY JUDGMENT OF ART

1

Chatel's article on Godard's film in *Socialisme ou Barbarie* #31 can be defined as film criticism dominated by revolutionary concerns. The analysis of the film takes as its point of departure a revolutionary perspective on society, confirms that perspective, and leads to the conclusion that certain tendencies of cinematic expression should be considered preferable to others in relation to the revolutionary project. It is obviously because Chatel's critique thus sets out the question in all its fullness, instead of debating various questions of taste, that it is interesting and calls for discussion. Specifically, Chatel finds *Breathless* a "valuable example" supporting his thesis that an alteration of "the present forms of culture" depends on the production of works that offer people "a representation of their own existence."

2

A revolutionary alteration of the present forms of culture can be nothing other than the supersession of all aspects of the aesthetic and technological apparatus that constitutes an aggregation of spectacles separated from life. It is not in its surface meanings that we should look for a spectacle's relation to the problems of the society, but at the deepest level, at the level of *its function as a spectacle*. "The relation between authors and spectators is only a transposition of the fundamental relation between directors and executants. ... The spectacle-spectator relation is in itself a staunch bearer of the capitalist order." (*Preliminaries Toward Defining a Unitary Revolutionary Program*.)

One must not introduce reformist illusions concerning the spectacle, as if it could be eventually improved from within, ameliorated by its own specialists under the supposed control of a better-informed public opinion. To do so would be tantamount to giving revolutionaries' approval to a tendency, or an appearance of a tendency, in a game that we absolutely must not play; a game that we must reject in its entirety in the name of the fundamental requirements of the revolutionary project, which can in no case produce an aesthetics because it is already entirely beyond the domain of aesthetics. It is a question not of engaging in some sort of revolutionary art-criticism, but of making a revolutionary critique of all art.

3

The connection between the predominance of the spectacle in social life and the predominance of a class of rulers (both based on the contradictory need for passive adherence) is no paradox or author's clever phrase. It is a factual correlation that objectively characterizes the modern world. It is here that the cultural critique issuing from the experience of the complete self-destruction of modern art meets up with the political critique issuing from the experience of the destruction of the workers movement by its own alienated organizations. If one really insists on finding something positive in modern culture, it must be said that its only positive aspect appears in its self-liquidation, its withering away, its witness against itself.

From a practical standpoint, what is at issue here is a revolutionary organization's relation to artists. The deficiencies of bureaucratic organizations and their fellow travelers in the formulation and use of such a relationship are well known. But it seems that a complete and coherent revolutionary politics must effectively unify these activities.

4

The greatest weakness of Chatel's critique is precisely that he assumes from the start, without even alluding to the possibility of any debate on the subject, that there is the most radical separation between the author of any work of art and the political analysis that might be made of it. Chatel's analysis of Godard is a particularly striking example of this separation. Having taken it for granted that Godard himself remains beyond any political judgment, Chatel never bothers to mention that Godard did not *explicitly* criticize "the cultural delirium in which we live" and did not *deliberately intend* to "confront people with their own lives." Godard is treated like a natural phenomenon, a cultural artifact. One thinks no more about the possibility of Godard having political, philosophical or other positions than one does about investigating the ideology of a typhoon.

Such criticism fits right in to the sphere of bourgeois culture—specifically within its "art criticism" sector—since it obviously participates in the "deluge of words that covers over every single aspect of reality." This criticism is one interpretation among many others of a work on which we have no hold. The critic assumes from the beginning that he knows *better than the author himself* what the author means. This apparent presumptuousness is in fact an extreme humility: the critic so completely accepts his separation from the artistic specialist in question that he despairs of ever being able to act on or with him

311

(which would obviously require that he take into consideration what the artist was explicitly seeking).

5

Art criticism is a second-degree spectacle. The critic is someone who makes a spectacle out of his very condition as a spectator—a specialized and therefore ideal spectator, expressing his ideas and feelings *about* a work in which he does not really participate. He re-presents, restages, his own nonintervention in the spectacle. The weakness of random and largely arbitrary fragmentary judgments concerning spectacles that do not really concern us is the lot of all of us in many banal discussions in private life. But the art critic makes a show of this kind of weakness, presenting it as *exemplary*.

6

Chatel thinks that if a portion of the population recognizes itself in a film, it will be able to "look at itself, admire itself, criticize itself or reject itself—in any case, to use the images that pass on the screen for its own needs." Let us first of all note that there is a certain mystery in this notion of using this flow of images to satisfy authentic needs. Just how they are to be used is not clear. It would seem to be necessary first to specify which needs are in question in order to say whether those images can really serve as means to satisfy them. Furthermore, everything we know about the mechanism of the spectacle, even at the simplest filmological level, absolutely contradicts this idyllic vision of people equally free to admire or criticize themselves by recognizing themselves in the characters of a film. But fundamentally it is impossible to accept this division of labor between uncontrollable specialists presenting a vision of people's lives to them and audiences having to recognize themselves more or less clearly in those images. Attaining a certain accuracy in describing people's behavior is not necessarily positive. Even if Godard presents people with an image of themselves in which they can undeniably recognize themselves more than in the films of Fernandel, he nevertheless presents them with a false image in which they recognize themselves falsely.

7

Revolution is not "showing" life to people, but making them live. A revolutionary organization must always remember that its objective is not getting its adherents to listen to convincing talks by expert leaders, but getting them to speak for themselves, in order to achieve, or at least strive toward, an equal degree of participation. The cinematic spectacle is precisely one of those forms of pseudocommunication—one which has been developed, in preference to other possibilities, by the present *class* technology—in which this aim is radically unfeasible. Much more so, for example, than in a cultural form like the university-style lecture with questions at the end, in which dialogue and audience participation, though placed in extremely unfavorable conditions, are not absolutely excluded.

Anyone who has seen a film-club debate has immediately noticed the lines of demarcation between the leader of the discussion, the professional talkers who speak up at every meeting, and the people who only occasionally express their viewpoints. These three categories are clearly separated by the degree to which they have mastered a specialized vocabulary that determines their place in this institutionalized discussion. Information and influence are transmitted unilaterally, never rising upward from the base. Nevertheless, these three categories are quite close to one another in their common confused powerlessness of spectators making a show of themselves, in relation to the real line of demarcation passing between them and the people who really make the films. The unilaterality of influence is still more strict in relation to this division. The considerable differences in the mastery of the conceptual tools of film-club debates are ultimately reduced by the simple fact that all of these tools are equally ineffectual. The film-club debate is a subspectacle accompanying the projected film; it is more ephemeral than written criticism, but neither more nor less separated. In appearance the film-club discussion is an attempt at dialogue, at social encounter, at a time when the urban environment isolates individuals more and more. But in fact it is the negation of this dialogue, since the people do not gather there in order to *decide* on anything, but in order to hold a discussion on a false pretext and with false means.

8

Leaving aside its external effect, the practice of cinematic criticism at this level immediately introduces two risks into a revolutionary organization.

The first danger is that certain comrades might be led to formulate other criticisms expressing their different judgments of other films or even of this one. Beginning from the same positions concerning the society as a whole, the number of different possible judgments of *Breathless*, though obviously not unlimited, is nevertheless fairly large. To give just one example, one could make a critique just as talented as Chatel's, expressing exactly the same revolutionary politics, but which would attempt to bring out Godard's own participation in an entire sector of the dominant cultural mythology: that of the cinema itself (shots of the tête-à-tête with the photo of Humphrey Bogart, cut to the Café Napoléon). Belmondo—on the Champs-Elysées, at the Café Pergola, at the Rue Vavin intersection—could be considered as the image (largely unreal, of course, "ideologized") that the microsociety of *Cahiers du Cinéma* editors (and not even the whole generation of French filmmakers who emerged in the fifties) projects of its own existence; with its paltry dreams of flaunted subspontaneity; with its tastes, its real ignorances, but also its cultural enthusiasms.

The other danger would be that the impression of arbitrariness given by this exaltation of Godard's revolutionary value might lead other comrades to oppose all intervention in cultural questions simply in order to avoid the risk of lacking in seriousness. On the contrary, the revolutionary movement must accord a central place to criticism of culture and everyday life. But any examination of these phenomena must first of all be disabused, not respectful toward the given modes of communication. The very bases of existing cultural relations must be contested by the critique that the revolutionary movement needs to really bring to bear on all aspects of life and human relationships.

GUY DEBORD
February 1961

THESES ON THE PARIS COMMUNE

1

"The classical workers movement must be reexamined without any illusions, particularly without any illusions regarding its various political and pseudotheoretical heirs, for all they have inherited is its failure. The apparent successes of this movement are its fundamental failures (reformism or the establishment of a state bureaucracy), while its failures (the Paris Commune or the Asturias revolt) are its most promising successes so far, for us and for the future." (*Internationale Situationniste* #7.)

2

The Commune was the biggest festival of the nineteenth century. Underlying the events of that spring of 1871 one can see the insurgents' feeling that they had become the masters of their own history, not so much on the level of "governmental" politics as on the level of their everyday life. (Consider, for example, the *games* everyone played with their weapons: they were in fact playing with power.) It is *also* in this sense that Marx should be understood when he says that "the most important social measure of the Commune was its own existence in acts."

3

Engels's remark, "Look at the Paris Commune—*that* was the dictatorship of the proletariat," should be taken seriously in order to reveal what the dictatorship of the proletariat as a political regime is not (the various forms of dictatorship over the proletariat in the name of the proletariat).

4

It has been easy to make perfectly justified criticisms of the Commune's incoherence, of its obvious lack of an *apparatus*. But as the problem of political apparatuses seems far more complex to us today than the would-be heirs of the Bolshevik-type apparatus claim it to be, it is time we examine the Commune not just as an outmoded example of revolutionary primitivism, all of whose mistakes are easily overcome, but as a positive experiment whose whole truth has not been rediscovered or fulfilled to this day.

5

The Commune had no leaders. And this at a time when the idea of the necessity of leaders was universally accepted in the proletarian movement. This is the first reason for its paradoxical successes and failures. The official organizers of the Commune were incompetent (if measured up against Marx or Lenin, or even Blanqui). But on the other hand, the various "irresponsible" acts of that moment are precisely what is needed for the continuation of the revolutionary movement of our own time (even if the circumstances restricted almost all those acts to the purely destructive level—the most famous example being the rebel who, when a suspect bourgeois insisted that he had never had anything to do with politics, replied, "That's precisely why I'm going to kill you").

6

The vital importance of the general arming of the masses was manifested practically and symbolically from the beginning to the end of the movement. By and large the right to impose popular will by force was not surrendered and left to any specialized detachments. This exemplary autonomy of the armed groups had its unfortunate counterpart in their lack of coordination: at no point in the offensive or defensive struggle against Versailles did the people's forces attain real military effectiveness. It should be borne in mind, however, that the Spanish revolution was lost—as, in the final analysis, was the civil war itself—in the name of such a transformation into a "republican army." The contradiction between autonomy and coordination would seem to have stemmed largely from the technological level of the period.

7

The Commune represents *the only realization of a revolutionary urbanism* to date—attacking on the spot the petrified signs of the dominant organization of life, understanding social space in political terms, refusing to accept the innocence of any monument. Anyone who reduces this to some "lumpenproletarian nihilism," some "irresponsibility of the *pétroleuses*," should specify what he believes to be of positive value in the prevailing society and worth preserving (it will turn out to be almost everything). "All space is already occupied by the enemy . . . . Authentic urbanism will appear when the absence of this occupation is created in certain zones. What we call construction starts there. It can be clarified by the *positive void* concept developed by modern physics." ("Elementary Program of Unitary Urbanism," *IS* #6.)

8

The Paris Commune succumbed less to the force of arms than to the force of habit. The most scandalous practical example was the refusal to use the artillery to seize the French National Bank when money was in such desperate need. Throughout the entire existence of the Commune the Bank remained a Versaillese enclave in Paris, defended by nothing more than a few rifles and the myth of property and theft. The other ideological habits proved in every respect equally disastrous (the resurrection of Jacobinism, the defeatist strategy of the barricades in memory of 1848, etc.).

9

The Commune shows how those who defend the old world always benefit, at one point or another, from the complicity of revolutionaries; and above all from those who *think out* the revolution and who turn out to still *think like* the defenders. In this way the old world retains bases (ideology, language, customs, tastes) among its enemies, and uses them to reconquer the terrain it has lost. (Only the thought-in-acts natural to the revolutionary proletariat escapes it irrevocably: the Tax Bureau went up in flames.) The real "fifth column" is in the very minds of revolutionaries.

10

The story of the arsonists who during the last days of the Commune went to destroy Notre-Dame, only to find themselves confronted by an armed batallion of Commune artists, is rich in meaning: it is a fine example of direct democracy. It shows, moreover, the kind of problems still to be resolved in the perspective of the power of the councils. Were those artists right to defend a cathedral in the name of eternal aesthetic values—and in the final analysis, in the name of museum culture—while other people wanted to express themselves then and there by making this destruction symbolize their absolute defiance of a society that, in its moment of triumph, was about to consign their entire lives to silence and oblivion? The artist partisans of the Commune, acting as specialists, already found themselves in conflict with an extremist form of struggle against alienation. The Communards must be criticized for not having dared to answer the totalitarian terror of power with the use of the totality of their weapons. Everything indicates that the poets who at that moment actually expressed the Commune's inherent poetry were simply *wiped out*. The Commune's mass of unaccomplished acts enabled its tentative actions to be turned into "atrocities" and the memory of it to be censored. Saint-Just's remark, "Those who make revolution half way only dig their own graves," also explains his own *silence*.

11

Theoreticians who examine the history of this movement by placing themselves at the omniscient viewpoint of God, which characterized the classical novelist, can easily prove that the Commune was objectively doomed to failure and could not have been fulfilled. They forget that for those who really lived it, the fulfillment *was already there*.

316

12

The audacity and inventiveness of the Commune must obviously be measured not in relation to our time, but in terms of the prevailing political, intellectual and moral attitudes of its own time, in terms of the *interdependence* of all the prevailing banalities that it blasted to pieces. In the same way, the interdependence of presently prevailing banalities (rightist or leftist) is a measure of the inventiveness we can expect of a comparable explosion today.

13

The social war of which the Commune was one moment is still being fought today (though its superficial conditions have changed considerably). In the task of "making conscious the unconscious tendencies of the Commune" (Engels), the last word is still to be said.

14

For almost twenty years in France the leftist Christians and the Stalinists have agreed, in memory of their national anti-German front, to stress the aspect of national disarray and offended patriotism in the Commune. (According to the current Stalinist line, "the French people petitioned to be better governed" and were finally driven to desperate measures by the treachery of the unpatriotic right wing of the bourgeoisie.) In order to refute this pious nonsense it would suffice to consider the role played by all the foreigners who came to fight for the Commune. As Marx said, the Commune was more than anything the inevitable battle, the climax of 23 years of struggle in Europe by "our party."

GUY DEBORD, ATTILA KOTÁNYI, RAOUL VANEIGEM
18 March 1962

THE SITUATIONISTS AND THE NEW FORMS OF ACTION IN POLITICS AND ART

(excerpts)

[. . .] Just as, on the one hand, we have been severe in preventing ambitious intellectuals or artists incapable of really understanding us from mingling in the situationist movement, and in rejecting and denouncing various falsifications (of which Nashist "situationism" is the most recent example), so, on the other hand, we recognize the perpetrators of new radical acts as being situationist, and are determined to support them and never disavow them, even if many among them are not yet fully conscious but are only moving toward the coherence of the revolutionary program of today.

We will limit ourselves to mentioning a few examples of acts of which we totally approve. On 16 January some revolutionary students in Caracas made an armed attack on an exposition of French art and carried off five paintings, which they declared they would return in exchange for the release of political prisoners. The forces of order recovered the paintings after a gun battle with Winston Bermudes, Luis Monselve and Gladys Troconis. A few days later some other comrades threw two bombs on the police van that was transporting the recovered paintings, which unfortunately did not succeed in destroying it. This is clearly an exemplary way to treat the art of the past, to bring it back into play in life and reestablish priorities. Since the death of Gauguin ("I tried to establish the right to dare everything") and of Van Gogh, their work, recuperated by their enemies, has probably never received from the cultural world an homage so true to their spirit as the act of these Venezuelans. During the Dresden insurrection of 1849 Bakunin proposed, unsuccessfully, that the insurgents take the paintings out of the museums and put them on a barricade at the entrance to the city, to see if this might inhibit the firing of the attacking troops. We can thus see how this skirmish in Caracas links up with one of the highest moments of the revolutionary rising of the last century, and even goes further. [. . .]

Finally, the action of the English comrades [the "Spies for Peace"] who in April divulged the location and plans of the "Regional Seat of Government #6" bomb shelter has the immense merit of revealing the degree already attained by state power in its organization of the terrain, its highly advanced establishment of a totalitarian functioning of authority. This totalitarian organization is not exclusively tied to the perspective of war. It is, rather, the universally maintained threat of a thermonuclear war which now, in the East and the West, serves to keep the masses submissive and to organize *shelters for state power*, to reinforce the psychological and material defenses of the ruling classes' power. [. . .]

The English have just made a decisive contribution to the study of this disease [the pathological excess expressed in the proliferation of bomb shelters] and thus also to the study of "normal" society. This study is itself inseparable from a struggle that has not feared to defy the old national taboos of "treason" by breaking the *secrecy* that is vital in so many regards for the smooth functioning of power in modern society, behind the thick screen of its glut of "information." The sabotage in England was later extended, in spite of the efforts of the police and numerous arrests: secret military headquarters in the country were invaded by surprise (and some officials present were photographed against their will) and forty telephone lines of British security centers were systematically blocked by the continuous dialing of ultrasecret numbers that had been publicized.

In order to salute and extend this first attack against the ruling organization of social space, we have organized this "Destruction of RSG 6" demonstration in Denmark.* [. . .]

GUY DEBORD
June 1963

ON THE POVERTY OF STUDENT LIFE

considered in its
economic, political, psychological, sexual
and especially intellectual aspects,
with a modest proposal for its remedy

by members of the Situationist International
and students of Strasbourg

AFGES, November 1966

To make shame more shameful still by making it public

It is pretty safe to say that the student is the most universally despised creature in France, apart from the policeman and the priest. But the reasons for which he* is despised are often false reasons reflecting the dominant ideology, whereas the reasons for which he is justifiably despised from a revolutionary standpoint remain repressed and unavowed. The partisans of false opposition, however, are aware of these faults—faults which they themselves share. They invert their real contempt into a patronizing admiration. Thus the impotent leftist intelligentsia (from *Les Temps Modernes* to *L'Express*) goes into raptures over the so-called "rise of the students," and the actually declining bureaucratic organizations (from the "Communist" Party to the UNEF) jealously contend for his "moral and material" support. We will show the reasons for this concern with the student and how they are rooted in the dominant reality of overdeveloped capitalism. We are going to use this pamphlet to denounce them one by one: the suppression of alienation necessarily follows the same path as alienation.

Until now all the analyses and studies of student life have ignored the essential issues. None of them go beyond the viewpoint of academic specializations (psychology, sociology, economics) and thus they remain fundamentally erroneous. Fourier long ago exposed this *"methodical myopia"* of treating fundamental questions without relating them to modern society as a whole. The fetishism of facts masks the essential category, and one can't see the *totality* for all the details. Everything is said about this society except what it really is: a society dominated by the *commodity* and the *spectacle*. The sociologists Bourderon and Passedieu, in their study *Les Héritiers: les étudiants et la*

319

culture, remain impotent in face of the few partial truths they have succeeded in demonstrating. For all their good intentions they fall back into professorial morality, the inevitable Kantian ethic of a *real democratization through a real rationalization of the teaching system*—that is, of the teaching of the system; while their disciples, the Kravetzes,[1] compensate for their petty-bureaucratic resentment with a hodgepodge of outdated revolutionary phraseology.

Modern capitalism's spectacularization[2] of reification allots everyone a specific role within a general passivity. The student is no exception to this rule. His is a provisional role, a rehearsal for his ultimate role as a conservative element in the functioning of the commodity system. Being a student is a form of initiation.

This initiation magically recapitulates all the characteristics of mythical initiation. It remains totally cut off from historical, individual and social reality. The student leads a double life, poised between his present status and the utterly separate future status into which he will one day be abruptly thrust. Meanwhile his schizophrenic consciousness enables him to withdraw into his "initiation group," forget about his future and bask in the mystical trance of a present sheltered from history. It is not surprising that he avoids facing his situation, particularly its economic aspects: in our "affluent society" he is still a pauper. More than 80% of students come from income groups above the working class, yet 90% of them have less money than the lowest worker. Student poverty is an anachronism in the society of the spectacle: it has yet to attain the new poverty of the new proletariat. In a period when more and more young people are increasingly breaking free from moral prejudices and family authority as they are subjected to blunt, undisguised exploitation at the earliest age, the student clings to his irresponsible and docile "protracted infancy." Belated adolescent crises may bring occasional brushes with his family, but he uncomplainingly accepts being treated as a baby by the various institutions that govern his daily life. (If they ever stop shitting in his face, it's only to come around and bugger him.)

Student poverty is merely the most gross expression of the colonization of all domains of social practice. The projection of all social guilty conscience onto the students masks the poverty and servitude of everyone.

But our contempt for the student is based on quite different reasons. He is contemptible not only for his real poverty, but also for his complacency in the face of every kind of poverty, his unhealthy propensity to wallow in his own alienation in the hope, amid the general lack of interest, of arousing interest in his particular lacks. The requirements of modern capitalism determine that most students will become mere *lower cadres* (that is to say, with a function equivalent to that filled

---

1. Marc Kravetz, a slick orator well known among the UNEF politicos, made the mistake of venturing into "theoretical research": in 1964 he published a defense of student unionism in *Les Temps Modernes*, which he then denounced in the same periodical a year later.

2. It goes without saying that we use the concepts of *spectacle*, *role*, etc., in the situationist sense.

320

by the skilled worker in the nineteenth century).[3] Faced with the evident poverty of this imminent "compensation" for his shameful present poverty, the student prefers to turn toward his present and decorate it with illusory glamor. The very compensation is too lamentable for him to look forward to it; tomorrow will be as dismal and mediocre as yesterday. So he takes refuge in an unreally lived present.

The student is a stoical slave: the more chains authority binds him with, the freer he thinks he is. Like his new family, the university, he takes himself for the most "independent" social being, whereas he is in fact *directly and conjointly* subservient to the two most powerful systems of social authority: the family and the state. He is their well-behaved and grateful child. Following the logic of the *submissive child*, he shares all the values and mystifications of the system and concentrates them in himself. The illusions that formerly had to be imposed on white-collar workers are now willingly internalized and transmitted by the mass of future lower cadres.

If the ancient social poverty produced the most grandiose systems of compensation in history (religions), the student, in his marginal poverty, can find no other consolation than the most shopworn images of the ruling society, the burlesque repetition of all its alienated products.

As an ideological being, the French student *always arrives too late*. All the values and enthusiasms that are the pride of his closed little world have long ago been condemned by history as laughable and untenable illusions.

Once upon a time the universities had a certain prestige; the student persists in the belief that he is lucky to be there. But he came too late. His mechanical, specialized education is as profoundly degraded (in relation to the former level of general bourgeois culture)[4] as his own intellectual level, because the modern economic system demands a mass production of uneducated students who have been rendered incapable of thinking. The university has become an institutional organization of ignorance; "high culture" itself is being degraded in the assembly-line production of professors, *all* of whom are cretins and most of whom would get the bird from any audience of highschoolers. But the student is unaware of all this; he continues to listen respectfully to his masters, conscientiously suppressing all critical spirit so as to immerse himself in the mystical illusion of being a "student," someone seriously devoted to learning *serious* things, in the hope that his professors will ultimately impart to him the ultimate truths of the world. Till then—a menopause of the spirit. The future revolutionary society will naturally condemn all the ado of the lecture halls and classrooms as mere *noise*, verbal pollution. The student is already a very bad joke.

The student is unaware that history is also altering even his "closed" little world. The famous "crisis of the university," that detail of a more

---

3. But without the revolutionary consciousness: the worker did not have the illusion of promotion.

4. We are referring to the culture of Hegel or the Encyclopédistes, not to that of the Sorbonne or the Ecole Normale Supérieure.

general crisis of modern capitalism, remains the object of a deaf-mute dialogue among various specialists. It simply expresses the difficulties of this special sector of production in its belated adjustment to the overall transformation of the productive apparatus. The remnants of the old liberal bourgeois university ideology are becoming banalized as its social basis is disappearing. During the era of free-trade capitalism, when the liberal state left the university a certain marginal freedom, the latter could imagine itself an independent power. But even then it was intimately bound to the needs of that type of society: notably the need to give the privileged minority an adequate general education before they took up their positions within the ruling class. Hence the ridiculousness of those nostalgic professors,[5] embittered at having lost their former function as guard-dogs serving the future masters for the considerably less noble function of sheep-dogs in charge of herding white-collar flocks to their respective factories and offices in accordance with the needs of the planned economy. These professors hold up their archaisms as an alternative to the technocratization of the university and imperturbably continue to purvey scraps of "general" culture to audiences of future specialists who will not know how to make any use of them.

More serious, and thus more dangerous, are the modernists of the Left and those of the UNEF led by the "extremists" of the FGEL, who demand a "reform of the university structure," a "reintegration of the university into social and economic life," i.e. its adaptation to the needs of modern capitalism. The various faculties and schools that once supplied "general culture" to the ruling class, though still retaining some of their anachronistic prestige, are being transformed into force-feeding factories for the accelerated rearing of lower and middle cadres. Far from contesting this historical process, which is subordinating one of the last relatively autonomous sectors of social life to the demands of the commodity system, these progressives protest against delays and inefficiencies in its completion. They are the partisans of the future cybernetized university, which is already emerging here and there.[6] The commodity system and its modern servants—these are the enemy.

But all these struggles naturally take place over the head of the student, somewhere in the heavenly realm of his masters. The whole of his life is out of his control, the whole of *life* is beyond him.

Because of his acute economic poverty the student is condemned to a paltry form of *survival*. But, always self-satisfied, he parades his very ordinary indigence as if it were an original "lifestyle": he makes a virtue of his shabbiness and affects to be a bohemian. "Bohemianism" is far from an original solution in any case, but the notion that one could live a really bohemian life without a complete and definitive

---

5. No longer daring to speak in the name of philistine liberalism, they invoke fantasized freedoms of the universities of the Middle Ages, that epoch of "democracy of non-freedom."

6. See "Correspondence with a Cybernetician" in *Internationale Situationniste* #9 and the situationist tract *La tortue dans la vitrine* directed against the neoprofessor A. Moles.

break with the university milieu is ludicrous. But the student bohemian (and every student likes to pretend that he is a bohemian at heart) clings to his imitative and degraded version of what is, in the best of cases, only a mediocre individual solution. Even elderly provincial ladies know more about life than he does. He is so "unconventional" that thirty years after Wilhelm Reich,[7] that excellent educator of youth, he continues to follow the most traditional forms of amorous-erotic behavior, reproducing the general relations of class society in his intersexual relations. His susceptibility to recruitment as a militant for any cause is an ample demonstration of his real impotence.

In spite of his more or less loose use of time within the margin of individual liberty allowed by the totalitarian spectacle, the student avoids adventure and experiment, preferring the security of the strait-jacketed daily space-time organized for his benefit by the guardians of the system. Though not constrained to separate his work and leisure, he does so of his own accord, all the while hypocritically proclaiming his contempt for "study fiends." He accepts every separation and then attends his religious, sports, political or union club to bemoan the absence of communication. He is so stupid and so miserable that he voluntarily submits himself to the University Psychological Aid Centers (BAPUs), those agencies of psycho-police control established by the avant-garde of modern oppression and naturally hailed as a great victory for student unionism.[8]

But the real poverty of student everyday life finds its immediate, fantastic compensation in the opium of cultural commodities. In the cultural spectacle the student finds his natural place as a respectful disciple. Although he is close to the production point, access to the real Sanctuary of Culture is denied him; so he discovers "modern culture" as an *admiring spectator*. In an era when *art is dead* he remains the most loyal patron of the theaters and film clubs and the most avid consumer of the packaged fragments of its preserved corpse displayed in the supermarkets for affluent housewives. Consuming unreservedly and uncritically, he is in his element. If the "Culture Centers" didn't exist, the student would have invented them. He is the living proof of all the platitudes of American market research: a conspicuous consumer, complete with artificially induced different attitudes toward products that are identical in their nullity, with an irrational preference for Brand X (Pérec or Godard, for example) and an irrational prejudice against Brand Y (Robbe-Grillet or Lelouch, perhaps).

And when the "gods" who produce and organize his cultural spectacle take human form on the stage, he is their main public, their perfect spectator. Students turn out *en masse* to their most obscene exhibitions. When the priests of different churches present their amorphous dialogues (seminars of "Marxist" thought, conferences of Catholic intellectuals) or when the literary debris come together to bear

---

7. See *The Sexual Struggle of Youth* and *The Function of the Orgasm*.

8. With the rest of the population, a straitjacket is necessary to force them to appear before the psychiatrist in his fortress asylum. But with students it suffices to let them know that advanced outposts of control have been set up in their ghetto: they rush there in such numbers that they have to wait in line to get in.

witness to their impotence (five thousand students attending a forum on "What are the possibilities of literature?"), who but students fill the halls?

Incapable of real passions, the student seeks titillation in the passionless polemics between the celebrities of Unintelligence: Althusser — Garaudy — Sartre — Barthes — Picard — Lefebvre — Levi-Strauss — Halliday — Châtelet — Antoine . . . and between their rival ideologies whose function is to mask real problems by expatiating over false ones: Humanism — Existentialism — Structuralism — Scientism — New Criticism — Dialectico-naturalism — Cyberneticism — *Planète*-ism — Metaphilosophism . . .

He thinks he is avant-garde if he has seen the latest Godard, or bought the latest Argumentist book,[9] or participated in the latest happening organized by Lapassade, that asshole. He discovers the latest trips as fast as the market can produce its ersatz version of long outmoded (though once important) ventures; in his ignorance he takes every rehash for a cultural revolution. His principal concern is always to maintain his cultural status. He takes pride in buying, like everyone else, the paperback reprints of important and difficult texts that "mass culture" is disseminating at an accelerating pace.[10] Unfortunately he doesn't know how to read. He contents himself with fondly gazing at them.

His favorite reading matter is the press that specializes in promoting the frenzied consumption of cultural novelties; he docilely accepts its pronouncements as guidelines for his tastes. He revels in *L'Express* or *Le Nouvel Observateur*; or perhaps he prefers *Le Monde*, which he feels is an accurate and truly "objective" newspaper, though he finds its style somewhat too difficult. To deepen his general knowledge he turns to *Planète*, the slick magical magazine that removes the wrinkles and blackheads from old ideas. With such guides he hopes to gain an understanding of the modern world and become politically conscious.

For in France, more than anywhere else, the student is content to be *politicized*. But his political participation is mediated by the same *spectacle*. Thus he seizes upon all the pitiful tattered remnants of a Left that was annihilated *more than forty years ago* by "socialist" reformism and Stalinist counterrevolution. The rulers are well aware of this defeat of the workers movement, and so are the workers themselves, though more confusedly. But the student remains ignorant of all that, and continues to participate blithely in the most laughable demonstrations that never draw anybody but students. This is political false consciousness in its virgin state, a fact that makes the universities a happy hunting ground for the manipulators of the dying bureaucratic organizations (from the "Communist" Party to the UNEF). These bureaucrats totalitarianly program the student's political options. Occasionally there are deviationary tendencies and slight im-

9. On the *Arguments* gang and the disappearance of its organ, see the tract *Into the Trashcan of History*, distributed by the Situationist International in 1963.

10. In this regard one cannot too highly recommend the solution already practiced by the most intelligent, which consists in stealing them.

pulses of "independence," but after a period of token resistance the dissidents are reincorporated into an order they have never fundamentally questioned.[11] The "Revolutionary Communist Youth," whose title is a case of ideological falsification gone mad (they are neither revolutionary nor communist nor young), pride themselves on having rebelled against the Party, then join the Pope in appealing for "Peace in Vietnam."

The student takes pride in his opposition to the "archaisms" of the de Gaulle regime, but he does this by unwittingly appealing to *older crimes* (such as those of Stalinism in the era of Togliatti, Garaudy, Khrushchev and Mao). His "youthful" attitudes are thus really even more *archaic* than the regime's—the Gaullists do after all understand modern society well enough to administer it.

But this is not the student's only archaism. He feels obliged to have general ideas on everything, to unearth a coherent world-view capable of lending meaning to his need for nervous activity and asexual promiscuity. As a result he falls prey to the last doddering missionary efforts of the churches. He rushes with atavistic ardor to adore the putrescent carcass of God and cherishes all the decomposing remains of prehistoric religions in the belief that they enrich him and his time. Along with elderly provincial ladies, students form the social category with the highest percentage of admitted religious adherents. Everywhere else priests have been insulted or beaten off, but university clerics openly continue to bugger thousands of students in their spiritual shithouses.

We should add that there do exist some students of a tolerable intellectual level. These latter easily get around the miserable regulations designed to control the more mediocre students, and they are able to do so precisely because they have *understood the system*, because they despise it and know themselves to be its enemies. They are in the educational system to get the best it has to offer: namely, grants. Exploiting the contradiction that, for the moment at least, obliges the system to maintain a small, relatively independent academic "research" sector, they are calmly going to carry the germs of sedition to the highest level: their open contempt for the system is the counterpart of a lucidity that enables them to outdo the system's own lackeys, especially intellectually. They are already among the theorists of the coming revolutionary movement, and take pride in beginning to be feared as such. They make no secret of the fact that what they extract so easily from the "academic system" is used for its destruction. For the student cannot revolt against anything without revolting against his *studies*, though the necessity of this revolt is felt less naturally by him than by the worker, who spontaneously revolts against his condition as worker. But the student is a product of modern society just like Godard and Coca-Cola. His extreme alienation can be contested only through a contestation of the entire society. This critique can in no way be carried out on the student terrain: the student, insofar as

---

11. The latest adventures of the "Union of Communist Students" and its Christian counterparts show that all these students are united on one fundamental principle: unconditional submission to hierarchical superiors.

he defines himself as such, identifies himself with a pseudovalue that hinders him from becoming aware of his real dispossession, and he thus remains at the height of false consciousness. But everywhere where modern society is beginning to be contested, young people are taking part in that contestation; and this revolt represents the most direct and thorough critique of student behavior.

It is not enough for theory to seek its realization in practice; practice must seek its theory

After a long period of slumber and permanent counterrevolution, the last few years have seen the first gestures of a new period of contestation, most visibly among young people. But the society of the spectacle, in its representation of itself and its enemies, imposes its own ideological categories on the world and its history. It reassuringly presents everything that happens as if it were part of the natural order of things, and reduces really new developments that herald its *supersession* to the level of superficial consumer novelties. In reality the revolt of youth against the way of life imposed on it is nothing other than a premonitory sign of a vaster subversion that will embrace all those who are feeling more and more the impossibility of *living* in this society, a prelude to the next revolutionary era. With their usual methods of inverting reality, the dominant ideology and its daily mouthpieces reduce this real historical movement to a socio-natural category: the Idea of Youth. Thus any new revolt of youth is presented as merely the eternal revolt of youth that recurs with each generation, only to fade away "when the young man becomes involved in the serious business of production and is given real, concrete aims." The "youth revolt" has been subjected to a veritable journalistic inflation that presents people with this spectacle of "revolt" so that they will forget to participate in it. It presents it as an aberrant but necessary social safety valve that has its part to play in the smooth functioning of the system. This revolt against the society reassures the society because it supposedly remains partial, pigeonholed in the *apartheid* of "youth problems" (analogous to "women's issues" or the "black question") and is soon outgrown. In reality, if there is a "youth problem" in modern society, it simply consists in the fact that youth feels the profound crisis of this society most acutely and tries to express it. This youth is a product par excellence of modern society, whether it chooses total integration into it or the most radical refusal of it. What is surprising is not that youth is in revolt, but that the "adults" are so resigned. But the reason for this is historical, not biological: the previous generation lived through all the defeats and swallowed all the lies of the long, shameful disintegration of the revolutionary movement.

In itself, "Youth" is a publicity myth profoundly linked to the capitalist mode of production, as an expression of its dynamism. This illusory primacy of youth became possible with the economic recovery after World War II resulting from the mass entry into the market of a whole new category of more pliable consumers; this consumer *role* carried with it an integration into the society of the spectacle. But the official ideology is once again finding itself in contradiction with socio-economic reality (lagging behind it), and it is precisely the youth who have first asserted an irresistible rage to live and are spontaneously revolting against the daily boredom and dead time that the old world continues to produce in spite of all its modernizations. The rebellious segment of youth expresses a pure, nihilist rejection without the consciousness of a perspective of supersession. But such a perspective is being sought and developed everywhere in the world. It must attain the coherence of theoretical critique and the practical organization of this coherence.

At the most primitive level, the deliquents all over the world express with the most evident violence their refusal to be integrated. But the abstractness of their refusal gives them no chance to escape the contradictions of a system of which they are a spontaneous negative product. The delinquents are produced by every aspect of the present *order*: the urbanism of the housing projects, the decomposition of values, the extension of an increasingly boring consumer leisure, the growing police-humanist control over every aspect of daily life, the economic survival of a family unit that has lost all significance. They despise work *but* they accept commodities. They want now everything the spectacle offers them, but they can't afford to pay for it. This fundamental contradiction dominates their entire existence and it smothers their strivings for real freedom in the use of their time, for self-assertion and for the formation of a sort of community. (Their microcommunities recreate a primitivism on the margin of developed society, and the poverty of this primitivism inevitably recreates hierarchy within the gang. This hierarchy, which can fulfill itself only in wars with other gangs, *isolates* each gang and each individual within the gang.) In order to get out of this contradiction the delinquent must come around to working in order to buy the commodities—and to this end a whole sector of production is devoted specifically to his recuperation as a consumer (motorcycles, electric guitars, clothes, records, etc.)—or else he is forced to attack the laws of the commodity, either in a rudimentary manner, by stealing it, or in a conscious manner by advancing toward a revolutionary critique of the world of the commodity. Consumption "mellows out" the behavior of these young rebels and their revolt falls back into the worst conformism. For the delinquents only two futures are possible: the awakening of revolutionary consciousness or blind obedience in the factories.

The *Provos* are the first form of supersession of the experience of the delinquents, the organization of its first political expression. They were born out of an encounter between a few dregs from the world of decomposed art in search of a career and a mass of young rebels in search of self-expression. Their organization enabled both sides to advance toward and achieve a new type of contestation. The "artists" contributed a few notions about play, though still quite mystified and decked out in a patchwork of ideological garments; the young rebels had nothing to offer but the violence of their revolt. From the inception of their organization the two tendencies have remained distinct; the theoryless masses have found themselves under the tutelage of a small clique of dubious leaders who have tried to maintain their "power" by developing an ideology of the "provotariat." Their neoartistic reformism has prevailed over the possibility that the delinquents' violence might extend itself to the plane of ideas in an attempt to supersede art. The Provos are an expression of the last reformism produced by modern capitalism: that of everyday life. Although nothing short of an uninterrupted revolution will be able to change life, the Provo hierarchy—like Bernstein with his vision of transforming capitalism into socialism by means of reforms—believes that a few improvements can alter everyday life. By opting for the fragmentary, the Provos end up accepting the totality. To give themselves a base, their leaders have concocted the ridiculous ideology of the provotariat (an artistico-political salad thrown together out of the mildewed leftovers of a feast they have never known). This new provotariat is contrasted with the supposed passivity and "bourgeoisification" of the proletariat (eternal refrain of all the cretins of the century). Because they despair of a total change, they despair of the only force capable of bringing about that change. The proletariat is the motor of capitalist society and thus its mortal threat: everything is designed to repress it—parties, bureaucratic unions, police (who attack it more often than they do the Provos), the colonization of its entire life—because it is the only really menacing force. The Provos have understood none of this; they remain incapable of criticizing the production system and thus remain prisoners of the system as a whole. And when an antiunion workers' riot inspired the Provo base to join in with the direct violence, their bewildered leaders were left completely behind and could find nothing better to do than denounce "excesses" and appeal for nonviolence. These leaders, whose program had advocated provoking the authorities so as to reveal their repressiveness, ended up by complaining that they had been provoked by the police. And they appealed over the radio to the young rioters to let themselves be guided by the "Provos," i.e. by the leaders, who have amply demonstrated that their vague "anarchism" is nothing but one more lie. To arrive at a revolutionary critique, the rebellious Provo base has to begin by revolting against its own leaders, which means linking up with the objective revolutionary forces of the proletariat and dumping people like Constant and De Vries (the one the official artist of the Kingdom of Holland, the other a failed parliamentary candidate and an admirer of the English police). Only in this way can the Provos link up with the authentic modern contestation of which they are already one of the fledgling expressions. If they really want to change the world, they have no use for those who are content to paint it white.

By revolting against their studies, the American students have automatically called in question a society that needs such studies. And their revolt (at Berkeley and elsewhere) against the university hierarchy has from the start asserted itself as a *revolt against the whole social system based on hierarchy and the dictatorship of the economy and the state.* By refusing to accept the business and institutional roles for which their specialized studies have been designed to prepare them, they are profoundly calling in question a system of production that alienates all activity and its products from their producers. For all their groping and confusion, the rebelling American youth are already seeking a coherent revolutionary alternative from within the "affluent society." Their movement remains largely attached to two relatively incidental aspects of the American crisis—the blacks and Vietnam—and the small "New Left" organizations suffer from this fact. Their form evinces authentic strivings for democracy, but the weakness of their subversive content continually causes them to fall into dangerous contradictions. Due to their extreme political ignorance and naïve illusions about what is really going on in the world, their hostility to the traditional politics of the old organizations is easily recuperated. *Abstract* opposition to their society leads them to admire or support its most conspicuous enemies: the "socialist" bureaucracies of China or Cuba. Thus a group like the "Resurgence Youth Movement" can in the same breath condemn the state and praise the "Cultural Revolution" directed by the most elephantine bureaucracy of modern times: Mao's China. At the same time, these semilibertarian and nondirective organizations, due to their obvious lack of content, are constantly in danger of slipping into the ideology of "group dynamics" or into the closed world of the sect. The mass consumption of drugs is an expression of real poverty and a protest against this real poverty: it is a fallacious search for freedom in a world without freedom, a religious critique of a world that has itself superseded religion. It is no accident that it is so prevalent in the beatnik milieu (that right wing of the youth revolt), where ideological refusal coexists with acceptance of the most fantastic superstitions (Zen, spiritualism, "New Church" mysticism and other rotten carcasses like Gandhiism and Humanism). In their search for a revolutionary program the American students make the same mistake as the Provos and proclaim themselves "the most exploited class in society"; they must henceforth understand that they have no interests distinct from all those who are subject to commodity slavery and the generalized oppression.

In the East, bureaucratic totalitarianism is also beginning to produce its own forces of negation. The youth revolt there is particularly virulent, but the only information on it must be derived from the denunciations of it in official publications and from the police measures undertaken to contain it. From these sources we learn that a segment of the youth no longer "respects" moral and family order (which still exists there in its most detestable bourgeois form), gives itself over to "debauchery," despises work and no longer obeys the Party police. The USSR has set up a special ministry for the express purpose of combating this new delinquency. Alongside this diffuse revolt, a more coherently formulated contestation is striving to express itself; groups and clandestine journals appear and disappear depending on the fluctuations of police repression. So far the most important act has been the publication of the *Open Letter to the Polish Communist Party* by the young Poles *Kuron* and *Modzelewski*, which expressly affirms the necessity of "abolishing the present production relations and social relations" and recognizes that in order to accomplish this, "revolution is inevitable." The Eastern intelligentsia is seeking to make conscious and clearly formulate the reasons of the critique that the workers have concretized in East Berlin, Warsaw and Budapest: the proletarian critique of bureaucratic class power. This revolt is placed in the difficult situation of having to pose and solve real problems at one fell swoop. In other countries struggle is possible but the goal remains mystified. In the Eastern bureaucracies the struggle is without illusions and the goals are known; the problem is to devise the forms that can open the way to their realization.

In England the youth revolt found its first organized expression in the antibomb movement. This partial struggle, rallied around the vague program of the *Committee of 100*—which was capable of bringing 300,000 demonstrators into the streets—accomplished its most beautiful action in spring 1963 with the "Spies for Peace" scandal.[12] For lack of radical perspectives, it inevitably fell back, recuperated by traditional political manipulators and nobleminded pacifists. But the specifically English archaisms in the control of everyday life have not been able to hold out against the assault of the modern world, and the accelerating decomposition of secular values is engendering profoundly revolutionary tendencies in the critique of all aspects of the prevailing way of life.[13] The struggles of the British youth must link up with those of the British working class, which with its shop steward movement and wildcat strikes remains one of the most combative in the world. The victory of these two struggles is only possible if they work out common perspectives. The collapse of the Labour government is an additional factor that could be conducive to such an alliance. Such an encounter will touch off explosions compared to which the Amsterdam Provo riot will be child's play. Only in this way can a real revolutionary movement arise that will answer practical needs.

Japan is the only advanced industrialized country where this fusion of student youth and radical workers has already taken place.

The *Zengakuren*, the well-known organization of revolutionary students, and the *League of Young Marxist Workers* are the two major organizations formed on the common orientation of the *Revolutionary Communist League.** This formation is already tackling the problem of revolutionary organization. Simultaneously and without illusions it combats Western capitalism and the bureaucracy of the so-called socialist countries. It already groups together several thousand students and workers organized on a democratic and antihierarchical basis, with all members participating in all the activities of the organization. The Japanese revolutionaries are the first in the world to carry on large organized struggles in the name of an advanced revolutionary program and with a substantial mass participation. In demonstration after demonstration thousands of workers and students have poured into the streets to wage violent struggle with the Japanese police. However, the RCL lacks a complete and concrete analysis of the two systems it fights with such ferocity. It has yet to define the precise nature of bureaucratic exploitation, just as it has yet to ex-

---

12. When the partisans of the antibomb movement discovered, made public and then invaded the ultrasecret fallout shelter reserved for members of the government.

13. One thinks here of the excellent journal *Heatwave*, which seems to be evolving toward an increasingly rigorous radicality.*

plicitly formulate the characteristics of modern capitalism, the critique of everyday life and the critique of the spectacle. The Revolutionary Communist League is still fundamentally a vanguard political organization, an heir of the best features of the classical proletarian organizations. It is presently the most important revolutionary grouping in the world, and should henceforth be a pole of discussion and a rallying point for the new global revolutionary proletarian critique.

To create at last a situation that goes beyond the point of no return

"To be avant-garde means to move in step with reality" (*IS #8*). The radical critique of the modern world must now have the *totality* as its object and its objective. This critique must be brought to bear on the world's real past, on its present reality and on the prospects for transforming it. We cannot grasp the whole truth of the present world, much less formulate the project of its total subversion, unless we are capable of *revealing* all its *hidden history*, unless we subject the entire history of the international revolutionary movement, initiated over a century ago by the Western proletariat, to a demystified critical scrutiny. "This movement against the whole organization of the old world came to an end long ago" (*IS #7*). *It failed.* Its last historical manifestation was the Spanish proletarian revolution, defeated in Barcelona in May 1937. But its official "failures" and "victories" must be judged in the light of their eventual consequences, and their essential truths brought back to light. In this regard we can agree with Karl Liebknecht's remark, on the eve of his assassination, that "some defeats are really victories, while some victories are more shameful than any defeat." Thus the first great "defeat" of proletarian power, the Paris Commune, is in reality its first great *victory* in that for the first time the early proletariat demonstrated its historical capacity to organize all aspects of social life *freely*. Whereas its first great "victory," the Bolshevik revolution, ultimately turned out to be its most disastrous defeat. The triumph of the Bolshevik order coincided with the international counterrevolutionary movement that began with the crushing of the Spartakists by German "Social Democracy." The commonality of the jointly victorious Bolshevism and reformism went deeper than their apparent antagonism, for the Bolshevik order too turned out to be merely a new variation on the old theme, a new guise of the old order. The results of the Russian counterrevolution were, internally, the establishment and development of a new mode of exploitation, *bureaucratic state-capitalism*, and externally, the growth of a "Communist" International whose spreading branches served the sole purpose of defending and reproducing their Russian model. Capitalism, in its bureaucratic and bourgeois variants, won a new lease on life, over the dead bodies of the sailors of Kronstadt, the peasants of the Ukraine and the workers of Berlin, Kiel, Turin, Shanghai, and finally Barcelona.

The Third International, ostensibly created by the Bolsheviks to combat the degenerate social-democratic reformism of the Second International and to unite the vanguard of the proletariat in "revolutionary communist parties," was too closely linked to the interests of its founders to ever bring about a *real socialist revolution* anywhere. In reality the Third International was essentially a continuation of the Second. The Russian model was rapidly imposed on the Western workers' organizations and their evolutions were thenceforth one and the same. The totalitarian dictatorship of the bureaucracy, the new ruling class, over the Russian proletariat found its echo in the subjection of the great mass of workers in other countries to a stratum of political and union bureaucrats whose interests had become clearly contradictory to those of their base. While the Stalinist monster haunted working-class consciousness, capitalism was becoming bureaucratized and overdeveloped, resolving its internal crises and proudly proclaiming this new victory to be permanent. In spite of apparent variations and oppositions, a single social form dominates the world, and the principles of the *old world* continue to govern our *modern world*. The tradition of the dead generations still haunts the minds of the living.

Opposition to the world offered from within it, on its own terrain, by supposedly revolutionary organizations is only an apparent opposition. Such opposition, propagating the worst mystifications and invoking more or less rigid *ideologies*, ultimately helps consolidate the dominant order. The unions and political parties forged by the working class as tools for its own emancipation have become mere safety valves, regulating mechanisms of the system, the private property of leaders working toward their own particular emancipation by using them as stepping stones to roles within the ruling class of a society they never dream of calling into question. The party program or union statute may contain vestiges of "revolutionary" phraseology, but their practice is everywhere *reformist*—and all the more so now that capitalism itself has become officially reformist. Wherever the parties have been able to seize power—in countries more backward than 1917 Russia—they have only reproduced the Stalinist model of totalitarian counterrevolution.[14] Elsewhere, they have become the static and necessary complement[15] to the self-regulation of bureaucratized capitalism, the token opposition indispensable for maintaining its police-humanism. Vis-à-vis the worker masses, they remain the unfailing and unconditional defenders of the bureaucratic counterrevolution and the docile creatures of its foreign policy. They are the bearers of the biggest lie in a world of lies, working to perpetuate the universal dictatorship of the economy and the state. As the situationists put it, "A universally dominant social system, tending toward totalitarian self-regulation, is only apparently being combated by false forms of opposition that remain on

---

14. The parties have striven to industrialize these countries through classic primitive accumulation at the expense of the peasantry, accelerated by bureaucratic terror.

15. For 45 years the French "Communist" Party has not taken a single step toward seizing power; and the same is true in all the advanced countries that have not fallen under the heel of the "Red" Army.

the system's own terrain and thus only serve to reinforce it. Bureaucratic pseudosocialism is only the most grandiose of these guises of the old world of hierarchy and alienated labor."

As for student unionism, it is nothing but the travesty of a travesty, the useless burlesque repetition of a long degenerated labor unionism.

The theoretical and practical denunciation of Stalinism in all its forms must be the basic banality of all future revolutionary organizations. It is clear that in France, for example, where economic backwardness has delayed awareness of the crisis, the revolutionary movement can be reborn only over the dead body of Stalinism. The constantly reiterated watchword of the *last* revolution of prehistory must be: *Stalinism must be destroyed.*

This revolution must *definitively* break with its own prehistory and derive all its poetry from the future. Little groups of "militants" claiming to represent the authentic Bolshevik heritage are voices from beyond the grave; in no way do they herald the future. These bits of debris from the great shipwreck of the "revolution betrayed" will always come around to defense of the USSR; this is their scandalous betrayal of revolution. They can scarcely maintain their illusions outside the famous underdeveloped countries,[16] where they serve to reinforce theoretical underdevelopment. From *Partisans* (organ of reconciled Stalino-Trotskyist currents) to all the tendencies and semi-tendencies squabbling over the dead body of Trotsky within and outside the *Fourth International*, the same revolutionary *ideology* reigns, with the same theoretical and practical incapacity to grasp the problems of the modern world. Forty years of counterrevolution separate them from the Revolution. Since this is not 1920, they can only be wrong (and they were already wrong in 1920).

The dissolution of the "ultraleftist" group *Socialisme ou Barbarie* after its division into two fractions—"Cardanist-modernist" and "traditional Marxist" (*Pouvoir Ouvrier*)—is proof, if any were needed, that there can be no revolution outside the modern, nor any modern thought outside the reinvention of the revolutionary critique (*IS #9*). Any separation between these two aspects inevitably falls back either into the museum of revolutionary prehistory or into the modernism of the system, into the dominant counterrevolution: *Voix Ouvrière* or *Arguments*.

As for the various "anarchist" groups, they possess nothing beyond this ideology reduced to a mere label, and they are all prisoners of this label. The incredible *Le Monde Libertaire*, obviously edited by *students*, attains the most fantastic degree of confusion and stupidity. Since they tolerate each other, they would *tolerate anything*.

The dominant social system, which flatters itself on its permanent modernization, must now be confronted with a worthy opponent: the equally modernized negation that it is itself producing.[17] Leave the dead to bury their dead. The practical demystifications of the historical movement are exorcizing the phantoms that haunted revolutionary

---

16. On their role in Algeria, see "The Class Struggles in Algeria" in *IS #10*.

17. "Address to Revolutionaries . . ." in *IS #10*.

consciousness; the revolution of everyday life is finding itself face to face with the immensity of its tasks. Both revolution and the life it announces must be reinvented. If the revolutionary project remains fundamentally the same—the abolition of class society—this is because the conditions giving rise to that project have nowhere been radically transformed. But this project must be taken up again with a new radicality and coherence, learning from the failure of previous revolutionaries, so that its partial realization will not merely bring about a new division of society.

Since the struggle between the system and the new proletariat can only be in terms of the *totality*, the future revolutionary movement must abolish anything within itself that tends to reproduce the alienation produced by the *commodity system*—the system dominated by commodity labor. It must be the living critique of that system, the negation embodying all the elements necessary for its *supersession*. As Lukács correctly showed, revolutionary organization is this necessary mediation between theory and practice, between man and history, between the mass of workers and the proletariat *constituted as a class*. (Lukács's mistake was to believe that the Bolshevik Party fulfilled this role.) If they are to be realized in practice, "theoretical" tendencies and differences must immediately be translated into organizational questions. Everything ultimately depends on how the new revolutionary movement resolves the organization question, on whether its organizational forms are consistent with its essential project: *the international realization of the absolute power of workers councils* as prefigured in the proletarian revolutions of this century. Such an organization must stress the radical critique of all the foundations of the society it combats: commodity production, *ideology* in all its guises, the state and the separations it imposes.

The rock on which the old revolutionary movement foundered was the separation of theory and practice. Only the supreme moments of proletarian struggles overcame this split and discovered their own *truth*. No organization has yet leaped this Rhodus, bridged this gap. *Ideology*, no matter how "revolutionary" it may be, always serves masters; it is the *alarm signal* revealing the presence of the enemy fifth column. This is why the critique of ideology must in the final analysis be the central problem of revolutionary organization. Lies are a product of the alienated world and they cannot appear within an organization claiming to bear the *social truth* without that organization thereby becoming one more lie in a world of lies.

All the positive aspects of the power of workers councils must already be embryonically present in any revolutionary organization aiming at their realization. Such an organization must wage a mortal struggle against the Leninist theory of organization. The 1905 revolution and the Russian workers' spontaneous self-organization into soviets was already a critique in acts[18] of that baneful theory. But the Bolshevik movement persisted in believing that working-class spontaneity could not go beyond "trade-union consciousness" and was in-

---

18. After the theoretical critique of it by Rosa Luxemburg.

capable of grasping "the totality." This amounted to decapitating the proletariat so that the Party could put itself "at the head" of the revolution. Contesting the proletariat's historical capacity to emancipate itself, as Lenin did so ruthlessly, means contesting its capacity to totally run future society. In such a perspective, the slogan "All power to the soviets" meant nothing more than the conquest of the soviets by the Party and the installation of the party state in place of the withering-away "state" of the armed proletariat.

"All power to the soviets" must once again be our slogan, but literally this time, without the Bolshevik ulterior motives. The proletariat can play the *game* of revolution only if the stakes are the *entire* world; otherwise it is nothing. The sole form of its power, *generalized self-management*, cannot be shared with any other power. Because it is the actual dissolution of all powers, it can tolerate no limitation (geographical or otherwise); any compromises it accepts are immediately transformed into concessions, into surrender. "Self-management must be both the means and the end of the present struggle. It is not only what is at stake in the struggle, but also its adequate form. ... It is itself the material it works on, and its own presupposition." ("The Class Struggles in Algeria.")

A unitary critique of the world is the guarantee of the coherence and truth of a revolutionary organization. To tolerate the existence of an oppressive system in one region or another (because it presents itself as "revolutionary," for example) amounts to recognizing the legitimacy of oppression. To tolerate alienation in any one domain of social life amounts to admitting an inevitability of all forms of reification. It is not enough to be for the power of workers councils in the abstract; it is necessary to demonstrate what it means concretely: the suppression of commodity production and therefore of the proletariat. Despite their superficial disparities, all existing societies are governed by the *logic of the commodity*; it is the basis of their totalitarian self-regulation. Commodity reification is the *essential* obstacle to a total emancipation, to the free construction of life. In the world of commodity production, praxis is not pursued in accordance with autonomously determined aims, but in accordance with the directives of external forces. Economic laws take on the appearance of natural laws, but their power depends *solely* on the "absence of consciousness of those who participate in them."

The essence of commodity production is the loss of self in the chaotic and unconscious creation of a world totally beyond the control of its creators. In contrast, the radically revolutionary core of generalized self-management is everyone's conscious direction of the whole of life. The self-management of commodity alienation would only make everyone the programmers of their own survival—squaring the capitalist circle. The task of the workers councils will thus be not the self-management of the existing world, but its uninterrupted qualitative transformation: the concrete supersession of the commodity (that enormous detour in the history of man's production of himself).

This supersession naturally implies the suppression of *work* and its replacement by a new type of free activity, and thus the abolition of one of the fundamental splits of modern society: that between an increasingly reified labor and a passively consumed leisure. Presently decomposing groups like *Socialisme ou Barbarie* or *Pouvoir Ouvrier*,[19] although adhering to the modern watchword of Workers' Power, continue to follow in the path of the old workers movement in envisioning a reformism of labor through its "humanization." But work itself must now be attacked. Far from being "utopian," the suppression of work is the first condition for the effective supersession of commodity society, for the abolition within each person's life of that separation between "free time" and "work time"—those complementary sectors of alienated life—that is a continual expression of the commodity's internal contradiction between use-value and exchange-value. Only when this opposition is overcome will people be able to make their vital activity subject to their will and consciousness and see themselves in a world they themselves have created. The democracy of workers councils is the solution to all the present separations. It makes "everything that exists outside individuals impossible."

The conscious domination of history by the people who make it—this is the entire revolutionary project. Modern history, like all past history, is the product of social praxis, the (unconscious) result of all human activities. In the era of totalitarian domination, capitalism has produced its own new religion: the *spectacle*. The *spectacle* is the terrestrial realization of *ideology*. Never has the world been so inverted. "And like the 'critique of religion,' the critique of the spectacle is today the essential precondition of any critique" (*IS* #9).

Humanity is historically confronted with the problem of *revolution*. The more and more grandiose material and technological means are equalled only by the more and more profound dissatisfaction of everyone. The bourgeoisie and its Eastern heir, the bureaucracy, are incapable of using this overdevelopment—which will be the basis of the *poetry* of the future—precisely because they both must strive to *maintain an old order*. The most they can use it for is to reinforce their police control. They do nothing but accumulate *capital* and therefore *proletarians*—a proletarian being someone who has no power over his life and who knows it. It is the new proletariat's historical fortune to be the only consequent heir to the valueless riches of the *bourgeois world*—riches that it must transform and *supersede* in the perspective of the project of the total man pursuing the total appropriation of nature and of his own nature. This realization of man's *nature* can only mean the infinite multiplication and full satisfaction of the *real desires* which the *spectacle* represses into the darkest corners of the revolutionary unconscious, and which it can realize only fantastically in the dreamlike delirium of its publicity. The actual realization of real desires—that is to say, the abolition of all the pseudoneeds and pseudodesires that the system manufactures daily in order to perpetuate its own power—cannot take place without the suppression and positive supersession of the commodity spectacle.

Modern history can be liberated, and its innumerable acquisitions can be freely put to use, only by the forces that it represses: the workers

---

19. In contrast, a group like ICO, by shunning any organization or coherent theory, condemns itself to nonexistence.

without power over the conditions, the meaning or the products of their own activities. In the nineteenth century the proletariat was already the heir of philosophy; now it has become the heir of modern art and of the first conscious critique of everyday life. It cannot suppress itself without at the same time realizing art and philosophy. To transform the world and to change life are one and the same thing for the proletariat, the inseparable passwords to its suppression as a class, the dissolution of the present reign of necessity, and the finally possible accession to the reign of freedom. The radical critique and free reconstruction of all values and patterns of behavior imposed by alienated reality are its maximum program, and free creativity in the construction of all moments and events of life is the only *poetry* it can acknowledge, the poetry made by all, the beginning of the revolutionary festival. Proletarian revolutions will be *festivals* or nothing, for festivity is the very keynote of the life they announce. *Play* is the ultimate principle of this festival, and the only rules it can recognize are to live without dead time and to enjoy without restraints.

This text may be freely reproduced, translated
or adapted, even without mentioning the source.*

UNTITLED PROGRAMATIC STATEMENTS

I

Internationale Situationniste is the journal of an international group of theorists who over the last few years have undertaken a radical critique of modern society—a critique of what it really is and of all its aspects.

As the situationists see it, a universally dominant system, tending toward totalitarian self-regulation, is only apparently being combated by false forms of opposition which remain on the system's own terrain and thus only serve to reinforce it. Bureaucratic pseudosocialism is only the most grandiose of these guises of the old world of hierarchy and alienated labor. The developing concentration of capitalism and the diversification of its machine on a global scale have given rise on one hand to the forced consumption of commodities produced in abundance, and on the other to the control of the economy (and all of life) by bureaucrats who own the state; as well as to direct and indirect colonialism. But this system is far from having found a definitive solution to the incessant revolutionary crises of the historical epoch that began two centuries ago, for a new critical phase has opened: in Berkeley and Warsaw, in the Asturias and the Kivu, the system is refuted and combated.

The situationists consider that the indivisible perspective of this opposition is the real abolition of all class societies, of commodity production, of wage labor; the supersession of art and all cultural acquirements by their reentry into play through free creation in everyday life—and thus their true realization; the direct fusion of revolutionary theory and practice in an experimental activity that precludes any petrification into "ideologies," which express the authority of experts and which always serve authoritarian expertise.

The factors put in question by this historical problem are the rapid extension and modernization of the fundamental contradictions within the existing system and between the system and human desires. The social force that has an interest in—and is alone capable of—resolving these contradictions is all the workers who are powerless over their own lives, unable to control the fantastic accumulation of material possibilities that they produce. Such a possible resolution has already been sketched out in the model of the democratic workers council that makes all decisions itself. The movement required from this new proletariat for it to form itself into a class, unmediated by any leadership, is the sum of intelligence of a world without intelligence. The situationists declare that they have no interest outside the whole of this movement. They lay down no particular principles on which to base a movement that is real, that is in fact being born before our very eyes. Faced with the struggles that are beginning in various countries over various issues, the situationists see their task as putting forward the whole of the problem, its coherence, its theoretical and therefore practical unity. In short, within the various phases of the overall struggle they constantly represent the interest of the whole movement.

1965*

II

The only reason the situationists do not call themselves communists is so as not to be confused with the cadres of pro-Soviet or pro-Chinese antiworker bureaucracies, leftovers from the great revolutionary failure that ultimately extended the universal dictatorship of the economy and the state.

The situationists do not constitute a particular party in competition with other self-styled "workers" parties.

The situationists refuse to reproduce internally the hierarchical conditions of the dominant world. They denounce everywhere the specialized politics of heads of hierarchical groups and parties, who base the oppressive force of their delusory future class power on the organized passivity of their militants.

The situationists do not put forward ideological principles on which to mold and thus direct the movement of proletarians. They consider that up to now revolutionary ideology has only changed hands: the point now is to dissolve it by opposing it with revolutionary theory.

338

The situationists are the most radical current of the proletarian movement in many countries, the current that constantly pushes forward. Striving to clarify and coordinate the scattered struggles of revolutionary proletarians, they help to draw out the implications of their actions. Striving to attain the highest degree of international revolutionary consciousness, with the new theoretical critique they have been able to predict everywhere the return of the modern revolution. They are feared not for the power they hold, but for the use they make of it.

The situationists have no interests separate from the interests of the proletariat as a whole. They expect everything and have nothing to fear from so-called "excesses," which signal the critical profundity of the new era and the positive richness of the liberated everyday life arising out of it.

In all the present struggles the situationists constantly bring to the forefront the question of abolishing "everything that exists separately from individuals" as the decisive question for the movement working to negate the existing society.

The situationists have nothing to hide of their views or their aims. They openly declare that their only interest and their only goal is a social revolution going to the point where all powers are concentrated in the international federation of workers councils, the power of everyone over all aspects of everyday life—over all aspects of the economy, of the society, of history. It is therefore a matter not of transforming private or state property, but of abolishing it; not of mitigating class differences, but of abolishing classes; not of "improving" the present society, but of creating a new society; not of some partial success that would give rise to a new division, but of a thorough rejection of every new disguise of the old world.

The situationists have no doubt that the only possible program of modern revolution necessarily entails the formation of councils of all the workers, who by developing a clear awareness of all their enemies, become the sole power.

Today revolutionaries turn their attention especially to Italy, because Italy is on the eve of a general uprising toward social revolution.

ITALIAN SECTION OF THE S.I.
1969

May 1968
Documents

COMMUNIQUÉ

Comrades,

Considering that the Sud-Aviation factory at Nantes has been occupied for two days by the workers and students of that city,

and that today the movement is spreading to several factories (Nouvelles Messageries de la Presse Parisienne in Paris, Renault in Cléon, etc.),

THE SORBONNE OCCUPATION COMMITTEE
calls for

the immediate occupation of all the factories in France and the formation of Workers Councils.

Comrades, spread and reproduce this appeal as quickly as possible.

Sorbonne, 16 May 1968, 3:30 p.m.

WATCH OUT FOR MANIPULATORS!
WATCH OUT FOR BUREAUCRATS!

Comrades,

No one must be unaware of the importance of the GA [general assembly] this evening (Thursday, 16 May). For two days individuals one recognizes from having previously seen them peddling their party lines have succeeded in sowing confusion and in smothering the GAs under a barrage of bureaucratic manipulations whose clumsiness clearly demonstrates the contempt they have for this assembly.

This assembly must learn to make itself respected, or disappear. Two points must be discussed in priority:

—WHO IS IN CONTROL OF THE SECURITY MARSHALS? whose disgusting role is intolerable.

—WHY IS THE PRESS COMMITTEE—which *dares to censor the communiqués* that it is charged to transmit to the agencies—composed of apprentice journalists who are careful not to disappoint the ORTF bosses or jeopardize their future job possibilities?

Apart from this: as the workers are beginning to occupy several factories in France, FOLLOWING OUR EXAMPLE AND WITH THE SAME RIGHT WE HAVE, the Sorbonne Occupation Committee issued a statement approving of this movement at 3:00 this afternoon. The

343

central problem of the present GA is therefore to declare itself by a clear vote supporting or disavowing this appeal of its Occupation Committee. In the case of a disavowal, this assembly will then have taken the responsibility of reserving for the students a right that it refuses to the working class; and in that case it is clear that it will no longer want to concern itself with anything but a Gaullist reform of the university.

OCCUPATION COMMITTEE OF THE
AUTONOMOUS AND POPULAR SORBONNE UNIVERSITY
16 May 1968, 6:30 p.m.

SLOGANS TO BE SPREAD NOW
BY EVERY MEANS

(leaflets, announcements over microphones, comic strips, songs, graffiti, balloons on paintings in the Sorbonne, announcements in theaters during films or while disrupting them, balloons on subway billboards, before making love, after making love, in elevators, each time you raise your glass in a bar):

OCCUPY THE FACTORIES

POWER TO THE WORKERS COUNCILS

ABOLISH CLASS SOCIETY

DOWN WITH THE SPECTACLE-COMMODITY SOCIETY

ABOLISH ALIENATION

ABOLISH THE UNIVERSITY

HUMANITY WON'T BE HAPPY TILL THE LAST BUREAUCRAT
    IS HUNG WITH THE GUTS OF THE LAST CAPITALIST

DEATH TO THE COPS

FREE ALSO THE 4 GUYS CONVICTED FOR LOOTING DURING
    THE 6 MAY RIOT

OCCUPATION COMMITTEE OF THE
AUTONOMOUS AND POPULAR SORBONNE UNIVERSITY
16 May 1968, 7:00 p.m.

TELEGRAMS

17 MAY 1968 / PROFESSOR IVAN SVITAK PRAGUE CZECHO-
SLOVAKIA / THE OCCUPATION COMMITTEE OF THE AUTONO-
MOUS AND POPULAR SORBONNE SENDS FRATERNAL SALU-
TATIONS TO COMRADE SVITAK AND TO CZECHOSLOVAKIAN
REVOLUTIONARIES STOP LONG LIVE THE INTERNATIONAL
POWER OF THE WORKERS COUNCILS STOP HUMANITY WON'T
BE HAPPY TILL THE LAST CAPITALIST IS HUNG WITH THE
GUTS OF THE LAST BUREAUCRAT STOP LONG LIVE REVOLU-
TIONARY MARXISM

17 MAY 1968 / ZENGAKUREN TOKYO JAPAN / LONG LIVE THE
STRUGGLE OF THE JAPANESE COMRADES WHO HAVE OPENED
COMBAT SIMULTANEOUSLY ON THE FRONTS OF ANTI-STALIN-
ISM AND ANTI-IMPERIALISM STOP LONG LIVE FACTORY OC-
CUPATIONS STOP LONG LIVE THE GENERAL STRIKE STOP
LONG LIVE THE INTERNATIONAL POWER OF THE WORKERS
COUNCILS STOP HUMANITY WON'T BE HAPPY TILL THE LAST
BUREAUCRAT IS HUNG WITH THE GUTS OF THE LAST CAPI-
TALIST STOP OCCUPATION COMMITTEE OF THE AUTONO-
MOUS AND POPULAR SORBONNE

17 MAY 1968 / POLITBURO OF THE COMMUNIST PARTY OF THE
USSR THE KREMLIN MOSCOW / SHAKE IN YOUR SHOES BU-
REAUCRATS STOP THE INTERNATIONAL POWER OF THE
WORKERS COUNCILS WILL SOON WIPE YOU OUT STOP HU-
MANITY WON'T BE HAPPY TILL THE LAST BUREAUCRAT IS
HUNG WITH THE GUTS OF THE LAST CAPITALIST STOP LONG
LIVE THE STRUGGLE OF THE KRONSTADT SAILORS AND OF
THE MAKHNOVSHCHINA AGAINST TROTSKY AND LENIN STOP
LONG LIVE THE 1956 COUNCILIST INSURRECTION OF BUDA-
PEST STOP DOWN WITH THE STATE STOP LONG LIVE REVO-
LUTIONARY MARXISM STOP OCCUPATION COMMITTEE OF
THE AUTONOMOUS AND POPULAR SORBONNE

17 MAY 1968 / POLITBURO OF THE CHINESE COMMUNIST
PARTY GATE OF CELESTIAL PEACE PEKING / SHAKE IN YOUR
SHOES BUREAUCRATS STOP THE INTERNATIONAL POWER OF
THE WORKERS COUNCILS WILL SOON WIPE YOU OUT STOP
HUMANITY WON'T BE HAPPY TILL THE LAST BUREAUCRAT IS

HUNG WITH THE GUTS OF THE LAST CAPITALIST STOP LONG LIVE FACTORY OCCUPATIONS STOP LONG LIVE THE GREAT CHINESE PROLETARIAN REVOLUTION OF 1927 BETRAYED BY THE STALINIST BUREAUCRATS STOP LONG LIVE THE PROLETARIANS OF CANTON AND ELSEWHERE WHO HAVE TAKEN UP ARMS AGAINST THE SO-CALLED PEOPLE'S ARMY STOP LONG LIVE THE CHINESE WORKERS AND STUDENTS WHO HAVE ATTACKED THE SO-CALLED CULTURAL REVOLUTION AND THE MAOIST BUREAUCRATIC ORDER STOP LONG LIVE REVOLUTIONARY MARXISM STOP DOWN WITH THE STATE STOP OCCUPATION COMMITTEE OF THE AUTONOMOUS AND POPULAR SORBONNE

REPORT ON THE OCCUPATION
OF THE SORBONNE

The occupation of the Sorbonne that began Monday, 13 May, has inaugurated a new period in the crisis of modern society. The events now taking place in France foreshadow the return of the proletarian revolutionary movement in all countries. The movement that had already advanced from theory to struggle in the streets has now advanced to a struggle for power over the means of production. Modernized capitalism thought it had finished with class struggle—it's started up again! The proletariat no longer existed—but here it is again.

In surrendering the Sorbonne, the government counted on pacifying the student revolt, which had already succeeded in holding a section of Paris behind its barricades an entire night before being recaptured with great difficulty by the police. The Sorbonne was given over to the students in the hope that they would peacefully discuss their university problems. But the occupiers immediately decided to open it to the public to freely discuss the general problems of the society. This was thus a prefiguration of a *council*, a council in which even the students broke out of their miserable studenthood and ceased to be students.

To be sure, the occupation has never been total: a chapel and some remnants of administrative offices have been tolerated. The democracy has never been complete: future technocrats of the UNEF claimed to be making themselves useful and other political bureaucrats have also tried their manipulations. Workers' participation has remained very limited and the presence of nonstudents soon began to be questioned. Many students, professors, journalists and imbeciles of other occupations have come as spectators.

In spite of all these deficiencies, which are not surprising considering the contradiction between the scope of the project and the narrowness of the student milieu, the exemplary nature of the best aspects of this situation immediately took on an explosive significance. Workers could not fail to be inspired by seeing free discussion, the striving for a radical critique and direct democracy in action. Even limited to a Sorbonne liberated from the state, this was a revolutionary program developing its own forms. The day after the occupation of the Sorbonne the Sud-Aviation workers of Nantes occupied their factory. On the third day, Thursday the 16th, the Renault factories at Cléon and Flins were occupied and the movement began at the NMPP and at Boulogne-Billancourt, starting at Shop 70. Now, at the end of the week, 100 factories have been occupied while the wave of strikes, accepted but never initiated by the union bureaucracies, is paralyzing the railroads and developing toward a general strike.

The only power in the Sorbonne was the general assembly of its occupiers. At its first session, on 14 May, amidst a certain confusion, it had elected an Occupation Committee of 15 members revocable by it each day. Only one of the delegates, belonging to the Nanterre-Paris Enragés group, had set forth a program: defense of direct democracy in the Sorbonne and absolute power of workers councils as ultimate goal. The next day's general assembly reelected its entire Occupation Committee, which had not been able to accomplish anything by then. In fact, all the specialized groupings that had set themselves up in the Sorbonne followed the directives of a hidden "Coordination Committee" composed of volunteer and very moderating organizers responsible to no one. An hour after the reelection of the Occupation Committee one of the "coordinators" privately tried to declare it dissolved. A direct appeal to the base in the courtyard of the Sorbonne aroused a movement of protests which obliged the manipulator to retract himself. By the next day, Thursday the 16th, thirteen members of the Occupation Committee had disappeared, leaving two comrades, including the Enragés member, vested with the only delegation of power authorized by the general assembly—and this at a time when the gravity of the moment necessitated immediate decisions: democracy was constantly being flouted in the Sorbonne and factory occupations were spreading. The Occupation Committee, rallying around it as many Sorbonne occupiers as it could who were determined to maintain democracy there, at 3:00 p.m. launched an appeal for "the occupation of all the factories in France and the formation of workers councils." To disseminate this appeal, the Occupation Committee had at the same time to restore the democratic functioning of the Sorbonne. It had to take over or recreate from scratch all the services that were *supposed* to be under its authority: the loudspeaker system, printing facilities, interfaculty liaison, security. It ignored the squawking complaints of the spokesmen of various political groups (JCR, Maoists, etc.), reminding them that it was responsible only to the general assembly. It intended to report to it that very evening, but the Sorbonne occupiers' unanimous decision to march on Renault-Billancourt (whose occupation we had learned of in the meantime) postponed the session of the assembly until 2:00 p.m. the next day.

During the night, while thousands of comrades were at Billancourt, some unidentified persons improvised a general assembly, which broke up when the Occupation Committee, having learned of its existence, sent back two delegates to call attention to its illegitimacy.

Friday the 17th at 2:00 p.m. the regular assembly saw its rostrum occupied for a long time by self-appointed marshals belonging to the FER; and in addition had to interrupt the session for the second march on Billancourt at 5:00.

That evening at 9:00 the Occupation Committee was finally able to present a report of its activities. It was completely unsuccessful, however, in getting its actions discussed and voted on, in particular its appeal for the occupation of the factories, which the assembly did not take the responsibility of either disavowing or approving. Confronted with such indifference and confusion, the Occupation Committee had no choice but to withdraw. The assembly showed itself just as incapable of protesting against a new invasion of the rostrum by the FER troops, whose putsch seemed to be aimed at countering the provisional alliance of JCR and UNEF bureaucrats. The partisans of direct democracy immediately declared that they no longer had anything to do at the Sorbonne.

At the very moment that the example of the occupation is beginning to be taken up in the factories it is collapsing at the Sorbonne. This is all the more serious since the workers have against them a bureaucracy infinitely more entrenched than that of the student or leftist amateurs. In addition, the leftist bureaucrats, echoing the CGT in the hope of being accorded a little marginal role alongside it, abstractly separate the workers from the students, whom "they don't need lessons from." But in fact the students have already given a lesson to the workers precisely by occupying the Sorbonne and briefly initiating a really democratic discussion. All the bureaucrats tell us demogogically that the working class is grown up, in order to hide the fact that it is enchained—first of all by them (now or in their future hopes, depending on which group they're in). They counterpose their lying seriousness to "the festival" in the Sorbonne, but it was precisely this festiveness that bore within itself the only thing that is serious: the radical critique of prevailing conditions.

The student struggle is now left behind. Even more left behind are all the second-string bureaucratic leaderships that think it's a good idea to feign respect for the Stalinists at this very moment when the CGT and the so-called "Communist" Party are *trembling*. The outcome of the present crisis is in the hands of the workers themselves if they succeed in accomplishing in the occupation of their factories the goals toward which the university occupation was only able to make a rough gesture.

The comrades who supported the first Sorbonne Occupation Committee—the Enragés–Situationist International Committee, a number of workers and a few students—have formed a Council for Maintaining the Occupations: the maintaining of the occupations obviously being conceivable only through their quantitative and qualitative extension, which must not spare any existing regime.

COUNCIL FOR MAINTAINING THE OCCUPATIONS
Paris, 19 May 1968

FOR THE POWER OF THE WORKERS COUNCILS

In the space of ten days workers have occupied hundreds of factories, a spontaneous general strike has totally interrupted the activity of the country, and de facto committees have taken over many buildings belonging to the state. In such a situation—which in any event cannot last but must either extend itself or disappear (through repression or defeatist negotiations)—all the old ideas are swept aside and all the radical hypotheses on the return of the revolutionary proletarian movement are confirmed. The fact that the whole movement was *really* triggered five months ago by a half dozen revolutionaries of the "Enragés" group reveals even better how much the objective conditions were already present. At this very moment the French example is having repercussions in other countries and reviving the internationalism which is indissociable from the revolutions of our century.

The fundamental struggle today is between, on the one hand, the mass of workers—who do not have direct means of expressing themselves—and on the other, the leftist political and union bureaucracies that (even if merely on the basis of the 14% of the active population that is unionized) *control the factory gates* and the right to negotiate in the name of the occupiers. These bureaucracies are not workers' organizations that have degenerated and betrayed the workers, they are a mechanism for integrating the workers into capitalist society. In the present crisis they are the main protection of this shaken capitalism.

The de Gaulle regime may negotiate—essentially (if only indirectly) with the PCF-CGT—for the demobilization of the workers in exchange for some economic advantages; after which the radical currents would be repressed. Or "the left" may come to power and pursue the same policies, though from a weaker position. Or an armed repression may be attempted. Or, finally, the workers may take the upper hand by speaking for themselves and becoming conscious of goals as radical as the forms of struggle they have already put into practice. Such a process would lead to the formation of workers councils making decisions democratically at the rank-and-file level, federating with each other by means of delegates revocable at any moment, and becoming the sole deliberative and executive power over the entire country.

In what way could the prolongation of the present situation lead to such a prospect? Within a few days, perhaps, the necessity of starting certain sectors of the economy back up again *under workers' control* could lay the bases for this new power, a power which everything is already pushing to burst through the constraints of the unions and parties. The railroads and printshops would have to be put back into operation for the needs of the workers' struggle. New de facto authorities would have to requisition and distribute food. If money became devalued it might have to be replaced by vouchers backed by those new authorities. It is through such a *practical process* that the consciousness of the profound will of the proletariat can impose itself— the class consciousness that lays hold on history and brings about the workers' domination over all aspects of their own lives.

COUNCIL FOR MAINTAINING THE OCCUPATIONS
Paris, 22 May 1968

ADDRESS TO ALL WORKERS

Comrades,

What we have already done in France is haunting Europe and will soon threaten all the ruling classes of the world, from the bureaucrats of Moscow and Peking to the millionaires of Washington and Tokyo. *In the same way we have made Paris dance*, the international proletariat will again take up its assault on the capitals of all states, on all the citadels of alienation. The occupation of factories and public buildings throughout the country has not only blocked the functioning of the economy, it has brought about a general questioning of the society. A deep-seated movement is leading almost every sector of the population to seek a real change of life. It is now a revolutionary movement, a movement which lacks nothing but *the consciousness of what it has already done* in order to triumph.

What forces will try to save capitalism? The regime will fall unless it threatens recourse to arms (accompanied by the promise of new elections, which could only take place after the capitulation of the movement) or even resorts to immediate armed repression. As for the possible coming to power of the left, it too will try to defend the old world through concessions and through force. In this event, the best defender of such a "popular government" would be the so-called "Communist" Party, the party of Stalinist bureaucrats, which has fought the movement from the very beginning and which began to envisage the fall of the de Gaulle regime only when it realized it was no longer capable of being that regime's main guardian. Such a transitional government would really be "Kerenskyist" only if the Stalinists were beaten. All this will depend essentially on the workers' consciousness and capacities for autonomous organization: those who have already rejected the ridiculous accords that so gratified the union leaders need only discover that they cannot "win" much more within the framework of the existing economy, but that they can *take everything* by trans-

350

forming all the bases of the economy on their own behalf. The bosses can hardly pay more; but they can disappear.

The present movement did not become "politicized" by going beyond the miserable union demands regarding wages and pensions, demands which were falsely presented as "social questions." It is beyond *politics*: it is posing *the social question* in its simple truth. The revolution that has been in the making for over a century is returning. It can assert itself only in its own forms. It is already too late for a bureaucratic-revolutionary patching up. When a recently de-Stalinized André Barjonet calls for the formation of a common organization that would bring together "all the authentic forces of revolution . . . whether they march under the banner of Trotsky or Mao, of anarchy or situationism," we have only to recall that those who today follow Trotsky or Mao, to say nothing of the pitiful "Anarchist Federation," have nothing to do with the present revolution. The bureaucrats may now change their minds about what they call "authentically revolutionary"; authentic revolution does not have to change its condemnation of bureaucracy.

At the present moment, with the power they hold and with the parties and unions being what they are, the workers have no other choice but to organize themselves in unitary rank-and-file committees directly seizing all aspects of the reconstruction of social life, asserting their autonomy vis-à-vis any sort of politico-unionist leadership, ensuring their self-defense and federating with each other regionally and nationally. By taking this path they will become the sole real power in the country, the power of the *workers councils*. Otherwise the proletariat, because it is "either revolutionary or nothing," will again become a passive object. It will go back to watching television.

What defines the power of the councils? Dissolution of all external power; direct and total democracy; practical unification of decision and execution; delegates who can be revoked at any moment by those who have mandated them; abolition of hierarchy and independent specializations; conscious management and transformation of all the conditions of liberated life; permanent creative participation of the masses; internationalist extension and coordination. The present requirements are nothing less than this. Self-management is nothing less. *Beware of the recuperators* of every modernist variety—including even priests—who are beginning to talk of self-management or even of workers councils without acknowledging this *minimum*, because they in fact want to save their bureaucratic functions, the privileges of their intellectual specializations or their future as petty bosses!

In reality what is necessary now has been necessary since the beginning of the proletarian revolutionary project. People struggled for the abolition of wage labor, of commodity production, of the state. It was a matter of acceding to conscious history, of suppressing all separations and "everything that exists independently of individuals." Proletarian revolution has spontaneously sketched out its adequate form in the councils, in St. Petersburg in 1905 as in Turin in 1920, in Catalonia in 1936 as in Budapest in 1956. The maintaining of the old society, or the formation of new exploiting classes, has each time been by way of the suppression of the councils. Now the working class knows its enemies and its own appropriate methods of action. "Revolutionary organization has had to learn that it can no longer *fight alienation with alienated forms*" (*The Society of the Spectacle*). Workers councils are clearly the only solution, since all the other forms of revolutionary struggle have led to the opposite of what was aimed at.

ENRAGÉS–SITUATIONIST INTERNATIONAL COMMITTEE
COUNCIL FOR MAINTAINING THE OCCUPATIONS
30 May 1968

Internal SI Texts
(1969–1971)

PROVISIONAL STATUTES OF THE S.I.

Participation in the SI and National Sections

1. The SI is an international association of *individuals* who, having demonstrated an equality of capabilities—in general, not in every detail—for our common theoretical and practical activity, are equal in all aspects of its democratic management. Majority decision is executed by everyone; the minority has the *duty* to break if the issue in dispute seems to it to concern a fundamental matter among the previously recognized bases of agreement.

2. The SI organizes its activity on the basis of a division into national sections. This "national" criterion is understood in both geographical and cultural terms; it is possible, and desirable, that each section be itself partially international in its composition. Each section is also "national" in the sense that it engages in a central advanced activity in a given country and does not seek to subdivide into regional subgroups in that country. A section might envisage such a subdivision within itself in certain exceptional geographical conditions, but the SI would continue to relate to the section only as a single unit.

3. A member of the SI is *ipso facto* a member of any national section where he expresses his decision to live and participate. Every member is responsible before the ensemble of the SI; and the SI is collectively responsible for the known behavior of each of its members.

4. The general assembly of all the members of the SI is the only decision-making power over all theoretical and practical choices. To the exact degree that there exist practical obstacles to the presence of everyone, the SI recognizes a system of delegates representing each of the members. These delegates may or may not bear specific, imperative mandates. Decisions made by delegates are revocable by those who have mandated them if the mandates have been general (left open); they are not revocable in cases in which a delegate has correctly executed a specific mandate.

Organization of National Sections

5. Each national section, on its own responsibility and within the general guidelines adopted by the whole of the SI, democratically decides on all its activities and tactics on its own terrain. It alone decides on all aspects of the publications, contacts and projects it sees fit to pursue. If possible it publishes a journal, the editorial management of which is entirely in its own hands. It goes without saying that personally undertaken projects or theoretical hypotheses cannot be lim-

355

ited by the section, nor by the SI as a whole—except in cases where they are manifestly hostile to the SI's very bases.

6. Each national section is the sole judge, in its region, of breaks with persons on the outside and of *admissions* to the section. It is only responsible to the whole of the SI for guarding against anything that might lower the general level of the SI (cf. Article #3) or introduce a notable inequality among participants. The entire SI automatically recognizes and upholds all these breaks and admissions as soon as it is informed of them.

7. Each section is master of its exclusions. It must immediately furnish the reasons and all pertinent documents to all the other sections. In cases where the *facts* are disputed by the excluded comrades, or in cases where another *section* requests a new discussion bearing on *the very basis* of the dispute, these exclusions are suspended until a general conference of the SI (or a meeting of delegates) makes the final decision. As a general rule it is not admissible that theoretical or programatic oppositions—even serious ones—be dealt with by exclusion before a general meeting of the SI can discuss the matter. But all practical failings must be dealt with on the spot. Any divergence or choice that does not require exclusion allows for resignation.

8. On any theoretical or tactical question that has not met with unanimity during a discussion, each member is free to maintain his own opinion (as long as he does not break practical solidarity). If the same problems and divergences are met with on several successive occasions, the members who are in agreement on one of the options have the right to openly constitute a *tendency*, and to draft texts to clarify and sustain their point of view, until final resolution (by rediscovered unanimity, by a break or by a practical supersession of the divergence). Such texts may be circulated throughout the SI and may also appear in the publications of one or more sections. A tendency bearing on a general tactical problem should normally itself be international (thereby tracing a division within several sections).

9. In exceptional cases in which a situationist finds himself isolated and yet active on a concrete terrain (a country where he alone acts in the name of the SI) he alone must determine his activity, while remaining answerable to the SI as a whole.

10. The present national sections can agree to temporarily divide their contacts or activities in certain countries where no SI section exists, in accordance with considerations of common language or geographical proximity. Such a division must not be institutionalized nor must it notably increase the importance of one of the sections relative to the others.

11. Each national section will organize its own complete financial autonomy; but in this domain too it will, as its means permit, show solidarity with other sections that might be in need.

12. The general conference of the SI should meet as often as possible with all members, or at least the greatest possible number of them who can get there. In no case will it be held without the presence of at least one delegate from the section that would have the greatest difficulty in getting there.

13. To coordinate the SI's activity in the periods between conferences, meetings of *delegates* from the sections will be held as often as necessary. Each delegate disposes of the exact number of votes as the number of situationists from the section that has mandated him. In cases where two different positions exist within a section, such a section would have to have two delegates, each representing the number of votes supporting his position. Any member of the SI can participate and vote in these delegate meetings: but with his vote only; his vote therefore could not also be accorded to a delegate.

14. A section that cannot send a delegate to these meetings has the right to have itself represented by a situationist it chooses from another section, who will bear a specific mandate. The selected delegate should be informed enough in advance to allow him to refuse to uphold a mandate if he disapproves of its content. The section that cannot attend must then ask another situationist to defend its point of view.

Adopted 30 September 1969 at the 8th SI Conference in Venice.

PROVISIONAL THESES FOR THE DISCUSSION OF THE NEW THEORETICO-PRACTICAL ORIENTATIONS IN THE S.I.

(excerpts)

[. . .] The "April Theses" [Debord's theses on the "Organization Question"] have defined the SI's direction of progress as having to stress the dissemination of theory more than its elaboration, though the latter must be continued. I want to call attention to the fact that in order to accomplish this, *theory must first of all be put in a condition in which it can be effectively disseminated.* The first step of theory's advance *toward practice* takes place within theory itself. The dissemination of theory is thus inseparable from its development. The task of giving all our formulated or implicit theses a systematic and completely dialectical development, one that will bring them not only to the point where no one can any longer be unaware of them, but also to the point where they circulate among the workers "like hotcakes" and finally spark a definitive awakening of consciousness (a scandal)— this is certainly a theoretical task. But it also has an immediately practical utility; more precisely, it is both necessary and banal at this time when the SI is more or less led to play double or nothing with history.

Let us consider, for example, the excellent project of a *Situationist Manifesto* ("situationist" in the sense that it is done by situationists). I think that some of the difficulty in conceiving or "imagining" it must be attributed to the fact that we have yet to attain a certain level of theoretical development. By this I mean: the SI's theory is solid and is already maturing without becoming old (it being the last theory, assuming that this epoch's decisive revolution is the last revolution). But beyond the fact that the SI's Manifesto must be translated into all the languages spoken by the modern proletariat and disseminated among the workers, it should be in a position to last *at least* as well as the *Communist Manifesto*, without having the latter's defects and insufficiencies. It thus clearly cannot be a book, or an article (like the "Address to Revolutionaries of All Countries," for example) that would arbitrarily be called a "manifesto"; rather, it must be the geometric locus of the theory of modern society and the constant reference point of any future revolution. In this sense the project proposed by Guy of settling our accounts with Marx, by precisely assessing the degree of accuracy of his analyses and predictions, is a preliminary project, though not a necessary one. More generally, our theory certainly runs through all the SI articles, from which it may easily be drawn; but in them our theory has to be *reconstructed* by the reader. Our theory must now be unified and synthesized; to this end some additional analyses will be in order. In particular, the new simplicity of language we are seeking will certainly not be able to make our language *familiar* in the short run. Thus, before the Manifesto we might undertake the intermediate task of *scientifically* developing all our previously outlined themes (articles, pamphlets, books).

In contrast, it seems to me that René-Donatien's proposal of a *Wildcat Striker's Handbook* should be realized in the near future. To the brief history of the wildcat movement and the confirmation of its critique in acts of the unions, we could add a critique of the worker milieu and a brief final programatic chapter (defeat of the revolutionary movement, bureaucracy, spectacle-commodity society, return of social revolution, workers councils, classless society). This would then be a followup to *Student Poverty* corresponding to a "Strasbourg of the factories"; and the premise for the *Manifesto*.

Finally, it seems to me that the *Manifesto* project is the way in which we consider the necessity of an overall advance in the relations among our theses as well as between them and the real movement, and that it thus presupposes the realization of virtually all the other projected theoretical works that have been formulated in the course of this debate. For example, René and Raoul's proposed pamphlet on workers councils and the critique of Pannekoek; of the four major projects presented by Guy, at least the analysis of the "two concomitant failures" (insofar as they concern the process of the formation of conscious revolutionary organizations and the critique of the present process of purely spontaneous struggle) and, linked to the critique of the councils of the past and of councilist ideology, the definition of the armed coherence (the outline of a program) of the new councils, which "will be situationist or nothing." Thus the "preface to the practical critique of the modernized old world" opens up the quest for a real antireformism and for new forms of mass or generalized action in the proletariat's development toward an autonomous movement, the first phase of which is manifested by sabotage, wildcat strikes and above all by the new, *modern* demands. Besides this, it will still be necessary to come back to the question of historical class determination, notably that of the working class and its revolutionary *nature*, since it continues, because of its material position in society, to bear the consciousness of humanity as a whole. (Tony: "We must affirm that the workers can become revolutionary and that they are the only ones who will be so effectively." Raoul: "The path of the worker is direct: because he holds the fate of the commodity in his hands, all he has to do in order to break free of his brutalization and stop being a worker is to become conscious of his power. His positivity is immediate. The intellectual is at best negative . . . . Our critique must now bear essentially on the worker milieu, the motor of the proletariat.") Essential chapters are thus: the analysis of American capitalism and American society with its new déclassés; the critique of the most modern ideologies in relation to the *supersession* in acts of political economy and to the *delay* of the revolution (urbanism as destruction of the city; automation as liberatory in itself; ecology as present-day society's moral crisis which compels it to envisage the necessity to *itself* transform production relations; and, linked to all the above, "situationism": the critique of everyday life conducted by power itself); the analysis of the material presence in work and in everyday life of all the fragmentary elements of the totality, of the entire historical project, of that which the disappearance of art, the withering away of philosophy and the bankruptcy of science were unable to abolish, but have on the contrary injected everywhere by making it a definitive acquisition of the workers who are henceforth becoming their conscious inheritors. In general, there is a need to pursue the international strategy of revolution by politico-historical articles on different countries, that is to say, to continue to translate *The Society of the Spectacle* into terms like those of *The Decline and Fall of the Spectacle-Commodity Economy*, and even further in that direction. (A good translation of the former has yet to appear in Italy.)

Another project I think it is useful to add is this: beginning with a quick run-through of past revolutions (like Marx does in the *Manifesto*, Engels in the Introduction to *The Class Struggles in France*, Trotsky in *1905*, Pannekoek in *Workers Councils*), to develop an answer to the question, "Why will the next revolution be the last one?" The history of the workers movement—aspects of which have been treated in numerous articles and whose line is most fully traced in "The Proletariat as Subject and Representation" along with Riesel's critique of its highest moments, the councils, in *IS #12*—is still far from being an outworn topic on which everything of consequence has already been said. But what seems to me of even greater interest is to clarify why modern revolutions are henceforth, and for the first time, *exclusively proletarian*, and this at a time that is witnessing a decisive transformation of the workers and of work itself. Thus the revolutions of the past failed to attain, except marginally, that without which the modern revolution cannot even begin: the fact that victory can be achieved only by demanding the totality is now also expressed in the fact that there are no longer even any struggles except for the totality. One could start from a definitive critique and a *justification* of Russian Bolshevism (of Trotsky and Lenin) in relation to the real conditions of the Russian proletariat, those conditions being in their turn considered in relation to the conditions of the modern proletariat, which simultaneously make Bolshevism impossible and the councils necessary, "no longer at the periphery of what is ebbing, but at the center of what is rising." This would also be a verification of Marx's general thesis: As long as the existing production relations are not exhausted and have not entered into contradiction with the development of the productive forces (in the total historical sense that includes the development of the revolutionary class itself and of the consciousness that produces history), the revolution runs the greatest risk, which so far has never been avoided, of being defeated and leading to a modernization of domination. Each revolution sets loose all possibilities (in 1789 as in 1871 and 1917), but *in the final analysis* realizes only those that correspond to the level attained by the development of productive forces. Out of all the possibilities each revolution opens up for itself, it always seems to choose the nearest. All the possibilities are *there before it*, but some of them remain invisible while others are in everybody's mind: it is obviously everyday life, the immediate relation with the existing world, that puts them there. This can just as well be expressed by saying that in all revolutions the negation is never absolute, that the *positive* plays a large part, whether as the positive or inversely as the *determination* of the negation: if the condition of victory consists in reducing the former, it also always consists in reinforcing the latter, in reducing the positive to its objective basis.

It also seems to me that we have arrived at a point where we must go over all of situationist theory from top to bottom and rewrite it, concerning ourselves with the mediations that were treated too rapidly and with the interstitial questions that were left open. The recognized value of writing books, for example (books that in the present period the workers should begin to read), obviously stems from this necessity of superseding the opening moment of hostilities on a new front of modern critique. [. . .]

In conclusion, we ourselves don't have a head start at this beginning of an era: it's the beginning of an era for us too. The SI was able to trace, condensed in a few phrases, a few of the fundamental alternatives and perhaps all of the modern directions of development; but it is *precisely for this reason* that it is virtually a question of beginning over again (except for the spectacle, the critique of everyday life, a few brief though excellent politico-historical texts on revolutions, and of course the analysis of May). Our most notable theoretical acquisition so far is our theoretical method, which must be verified on a number of concrete aspects by deepening the theory itself in a decisive manner, precisely because "the force of spirit is only as great as its externalization." We have already written, in installments, our *German Ideology*, but our *1844 Manuscripts* will be the text Guy proposes for the historical detournement of Marx. We are beginning to consider our *Manifesto* at the same time as our *Critique of the Gotha Program*. Moreover, we don't come only from Hegel and Marx. The *Treatise on Living* has only opened the way; antiutopia is an unexplored territory from which no one has returned so far. It is this antiutopia, made possible on the bases of modern society, that must fill in the gaps left by Marx's "insufficiencies," just as it must itself be rendered dialectical and find a practical use. [. . .]

PAOLO SALVADORI
Milan, May 1970

REMARKS ON THE S.I. TODAY

(excerpts)

1

I am in agreement with Paolo's text ("Provisional Theses," May 1970) apart from two slight differences. First, on page 5 of the French translation, I think it is necessary to dialectize somewhat more the question of the relation of Bolshevism with the backwardness of productive forces in Russia, by pointing out the very role of Lenin's Bolshevism as a factor of retardation and regression for that central part of the productive forces: the revolutionary class's *consciousness*. Elsewhere (page 7) Paolo characterizes this formulation regarding what the SI has so far been able to accomplish—"the element of *promise* still surpasses the element of realization"—as a "slight exaggeration." On the contrary, I find this phrase to be completely true, without any exaggeration. With these theses of Paolo and a number of those expressed by various comrades, notably Raoul, René and Tony (as well as Gianfranco's very correct insistence on our developing certain economic analyses more concretely), it seems to me that we have a substantial basis from which we can more and more concretely develop both our strategical analysis and our theoretico-practical activity.

2

However, a few points remain to be dealt with that are *preliminary* to this debate (although they have already been touched on in texts by René, René-Donatien and myself). Paolo was right to parenthesize these preliminaries, for they have little direct relation with his programatic outline; and he has taken care, in a final note, to make the very significance of his text *contingent* on their practical resolution. We must thus now make an effort to define more concretely these difficulties, which are simultaneously *archaisms* in our own historical development and preconditions that we have to master before *really* undertaking the realization of a more advanced perspective. [. . .]

4

After four months of this orientation debate we have not seen any theoretical divergences appear; and this was fairly predictable. But one begins to wonder if these texts—which go in the same general direction and many of which contain excellent points—are not piling up like so many monologues *while scarcely being used*. To clarify what I mean regarding this underuse of theory: Just as Magritte could paint a pipe and then write on the painting, "This is not a pipe," to declare that one does not separate theory and practice *is not yet to practice theory*; and putting revolutionary theory into practice is not at all messianically postponed until the victory of the revolution, it is required throughout the *entire process* of revolutionary activity. Similarly (and this too is only a theoretical observation, but a necessary one), we all naturally refuse to consider even the most fundamentally theoretical activity as practically separable from even the most distinctly practical activity. To formulate the most general revolutionary theory is inconceivable without a very precise practice, and vice versa. And even in street fighting you still have to think! But if we leave aside these dialectical truisms on limiting cases, we can consider the most common *concrete* situation in which dialecticians reveal themselves as such (even if many of them don't have the intellectual background enabling them to *talk* about dialectics or to *write* theory at the dialectical level). People meet each other. They talk about how they understand the world and what they think they can do in it. They judge each other while judging their world; and each judges the judgments of the others. They agree with or oppose each other's projects. If there is a common project they have to know at different moments what this project has *become*. Their success or failure is measured by practice and their *consciousness of practice* (they may themselves, rightly or wrongly, characterize their failures and successes as secondary or decisive; the result may later be reversed and they may be aware of this or have forgotten it). Etc., etc. In a word, it is in this concerted and theorized action (which is also theory tested in action) that revolutionary dialecticians have to recognize as well as possible the *decisive elements* of a complex problem; the probable or modifiable (by them) *interaction* of these elements; the *essential character* of the moment as result, as well as its progressive negation. This is the *territory of the qualitative* where individuals, their acts, meaning and life know each other—*and where it is necessary to know how to know*. This is the presence of history in the everyday life of revolutionaries. You comrades will certainly say that the preceding lines are very banal; and this is quite true. [. . .]

6

Leaving aside the fact that all the *IS* issues have included some personal contributions (often notable and sometimes even discordant), it

362

can be said that for the most part the anonymous portions of issues 1–5 were produced in a truly collective manner. Issues 6–9 were still done relatively collectively, mainly by Raoul, Attila and me. But from number 10 on I have found myself left with *almost the entire responsibility* for preparing each publication. And what seems to *me* even more alarming and unhealthy is that I consider—unbiasedly, I hope—these three issues as precisely the best ones of the series! This situation was still somewhat obscured for me in numbers 10 and 11 by a small (but welcome) amount of collaboration from Mustapha (I'm still referring to the articles published without signature). We know that the disappearance of Mustapha right in the middle of the preparation of number 12 (though after he had turned in the article on Czechoslovakia) pushed things to a scandalous point, since at the same time the membership of the French section had doubled. I thus soon after resigned from the "direction" of the journal, mainly in order not to be an accomplice to a sort of spectacular lie, since we all had plenty of opportunity to be aware of our distance in this regard from our stated principles. A year has now gone by since this problem was posed, and the comrade editors are now beginning to put themselves in a position to resolve it. They will no doubt succeed by finally appropriating the methods that have "officially" been theirs for several years. [. . .]

8

This deficiency of *collective* activity (I don't mean to say, of course, that we haven't collectively discussed, decided on and carried out a certain number of actions or writings, even during the last two years) is mainly noticeable—in the French section—by a sort of general aversion to any critique aimed at a specific fact or at one of us. This was quite evident at the 14 July meeting. The slightest critique is felt as a total calling into question, an absolute distrust, a manifestation of hostility, etc. And this emotional reaction is not only expressed by the criticized comrade. The SI comrades are very quick and adept at judging the pro-situs* (the successive writings of the poor GRCA, for example), that is to say, something of very little importance. But almost everyone manifests a strange reluctance when it comes to judging anything about a member of the SI. They are visibly uneasy even when someone else of us does so. I cannot believe that some hollow politeness is at the origin of this. It must therefore be a certain fatigue that sets in at the moment of broaching the questions that really mark our *movement*: things we *risk* succeeding or failing in. In any case a critique is never *carried further* by other comrades and no one (except occasionally the criticized comrade) works to draw from it any conclusions that would be useful for our subsequent collective action. Thus the SI has a tendency to freeze into a sort of perpetual and admirable present (as if a more or less admirable past was continued in it). This not very historical or practical harmony is only broken in two situations, in one case really, in the other only apparently. When a critique is really taken seriously and given practical consequences (because the event is so glaring that everyone demands this conclusion) an individual is excluded. He is cut off from the harmonious communion, perhaps even without ever having been criticized before, or only once briefly. The *apparent* break in our habitual comfort happens this way: A critique is made or a defect of our action is pointed out. Everyone goes along with this critique, often *without even bothering to express themselves* on it; the point seems clear and undeniable, but boring (and little attention is given to really remedying it). But if someone has insisted on the point, everyone admits that the detail is indeed a bad thing. And everyone immediately decides that it must not continue, that things must change, etc. But since no one bothers with the practical ways and means, this remains a pious hope and the thing may well recur ten times; and by the tenth time everyone *has already forgotten the ninth*. The general feeling, expressed not so much in the responses as in the silences, is clearly: "Why make a drama out of it?" But this is a false idea because it's not a question of a drama and the choice is not between drama and passivity. But in this way the problem, when it eventually is dealt with, is dealt with only dramatically, as many of our exclusions have shown. [. . .]

9

[. . .] I have mentioned the prompt critique of the errors of the pro-situs, not in order to say that it is not in itself justified, but in order to note that the pro-situs are not our principal reference point (any more than ICO or the leftist bureaucrats). Our principal reference point is ourselves, it is *our own operation*. The underdevelopment of internal criticism in the SI clearly signifies, at the same time that it contributes toward, the underdevelopment of our (theoretico-practical) action. [. . .]

11

I think that all this is only a symptom of a correctible deficiency: several situationists' *lack of cohabitation with their own practice*. I almost always remember the times I have been mistaken; and I acknowledge them rather often *even when no one reminds me of them*. I am led to think that this is because I am rarely mistaken, having never concealed the fact that I have nothing to say on the numerous subjects in which I am ignorant, and habitually keeping in mind several contradictory hypotheses on the possible development of events when I don't yet discern the qualitative leap. In speaking here for myself I would nevertheless like to believe that, as Raoul would put it, I am also speaking for some others. And, by anticipation, for all those comrades who will decide to consciously self-manage their own basic activity. [. . .]

15

The style of organization defined by the SI and that we have tried to realize is not that of the councils or even that which we have outlined for revolutionary organizations in general; it is *specific*, linked to our task as we have understood it so far. This style has had obvious successes. Even now it is not a question of criticizing it for lacking effectiveness: if we successfully overcome the present problems of the phase of entering into a "new era" we will continue to be more "effective" than many others; and if we don't overcome them it doesn't much matter if we have carried out a few publications and encounters a little slower or a little faster. I am thus not criticizing any ineffectiveness of this style of organization, but the essential fact that at the moment this style is not really being applied among us. If, in spite of all its advantages, our organizational formula has this sole fault of *not being real*, it is obvious that we must at all costs make it real or else renounce it and devise another style of organization, whether for a continuation of the SI or for a regroupment on other bases, for which the new era will sooner or later create the conditions. In any case, to take up Paolo's phrase, most of us "will not stop dancing." We must only stop pretending.

16

Since the present problem is not at the *simply theoretical* level (and since it is dissimulated when we carry on theoretical discussions, which are moreover virtually contentless since they immediately lead to a consequenceless unanimity), I don't think we can settle it by constituting formal tendencies (*and still less by forgetting about it*). I think that each of us might first try to find with one other situationist, chosen by affinity and experience and after very *complete* discussion, a theoretico-practical accord that takes account of all the elements we are already aware of (and of those that may appear in the process of continuing this discussion). This accord could then, with the same prudence, be extended to another, etc. We could in this way perhaps arrive at a few regroupments that would be capable of dialoguing with each other—to oppose each other or to come to an agreement? The process could be long (but not necessarily so) and it would probably be one way to put into practice the perspective evoked a few months ago but scarcely developed since of "rejoining the SI" (without formally suspending the present accord, but by here and now preparing *its future*). Suffice it to say that it is time to seek concrete individuals behind the now-evident *abstraction* of the "SI organization"; and to find out what they really want to do and can do. Without claiming that this will produce a stable assurance for the future, it would at least make it possible to bring into the open and deal with all the difficulties and discouraging impressions that have already been noted. We still have to talk about all this until acts permit us to shut up.

GUY DEBORD
27 July 1970

DECLARATION

The crisis that has continually deepened in the SI in the course of the last year, and whose roots go much further back, has ended up revealing all its aspects; and has led to a more and more glaring increase in theoretical and practical inactivity. But the most striking manifestation of this crisis (ultimately revealing what was precisely its original hidden center) has been several comrades' *indifference* in the face of its concrete development, month after month. We know quite well that no one has at all *expressed* this indifference. And that is precisely the heart of the problem, for what we have really been experiencing, behind an abstract proclamation of the contrary, is this refusal to take any responsibility whatsoever in participating in either the decisions or the implementation of our *real* activity, even at a time when it has been so indisputably threatened.

Considering that the SI has carried out an action that has been at least substantially correct and that has had a great importance for the revolutionary movement of the period ending in 1968 (though with an element of failure that we must account for); and that it *can* continue to make a significant contribution by lucidly comprehending the conditions of the new period, including its own conditions of existence; and that the deplorable position in which the SI has found itself for so many months must not be allowed to continue—we have constituted a tendency.

Our tendency aims to break completely with the *ideology of the SI* and with its corollary: the miserable vainglory that conceals and maintains inactivity and inability. We want an exact definition of the SI organization's collective activity and of the democracy that is *actually possible* in it. We want the *actual application* of this democracy.

After everything we have seen these last several months, we reject in advance *any abstract response*, any response that might still aim to simulate a comfortable euphoria by finding nothing specific to criticize or self-criticize in the functioning—or nonfunctioning—of a group in which so many people know so well what they have lacked. After what we have all seen for months regarding the question of our common activity, nothing can any longer be accepted as before: routine optimism becomes a lie, unusable abstract generalization becomes a dodge. Several of the best situationists have become *something else*; they don't talk about what they know and they talk about what they don't know. We want a radical critique—a critique *ad hominem*.

Without prejudging any later, more considered and serious responses they may make, we declare our disagreement with the American comrades, who have constituted a tendency on completely futile bases. At the present moment the infantile futility of pseudocritiques is a bluff as unacceptable as the noble generality of pseudocontentment; both are evasions of real criticism. Other comrades have for months never undertaken to respond in any manner whatsoever to the mass of clearly burning questions pointed to *by facts themselves* and by the first, and *increasingly specific*, written critiques that we have been formulating for months. The very terrain of the scandal and of its denunciation have *expanded together* and any silence makes one a direct accessory to all the deficiencies. Let no one believe in our naïveté, as if we were putting forward here some new exhortation aimed at arousing the members against some incomprehensible and paralyzing fatality—an exhortation that would meet with the same absence of response as all the preceding ones! We are quite aware that some of you have not wanted to respond.

This shameful silence is going to stop immediately because *we demand*, in the name of the rights and duties given us by the SI's past and present, that each member accept his responsibilities right now.

It is certainly useless at this point to reiterate the central questions regarding which we await responses. Everyone is aware of them and they have already been put in writing. Let us simply say that we will naturally accept no response that is in contradiction with the real existence of the person who formulates it.

If certain members have *hidden* goals different from ours, we want those goals to be brought out into the open and to be expressed, as they should be naturally, in distinct actions carried out under distinct responsibilities. And if anyone doesn't *have* any real goals, as strange as it seems to us that anyone would want to conserve the miserable *status quo ante*, let us only say that we will not contribute to covering for some glorified pseudocommunity of "retired thinkers" or unemployed revolutionaries.

Our tendency is addressing this declaration to all present members of the SI without distinction or exception. We clearly state that we are not seeking the exclusion of anyone (and much less will we be satisfied with the exclusion of some scapegoat). But since we consider it very unlikely that a genuine accord can be arrived at *so belatedly* among everyone, we are prepared for any split, the dividing lines of which will be determined by the forthcoming discussion. And in that eventuality we will for our part do everything possible to make such a split take place under the most proper conditions, particularly by maintaining an absolute respect for truth in any future polemics, just as all of us have together maintained this truth in all the circumstances in which the SI has acted until now.

Considering that the crisis has attained a level of extreme gravity, we henceforth reserve the right—in accordance with Article 8 of the statutes voted at Venice—to make our positions known outside the SI.

DEBORD, RIESEL, VIÉNET
Paris, 11 November 1970

UNTITLED TEXT

(excerpts)

Comrades,

In casting back into their nothingness the contemplatives and incompetents who counted on a perpetual membership in the SI, we have taken a great step forward. We must continue to advance; because now an era is over *for the SI too*, and is *better understood*. The undeniable success that we have registered in this case was so *easy*, and so *belated*, that certainly no one will think we have the right to settle back for a few weeks to gloat over it. Yet already over the last few weeks a certain lethargy has begun to manifest itself again (without, in my opinion, any longer having the previous excuses or semijustifications) when it comes to developing our present positions. [. . .]

1) The SI recently was in danger of becoming not only inactive and ridiculous, but recuperative and counterrevolutionary. The lies multiplying within it were beginning to have a mystifying and disarming effect outside. The SI could, in the very name of its exemplary actions in the preceding period, have become *the latest form of revolutionary spectacle*, and you know those who would have liked to maintain this role for another ten or twenty years.

2) The process of alienation gone through by various past emancipatory endeavors (from the Communist League to the FAI, or even, if this aspect should be evoked in our case, surrealism) was followed by the SI in all its easily recognizable forms: theoretical paralysis; "party patriotism"; lying silence on increasingly evident faults; imperious dogmatism; wooden language addressed to the miners of Kiruna—still rather far off, fortunately—and to Iberian exiles; invisible titles of ownership possessed by little cliques or individuals over one or another sector of our relations or activities, on the basis of their being "SI members" like people used to be "Roman citizens"; ideology and dishonesty. Naturally this process took place this time *in the present historical conditions*, that is to say, to a large extent in the very conditions created by the SI; so that many features of past alienations were precluded. This set of conditions could have made a counterrevolutionary subversion of the SI all the more dangerous if it had succeeded, but at the same time it made such a success difficult. I think that this danger virtually no longer exists: We have so well *smashed* the SI in the preceding months that there is scarcely any chance that that *title* and *image* could become harmful in bad hands. The situationist movement—in the broad sense of the word—is now diffused more or less everywhere. And any of us, as well as some of the excluded members, could at any time, in the name of the SI's past and of the radical positions presently needing to be developed, speak *by himself* to the revolutionary current that listens to us; but that is just what Vaneigem will be unable to do.* On the other hand, if a neo-Nashist

368

regrouping dared to form, a single pamphlet of 20 pages would suffice to demolish it. To smash the SI and reduce to nothing the miserable pretensions that would have been able to preserve it as an alienated and alienating model—this had become *at least* our most urgent revolutionary duty. On the basis of these new measures of security we have fortunately implemented, we can now probably do better.

3) The SI had (and still has, but fortunately with less of a monopoly on it) the most radical theory of its time. On the whole it knew how to formulate it, disseminate it and defend it. It often was able to *struggle well* in practice; and some of us have often even been capable of conducting our personal lives in line with that theory (which was, moreover, a necessary condition to enable us to formulate its main points). But the SI has not applied its own theory *in the very activity of the formulation of that theory* or in the *general conditions of its struggle*. The partisans of the SI's positions have for the most part not been their creators or their real agents. They were only more official and more pretentious pro-situs. This has been the SI's main fault (avoidable or not?). To have gone so long without being aware of it has been its worst error (and to speak for myself, *my* worst error). If this attitude had prevailed, it would have been the SI's ultimate crime. As an organization the SI has *partly failed*; and this has been the part in which it has failed. It was thus necessary to apply to the SI the critique it had applied, often so well, to the dominant modern society. (It could be said that we were rather well organized to propagate our program, but not our organizational program.)

4) The numerous deficiencies that have marked the SI were *invariably* produced by individuals who *needed the SI* in order to personally be something; and that something was never the real, revolutionary activity of the SI, but its opposite. At the same time, they pushed the praise of the SI to the extreme, both to make it seem that they subsisted in it like fish in water and to give the impression that their personal extremism was above any vulgar corroboration of facts and acts. And yet the alternative has always been quite simple: either we are fundamentally equal (and prove it) or we are *not even comparable*. As for us here, we can take part in the SI *only if we don't need it*. We must first of all be *self-sufficient*; then, secondarily, we may lucidly combine our *specific* (and specified) desires and possibilities for a collective action which, on that condition, *may* be the correct continuation of the SI [. . .]

GUY DEBORD
28 January 1971

TRANSLATOR'S NOTES

4. "Ivan Chtcheglov participated in the ventures that were at the origin of the situationist movement and his role in it has been irreplaceable, both in its first theoretical endeavors and in its practical activity (the dérive experiments). In 1953, at the age of 19, he had already drafted—under the pseudonym Gilles Ivain—the text entitled "Formulary for a New Urbanism," which was later published in the first issue of *Internationale Situationniste*. Having passed the last five years in a psychiatric clinic, where he still is, he reestablished contact with us only long after the formation of the SI. He is currently working on a revised edition of his 1953 writing on architecture and urbanism. The letters from which the following lines have been excerpted were addressed to Michèle Bernstein and Guy Debord over the last year. The plight to which Ivan Chtcheglov is being subjected can be considered as one of modern society's increasingly sophisticated methods of control over people's lives, a control that in previous times was expressed in atheists being condemned to the Bastille, for example, or political opponents to exile." (Introductory note to Chtcheglov's "Letters from Afar," *IS* #9, p. 38.)

8. The French word *détournement* means diversion, deflection, turning aside from the normal course or purpose (often with an illicit connotation). It has sometimes been translated as 'diversion', but this word is confusing because of its more common meaning of idle entertainment. I have chosen simply to anglicize the French word, which already has a certain currency in America and England.

13. In the first imagined scene a phrase from a Greek tragedy is put in the mouth of Maximilien Robespierre; in the second, a phrase from Robespierre is put in the mouth of a truckdriver.

21 (first note). The final break was provoked when the radical tendency disrupted a Charlie Chaplin press conference in October 1952. The aesthete lettrists, including the founder of lettrism, Isidore Isou, disavowed the act. The disrupters responded in an open letter: "We believe that the most urgent exercise of freedom is the destruction of idols, especially when they present themselves in the name of freedom. The provocative tone of our leaflet was an attack against a unanimous, servile enthusiasm. The disavowal by certain lettrists, including Isou himself, only reveals the constantly reengendered incomprehension between extremists and those who are no longer so . . . ."

21 (second note). In a previous passage omitted in this translation Debord had quoted a speech of Andrei Zhdanov (head of culture under Stalin in the 1940s), who defended the USSR's suppression of avant-garde artists on the grounds that the latter represented the "liquidation" of classical art.

22. The SI subsequently renounced any such "infiltration" of other groups, considering that any simultaneous membership in two organizations inevitably leads to manipulation.

25. *Report on the Construction of Situations* was one of the preparatory texts for the July 1957 conference at Cosio d'Arroscia, Italy, at which the SI was founded.

29. *On the Passage . . .*, which is concerned with the lettrist experiences at the origin of the situationist movement, opens with shots of the Paris district frequented by the lettrists in the early fifties.

36. *enfants perdus*: soldiers sent on a virtually suicidal mission; literally, 'lost children'.

52. "The *dérive* (with its flow of acts, its gestures, its strolls, its encounters) was *to the totality* exactly what psychoanalysis (in the best sense) is to language. Let yourself go with the flow of words, says the analyst. He listens, until the moment when he rejects or modifies (one could say *detourns*) a word, an expression or a definition. The dérive is certainly a technique, almost a therapeutic one. But just as analysis without anything else is almost always *contraindicated*, so the continual dérive is dangerous to the extent that the individual, having gone too far (not without bases, but . . .) without defenses, is threatened with explosion, dissolution, dissociation, disintegration. And thence the relapse into what is termed 'ordinary life,' that is to say, in reality, into 'petrified life.' In this regard I now repudiate the Formulary's propaganda for a *continual dérive*. Yes, continual like the poker game at Las Vegas, but continual for a certain period, limited to Sunday for some, to a week as a good average; a month, that's a lot. In 1953–1954 we dérived for three or four months; that's the extreme limit, the critical point. It's a miracle it didn't kill us." (Ivan Chtcheglov, "Letters from Afar," *IS* #9, p. 38.)

54. A slightly different version of this article was published in *Les Lèvres Nues* #9 (November 1956), along with accounts of two dérives.

64. A later issue (*IS* #11, p. 64) has the following note on Solidarity: "The majority of the British *Solidarity* group apparently demanding this boycott of the situationists are very combative revolutionary workers. We feel confident in stating that its shop-steward members have not yet read the SI, certainly not in French. But they have an ideologue, their specialist of nonauthority, Dr. C. Pallis, a well-educated man who has been aware of it for years and who has been in a position to assure them of its utter unimportance. His activity in England has instead been to translate and comment on the texts of Cardan, the thinker who presided over the collapse of *Socialisme ou Barbarie* in France. Pallis knows quite well that we have for a long time pointed out Cardan's unmistakable progression toward revolutionary nothingness, his swallowing of every kind of academic fashion and his ending up becoming indistinguishable from any ordinary sociologist. But Pallis has brought Cardan's thought to England like the light that arrives on Earth from stars that have already long burned out—by presenting his least decomposed texts, written years before, and suppressing their regressive development. It is thus easy to see why he would like to prevent this type of encounter."

65. The French word *urbanisme* is equivalent to 'city planning' but also connotes the overall accompanying ideology.

88. *recuperation*: used in the sense of the system's recovering something that was lost to it, bringing back into the fold a potential revolt against it. The term 'cooption' is similar but more limited. Thus, a reformist demand is coopted (and recuperated) by being taken over and implemented by the state. But a more radical act or idea can be recuperated by being pigeonholed within the dominant categories, integrated into the spectacle as a confusionist or extremist foil which thus serves to complement and reinforce the system, while not necessarily obtaining the approval or implementation implied by cooption.

111. In 1961–1962 the German situationists were subjected to a series of police harassments—searches, confiscation of SI publications, arrests for immorality, pornography, blasphemy, incitement to riot, etc. The SI conducted an international campaign on their behalf, even after the majority of them had been excluded from the SI for moderation and compromises in other regards. Uwe Lausen, who had not been excluded, was the only one to eventually be jailed (for three weeks); the others got fines and suspended sentences. (See *IS* #6, p. 6; #7, p.51; #8, p. 64.)

113. An example of the gross results: "The ex-situationist Constant, whose Dutch collaborators had already been excluded from the SI for having agreed to construct a church, now himself presents *models of factories* in his catalogue published in March by the Municipal Museum of Bochum. Apart from plagiarizing two or three poorly understood fragments of situationist ideas, this slippery character has nothing better to propose than to act as a public relations man in integrating the masses into capitalist technological civilization; and he reproaches the SI for having abandoned his whole program of transforming the urban milieu, which he alone is carrying out. Under these conditions, yes!" (*IS* #6, p. 6.) Constant resigned from the SI in 1960. He is the same person later mentioned in *Student Poverty* as a member of the Provo hierarchy.

115. *Information* is also the French word for 'news'.

133. *Declaration of the 121*: a "Declaration on the Right To Resist the Algerian War" signed by 121 French artists and intellectuals September 1960. The French government responded with arrests and firings, and even prohibited news media from mentioning the name of any signer; which only resulted in more people signing. The Declaration polarized the intellectual community and contributed toward arousing French public opinion (the first demonstration against the war came a month later). See *IS* #5, pp. 5–7, 12.

136. Trocchi's article, which proposed a sort of coherent linking up of countercultural artists and dissidents, is not included in this anthology. The English version, "A Revolutionary Proposal," appeared in *New Saltire* #8 (London, June 1963) and *City Lights Journal* #2 (San Francisco, 1964), the latter also containing a subsequent more detailed program for his "Project Sigma." *IS* #10 contains this note:

"Upon the appearance in London in autumn 1964 of the first publications of the 'Project Sigma' initiated by Alexander Trocchi, it was mutually agreed that the SI could not involve itself in such a loose cultural venture, in spite of the interest we have in dialogue with the most exigent individuals who may be contacted through it, notably in the United States and England. It is therefore no longer as a member of the SI that our friend Alexander Trocchi has since developed an activity of which we fully approve of several aspects."

139. See, for example, the SI's critique of the Spanish *Acción Comunista* group in "Contribution au programme des conseils ouvriers en Espagne" (*IS* #10, pp. 27–32).

142. The SI stated that it had no objections to publishers, film producers, patrons, etc., interested in financing situationist projects, whether disinterestedly or in the expectation of making profits, as long as it was understood that the situationists would retain total control over the form and content of the projects.

Regarding the publication of radical texts *IS* #10 (p. 70) has this remark: "It is clear that there are presently only four possible types of publishing: state-bureaucratic; bourgeois semicompetitive (though subject to a tendency toward economic concentration); independent (wherever radical theory can be legally self-published); and clandestine. The SI—and any critical current anywhere—uses and will use the latter two methods; it *may* in many cases use the second one (to obtain a qualitatively different level of distribution) because of the contradictions left open by anarchic competition and the lack of enforced ideological orthodoxy; and it is of course totally incompatible only with the first one. The reason is very simple: the competitive bourgeois type of publishing does not claim to guarantee any consistency between itself and its different authors; the authors are not responsible for a publishing firm's operation and, conversely, the publisher has no direct responsibility for their life or ideas. Only state-bureaucratic publishing (or that of parties representing such a bureaucracy in formation) is in complete solidarity with its authors: it has to endorse its authors in everything and its authors also have to endorse it. Thus it represents a *double* impossibility for any revolutionary expression."

150. "The discoveries of psychoanalysis have, as Freud suspected, turned out to be unacceptable for the ruling social order—or for any society based on repressive hierarchy. But Freud's 'centrist' position, stemming from his absolute and supratemporal identification of 'civilization' with repression by exploitation of labor, and thus his carrying out of a partially critical research within an uncriticized overall system, led psychoanalysis to be officially 'recognized' in all its degraded variants without being accepted in its central truth: its *potential* critical use. This failure is of course not exclusively attributable to Freud himself, but rather to the collapse in the 1920s of the revolutionary movement, the only force that could have brought the critical findings of psychoanalysis to some fulfillment. The subsequent period of extreme reaction in Europe drove out even the partisans of psychoanalytic 'centrism.' The psychoanalytic debris who are now in fashion (in the West, at least) have all developed from this initial capitulation, in which an unacceptable critical truth was turned into acceptably innocuous verbiage. By surrendering its revolutionary cutting edge, psychoanalysis exposed itself *both* to being used by all the guardians of the present Sleep and to being disparaged for its insufficiencies by run-of-the-mill psychiatrists and moralists. [. . .] Cardan, who here as elsewhere seems to think that it suffices to speak of something in order to have it, vaguely blathers on about 'the imagination' in an attempt to justify the gelatinous flabbiness of his thought. He seizes on psychoanalysis (just as does the official world nowadays) as a *justification* of irrationality and of the profound motivations of the unconscious, although the discoveries of psychoanalysis are in fact a weapon—as yet unused due to obvious sociopolitical reasons—for a *rational critique* of the world. Psychoanalysis profoundly ferrets out the unconscious, its poverty and its miserable repressive maneuvers, which only draw their force and their magical grandeur from a quite banal practical repression in daily life." (*IS* #10, pp. 63 & 79.)

194. "Nothing is so blatant, however, as the bloody downfall of Indonesian Stalinism, whose bureaucratic mania blinded it to the point of expecting to seize power only by way of plots and palace revolution, although it was in control of an immense movement—a movement it led to annihilation without even having led it into battle (it is estimated that there have been over 300,000 executions)." (*IS* #10, p. 65.)

214. "From the strategical perspective of social struggles it must first of all be said that one should never *play with terrorism*. But even serious terrorism has never in history had any salutary effectiveness except in situations where complete repression made impossible any other form of revolutionary activity and thereby caused a significant portion of the population to side with the terrorists." (*IS* #12, p. 98.)

227. "Katangans": nickname given to ex-mercenaries and other toughs who took part in the May movement.

228. In 1960 the SI initiated a boycott of anyone who collaborated with the journal *Arguments*, "in order to *make an example* of the most representative tendency of that conformist and pseudoleftist intelligentsia that has up to now laboriously organized a conspiracy of silence regarding us, and whose bankruptcy in all domains is beginning to be recognized by perceptive people" (*IS* #5, p. 13). The SI noted various evidences of this bankruptcy and predicted its imminent demise from sheer incoherence and lack of ideas; which was precisely what happened in 1962. It so happened that the last issue of *Arguments* contained an article by Henri Lefebvre on the Paris Commune that was almost entirely plagiarized from the SI's "Theses on the Commune." The SI issued a tract, *Into the Trashcan of History*, calling attention to the contradiction that the lead article of a guest writer himself far above the general level of this journal—a journal pretending that the SI was of so little interest as to not be worth mentioning—was merely a watered-down version of a text three situationists had written in a few hours. This tract was reprinted in *IS* #12 in response to the numerous commentators who attributed to Lefebvre an important influence on the May 1968 movement due to "his" theses on the festive nature of the Commune, etc.

229. "Those who spoke of Marcuse as the 'theorist' of the movement did not even understand Marcuse, much less the movement itself. Marcusian *ideology*, already ridiculous, was pasted onto the movement in the same way that Geismar, Sauvageot and Cohn-Bendit were 'designated' to represent it. But even they admitted their ignorance of Marcuse. In reality, if the May revolutionary crisis showed anything, it was precisely the opposite of Marcuse's theses: it showed that the proletariat has not been integrated and that it is the main revolutionary force in modern society. Pessimists and sociologists will have to redo their calculations, along with the spokesmen of underdevelopment, Black Power and Dutschkeism." (Viénet, *Enragés et situationnistes dans le mouvement des occupations*, pp. 153–154.)

233. By 20 May six million workers were on strike; within a few days the number had risen to ten million.

238. "The March 22nd Movement was from the beginning an eclectic conglomeration of individuals who joined it as individuals. They all agreed on the fact that it was impossible for them to agree on any theoretical point, and counted on 'collective action' to overcome this deficiency. There was nevertheless a consensus on two subjects, one a ridiculous banality, the other a new exigency. The banality was anti-imperialist 'struggle,' the heritage of the contemplative period of the little leftist groups that was about to end—Nanterre, that suburban Vietnam, resolutely supporting the just struggle of insurgent Bolivia. The novelty was direct democracy in the organization. This was only very partially realized in the March 22nd Movement because of the dual membership, discreetly unmentioned or never taken into consideration, of the majority of its members. [...] All the sociological and journalistic trumpeting of the 'originality' of the March 22nd Movement masked the simple fact that its leftist amalgam, while new in France, was a direct copy of the American SDS, itself equally eclectic and democratic and frequently infiltrated by various old leftist sects." (Viénet, *op. cit.*, pp. 37–39.)

"Cohn-Bendit himself belonged to the independent semitheoretical anarchist group around the journal *Noir et Rouge*. As much from this fact as because of his personal qualities, he found himself in the most radical tendency of the March 22nd Movement, and more truly revolutionary than the whole rest of the group whose spokesman he was to become and which he therefore had to tolerate. (In a number of interviews he has increased his concessions to Maoism, as for example in *Le Magazine Littéraire* of May 1968: 'I don't really know that much about what Maoism really is! I've read some things in Mao that are very true. His thesis of relying on the peasantry has always been an anarchist thesis.') Insufficiently intelligent, informed confusedly and at second hand regarding present-day problems, skillful enough to entertain a student audience, frank enough to stand out from the arena of leftist political maneuvers yet flexible enough to come to terms with its leaders, Cohn-Bendit was an honest revolutionary, but no genius. He knew much less than he should have, and did not make the best use of what he did know. Moreover, because he accepted without a critique the role of a star, exhibiting himself for the mob of reporters from the spectacular media, his statements, which always combined a certain lucidity with a certain foolishness, were inevitably twisted in the latter direction by the deformation inherent in that kind of communication." (Viénet, *op. cit.*, pp. 38–39.)

244. "In the name of the Enragés, René Riesel immediately demanded the expulsion of two observers from the administration and of the several Stalinists who were present. An anarchist spokesman and regular collaborator of Cohn-Bendit asserted, 'The Stalinists who are here this evening are no longer Stalinists.' The Enragés immediately left the meeting in protest against this cowardly illusion." (Viénet, *op. cit.*, p. 34.)

248. Besides numerous SI and Enragé texts, Viénet's book reproduces a critique of medicine by the National Center of Young Doctors, a critique of advertising by a group of ad designers, a manifesto against the commercial manipulation of soccer by the Soccer Players Action Committee, and leaflets by a Yugoslavian woman, by the North African Action Committee, by the strike committee of a large department store, by Sud-Aviation workers, by postal workers and by several revolutionary groups.

279. *anarcho-trenchists*: term applied to anarchists who rallied to the support of World War I.

293. Morea and Allan Hoffman later formed the New York "Motherfuckers" group.

295. It should perhaps be stressed that the SI made an example of Maitron because of his revolutionary pretensions and credibility as an "anarchist" historian—and this only after his refusing to make a public rectification of demonstrated falsehoods which any person of good faith would have readily granted. The situationists did not attack people physically merely because they criticized or disagreed with the SI. And even in the innumerable instances of deliberate falsification of the SI's positions or activities, they almost always confined themselves to publicly pointing out the falsification. In a related connection (apropos of the French government's dissolution of Maoist and Trotskyist groups after May 1968): "The SI's position on this point is quite clear: we obviously defend, in the name of our principles, the right of these people to free expression and association—a right they would refuse us in the name of their own principles if they were ever in a position to do so." (*IS #12*, p. 98.)

296 (first note). As Raspaud and Voyer have shown in their "Index of Insulted Names," it is a gross exaggeration to say that the SI criticized everybody: out of 940 persons mentioned in the twelve *IS* issues, only 540 were insulted—less than 58%.

296 (second note). The SI had an average membership of around ten or twenty. In all, 63 men and 7 women from 16 different countries were members at one time or another.

297. The lettrist films of the early fifties, for example, frequently contained such blank-screen passages, culminating in Debord's first film, *Hurlements en faveur de Sade* (1952), which has no images whatsoever and only a sporadic soundtrack.

310. Pierre Canjuers was at this time a member of the *Socialisme ou Barbarie* group. This text is described in *IS #5* as "a platform for discussion within the SI, and for its link-up with revolutionary militants of the workers movement."

318. "In June 1963 the SI organized a 'Destruction of RSG 6' demonstration in Denmark, under the direction of J.V. Martin. On this occasion the situationists distributed a clandestine reissue of the English tract *Danger: Official Secret—RSG 6*, signed 'Spies for Peace,' which revealed the plan and function of 'Regional Seat of Government #6.' A theoretical text, *The Situationists and the New Forms of Action in Politics and Art*, was also issued in Danish, English and French. In one area an ugly reconstruction of a bomb shelter was set up; in another were exhibited Martin's 'Thermonuclear Maps,' detournements of pop art representing various regions of the globe during World War III." (*IS* #9, pp. 31–32.)

319. In some passages in this anthology I have followed the recent tendency of phasing out masculine terms for sex-neutral senses (e.g. by changing 'men' to 'people'). In most cases, however, as in *Student Poverty*, I have retained the he/his forms in order to avoid a complicated recasting of the text.

330 (footnote). Obsolete address omitted. The *Heatwave* group soon after formed part of the short-lived British SI section.

330. Obsolete addresses omitted. The SI's judgment of the Revolutionary Communist League turned out to be mistaken in some respects. The RCL Zengakuren was not "the" Zengakuren, but only one of several rival ones (another was dominated by the Japanese CP, others by various combinations of Trotskyists, Maoists, etc.). In the early sixties the Zengakuren faction that was to form the RCL certainly had many of the positive features the SI attributed to it: it had a political platform distinctly to the left of Trotskyism, participated militantly in practical struggles on many fronts and seems to have had a fairly experimental approach to organizational and tactical questions. In 1963 it sent some delegates to Europe who met the situationists, and it later translated a few situationist texts into Japanese. At least by 1970, however, when an SI delegate visited Japan, the RCL had devolved into a largely Leninist position and turned out to be not very different from leftist sects everywhere else.

337. A similar statement appeared at the beginning of each SI journal. *On the Poverty of Student Life* is in fact the most widely circulated situationist text. It has been translated into Chinese, Danish, Dutch, English, German, Greek, Italian, Japanese, Portuguese, Spanish and Swedish, and its total printing so far is in the neighborhood of half a million.

338. This text was originally appended to the first edition of "The Class Struggles in Algeria." It was subsequently reprinted and adapted by the SI as a separate text. I haven't seen the French version; I have simply made a few stylistic modifications to an earlier English translation.

363. *pro-situ*: pejorative term referring to followers (passive or active) of the SI. See "Theses on the SI and Its Time" nos. 25–38 (in *La véritable scission*).

368. Raoul Vaneigem resigned from the SI on 14 November 1970 in response to the Debord-Riesel-Viénet "Declaration." His letter of resignation, along with the SI's "Communiqué Concerning Vaneigem," is reproduced in *La véritable scission dans l'Internationale*. Vaneigem has since put out three books—*De la grève sauvage à l'autogestion généralisée* (Editions 10/18, 1974, under the pseudonym Ratgeb), *Histoire désinvolte du surréalisme* (Editions Paul Vermont, 1977, pseudonym Jules-François Dupuis) and *Le livre des plaisirs* (Encre, 1979)—but these are not on the same level as his earlier writings.

UPDATED BIBLIOGRAPHY

Since 1968 dozens of books and innumerable pamphlets, journals, leaflets, etc., by non–SI members have appeared that can be considered more or less situationist in the broad sense of the term, in that, well or poorly, they have adopted the SI's perspectives and methods. This bibliography, however, mentions only the main publications of the SI itself, the pre- and post-SI works of some of its members, and some of the books about the SI.

PRE–S.I. TEXTS

Guy Debord (ed.), *Potlatch: 1954–1957* (Lebovici, 1985) is currently out of print. Gérard Berreby (ed.), *Documents relatifs à la fondation de l'Internationale Situationniste: 1948–1957* (1985; Éditions Allia, B.P. 90, 75862 Paris cedex 18), a huge (650 8″×11″ pages) and lavishly illustrated collection, includes not only all the issues of *Potlatch* but numerous other texts from Cobra, the Lettrist International and the Movement for an Imaginist Bauhaus, along with Asger Jorn's *Pour la forme* and Jorn and Debord's *Fin de Copenhague*. Another early Jorn-Debord collaboration, Debord's *Mémoires* (1958), which consists entirely of detourned elements, has recently been reprinted (Pauvert, 1993). Except for the half-dozen pre-SI articles in the present anthology, virtually none of these texts have been translated.

GUY DEBORD'S FILMS

Hurlements en faveur de Sade (Films Lettristes, 1952, 90 minutes).

Sur le passage de quelques personnes à travers une assez courte unité de temps (Dansk-Fransk Experimentalfilmskompagni, 1959, 20 minutes).

Critique de la séparation (Dansk-Fransk Experimentalfilmskompagni, 1961, 20 minutes).

La société du spectacle (Simar Films, 1973, 80 minutes).

Réfutation de tous les jugements, tant élogieux qu'hostiles, qui ont été jusqu'ici portés sur le film "La société du spectacle" (Simar Films, 1975, 30 minutes).

In girum imus nocte et consumimur igni (Simar Films, 1978, 80 minutes).

All are 35mm, B&W. *Oeuvres Cinématographiques Complètes: 1952–1978* (Champ Libre, 1978; Gallimard, 1994) contains illustrated scripts for all six films, with descriptions of every shot. Translations of the first five are available in *Society of the Spectacle and Other Films* (Rebel, 1992). *In girum* has been translated by Lucy Forsyth (Pelagian, 1991).

In 1984 Debord removed all his films from circulation in France as a protest against the reaction of the French press and public to the assassination of his friend and publisher, Gérard Lebovici. Some time later he specified that they would in fact never again be shown anywhere. Shortly before his suicide in November 1994 (he had a painful terminal illness) Debord and Brigitte Cornand made a 60-minute "antitelevisual" video, *Guy Debord, son art et son temps*, which was shown January 1995 on an alternative French television channel along with *La société du spectacle* and *Réfutation de tous les jugements*. Information on the video (currently available only in French) can be obtained from Brigitte Cornand, c/o Canal Plus, 85/89 Quai André Citroën, 75711 Paris cedex 15. It is not clear at this time if Debord's films will ever become available again, although needless to say numerous videocopies of the three televised works are now in pirate circulation around the world.

FRENCH S.I. BOOKS

Internationale Situationniste: 1958–1969 (Van Gennep, 1970; Champ Libre, 1975). 700 pages, illustrated. Reissue of all twelve French journals in the original format. Selections were translated by Christopher Gray in *Leaving the Twentieth Century: The Incomplete Work of the Situationist International* (Free Fall, 1974). The present anthology includes more accurate translations of most of the articles in Gray's long out-of-print collection.

Raoul Vaneigem, *Traité de savoir-vivre à l'usage des jeunes générations* (Gallimard, 1967). Translated as *The Revolution of Everyday Life* by Donald Nicholson-Smith (Rebel/Left Bank, 1983; revised 1994).

Guy Debord, *La société du spectacle* (Buchet-Chastel, 1967; Champ Libre, 1972; Gallimard, 1992). Translated by Fredy Perlman and John Supak as *The Society of the Spectacle* (Black & Red, 1970; revised 1977); and by Donald Nicholson-Smith (Zone, 1994).

378

René Viénet, *Enragés et situationnistes dans le mouvement des occupations* (Gallimard, 1968). Includes numerous documents and illustrations. Translated as *Enragés and Situationists in the Occupation Movement, May '68* (Autonomedia, 1992).

Guy Debord and Gianfranco Sanguinetti, *La véritable scission dans l'Internationale* (Champ Libre, 1972). Analysis of post-1968 SI crises. Translated as *The Veritable Split in the International* (Piranha, 1974; revised: Chronos, 1990).

Débat d'orientation de l'ex-Internationale Situationniste (Centre de Recherche sur la Question Sociale, 1974). Internal documents, 1969–1971. Not translated except for the few selections in the present anthology.

S.I. PUBLICATIONS IN OTHER LANGUAGES

Most of the more original and important SI texts appeared in French. (The present anthology is drawn entirely from French texts except for the one piece by the Italian section on pp. 338–339.) SI publications in other languages often represented the more artistic and opportunistic tendencies (notably in Italy, Germany, Scandinavia and the Netherlands) that were repudiated early in the SI's history. In the later period, the British section never got off the ground and the American and Italian sections scarcely lasted much longer, coming as they did right in the middle of the post-1968 crises that were soon to lead to the SI's dissolution.

The American section's main publications were Robert Chasse's pamphlet *The Power of Negative Thinking* (New York, 1968; a critique of the New Left, actually published shortly before Chasse joined the SI) and one issue of a journal, *Situationist International* #1 (New York, 1969; notably including critiques of Marcuse, McLuhan, Bookchin, Baran and Sweezy, etc.). The journal has been reissued by Extreme Press. After their December 1969 resignation/exclusion, Chasse and Bruce Elwell produced an extensive critical history of the American section, *A Field Study in the Dwindling Force of Cognition* (1970), which the SI never answered.

The Italian section published one issue of a journal, *Internazionale Situazionista* #1 (1969), and carried out a number of interventions in the crises and struggles in Italy. None of the Italian texts have been translated into English, but there is a complete French edition, *Écrits complets de la Section Italienne de l'Internationale Situationniste (1969–1972)*, translated by Joël Gayraud and Luc Mercier (1988; Contre-

Moule, Cedex 2461, 99246 Paris-Concours).

The Scandinavian section published three issues of the Danish journal *Situationistisk Revolution* (1962, 1968, 1970). Some of its other activities are described in *I.S.* #10, pp. 22–26.

Most of the major SI writings have been translated into English, German, Greek, Italian and Spanish; some have also been translated into Arabic, Chinese, Danish, Dutch, Japanese, Polish, Portuguese, Swedish, and by now probably several other languages.

POST–S.I. WORKS

GUY DEBORD, *Préface à la quatrième édition italienne de "La Société du Spectacle"* (Champ Libre, 1979; reprinted in the Gallimard edition of *Commentaires*). Translated as *Preface to the Fourth Italian Edition of "The Society of the Spectacle"* by Frances Parker and Michael Forsyth (Chronos, 1979).

—*Considérations sur l'assassinat de Gérard Lebovici* (Lebovici, 1985; Gallimard, 1993). Not translated.

—(with Alice Becker-Ho), *Le "Jeu de la Guerre": Relevé des positions successives de toutes les forces au cours d'une partie* (Lebovici, 1987). Account of a board game with strategical commentaries. Not translated.

—*Commentaires sur la société du spectacle* (Lebovici, 1988; Gallimard, 1992). Translated as *Comments on the Society of the Spectacle* by Malcolm Imrie (Verso, 1990).

—*Panégyrique, tome premier* (Lebovici, 1989; Gallimard, 1993). Translated as *Panegyric, Volume I* by James Brook (Verso, 1991).

—*"Cette mauvaise réputation..."* (Gallimard, 1993). Not translated.

—*Des contrats* (Le Temps Qu'il Fait, 1995). Debord's film contracts. Not translated.

Some Debord letters are included in the two volumes of published Champ Libre *Correspondance* (1978 & 1981).

GIANFRANCO SANGUINETTI (pseudonym Censor), *Rapporto veridico sulle ultime opportunità di salvare il capitalismo in Italia* (Milan, 1975). Translated into French by Guy Debord as *Véridique rapport sur les dernières chances de sauver le capitalisme en Italie* (Champ Libre, 1976). Not translated into English.

—*Del terrorismo e dello stato* (Milan, 1979). Translated as *On Terrorism and the State* by Lucy Forsyth and Michel Prigent (Chronos, 1982).

RAOUL VANEIGEM (pseud. Ratgeb), *De la grève sauvage à l'autogestion généralisée* (Éditions 10/18, 1974). Partially translated as *Contributions to the Revolutionary Struggle* by Paul Sharkey (Bratach Dubh, 1981; Elephant, 1990).

379

—(pseud. J.F. Dupuis), *Histoire désinvolte du surréalisme* (Paul Vermont, 1977). Translated by Donald Nicholson-Smith (AK, 1995).

—*Le livre des plaisirs* (Encre, 1979). Translated by John Fullerton as *The Book of Pleasures* (Pending Press, 1983).

—*Le mouvement du Libre-Esprit* (Ramsay, 1986). Translated by Ian Patterson as *The Movement of the Free Spirit* (Zone, 1994).

—*Adresse aux vivants sur la mort qui les gouverne et l'opportunité de s'en défaire* (Seghers, 1990). Not translated.

RENÉ VIÉNET, *La dialectique peut-elle casser des briques?* (1973). 90-minute kungfu film with altered soundtrack. A videocopy with English subtitles (translation: Keith Sanborn), *Can Dialectics Break Bricks?*, is available from Drift Distribution (219 E. 2nd St. #5E, New York, NY 10009).

Of the various above-mentioned translations, Nicholson-Smith's versions of *The Revolution of Everyday Life* and *The Society of the Spectacle* are the most fluent, but rather free. Such liberties may be appropriate in the case of Vaneigem's relatively "lyrical" work, but they sometimes obscure the rigorous dialectical structure of Debord's original text. The Black & Red version sticks closer to the original, though it contains numerous minor errors. Considering the central importance of Debord's book, the serious reader might do well to study both versions together.

At the opposite extreme, the translations published by Chronos are clumsily overliteral, often to the point of unreadability. The various other translations fall somewhere in between, generally sufficing to give a pretty good idea of the originals, but all containing innaccuracies and stylistic infelicities. Those of Debord's *Comments* and *Panegyric* are among the most accurate; that of Viénet's *Enragés and Situationists* contains quite a few careless errors.

BOOKS ABOUT THE S.I.

Jean-Jacques Raspaud and Jean-Pierre Voyer's *L'Internationale Situationniste: protagonistes, chronologie, bibliographie (avec un index des noms insultés)* (Champ Libre, 1971) is a handy reference to the French journal collection. Jean-François Martos's *Histoire de l'Internationale Situationniste* (Lebovici, 1989) recounts the SI's development and perspectives largely in its own words. Pascal Dumontier's *Les situationnistes et Mai 68* (Lebovici, 1990) is a competent account. Elisabeth Sussman (ed.), *On the Passage of a Few People Through a Rather Brief Moment in Time: The Situationist International, 1957–1972* (MIT/Institute of Contem-

porary Art, 1989), an illustrated catalog of the 1989–90 exhibition on the SI in Paris, London and Boston, includes several previously untranslated SI texts along with an assortment of scholarly articles devoted almost exclusively to the early artistic-cultural aspects of the SI's venture. Greil Marcus's *Lipstick Traces: A Secret History of the Twentieth Century* (Harvard, 1989, illustrated) concentrates even more on the presituationist ventures of the 1950s, which the author relates rather impressionistically to other extremist cultural movements such as Dada and early punk. Iwona Blazwick (ed.), *An Endless Adventure, an Endless Passion, an Endless Banquet: A Situationist Scrapbook* (Verso/ICA, 1989, illustrated) includes an assortment of texts illustrating the (for the most part rather confused) influence of the SI in England from the 1960s through the 1980s. The first half of Sadie Plant's *The Most Radical Gesture: The Situationist International in a Postmodern Age* (Routledge, 1992) is a fairly competent summary of the main situationist theses; the second half will be of interest primarily to those who are so ill-informed as to imagine that the situationists had some resemblance to the "postmodernists" and other fashionably pretentious ideologists of confusion and resignation. Simon Ford's *The Realization and Suppression of the Situationist International: An Annotated Bibliography 1972–1992* (AK, 1995) lists over 600 texts, mostly in English, about or influenced by the SI. Ken Knabb's forthcoming *New and Collected Writings, 1970–1996* (Bureau of Public Secrets, 1996) will include some relevant material.

PUBLISHERS AND DISTRIBUTORS

Éditions Champ Libre was renamed Éditions Gérard Lebovici in memory of its founder-owner, who was assassinated in 1984. (The assassins were never identified.) Besides the books mentioned here it has published many other situationist-influenced authors along with a wide range of works of related interest. After yet another change of name and address, it is now Éditions Ivrea, 1 Place Paul Painlevé, 75005 Paris.

Guy Debord recently shifted from Champ Libre to Éditions Gallimard (5 rue Sébastien-Bottin, 75007 Paris), which is in the process of reprinting all his books.

Most situationist texts in English are available from Left Bank Distribution (4142 Brooklyn NE, Seattle, WA 98105); Perennial Books (Box B14, Montague, MA 01351); and AK Distribution (P.O. Box 40682, San Francisco, CA 94140, *or* 22 Lutton Place, Edinburgh EH8 9PE, Scotland).

THE BLIND MEN AND THE ELEPHANT

(Selected Opinions on the Situationists)

But even if this were not so, there would still be no reason to accept the tutelage of science, as is proposed, for example, by a self-styled "Situationist International," which imagines it is making a new contribution when in fact it is merely creating ambiguity and confusion. But is it not in such troubled waters that one fishes for a situation?

—Benjamin Péret in *Bief* #1, 1958

This young group sees only one way out of this impasse: to renounce painting as an individual art in order to use it within a new "situationist" framework. What a monstrous word! Such manifestos are interesting as symptoms of inquietude and malaise. This particular one contains a few trivial truths, but its authors cling too closely to phenomena and slogans, with the result that essential truth escapes them.

—*Die Kultur,* October 1960

Their principal activity is an extreme mental derangement. . . . In the maximum possible number of languages the Situationist International sends letters from foreign countries filled with the most filthy expressions. In our opinion the Munich court gave them too much credit in condemning them to fines and imprisonment.

—*Vernissage* #9–10, May-June 1962

The situationist critics who hope to seize all the means of communication without having created any at any level, and to replace its diverse creations and trivialities with their unique and enormous triviality—these cretins, we say, are excretions of the Hitlerist or Stalinist type, one of the manifestations of its present extreme impotence, of which the most well-known examples are the Nazi gangs of America and England.

—*Les Cahiers du Lettrisme* #1, December 1962

As previously happened with surrealism, the internal development of the Situationist International shows that when the crisis of language and poetry is pushed beyond certain limits it ends up putting in question the very structure of society.

—*La Tour de Feu* #82, June 1964

This movement, supported by M. Bernstein and G. Debord among others, whose concerns are in some sense comparable, a hundred years later, to those of the Young Hegelians and especially to the Marx of the *1844 Manuscripts* . . . that is to say, they imagine a revolution is possible and their program is aimed at making one.

—*Arts,* 9 June 1965

Behind the angry young men of Amsterdam we find an occult International. . . . The Provos provide the previously isolated theorists of the Situationist International with troops, with "intelligent supernumeraries" capable of constituting the secular arm of an organization which itself prefers to remain more or less behind the scenes.

—*Figaro Littéraire,* 4 August 1966

These students have insulted their professors. They should be dealt with by psychiatrists. I don't want to take any legal measures against them—they should be in a lunatic asylum. . . . As for their incitement to illegal acts, the Minister of the Interior is looking into that.

—Rector Bayen, Strasbourg University, November 1966

Their doctrine, if this term can be used in describing their delirious lucubrations, . . . is a sort of radical revolutionarism with a nihilist basis. . . . A monument of imbecilic fanaticism, written in a pretentious jargon, spiced with a barrage of gratuitous insults both of their professors and of their fellow students. It constantly refers to a mysterious "Situationist International."

—*Le Nouvel Alsacien*, 25 November 1966

This well-written text constitutes a systematic rejection of all forms of social and political organization in the West and the East, and of all the groups that are currently trying to change them.

—*Le Monde*, 9 December 1966

The accused have never denied the charge of misappropriating the funds of the Strasbourg Student Union. Indeed, they openly admit to having made the union pay some 5000 francs for the printing and distribution of 10,000 pamphlets, not to mention the cost of other literature inspired by the "Situationist International." These publications express ideas and aspirations which, to put it mildly, have nothing to do with the purposes of a student union. One has only to read what the accused have written for it to be obvious that these five students, scarcely more than adolescents, lacking any experience of real life, their minds confused by ill-digested philosophical, social, political and economic theories, and bored by the drab monotony of their everyday life, make the empty, arrogant and pathetic claim to pass definitive judgments, sinking to outright insults, on their fellow students, their professors, God, religion, the clergy, and the governments and political and social systems of the entire world. Rejecting all morality and legal restraint, these cynics do not hesitate to commend theft, the destruction of scholarship, the abolition of work, total subversion and an irreversible worldwide proletarian revolution with "unrestrained pleasure" as its only goal.

—summing-up of Judge Llabador, Strasbourg, 13 December 1966

The verbal gesticulations of the situationists do not hit home. . . . It is, moreover, curious to see the bourgeois press, which refuses to print information coming from the revolutionary workers movement, rushing to report and popularize the gesticulations of these buffoons.

—*Le Monde Libertaire*, January 1967

A new student ideology is spreading across the world: a dehydrated version of the young Marx called "situationism."

—*Daily Telegraph*, 22 April 1967

Then appeared for the first time the disquieting figures of the "Situationist International." How many are there? Where do they come from? No one knows.

—*Le Républicain Lorrain*, 28 June 1967

Situationism is, of course, no more the specter that haunts industrial society than was communism the specter that haunted Europe in 1848.

—*Le Nouvel Observateur*, 3 January 1968

It's the tune that makes the song: more cynical in Vaneigem and more icy in Debord, the negative and provocative violence of their phraseology leaves nothing standing among what previous ages have produced—except perhaps Sade, Lautréamont and Dada. . . . A snarling, extravagant rhetoric that is always detached from the complexity of the facts upon which we reason not only makes the reading disagreeable but also staggers thought.

—*Le Monde*, 14 February 1968

M. Debord and M. Vaneigem have brought out their long-awaited major texts: the *Capital* and *What Is To Be Done?*, as it were, of the new movement. This comparison is not meant mockingly. . . . Under the dense Hegelian wrappings with which they muffle their pages several interesting ideas are lurking. M. Debord and M. Vaneigem are attempting, for the first time, a comprehensive critique of alienated society. .... Their austere philosophy, now authoritatively set forth, may not be without influence on future Committees of 100, Declarations of the 121, and similar libertarian manifestations.

—*Times Literary Supplement*, 21 March 1968

These commando actions undertaken by a group of anarchists and "situationists," with their slogan: *"Never work!"* ... How has a handful of irresponsible elements been able to provoke such serious decisions, affecting 12,000 students in Letters and 4000 in Law?

—*Humanité*, 29 March 1968

Those who want to understand the ideas lying behind the student revolts in the Old World ought to pay serious attention not only to the writings of Adorno and of the three M's—Marx, Mao and Marcuse—but above all to the literature of the Situationists. ... Debord's book ... rejects the idea of proletarian revolution in the same way as it repudiates Socialist democracy, Russian or Chinese Communism, and traditional "incoherent anarchism." ... One has to destroy all authority, especially that of the state, to negate all moral restrictions, to expose fossilized knowledge and all "establishments," to bring truth into the world of semblance, and to achieve what Debord calls "the fulfillment of democracy in self-control and action." He fails to say how to achieve this program.

—*New York Times*, 21 April 1968

The situationists ... are more anarchist than the anarchists, whom they find too bureaucratic.

—*Carrefour*, 8 May 1968

WARNING: Leaflets have been distributed in the Paris area calling for an insurrectionary general strike. It goes without saying that such appeals have not been issued by our democratic trade-union organizations. They are the work of provocateurs seeking to provide the government with a pretext for intervention. ... The workers must be vigilant to defeat all such maneuvers.

—*Humanité* (paper of the French Communist Party), 20 May 1968

... Daniel Cohn-Bendit, leader of the "enragés," whom the leftist intellectuals have presented as being disciples of the American Marcuse, although anyone who reads the French books of the "situationist" writers Vaneigem and Debord can see where Dany and his friends got their inspiration.

—*Le Canard Enchainé*, 22 May 1968

Inside, in jampacked auditoriums, thousands applauded all-night debates that ranged over every conceivable topic, from the "anesthesia of affluence" to the elimination of "bourgeois spectacles" and how to share their "revolution" with the mass of French workers. ... There were Maoists, Trotskyists, ordinary Communists, anarchists and "situationists"—a tag for those without preconceived ideologies who judge each situation as it arises.

—*Time*, 24 May 1968

This explosion was provoked by a few groups in revolt against modern society, against consumer society, against technological society, whether communist in the East or capitalist in the West—groups, moreover, that do not know what they would put in its place, but that delight in negation, destruction, violence, anarchy, brandishing the black flag.

—Charles de Gaulle, televised speech, 7 June 1968

The fact that the uprising took everyone by surprise, including the most sophisticated theoreticians in the Marxist, Situationist and anarchist movements, underscores the importance of the May-June events and raises the need to re-examine the sources of revolutionary unrest in modern society.

—Murray Bookchin, "The May-June Events in France" (July 1968)

Who is the authentic representative of the Left today: the Fourth International, the Situationist International or the Anarchist Federation? Leftism is everything that is new in Revolutionary history, and is forever being challenged by the old. . . . The Strasbourg pamphlet . . . acted as a kind of detonator. And although we, in Nanterre, did not accept the Strasbourg interpretation of the role of minority groups, i.e. university students, in the social revolution, we did all we could in helping to distribute the pamphlet.

—Daniel & Gabriel Cohn-Bendit,
Obsolete Communism: The Left-Wing Alternative (1968)

The notion of "spectacle" (drama, happening, mask) is crucial to the theories of what is probably the furthest out of the radical factions. . . . In our consumer-technologies, life is merely a bad play. Like Osborne's Entertainer, we strut about in a bankrupt sideshow playing parts we loathe to audiences whose values are meaningless or contemptible. Culture itself has become frippery and grease-paint. Our very revolutions are melodrama, performed under stale rules of make-believe; they alter nothing but the cast. . . . Compared to the Strasbourg absolutists, Monsieur Cohn-Bendit is a weather-beaten conservative.

—*The Sunday Times*, 21 July 1968

. . . "situationists" (whose main contributions to the May Revolution were graffiti, joyful and nonsensical). . . . A group of "International Situationists"—a latterday incarnation of surrealism—seized the university loudspeaker system for a time and issued extravagant directives.

—Seale & McConville, *Red Flag, Black Flag: French Revolution 1968* (1968)

It would be wrong to underestimate certain antecedents, in particular the November 1966 takeover of the Strasbourg Student Union. . . . The observer cannot help being struck by the rapidity with which the contagion spread throughout the university and among the nonuniversity youth. It seems that the watchwords propagated by a small minority of authentic revolutionaries struck some sort of indefinable chord in the soul of the new generation. . . . This fact must be stressed: we are witnessing the reappearance, just like fifty years ago, of groups of young people consecrating themselves entirely to the revolutionary cause who, in accordance with tested technique, know how to await the favorable moments to trigger or aggravate disturbances of which they remain the masters, then to go back into clandestinity and continue the work of undermining or of preparing other sporadic or prolonged upheavals, so as to slowly disorganize the social edifice.

—*Guerres et Paix* #4, 1968

. . . the Situationist International, which has its base in Copenhagen and which is controlled by the security and espionage police of East Germany.

—*Historama* #206, December 1968

The situationists . . . make use of street theater and spontaneous spectacles to criticize society and denounce new forms of alienation. . . . Even though the small situationist group concentrated principally on the student situation and the commercialization of mass culture, the spring revolt was less a questioning of culture than a political criticism of society.

—Alain Touraine, *The May Movement: Revolt and Reform* (1968)

Their manifesto is the now famous book by Guy Debord, *The Society of the Spectacle.* In order to criticize the system radically, Debord, in an epigramatic and Adornian style, constructs a concept of "spectacle" derived from Marx's, and especially Lukács's, conceptions of "commodity fetishism," alienation and "reification."

—*L'Espresso*, 15 December 1968

Their general headquarters is secret but I think it is somewhere in London. They are not students, but are what are known as situationists; they travel everywhere and exploit the discontent of students.

—*News of the World*, 16 February 1969

You know, I more or less agree with the situationists; they say that it's all finally integrated; it gets integrated in spectacle, it's all spectacle.

—Jean-Luc Godard, interview, March 1969

The occupation committee, which was re-elected every day, was not able to guarantee continuity, in addition to which situationist factions had gained a certain influence. On Thursday the 16th, the latter distributed a leaflet denouncing the "bureaucrats" who disagreed with their slogans and working methods. . . . The situationists set up a "council to maintain the occupations" which, in their inimitable Hegelianistic-Marxist terminology, expatiated on the same themes.

—Alain Schnapp & Pierre Vidal-Naquet, *The French Student Uprising* (1969)

We should add that Vaneigem's very style is that of the slogans of May. He seems, moreover, to have been at the origin of many of the most successful and poetic phrases. . . . The author of the *Treatise on Living* gives us a key for understanding the role and place of the *paranoic mechanisms of our civilization.*

—André Stéphane, *L'Univers contestationnaire* (1969)

Historically, few doctrines have attempted to follow the thread we have been pursuing. I know of only two: personalism and, in the contemporary scene, situationism. . . . Built on ideological premises utterly opposed to those of personalism (the latter is strongly influenced by Christianity, which situationists reject), the movement actually advances (despite its criticism) the tenets of surrealism, which were genuinely revolutionary at the start and closely resembled those of situationism. . . . Situationism should be credited for advocating individual decision-making and the exercise of imagination free of the irrationality we have discussed. The individual is committed to scrutinize his daily existence and to create a potential new one.

—Jacques Ellul, *Autopsy of Revolution* (1969)

An advertising specialist summed up the action of the graffiti writers with this formula: "They are fighting advertising on its own terrain with its own weapons." . . . Those responsible are a small group of revolutionary students, half lettrist, half situationist.

—France-Soir, 6 August 1969

Too èxtreme for those of the old left intelligent enough to understand it, and too incomprehensible for those of the new left extreme enough to live it.

—Grove Press position on *Enragés and Situationists . . .*, 1969

It seems to me that the Situationist International's influence has been considerably underestimated by commentators on the May events. (It should be said that, sparing nothing and nobody, the *Situationists* devote a good deal of their activity to virulent attacks on those who are closest to their own thinking, and have thus alienated a good many intellectuals who would otherwise be sympathetic to their views.) . . . Distortion [i.e. detournement], which was adopted and widely used first by the Situationists— especially, though not exclusively, in strip cartoons—consists in adding to a drawing, for example, certain words or phrases that distort the original meaning. . . . If the new meaning dominates or at least disturbs the meaning usually perceived by the reader of the original, the desired aim is achieved. It may involve a sudden awareness, an invitation to reflection, to doubt, or at least to participation in the game that will produce a certain detachment from the thing criticized. . . . This practicable and cheap technique of counter-manipulation is all the more effective in that it is placed in the context of an event, a production, etc., that already possess an audience.

—Alfred Willener, *The Image-Action of Society* (1970)

The Situationist pamphlet "Theses on the Commune" refers to the Commune as the greatest carnival of the nineteenth century, but to try to burn down the Louvre is merely symbolic. Revolutionary activity has to move beyond the symbolic into the phase of literalization of the stasis of "working" institutions in bourgeois society.

—David Cooper, *The Death of the Family* (1970)

385

Diderot wrote the preface to a Revolution and so the surrealists and the situationists have written the preface to a new Revolution. . . . Claims grew into *contestation*; the games and the playful demonstrations of the anarchist-situationist mini-group gave way to more serious activity.

—*Reflections on the Revolution in France: 1968*, ed. Posner (1970)

Although the language and tone of the essay are markedly similar to those of the Situationist manifesto, there are important differences between Bookchin and the Situationists. He explains these (in a personal letter to the editor) as follows: "The Situationists have retained very traditional notions about the workers' movement, Pannekoek's 'council communism,' almost Stalinist forms of internal organization (they are completely monolithic and authoritarian in their internal organization), and are surprisingly academic."

—*"All We Are Saying . . .",* ed. Lothstein (1970)

In those mystical days of May . . . the poets of Paris were the International Situationists, who have attained a similar state of frenzied anti-doctrinal comic anarchism to the yippies, though suckled on Dada, not L.S.D.

—Richard Neville, *Play Power* (1970)

In the extreme case, the anarcho-situationist groups all but deny the persistence of traditionally recognized forms of oppression, and put forward a model of contemporary capitalism as dependent solely on psychological oppression, a strategy that sees class society defeated by the "return of the repressed," and an organization and tactics confined to the symbolically terrorist actions of small groups.

—*New Left Review* #64, November 1970

We are here concerned with only two small groups who alone set the scene for the May events and provided the insurrection with a dialectical backbone. These few outlaws, the *Enragés* and the *Situationists*, universally despised by political organizations and student bodies, have their base on the surrealistic fringes of the Left Wing. From there they have nurtured one of the most advanced, coherent revolutionary theories (though often plagued by academic arrogance and "in" references), which provoked a near-liquidation of the State.

—*BAMN (By Any Means Necessary)*, ed. Stansill and Mairowitz (1971)

When one reads or rereads the *Internationale Situationniste* issues it is quite striking to what degree and how often these *fanatics* have made judgments or put forward viewpoints that were later concretely verified.

—*Le Nouvel Observateur*, 8 February 1971

Internationale Situationniste 1958–69 . . . provides a fascinating record of this groupuscule which began in the French tradition of political-cultural sectarianism and ended by playing a prominent part first in the disturbances at Strasbourg University in 1966 and then in the more dramatic "events" of May 1968. Many of the slogans which achieved fame on the walls of Paris may be found here in some form, and the ideas which influenced the rebels so much were being worked out in these pages during the previous ten years. There is a certain irony in such a publication . . . here they are neatly packaged as a highly marketable commodity in a clearly spectacular way.

—*Times Literary Supplement*, 19 February 1971

The concept of the spectacle, which derives from the French Situationists . . . is a useful analytic device: it simplifies a world of phenomena that seem otherwise disparate. Surely the spectacle is conspicuous, once one learns to see it in its many dimensions.

—Todd Gitlin in *Liberation*, May 1971

This revolt must be attributed to an awakening of consciousness regarding the real nature of "consumer society"—an awakening of consciousness (and its articulation) that has its source in the intellectual (and practical) activities of a small group of insolent but lucid insurgents: the Situationist International. Now, by a paradox to which history holds the secret, the SI remained practically unknown in this country for over ten years, a phenomenon which verifies Hegel's reflection: "Every important revolution that leaps into view must be preceded in the spirit of an era by a secret revolution that is not visible to everyone and still less observable to contemporaries, a revolution that is as difficult to express in words as it is to comprehend."

—Le Nouveau Planète #22, May 1971

The resolution unanimously passed by the Anarchist Congress calls for some explanation. The influence of the Situationist International, particularly negative on numerous Scandinavian, North American and Japanese extraparliamentary groups, has been active in France and Italy since 1967–68 with the aim of destroying the federated anarchist movement of these two countries—in the name of a theoretical discourse that the situationists generally submerge in a barrage of insolences and vague and tortuous phraseology.

—communiqué of the Italian Anarchist Federation, *Umanità Nuova*, 15 May 1971

At the beginning of 1968 a critic discussing situationist theory mockingly characterized it as a "glimmer wandering vaguely from Copenhagen to New York." Alas, the glimmer became, that same year, a conflagration that spread through all the citadels of the old world. . . . The situationists have uncovered the theory of the subterranean movement that torments the modern age. While the pseudoinheritors of Marxism forgot the role of the negative in a world swollen with positivity, and simultaneously relegated dialectics to the museum, the situationists announced the resurgence of that same negative and discerned the reality of the same dialectics, whose language, the "insurrectional style" (Debord), they rediscovered.

—Les Temps Modernes #299–300, June 1971

It was not in America but among the Western European student movements that the recent renaissance of interest in Reich first began. In France, where he was practically unknown, his theories were initially rediscovered by the Situationists.

—Liberation, October 1971

The Society of the Spectacle . . . has led the discussion of the entire ultraleft since its publication in 1967. This work, which predicted May 1968, is considered by many to be the *Capital* of the new generation.

—Le Nouvel Observateur, 8 November 1971

The situationists, although in many ways they are the heirs of surrealism, dadaism and some millenarian trends, rejoin the modern currents in post-Marxism and even go further in their quasi-Marcusian analyses of alienation in capitalist-bureaucratic society, which is the purely political aspect of their ideas. . . . The *enragés* and the situationists had the chance to put their ideas into practice in the first Committee of Occupation of the Sorbonne (14–17 May 1968) which, under their influence, set up total direct democracy in the Sorbonne. . . . The members of the Situationist International go so far as to deny that they have any ideology at all since any ideology is alienating.

—Richard Gombin in *Anarchism Today*, ed. Apter & Joll (1971)

But the situationists never arrived at an adequate practice. Afraid to get their hands dirty in the confusion of radical activity (which they scorned as "militantism") they confined their interventions to the theoretical level.

—Anarchy #7, Winter 1972

The Situationists . . . constantly talk of "workers" (sic) councils . . . while demanding the abolition of work! Unfortunately they seem to confuse attacks on the *work ethic* and on alienated labor, both of which are justified and necessary, with attacks on work itself.

—Workers' Councils and the Economics of a Self-Managed Society,
Solidarity (England), March 1972

Miss Martin said the "situationists" were a political movement active in France in the 18th century, and that there had been "talk" on the campus of a revival under that name in Berkeley.

—*San Francisco Examiner*, 18 May 1972

The manifesto published by the Strasbourg students did little more than restate the troubling dilemmas already examined by the radical existentialists. Its content was not particularly original—except, perhaps, in its interpretation of the capitalist system as a vast, cretinizing spectacle. . . . When all was said and done, the "theory" of the situationists was rather uninspiring. . . . The situationists described their "situation" but presented no real, strategic perspective for its transformation. The task of forging concrete solutions was left to Daniel Cohn-Bendit, the principal ideologue of the May revolt.

—Richard Johnson, *The French Communist Party Versus the Students* (1972)

The S.I., although it presented the "most developed, most comprehensive, most modern" revolutionary theory yet to be found anywhere, is still not the end-all of revolutionary theory and practice. The sexual politics of the new women's movement, coupled with the communal lifestyles and counter-institutions which have emerged, are among the American contributions which can aid in the development of a coherent post-Situationist critique of our conditions.

—*New Morning*, February 1973

I could understand it, but it would be over the heads of our readers. Besides, why would they be interested in something that happened in *France* in 1968?

—editor at Straight Arrow Books, April 1973

The notion of *recuperation*, first introduced by the Situationists, refers to the manner in which the repressive system seeks to neutralize or contain the attacks launched against it by *absorbing* them into the "spectacle" or by *projecting* its own meanings and goals onto these oppositional activities.

—Bruce Brown, *Marx, Freud and the Critique of Everyday Life* (1973)

In the confusion and tumult of the May Revolt the slogans and shouts of the students were considered expressions of mass spontaneity and individual ingenuity. Only afterward was it evident that these slogans were fragments of a coherent and seductive ideology and had virtually all previously appeared in situationist tracts and publications. . . . Mainly through their agency there welled up in the May Revolt an immense force of protest against the modern world and all its works, blending passion, mystery, and the primeval.

—Bernard E. Brown, *Protest in Paris: Anatomy of a Revolt* (1974)

Brown . . . portrays (and unsympathetically so) the elements of the French intelligentsia who raised the banners of unreason, passion and primitivism. The anarchists and the "situationists" upon whom he concentrates most, represent in this interpretation a traditional force of romantic but destructive politics, determined to resist progress.

—*New Republic*, 16 March 1974

Pillaging and detourning in a lively and unconstrained manner a wealth of newsclips, sequences filmed in the streets, ads with naked women, press photos, scenes from American westerns, secondrate war films, Soviet and Polish films, flashes from fashion ads, mixing in quotations from Clausewitz, Marx, Machiavelli, etc., interrupting the narrative to wickedly announce to the spectator that if the rhythm he has given the images continued it would be seductive, "but it won't continue," Debord develops the argument of his book without limiting himself to "illustrating" it. . . . If war, according to Clausewitz, is a continuation of politics by other means, the cinema, according to Debord, is a continuation of theory with other weapons. One must have seen the film two or three times to enumerate all the carefully calculated strokes of genius, the riches lavished with a subtle irony and the outbursts of a lyricism of rage that suddenly grips the heart. . . . Debord's indignation (the word is too feeble) splashes out in superb images of contemporary subversion: from the Asturias to Gdansk and Gdynia, from Poznan to Budapest, from police actions all over the world to May 68. It is no longer a matter of filming the world, the point is to change it. .... Brecht dreamt all his life of adapting *Capital* to the stage. Guy Debord has found a producer crazy enough and wise enough to permit him to *re-form* his *Society of the Spectacle* on the screen. See it.

—Le Nouvel Observateur, 29 April 1974

In his film *The Society of the Spectacle*, situationist Guy Debord has undertaken "a total critique of the existing world, that is, of all aspects of modern capitalism and its general system of illusions." In bringing his book to the screen, the author has fulfilled his aim of creating a *theoretical* film. .... Imagine a work of the same sort as *Capital* presented in the form of a western and you will get some idea of what Guy Debord's film is like. The sequences of this theoretical western are accompanied by a narration read from the book. The film is a montage of fashion ads, newsclips, quotations from Marx, Machiavelli, Tocqueville, Clausewitz, and fragments from diverse films that have marked the history of the cinema: *Potemkin, Ten Days That Shook the World, New Babylon, We from Kronstadt, Shanghai Gesture, La Charge Fantastique, For Whom the Bell Tolls, Rio Grande, Johnny Guitar* and *Mr. Arkadin.*

—Le Monde, 9 May 1974

The Makhnist Situationist International pig countergang created by the CIA from scratch in 1957 in France under the slogans "Kill the Vanguards!," "Workers Councils Now!," and "Create Situations!," is the paradigm example of a CIA synthetic all-purpose formation. The loose and programless anarchist "left cover" countergang on the SI model is ideal for the CIA for the recruitment of new agents, the launching of psywar operations, the detonation of riots, syndicalist workers' actions (e.g., LIP strike), student power revolts, etc., the continual generation of new countergang formations, and infiltration, penetration and dissolution of socialist and other workers' organizations. .... During the 1968 French general strike the Situationists united with Daniel Cohn-Bendit and his anarchist thugs in preventing any potential vanguard from assuming leadership of the strike—thus guaranteeing its defeat. In the U.S. Goldner and his Situationist International offshoot group Contradiction have been assigned to play the same kind of role: namely to stop the Labor Committees from developing into a mass-based working-class party.

—New Solidarity (paper of the National Caucus of Labor Committees),
28 August and 6 September 1974

What was basically wrong with the S.I. was that it focused exclusively on an intellectual critique of society. There was no concern whatsoever with either the emotions or the body. .... In the last analysis they made the same mistake as all left-wing intellectuals: *they thought that everyone was plain thick.* The poor workers don't know what's going on, they need someone to tell them. But people in the streets, in the offices and factories know damn well what's going on, even if they can't write essays about all its theoretical ramifications. *The point is that they can't do anything about it.* .... Ultimately the problem is an *emotional,* not an intellectual one.

—Christopher Gray, *Leaving the Twentieth Century* (1974)

The revolutionary hopes of the 1960s, which culminated in 1968, are now blocked or abandoned. One day they will break out again, transformed, and be lived again with a different result. .... When that happens, the Situationist programme (or anti-programme) will probably be recognized as one of the most lucid and pure political formulations of that earlier, historic decade, reflecting, in an extreme way, its desperate force and its privileged weakness. What then was its privileged weakness? .... They ignored the everyday fact of tragedy, both on a world and personal scale. They refused to face the need to find meaning in tragedy.

—John Berger in *New Society,* 6 March 1975

Apart from a lot of the dialectical jargon, which is just rubbish, there is much that is a bad case of "excuse me but didn't Hegel say that?" The grandeur of the rhetoric shows up the bathos of the suggested "practice" (e.g. creating situations, whatever that may mean), while the "revolutionary project" itself seems to lack any clear goals.

—Time Out, 4 April 1975

Coming from the decomposition of "left" lettristes and cultural dilettantes of the 50s, the Situationists simply carried to their logical conclusions the bourgeois "critiques" of capitalism contained in Dadaism and Surrealism. Parrotting what *Socialisme ou Barbarie* had taught them about economics, about the "workers councils" and "generalized self-management," the Situationists became the most coherent expression of petty bourgeois radicalism in the whole modernist carnival which accompanied May '68. . . . But the proletariat did not begin a communist revolution in Paris '68. The Situationists and other modernists did not fail to notice this omission and from then on the viciousness of their anti–working class outbursts knew no limits. . . . In *The Decline and the Fall of the "Spectacular" Commodity-Economy* (1965) the Situationists had already begun to talk about "the integration of the classical proletariat" to the "society of the spectacle."

—*World Revolution #3*, April 1975

But of course, it should have been obvious from the start that the Situationists do not have the slightest *genuine* concern with freedom. Their mask is far too transparent to conceal that familiar, vicious and authoritarian face beneath, the same old desire to dominate, rule and coerce other people. . . . It is indeed fortunate for the human race, however, that there now exist truly radical individualist and libertarian movements which are actually dedicated to leading it out of the Twentieth Century—*into the Twenty First*, into a new world of greater freedom and prosperity and not, as would the Situationists, back into the Dark Ages of slavery and poverty.

—Chris R. Tame, *The Politics of Whim* (Radical Libertarian Alliance, 1975)

Situationism seems to have "caught on" in the U.S.A., particularly in California, that playground of the ideologies. . . . The American situationists seem to be repeating the pattern of mutual exclusion and criticism as occurred in Europe, and to be employing a fairly impenetrable Hegelian vocabulary. . . . Debord and Vaneigem are worth reading for their critique of modern consumer-culture (if you can arrange a few weeks free of work and booze).

—*Freedom*, 10 May 1975

Their strategy of interrupting the routines of daily life with guerrilla theatre in order to "create situations" was traceable to Lefebvre, although they asserted that he also took much from them. . . . The Situationists created a mini-May in 1966, disrupting the university and publishing a very popular pamphlet, *De La Misère en milieu étudiant*, which was an application of the theory of the *Arguments* group to student life.

—Mark Poster, *Existential Marxism in Postwar France* (1975)

What is hidden behind the Censor case, where will the Censor scandal lead? First let us explain: Censor is the author of a book entitled *True Report on the Last Chance To Save Capitalism in Italy*, circulated in a limited edition in August among the men of power, then in October among the literati. At the time, everyone wondered who Censor was. Everyone assumed he had to be himself a man of power: Merzagora, Carli, Mattioli. The things he knew were too important and too precise. He had to be one of these three men. Instead, here is the surprise: a few days ago the real author revealed himself. He is not a man of power, but a little-known young man in his twenties by the name of Gianfranco Sanguinetti. "The first duty of the press today is to undermine all the bases of the constituted political order," wrote Marx in 1849. Sanguinetti-Censor has set out to accomplish precisely this task with his book. He is not modest, but on the whole he has done so effectively. . . . Anyone who is familiar with the situationists knows that the immediate objectives of their philosophy are provocations and scandals carried out with coolness and precision. With his Censor coup, Sanguinetti has simply given a crowning manifestation of the situationist technique of scandal.

—*L'Europeo*, 6 February 1976

Situationalism: Species of Marxist cultural and political criticism propounded by L'Internationale Situationaliste, a tiny group of intellectual terrorists formed from the fusion of the Romanian surrealist Isidore Ison's Mouvement Lettriste with other nihilist and anti-cultural avant-gardists in 1957. Influenced by the Trotskyist surrealists Breton and Péret, as well as Lefebvre, de Sade, Lautréamont and Lewis Carroll. Specialists in staccato, sarcastic and heavily Hegelian denunciations of the Spectacle, art, advertising and consumption. ... In its simplified form became a rationale for "action" and the propaganda of the deed during the decline of the student Left. Its executive has had British members, including the Scots novelist and junkie Alex Trocchi, but they have usually been swiftly expelled.

—David Widgery, *The Left in Britain: 1956–68* (1976)

Jorn's role in the Situationist movement (as in COBRA) was that of a catalyst and team leader. Guy Debord on his own lacked the personal warmth and persuasiveness to draw people of different nationalities and talents into an active working partnership. As a prototype Marxist intellectual Debord needed an ally who could patch up the petty egoisms and squabbles of the members. Their quarrels came into the open the moment Jorn's leadership was withdrawn in 1961. ... Finally, 1966–8 saw the vindication of Debord's policy, sustained against every kind of opposition, of adhering rigidly to the uncompromising pursuit of a singleminded plan. When the time came—in Strasbourg in November 1966 and in Paris in May 1968—Debord was ready, with his two or three remaining supporters, to take over the revolutionary role for which he had been preparing during the last ten years. Incredible as it may seem, the active ideologists ("enragés" and Situationists) behind the revolutionary events in Strasbourg, Nanterre and Paris, numbered only about ten persons.

—Guy Atkins, *Asger Jorn, the Crucial Years: 1954–1964* (1977)

Paris 1968 was rich in nameless wildness. ... It was marred by a small group of embittered scene-creamers, who called themselves the Situationists, and who tried in typically French fashion to intellectualize the whole mood out of existence, and with their very name tried to colonize it. Failed activists and mini-Mansonettes who boasted that all their books and pamphlets (Leaving the 20th Century, The Veritable Split in the Fourth International, etc.) had been produced from the proceeds of a bank robbery when even the most lavish of them could have been produced for the price of a few tins of cat-food from Safeways (one tiny exception being "Ten Days that Shook the University" by Omar Khayati). ... Their heroes are a legion of mad bombers: Ravachol, Valerie Solanas, Nechayev, the IRA, et al.

—Heathcote Williams in *International Times*, Autumn 1977

Ducasse in one sense leads to the Orwell of *Politics and the English Language* and beyond, to Vaneigem and the Situationists who by shrewd use of collage and juxtaposition exposed both the poverty and richness of slogans, and the thinly veiled hypocrisy of a society which by not respecting words abuses people, and by insulting the intelligence creates a state of political cretinisation in which the various forms of authoritarian control may dominate.

—Alexis Lykiard, introduction to his translation of *Poésies* (1978)

Guy Debord rejects praise as well as blame. ... Far from currying favor with his contemporaries, Debord denounces their compromises and resignations with the ferocity of a grand inquisitor. ... The seduction of this author stems precisely from the rigor of his critique and the sovereign form he gives to it. The publication of his *Oeuvres cinématographiques complètes*, and particularly of the text of his latest film, *In girum imus nocte*, confirms his position in the line of French writers—Pascal, Bossuet, Chamfort—who combine elegance, passion and firmness. ... We are going to die one day, soon. Let us therefore not be unworthy of our pride and our ambitions. This, I believe, is Guy Debord's message.

—*Le Monde*, 20 January 1979

In exploiting the hysteria of the record companies and the public over the Pistols, McLaren was drawing upon an avant garde movement too playful and fluid to be doctrinal. This was the Situationist International, or Situationism. ... So, although professing the obligatory sympathy with the proletariat, the Situationists rejoiced, like students at a rag day, in scandal and shock tactics. ... In this evaluation one may see the models for the subsequent behavior of Malcolm McLaren and the Pistols. ... Mc-

Laren and Jamie Reid took Situationism to Glitterbest with more success. "It's wonderful to use it in rock n' roll," McLaren said.

—Melody Maker, June 1979

Meanwhile, the notion of the spectacle elaborated by the S.I. falls behind what Marx and Engels understood by the term "ideology." Debord's book *The Society of the Spectacle* presents itself as an attempt to explain capitalist society and revolution, when in fact it only considers their forms, important but not determinant phenomena. . . . Its contradiction, and, ultimately, its theoretical and practical dead-end, is to have made a study of the profound through and by means of the superficial appearance. The S.I. had no analysis of CAPITAL: it understood it, but through its effects. . . . The S.I. saw the revolution as a calling into question more of the relations of distribution (cf. the Watts riot) than of the relations of production. It was acquainted with the commodity but not with surplus value.

*—Jean Barrot, "Critique of the Situationist International" in *Red-Eye* #1 (Fall 1979)

Situationism is a product of the student rebellion, a glorification of the spontaneous happenings which it is felt will spring out of the favoured role of the student within society. It picks up phrases, here from Marxism and there from anarchism. It has an affinity with Blanquism and, when it does, often parades as Maoism or a revised form of Marxism-Leninism—to the indignation of orthodox Maoists or other Marxist-Leninists. But the situationists were virtually non-existent between situations, and unlikely ever to get around to doing anything so positive as attacking a Cabinet Minister.

*—Stuart Christie, *The Christie File* (1980)

Shot in March 1978, this situationist maceration [*In girum imus nocte*] is now finally presented to the *vulgum pecus* of the Latin Quarter, Montparnasse and the Olympic. . . . In 1973 Guy Debord presented his first film, *The Society of the Spectacle*, adapted from his book of the same name. Its moral: smash everything, hock the cinema, we have to live today. A detournement of the spectacle and thus of the cinema, a return to the essential, to immediate life. *In girum*: . . . a pavane for a disappointed love of the cinema, often irritating because of his self-satisfied indulging of his dear little ego. Strictly for in-group devotees.

—Le Monde, 11 May 1981

In girum imus nocte was completed in March 1978. . . . It was subjected to a complete blackout for the next three years. . . . Debord begins by attacking the spectators, the audience. The first image of the film is a photo of a "present-day film audience staring fixedly ahead," so that "the spectators see nothing but a mirror image of themselves on the screen." . . . But in his film Debord does not talk only about the cinema public. He talks about himself. . . . The same people who go into ecstasies over the self-portraits of famous painters, the memoirs of someone or other or even Bakunin's *Confession* are suddenly outraged at having Debord "inflict his ego" on them. . . . Yet Debord recounts his life and loves quite simply. . . . And who better than he can render homage to his friends of long ago such as Ivan Chtcheglov . . . or expose the devastation that has since hit Paris? . . . But enough of all these incoherent quotations from the text of the film. If you can't catch the pirate showing of it tonight on channel 68, go see it at the cinema.

—Libération, 3 June 1981

INDEX

Hollon, Bobbi, 155–156
Hong Kong, 196
How To Be a Good Communist (Liu Shao-ch'i), 193
humanism, 99, 159, 324, 329
Humanité (PCF daily paper), 72
Humphrey, Hubert H., 195
Humpty Dumpty, 114
Hung, General, 191
Hungarian revolution (1956), 15, 147, 152, 166, 180, 236, 259, 264, 274, 330, 345, 351
Husák, Gustáv, 263
Hussein (king of Jordan), 202–203

Iberian Anarchist Federation (FAI), 278–279, 368
ICO (Workers' News and Correspondence), 238–240, 279–280, 336, 364
iconoclasts, 93
Imagination au pouvoir, L' (Lewino), 241
Immediate Tasks of the Soviet Government, The (Lenin), 275
Ince, Thomas, 215
Incitement to Murder and Debauchery (proposed film), 215
India, 185, 194, 221
Indochinese Communist Party, 198
Indonesian Stalinism, 194, 374
Informations, Correspondance Ouvrières (ICO), 238–240, 279–280, 336, 364
INSA (National Institute of Applied Sciences), 238
"Instructions for Taking Up Arms" (SI), 102
Internationale Situationniste (IS), 123, 143, 213, 228, 268, 337, 362–363 (quotations from it not indexed)
International Movement for an Imaginist Bauhaus, 14–16, 21
International Workingmen's Association (First International), 84, 142
Into the Trashcan of History (SI), 228, 324, 375
IPN (National Pedagogical Institute), 238–239, 247
Islam, 149, 151, 167, 169
Isou, Jean-Isidore, 144, 371
Israel, 151, 194–195, 199–204
Italian Anarchist Union, 273
Italian Communist Party, 185, 255, 264
Italian Socialist Party, 272–273
Italy, 21, 83, 255, 264, 272–273, 280. *See also* Turin council movement
Izvestia, 185, 196

Jacobinism, 316
Jacopetti, Gualtiero, 298
Jacqueries, 93, 147, 169
Japan, 21, 41, 139, 152, 194, 198, 254, 330–331, 345, 377

JCR (Revolutionary Communist Youth), 237, 246, 325, 347–348
Jews, 195, 199–201
Jiefang Ribao, 190
Jong, Jacqueline de, 61, 88–89
Jordan, 203
Jorn, Asger, 14–15, 17, 47–48, 55–56, 61–62
Joyce, James, 114, 169, 172
Judaism, 199
June 19th Declaration (accompanying Boumedienne's coup), 149, 163–164

Kádár, János, 262
Kamenev, Lev, 270
KAPD, 277–278
Karol, K.S., 193
Kassem, Abd-ul-Karim, 202
Katanga, 103, 151
"Katangans" (France, May 1968), 227, 231, 374
KAUD, 278
Kaupp, Katia, 179
Kautsky, Karl, 274–275
Keller, George (pseudonym of Asger Jorn), 87
Kennedy, John F., 77, 80
Kerensky, Alexander, 234, 350
Khatib, Abdelhafid, 48
Khayati, Mustapha, 175, 205–207, 209, 212, 222, 363
Khrushchev, Nikita, 180, 187, 325
Khrushchevo-Brezhnevists, 165
kibbutzim, 200
Kiel mutiny (1918), 116, 331
Kierkegaard, Søren, 169
King, Martin Luther, Jr., 154
King Mob, 294
Kivu (region of the Congo), 337
Klossowski, Pierre, 174
Koran, 152
Korun, Walter, 48–49
Kosygin, Alexei, 185, 264
Kotányi, Attila, 59, 61–62, 67, 88–89, 217, 317, 363
Kotik, Jan, 14–15
Koutchoum, 185
KPD, 278
Kravetz, Marc, 231, 320
Krivine, Alain, 240
Kronstadt Izvestia, 270
Kronstadt revolt (1921), 84, 93, 116, 169, 232, 270–271, 275–276, 331, 345
Kropotkin, Piotr, 279
Ku Klux Klan, 12
Kulturni Tvorba, 259
Kunzelmann, Dieter, 88
Kurds, 151
Kuron, Jacek, 329

Labour government (England), 158, 254, 330

397

401

INDEX TO DEBORD'S
"SOCIETY OF THE SPECTACLE"

Arabic numerals refer to theses, Roman numerals to chapter epigraphs.

INDEX TO VANEIGEM'S
"TREATISE ON LIVING"

References are to chapters and subchapters.